Epic Series Vol.2

2022 & Beyond
ROSESTORM

Return of the Feminine

9/11 20th Anniversary Commemoration

WILLOW WILLIS

Copyright © 2020 Willow Willis

All rights reserved.

Willow Willis asserts the moral right to be identified as the author of this work.

willowwillis.com
Fb/2020&beyond

No part of this book may be reproduced or transmitted in any form or by any means without permission from the author. This book contains mature content and some course language, however, this book is for everyone. Fair use is implied throughout this work for educational purposes.

Cover art:

ISBN: 978-0-9953951-3-8

DEDICATION

I dedicate this book to the future of Humanity & to
Mother Earth, without hope for, there is
simply no point to existence.

This is for you.

CONTENTS

    Forward

1   Et tu, Brute`?   1
    'And You Brutus?'

2   Et Iterum, Brute`?   29
    'And Again, Brutus?'

3   Osiris & Isis   49

4   King Kennedy   93

5   Orpheus Eurydice Hermes   130

6   The Goddess   133

7   Lady Liberty, The Light Bearer   174

8   The Green Man   217

9   The Phoenix Returns   252

10   The Virgin-Whore Paradox   261

11   The Woman Haters   277

12   The Messenger   294

    Epilogue   312

    ABOUT THE AUTHOR   313

For my family & for your family
wherever you may be,
whatever 'time' you find yourself in

FORWARD

There is a secret so profound, so near to our hearts and right in our faces that we have been unable, as individuals and as a collective, to acknowledge the full truth of who we *really* are and what we are *really* involved in here. There is a lie *so* pervasive and *so* enormous we have been unable to not only grasp this lie but to believe that such a *huge* lie can even exist for so long and go undiscovered in a *conspiracy of illusion*.

We are about to step up to the plate in a long-prophesised date with destiny that will level the playing field and set humanity free once and for all. No more with the 'children of god' garbage which is nothing more than cheating alien controllers that have kept humanity on a hamster wheel of slavery and devastation for eons in an endless dreamscape of mind games and cruelty so they can play Big Daddy or 'god'.

It's time to face reality once and for all. It's time to face the truth of our potential and our worth, the truth of our hearts. It's time to overthrow the slave master's and seek justice for all those who have suffered under their heel generation after generation. It's time to set ourselves free and see the enormity of our importance as a species not only of Mother Earth but in the context of the *entire Universe*. Yes, that's how big this is and you are *far more important* than you have ever been told!

There is no cavalry for this on. No 'saviour' the way we've been told. There is no one answer. Yet the human race is brave enough, having our bravery and honour wasted on useless wars and childish infighting for eons, to emerge victorious not only to save ourselves but to assist other planets in a similar predicament to save *themselves too!* This job *will* be done one way or another and the only advice to those trying to stop us is, get out of the way.

There really isn't a great deal of philosophy to bloviate endlessly about and so, with no further ado, I will only say let's get on with it. Its time. In the end we will free ourselves and, ironically, the very keys to our liberation were within us the *entire time*.

Tuesday 25th April 2021

Willow Willis

PART ONE

*The illusion is over
believe in yourself*

CHAPTER ONE

ET TU, BRUTE`?

"And you, Brutus?" from The Tragedy of Julius Caesar upon recognising the betrayal of his friend as one of the assassins by William Shakespeare.

Betrayal would have to be the single worst outcome for any just person or noble cause ever accounted for in the expanse of historical record. From Julius Caesar to William Wallace to President Kennedy. There is no greater wound than betrayal. Even the murder of a complete stranger, however senseless and outrageous, if the assailant is apprehended, at least leaves the bereft with a finger of accusation to point at *someone*. The perpetrator, a focal point of rage and despair, is a monster to pin loss and hatred on allowing the bereft to at least diffuse *some* of their pain across a broader community of friends, family and neighbours as they come together united in their fortitude against such *monumental* and enduring injustices! Tragedy often brings out the best in people. We're known for it. It's sad but true. Beyond the tragedy though it is often the case that, post the event, the *betrayal* of the judicial system is a crime in *itself* leaving many who remain behind with a twisted knot of bitterness forever planted in their gut, a bitterness that reaches far beyond the horror of the initial crime long after it has been committed.

There are many different levels of betrayal yet however deep, broad or small that the betrayal *may* be, it's effects inevitably last to the crushing end of those who must prevail against it until a new generation with fresh **experiences** and new hopes wipe clean our collective memories as the hurts fade and the **betrayals of those who perpetrated them against us are forgotten.** But betrayal always comes back like an old lover foraging for whatever's left over, it returns, digging through the garbage like the last rogue bear gutsing whatever it can before the finality of winter and hibernation eventually conquers it. "Et tu, Brute`?" Maybe more aptly we should be crying, 'Et iterum, Brute`?' meaning 'And *again*, Brutus?!' Et iterum! Et iterum! Et iterum! And again! And again! And again! How many times can you be stabbed in the back? How many times can the assassins return for *another* jab? And another! And another! God it never ends! At this time in history our world sinks into a quagmire of epic betrayals worthy of biblical proportions, *literally*, as we round off against the monumental *betrayal* of the worldwide population by the *obvious* and fumbling attempts of an ever-failing *traitorous* body politic *posing* as your leaders, secretly siding with megalomaniacal corporations, scheming in private and unabashedly *selling you a lie* that rapidly falls apart by the day! The Grand Public now contemptuously scrutinises a rather *convenient* pandemic and rollout of a sudden *global* 'vaccine' after *two decades* of frankly farcical in-your-face conspiracies since 9/11 that have left even the *dullards* of mainstream media shuffling awkwardly in the direction of the once wretched conspiracy nuts. Safety in numbers, hey guys? Let's hope so.

But there is a story beyond the story. Always is. There is a root cause to all this chaos although we have summarily forgotten that root cause as its players fade into the litany of faces and names welling up in endless numbers from the mill of even our most *recent* social and political past. Once again, we find the Brutus's in our ranks. We discover the Robert the Bruce's on our side during daylight hours yet wearing the armour of the enemy by night switching sides whenever it suits them. "I want *them* to see what *they* have done to Jack" said Jackie Kennedy in her blood-stained pink Chanel suit. "Et tu, Brute`?" It's the same fucken story and we're sick of it. We're crumpling under never-ending betrayals some not yet even known to us as we jointly suffer mass battle fatigue. We're tired. "I shall attack them from all sides" said Satan in the Quran. This has gone on too long and just when we thought we were emerging into our hard-won freedom…no. Once more waylaid, we are! It's on *again*. Like an abusive relationship with a spouse who promises to change their ways and just never does. Always letting us down. Unable to change. We've finally concluded, however much it hurts, and at long last…it's them or us. We're sick of the endless wars and yet *more* looming mass disasters that go on and on. We voted hard, man. We prayed. We got existential on their asses! We've gotten philosophical, biblical, socially responsible, informed, even, dare I say, 'progressive' (gently hand me the vomit bag, would you, luv?). We've petitioned. We've even memed. Yet nothing works. It is a terrible conclusion we face. It is a sad end.

But I know a story, it is my own, and it plays very much into what we are all collectively experiencing *now* and once you know my story and my lifelong battle to tell it, maybe you too will understand there is far, far more than meets the eye going on here and we about to come face to face with our ultimate nightmare. We did everything we could to negotiate with it. To avoid the disaster on our path. We trusted them and *still* the monumental betrayal returns! To coin a phrase, 'You can't negotiate with terrorists' and these guys (and they are, by and large, males although I wouldn't call them 'men') are the worst most heavily armed and savvy terrorists in the history of the known world! We, on the other hand, us humans, however puny we may seem, have our computers, our voices, and the dream humanity has dared to dream since this whole wretched farce first reared its ugly head *ten thousand* years ago. *We will go on!* They can damn us to hell and back again and we will *still* go on. Our ancestors faced these motherfuckers *many times* and so shall we! I say this to you now, don't whimper, don't shy away and most certainly, don't run.

You see, most people view the monster as audaciously looming up at this time of despair *because* it is unbeatable. Like all those who went before us, at *some* time, they all faced the same monster and it appears the same monster has always prevailed because, well, it's still here. That said, we've always kept it at bay until it comes around again. We face yet another time of dread at what has arrived on our doorstep once more and never before have we been more weakened by this relentless foe, poisoned with their lies, nutritionally depleted and injected with toxins disrupting our nervous systems. Most of us are emotional wrecks and that's on a good day even *before* the shit kicks off! We're prone with confusion as the voices of society's once calm 'intellectuals' languidly discussing growing global issues now rise in hysterical pitch etched with palpable fear as they lose their shit and crumble with bewilderment. Debate's over, kids. The mass media 'critics' weren't so intellectual after all and their 'rational' lines of logic increasingly fail to explain the horror we are witnessing as an absurd truth weirdly becomes our new reality. Snap! Gotcha! The laughably impossible is, after all, possible as we come to terms with things that we are finding we have no defenses against, for example, demons, ghosts, aliens, cryptids, phenomena, portals, slips in time, *time travel*, overlaying/downloading a person's consciousness into another person's body, human harvesting, soul transfer, witchcraft, black magic, voodoo. All of it militarized and all of it practiced on this planet for eons right in front of our faces only we were too immature to accept it was happening let alone deal with it. We must deal with it now. We must. There is no other option. The same people who told us these things were rubbish are the same ones doing it to us. It's hilarious for them. They love our naivete. They get a kick out of their power trip over a sentient species, humans, that is, by all other accounts, better than them on every conceivable level. That's why they hate us. They're jealous.

Many people are learning the hard way that there are *still* too many questions left unanswered despite all our technology in the 'information' age. Oh yes, we are going to explore subjects that *many* are struggling to comprehend while others aim their misdirected anger in a self-flagellation of self-medicated alcoholism and drugs abuse to numb the pain of it all. But truly, I tell you, never before has a greater opportunity presented itself to see the beast outside of its lair, out in the open, where we can *truly* see it for what it *really* is and *this* time formulate a *real* plan. Let it come. This horrendous beast has sent forth it's cronies and gofers for decades even hundreds, *thousands*, of years in advance, to make sure the that the people have been adequately buttered-up for its grand entrance and final takeover. That's because the beast is secretly a coward. It is afraid. This long lead up to its arrival is just *another* gimmick of psychological warfare. Genghis Kahn had a successful military tactic. He would lay waste to a few people's, crush most brutally those who opposed him even invite them to oppose him and using their example of obliteration, he would send his emissaries to give others a forewarning, a chance, to give in to him before he arrived. It saved him on military expenditures, energy of troops and supplies stockpiling his resources for further expansion *after* his initial conquest. He did well. He will go down in history as one of the most convincing and calculating military minds of all time. But it only lasted one generation his son unable, as often happens, to match his father's prowess and the once great empire fell to the wretched politicians again! The schemers always lurking in the wings like vultures waiting for the King to weaken and even seeking to weaken him. They all want to be top dog. This is the very same tactic as the beast that moves upon us now. To inflate itself out of all proportion. To scare the enemy, us, with its *potential*. To kill us *in our minds* first, to crush us *in our hearts*, before it grinds us unto dust in the physical!

I am going to tell you a story now and I encourage you to hear me out and although it may seem a little dire, it's fitting for what we now experience and may give you some inspiration, even resolve, to do what must be done. Your story, like most people's, has a similar plotline in that your parents met, got involved, set up a home, started a family. You were born. You were named. Baby photos were taken. You outgrew your diapers, shorts, pants. You attended school. You became a child, a teenager, a young adult. You variously attended high schools and universities or trade schools or entered the work force. Some travelled. Some stayed home. It is the story of basically everyone particularly in 1st and 2nd world countries with generally westernized social ambitions. The themes aren't too exciting but hey, the world is an amazing place. The world is your oyster! At least, that's what we were led to believe. I'm gonna cut to the chase to save you some time. If you've read the first installment of my book, Epic Series Vol.1 *2020 & Beyond – This is Not a Drill*, then what I am about to say to you is nothing new. For those of you who are reading this for the first time, I highly recommend you get some context and read the first book or take a look at two videos I posted on YouTube titled under the same name, otherwise, I may appear to be a complete and utter nut-job. Either way, it's up to you.

Science and the weirdness of what they've been doing behind the scenes *unchecked* is slowly unraveling by the day and a *very* disturbing picture is emerging. You would be *amazed* how many 'ordinary' people are *unwittingly* involved in secret science projects and don't even know it. Some big. Some small. Science is cruel. Religion is cruel. Politics is cruel. We need something totally different from these three models of commerce and control. So, let me start at the start. In the beginning…just kidding…that's lame. Let me start by saying that, like you, yes, a baby was born – *moi* - my parents selected a name. Baby photos were taken, well, *one* baby photo was taken that may or may not be me. Yet my life goes back before then. This body was born, but *I*, my consciousness, *me*, was beamed in. Yes, *beamed* in. They got their 'soul transfer' technology from treaties with ET's and throughout this book I'm going to reference movies and TV shows to help you understand what I'm talking about and I *highly* encourage you to take a look at these productions as it's all part of the *massive* manipulation program to take ownership of Humanity and Mother Earth emanating from shady agencies worldwide. To dress up fundamental truths as 'fiction' and 'fantasy' then hide these things in plain sight, in pop culture as movies and TV shows so you won't believe it if it *really* happens. Its diabolical albeit basic psychology though. Therefore, take a look at a film called *Self/less* with Ryan Reynolds and Ben Kingsley about a rich mogul dying of cancer who pays to have his consciousness transferred into a young healthy man. You also need to take a look at a 1966 film, *Seconds,* starring Rock Hudson (no wonder they destroyed him) which details how wealthy bored men can have their deaths faked by a secret agency then have their *entire identities* changed to live the high life elsewhere. The catch is there's no going back once they've signed up and they don't get a choice as to who they are selected to become called 'Reborns'. Great flick. They do really crazy things so if you try to expose them you just wind up looking really crazy. It's evil genius. Bravo. *Sound of one hand clapping.* Stares blankly.

At *this* time in modern history we are now seeing the third and fourth waves of *industrialised* mind-controlled generations of people who have been programmed with different objectives to suit this *unbelievable* unfolding narrative in an *incredible* cosmic script that literally stretches offworld! Yes, it's about to get weird. Hang in there. So, I remember being beamed into this reality from a place outside my body, not from before I was born, but *outside* my current body. I was supposed to believe the place I remember was some sort of space-platform orbiting Earth, possibly alien like a mothership or something. Maybe it was? I don't know. I can tell you though that it has very real-world ramifications about to shake things up on a global scale as people's *real* memories return and they experience what's called Total Recall. No, this isn't just a shitty Hollywood sci-fi. This is really happening! I was part of a program that was, and is, *massive* and one of, if not the *most*, secretive and outlandish programs in the world directly attempting to install the 'Anti-Christ' and/or 'Messiah' depending what mood they're in on the day. Bill Cooper blew the whistle on this in the 1990's and, among other things, it cost him his life. I note recently, Wilfred Wong, a British barrister, satanic cult-hunter and whistleblower made mention of the conspiracy to install an Anti-Christ-One World Leader and now he finds himself in the clink under rather spurious circumstances. Yes, a barrister. No one is safe now. Please support him. We need more courageous people like him.

When it comes to this plan to install the anti-Christ, *they're all in on it* from Hollywood royalty to Euro-British royalty to politicians to global clergy in every country, *worldwide,* all vying to be the father of this faker. And because they can transfer souls, the father becomes the son, *literally!* It's their satanic take on the organic functions of Mother Nature. Their ego is beyond comprehension. If they think that this world is going to go around for another turn on the fake one-male-god merry-go-round then frankly, their *idiocy* is scary in and of itself! The seams are about to burst wide open on this one and I'm happy to help it along! Bring it. This secret is *so big* and right in front of us that it beggar's belief how they can keep a lid on this stuff! It's like some mass Jedi mind trick that people are, even still, unaware of despite how obvious it *should* be. And anyone in-the-know who develops loose lips? Their ship sinks pretty damn quick! Many have paid with their lives for this. This is why it requires someone who is on the 'outside' like myself who never profited and suffered *deeply* for what I am about to tell you. They've secretly tried to kill me *many* times as I remained loyal to a program that was *not* loyal to me.

I thought we were helping.

Firstly, there is no 'we'. They didn't intend for me to achieve my objectives. I was *supposed* to fail. Therefore, having survived their *insanity* I owe them nothing conversely, they owe me *everything* but I *aint* holding my breath! Yes, bitter betrayal. It's a big story to tell so I'll break it down into manageable chunks for you. It's hard for me to even believe it myself let alone ask you to believe it and yet it will all come out in the end and it will change *everything.* Honestly, at this point I don't know the name of the program but two programs mentioned by Max Spiers piqued my interest. He unfortunately got himself killed rather conveniently for those he was about to expose. I am always looking for more information so if you think you know something or any online link, please, send them on. Project Ibis and Project Oaktree were apparently two projects designed to manifest certain souls into certain bloodlines via certain mothers 'star seeds' born during the 70's & 80's but it goes back further than that possibly to the 1920's and no doubt have continued on. It's tied up with Tesla technology. Most people's memories begin as a toddler, my memories begin at some science facility *prior* to being 'beamed' into this body. I don't know where this facility is or what it's called although, increasingly, it *appears* to have been based out of or has direct connection to the US specifically, New Orleans, Louisiana. Interestingly, this is where they set the movie *Self/less* which allows them to claim 'plausible deniability' brushing off anyone who tries to expose this *real program* as suffering from a 'mental illness' triggered by movies. 'You must have seen it on TV'. 'You're an obsessed fan'. 'Wannabe starlet'. 'What' *wrong* with you?'. 'We've got a pill for that' or worse an injection. Can you believe it's come to this? It's like the whole world has become cold-war

Russia. Stoke up the KGB! We must now be afraid of some psycho nurse or Nazi doctor looming up with a hypodermic! We have arrived. Christ! No pun. This *epic* conspiracy has *massive* ties to mainstream global religions, major American politics, A-list entertainment and *their* secret religion and the arrival of the 'new-age' of Aquarius and the 'prophesised' second coming of another male god-messiah all primed in advance for *billions* of religious people *worldwide* to say, *'I tolja so!'* and all the shit show that goes along with *that*. The 'ascension' is turning into a cult and people are scrambling to get onboard. The evil plans to manipulate the new-age *must be derailed* and I have gone through hell and high water to help do so.

Just over four decades ago I recall being ushered into a room. It was fairly ordinary. The décor was 1970's tre` shit couture with lots of burnt oranges and browns. Fifty shades of brown. Which is why I don't believe it was a super-advanced orbiting space platform from the future. Little clues, folks. It wasn't like these sci-fi movies with all this fancy equipment, it was very simple, from memory. I entered the room, turned right and viewed a trapezoidal shaped computer screen where I was shown images of my soon-to-be family via 'keyhole in your ceiling' technology that made me feel like I was actually there in 3D. They specifically showed me images of what appeared to be a functional happy-go-lucky family. They gave me 'the spiel' and it is etched into my mind in ways that is different from normal memories. It goes like this, 'There's a spot coming up in this family. It's yours if you want it. It's a good one. You'll be given all the tools you need to do the job but remember, it's not going to be easy'. Telling someone that a task isn't going to be easy as opposed to telling them it's going to be *impossible* is two *very* different things. To tell someone 'this hill isn't going to be easy to climb but it *can* be done' gives one the impetus to at least *try*. Telling someone 'this hill is impossible to climb with bracken and sharp rocks, you will be injured, fall down and wish you hadn't bothered' will basically eliminate most people from attempting it. Later in life when all this started unfolding, I realized their monumental *betrayal* in that I was sent in not to achieve some altruistic objective, no, I was sent in to *suffer and die* and there are *big* reasons *why* they would do this hating women being one of them but we'll get to that. I was given one choice and one choice only this life and body or nothing at all. Although the family they selected looked like a happy bunch/, I wasn't initially convinced that I wanted to be a part of it unsure of whether I should 'come in'. So, they showed me another clip this one very convincing which tugged at my heartstrings and my 'helper' psychology. The underdog warrior. The David and Goliath routine. Impossible odds? Little chance of success? Where do I sign up? So, I decided I would give it a go. But what was I signing up for? I was only aware that something *really big* was coming and whatever needed to be done could basically save the *whole* world and the future of humanity. I would be some sort of lifelong secret undercover agent in that I would be one of however-many-others sent in to perform certain tasks at this time that was, ultimately, a *really* good cause. It was a standard Hollywood-style 'suicide mission' but a mission nonetheless. I remember thinking 'just get me in there, we'll knock this over no worries at all!' It *should* have been pretty straightforward.

I recall at some point standing in someone's office or certainly standing in front of a large painting or photograph of a *speed-hump* overlaid with a *maroon* filter. By way of clues to assist me, I was given three symbols, the word a *trapezoid*, *Wednesday* as well as the *speed-hump* and the colour *Maroon*. That's all I got to navigate this shit-hole. Every other memory, the backstory of this entire thing and what they were doing, who was involved and indeed who *I* was, was wiped, erased, from my memory. I attempted to do some research on these hints during the course of my life but without some crucial context, it was all just gibberish. For example, in mythology, Wednesday is ruled over by the god Hermes the god of *speed*. In Eastern philosophy the colour maroon is the colour of the root chakra. Hermes. Root chakra. Speed. And? What does that mean? It meant nothing to me until a couple of *crucial* details were revealed to me after much hardship, pain and suffering nearing the end of my apparent 'initiation' period of *forty fucking years* to line me up with this new age 'cycle' of Aquarius. This involved the *deliberate* sabotage and brutal wastage of my entire life *and* family. When I was received these small yet *critical* insights, I took off like a rocket. I can run on the sniff of an oily rag indeed and an astrologer said to me I had this 'big job' coming up and that I was 'built for this'. I didn't need an astrologer to tell me something *big* was coming. I always knew that. When I was a kid I tried to probe the future with one of my many psychic talents and it appeared as a *massive* maroon coloured 'sandstorm', *the rose storm*, silent, ever encroaching, from horizon to horizon, from ground to sky.

See You Next Wednesday is a Masonic inside joke found in many movies as a take on the phrase C U Next Tuesday or *CUNT*. I've discovered the codes of an entire secret satanic religion based on ancient mythology built into pop culture. Famous artists are known historically for coding their secrets into art hiding in it  in plain sight. This old Masonic trick now successfully exposes them as we gather more tools and information to piece this together and while interesting, these guys aint no Rembrandt. What we are about to face is something *so* enormous nothing like it has ever been seen before on Planet

Earth so, buckle up, Dorothy! To say it is 'epic' is a bit of an understatement. *Hold on*. We're going to get through this. They don't want you to know that.

After they showed me my family and I agreed to 'come in', I was led up a corridor and as we were walking one of the guys escorting me laughed and said, 'Oh, by the way, don't bother trying to remember. *Nobody* remembers!' So, there's others? 'I *will* remember', I thought to myself and I did. We turned right and entered another room that had soft lighting and faceted walls with a blue hue. Years later I would see images of the 'golf-ball' geodesic domes photographed at secret science facilities located in the desert. I knew I was about to do something *extremely important* and as I took my position, I looked around taking a mental snapshot of the room then focused *intently* on my heart centre, *my heart chakra*. I closed my eyes and repeated in my mind, 'you have to remember this, you have to remember this, you have to remember this!' *I hung on for dear life*. Next thing I know I open my eyes and I am in a totally different environment. I recall my curiosity like I had literally been beamed into another world or dimension. It's *literally* like the movie The Matrix the only difference being Neo, *note*, the name The One was busted out then inserted *back* in and could come and go from the construct at will. I, on the other hand, was just beamed in, no prior experience, no getting out and *no choice* as to whom I was being beamed into! I was utterly fascinated despite the fact that it wasn't a particularly exciting environment. It was a simple room in a simple house, yet I was absolutely enthralled! I looked up at the enormous door sailing above me. The door handle might well have been four stories high! For some reason I remember I was fascinated by the wood of the door frame like it was *actual* wood! It was as if I hadn't seen wood before. It was *amazing*, although simple, the details were incredible! I was gob smacked, 'They said they would do it...and they did!' It was *literally* a 'matrix', a virtual reality.

As I was growing up, I was intrigued to see that what was broadcasting as 'fiction' on TV actually bears a *striking* resemblance to what I had experienced. Yes, it's big, it's multilayered and you are about to have your mind blown so get ready. The opening credits and music of Dr Who scared the hell out of me. The series 'V' was like watching the future and I knew, 'that's going to happen one day'. When I saw Star Trek's 'beam me up Scotty' I was literally beside myself as I gestured vigorously at the TV and then at myself unable to even verbalise my excitement. I just kept pointing at the TV and at myself going 'ugh! Ugh! UGH!' Trying to tell my family 'that happened to me!' Many people claim aspects of their lives or programs they were involved in were found in TV shows growing up. It's all a part of the mind-fuck like 'who's going to believe me? It's on the TV for gods sake!' TV is hacking our perceptive functions like a computer virus. It's evil genius. It's maddening. Therefore, one man's fact is another man's fiction and vice versa. There is actually a program called Operation Mind-Fuck and when people can't tell the difference between what's real and what's not they will unleash the Old Ones, ancient evil 'gods' - *aliens!* Your enemies are aliens from the demonic realm. Same thing. Their IQ's measure in the four, five and six digits and as much as we hate to admit it, we're no match for them *intellectually*. Yet there is a *big* secret that I will tell you about in this book and it will level the playing field once and for all so hang on. Shit just got real.

I *distinctly* remember my first impression, 'it's very convincing, no wonder they believe it'. It was night-time as I became aware that it was dark and creepy and immediately felt an explosion of 'fear' in my gut chakra as my solar plexus logged onto this bio-frequency/matrix. I suddenly panicked and realised I'd made a *big* mistake, 'I don't want to do this! I want to go back! This is all wrong!' But it's a one-way ticket. There is no going back. I felt trapped but quickly had to resign myself to the business of getting about being an ordinary kid in an ordinary family. I must have had training or was selected for certain traits that I retained after my insertion as I militarily got about my mission from the *earliest* age. Despite being highly sensitive my behaviour over the years indicates a practical almost matter-of-fact approach to the difficulties I faced literally like a special reconnaissance agent sent into the field gathering information. In the Matrix they speak about Agent Smith and being 'one of them' and 'if you see one…run'. Even as a toddler if I saw an officer I suddenly felt the strong desire to break into a run.. They are agents of the dark order even if they don't know it themselves yet.

I've also received ongoing 5D auric energy-field treatments, downloads, upgrades and reinforcements that I shouldn't have remembered during sleep states all shrouded through a maroon filter. I have retained a never-say-die attitude that would render most people incapacitated *very* early on in life under the same circumstances. In fact, sometimes I can't believe how weak and self-indulgent people are. If only you knew what was at stake you would put aside most of this *emotional* new-age sewage and fight like hell. There is a big fight over me right now in secret places and however ordinary, even dull, my life may seem there are things happening in the wings that is nothing short of a science fiction shit-fight as they scramble to either make me or break me. As I sit in my little studio typing this, one couldn't conceive of the absurdity of it all. Sigh. Sometimes I would say to my family, "they beamed me in! I remember! But I'm the same person there that I am here but how can that be?" It didn't make any sense. You are *literally* being blanketed by frequencies of fear (nervous stomach) as this reality locks into all your chakras at various levels plugging you in like a multi-socket electrical power board. Everything is electricity and we are increasingly understanding that we must be plugged into an alien matrix that syncs us into *their* preferred reality via our brain, DNA and meridians where your physical body becomes your cellular body and chemical processes, electrochemical signals and finally, dissipate into the subatomic, energetic and metaphysical planes. *These* are the different 'dimensions' and we are already interacting with them on *many* levels. Therefore, we must be unlocked, unplugged *somehow*, to 'get out' of their energetic trap. It's a metaphysical jail break! When confronted with the *idiocy* of the masses, remind yourself, people have been *locked* into their lower frequencies and however impossible it may seem, *once energetically liberated*, humanity will do incredible things. Wait and watch. It's coming, folks. Hold on!

The fact that we only use about 5% of our brain, chakras and DNA *ought to raise some eyebrows*. Twice is coincidence, three times is enemy action. We've been shut out of ourselves. Our higher functions have been locked down by a diabolical *alien enemy* to keep us prisoner, pets even, to their demands as they whimsically indulge their *every desire* at our expense, like gods indeed *they are* the 'gods' of myth and legend. Liars. Frauds. Stand-ins. Interlopers. Impostors of the lowest order regaling themselves in the face of a once great species, humanity, reduced in capacity like cosmic retards who were once the *true royalty* of our beautiful planet become peasants in their sick alien empire! We are captive to their egomaniacal *need* to be worshiped. As a spiritually higher species, these concepts are literally alien to our higher cognitive functions as human beings as we still retain long lost memories of our once great former selves. We suffer a sort of collective dementia triggered by an innate sense they cannot seem to destroy, a sense that reminds us we were once wonderful and will be again! These higher functions were described by Greek poet Hesiod as the 'Higher State of Man'. It's this *will* to resist them that still lies buried in our collective psyches despite all that they have done to us. This is why we keep trying to break out despite our willingness to be compliant and 'go along' with the madness (to a point) as we are at heart non-confrontational. We contradictorily fight like hell against their psychotic rule *because* we are not like them. As such, in this transitional phase we are in a state of flux trying to understand our position in all this. It will pass. We will prevail against them. Their time is near and they know it.

Humans are *fundamentally* a different species specifically when it comes to spirituality. We are from the light. They are from the dark. We are sun people we *literally* live in the light of the sun and are *warm* blooded. They are cold blooded and like snakes that lie in the hot sunshine to get their warmth, they must attach to light beings, *us*, to get *their* source of light otherwise they will sink to darkness and die. But true to their nature they can't live in balance, they can't just be here *undetected*. No. They must consume us and act in our place as a weird cosmic clone. As such, when they access our light broadcast from the sun ultimately harnessed from the centre of the galaxy, their patriarchal hyper-masculine obsession kicks in and, awed by the power of the light, has spawned generations of the 'sun kings' and solar deities 'gods' which I'll get to soon. The egomania of these creatures to hack into the light via us and then use *our* light *against us* to position themselves as false 'gods' gives you an indication of their level of their *insidiousness*. In this way we may understand that the cryptic lies we have been told via religion regarding 'angels' and 'demons' is actually describing *us and them*. *We* are the 'angels' of old. *They* are the devils, *demons*, of old. It is not 'out there' as described in every Abrahamic religion and *all* major religious institutions and governments have *some serious answering to do* given that if a person like myself can figure this out, the obvious question is, why haven't they? They *know* it's all lies, a *deliberate* lies that has worked *very well* for their power mongering and ruthless ambitions to *become* an idealised *preconceived* version of *their* idea of 'god' *as benefits them*. It is this power mongering, lying, entrapment and cruelty that they *will* answer for. This knowledge of good and evil, light and dark, angels and demons, and the *power* this knowledge unleashes is patently *inside* us. You must try to understand *this* is what defines us as separate entities from them and it is *why* we continue to resist them after eons of their brutality and deliberate manipulation of the highest order. They are cosmic criminals and justice, one way or another, will be served. It can be no other way. After a reign of terror, if we are to survive, there must be balance and that balance calls, firstly, for them to cease operations at the current level they are operating and get the fuck out of our planet once and for all!

It is innate to the very substance of our existence to *not* fall into their final criminal act which is to turn humanity into something that is not even human anymore - cybernetically implanted genderless sterile mutants all in the name of progress! We seem to have forgotten the term 'transhuman' – which means *beyond* human - was being widely used only a few years ago along with the term 'Agenda 21'. So now we're in 2021 and hundreds of millions of people are lining up for injections that will bring into effect the largest unknown biological alteration of human DNA the world has ever seen but there's no connection? All on the 20th anniversary of 911 and we have COVID-19 or is it COVID-911? Anyone? The human race is so morbidly stupid it's a wonder how anyone will get out of this and yet we do in a trick of fate as a last minute change. Their vast sweeping alien empire that stretches throughout our solar system into the Milky Way and beyond. From what I understand it's a series of interlocked 'royal' alien space corporations, syndicates, that target certain planets for their resources as well as these aliens' compatibility with the host *sentient* species found on said planets. They move in on the target population using sonic technology to prepare the host sentient species for their infiltration on every level blasting the inhabitants until they are practically vegetative. Once incapacitated, they move in on the target population genetically fusing with the sentient species' genetics appearing to be, look and act *exactly* like their victims to take them *over from the inside out*. Invasion of the body snatchers! Its tactical. They are militants. It's classic parasitism. They are some sort of alien larva-parasite, a cosmic virus, integrating with selected species throughout the galaxy and *becoming* them over time until there is no *obvious* differences like a changeling, a cuckoo, replacing the *original* species with something not of its former nature to trick the universe into believing *they* are the rightful sentient species of this planet, *morphing us to them,* and *posing* in our place. It's multilayered beyond most people's comprehensions and why the necessity to go to *such lengths* which strongly indicates there *must* be some sort of repercussions if they are ever found out otherwise, why the big parade? Why the *protracted* process? The dullards muse, 'but why haven't they just taken us over already?' It's because, and you'll be grateful for this one day, there are *rules* to the cosmos, *Universal Laws* of fair play, protect us from those who dare to break those rules. There are recoil effects they are *terrified* of and it's the *knowing* that makes what they do so risky. They cannot plead ignorance. They skate close to the edge. Thrill-seekers. Otherwise, they would have simply used their advanced weaponry consume us already and easily so. The rigmarole, games and *huge* charade is *because* there are other things going on beside them. Things that are bigger. Better. Faster. Stronger.

It's *very much* like the movie Dune what is happening to us. When they use up a planet of its resources and it is dead, they move on. Like the Borg in Star Trek. It's all romanticized and animated with all the cutesy touchy-feely themes emanating out of Hollywood just *one* of their many control tendrils. It's creepy. This is the mind fuck we're currently battling. You have emotions *because* you are warm-blooded. They are cold-blooded and therefore have no emotions. I hazard a guess all living planets have at least *one* sentient species and it's *because* these aliens lack the 'light body', the sun body, of the chakras and the meridians that they breed with or genetically alter/splice themselves with certain sentient species who *do* harbour the chakra systems. They then hack into the higher dimension *through* us. Otherwise, they're trapped in lower vibrational 'dark', *cold*, dimensions which is why wherever they show up good shit goes bad, light turns to dark. But not as bad as their *true* dimensional state, which is pure chaos, pure evil. Yet some of them see an opportunity to get out for good but I don't want to get too far ahead of myself as there is just *so much to cover.* As I piece all this together try to understand the *expanse* of this *unbelievably enormous* ET syndicate. The depth and breadth of it can be overwhelming so, we'll just focus on one thing at a time. Manageable chunks.

So, there I was beamed into the body of a toddler and suddenly very small! It was all was quite confusing yet exciting as I had just come from being a full-sized adult into a body about three and half years old, yet I still carried a lot of my adult 'maturity' with me. Its mind blowing as I get older and comprehend the enormity of this. I had some shocking flashbacks as a kid as temporarily my *conscious* mind fought this 'reality' as if clashing with my subconscious mind and *deeper* knowledge hidden there like two opposing energy fields causing occasional static. One time when I was about five years old, I was sitting at the breakfast table eating my soggy Vita-Brits when suddenly, I looked around at my siblings and my parents and began to feel *real* panic. What was this place? Where am I? What's going on?! WHO ARE THESE PEOPLE?! Whenever this fracture occurred, a gentle voice, my own mature voice, would come into my mind saying, 'Calm down. It's going to be okay. Don't say anything'. It was *very important* not tell anyone. To say anything was *very* dangerous it was a 'big no, no' and I had to be on the alert *all the time* and have remained so ever since. What a job.

The child I was beamed into was small and uncoordinated lacking real speech or real personality at the time therefore, the family would *never* suspect let alone notice that someone *else* was now inhabiting their kid. It's being done all the time with scientific methods and also entity attachments and black magic, in fact, it's left me wondering just how much of ourselves *we* actually are! There are many programs on and off world that are doing this. Kids are easy targets at that age as their personality hasn't set in yet and they can't physically articulate anyway so there is little chance anyone will notice except for a few minor things passed off as developmental quirks. The movie Being John Malkovich is creepy as shit! And the end where the guy gets beamed into a kid's body and loses himself inside the mind of the emerging child's personality? Phew! I came in at three and a half which is old enough to remember what you're actually doing and generally who you are. Anything earlier than that and, yes, I can see how one could be absorbed and *forgotten*, forever deleted, inside the psyche of the developing brain. *Remembering is everything.* I can tell you now, all these years later, Hollywood is a nest of science experiments and all manner of weird alien matrix programs, mind control, black magic, witchcraft, secret science and unbelievable out-of-this-world members of a space syndicate granting themselves *the best* positions in the world! What did Donald Trump say? 'When you're a 'star' *they* let you do anything!' Who are *they*, Donny? More on *that* soon. And reptilians? We'll get to *that* too.

This book is being written because you are about to get a rude awakening as the reality of what I am saying is increasingly bought out into the light of day. To that end, we face a rare opportunity to reveal the *actual* truth of the matter and celebrities are crucial to this process as they take a firm grip on their balls and…tell all. They like a scandal? They're gonna lu-urv this! One of the reasons they really sold me the idea to come into my family was largely due to practicality. My father was a multi-instrumentalist and jack of all trades, there wasn't anything he couldn't do and I witnessed many of his marvels. My mother was a fashion designer and a singer who owned two fashion design houses in her early twenties called *Anne's Creations*. She was deeply interested in *everything*. They were a real pair, my parents. Talk about the odd couple. They were both highly intelligent, talented and very attractive. They were really something I can tell you. They would dance to the old 1940's tunes and taught me everything I know including tap-dancing, various other dance styles, fashion, sewing, design, singing, drawing, sketching, writing, poetry, musical instruments - you name it. Our home was a creative powerhouse and it appears the *best* artists in the world, including my parents, don't get their due props, passed up for well-connected louts! Our shelves were piled with old books and strange ancient mechanism's like antique typewriters oozing craftsmanship and sophisticated detail that has all but disappeared from the aptitudes of late 20th early 21st century people. With barely any wall space left, original paintings done by various family members lined every available area and unending drawers and cupboards were filled with interesting oddities and strange marvels a little curious girl could really sink her creative teeth into. It was Dickensian to say the least! Coupled with this, my father and mother both had their fair share of 'psychic' abilities although we never really called it that but they both had stories about unusual shared happenings.

My dad was 54 when I was born and, in keeping with the *symbolic* script, he was born on 5th November 1923. Guy Fawkes Day. In 2023 he will have been born *100 years ago*. Time is not what *you* think it is. He had a rose coloured love-heart shaped birthmark on his upper left bicep. He died around 4am on 04.04.04. My mother was born on 28th July 1942, the beginning of the Lions Gate when Earth, Sirius and the Galactic Centre are in alignment. Oh yes, there's reasons for *all* this. I was the youngest of five kids and this will become important as I reveal more of the previously mentioned *enormous* mythical ritual our *whole world* is engaged in and how they recreate and replicate the past in their twisted astro-plot *trying* to trick the universe that this is 'normal'. All up we were seven and two dogs, Woof & Jellybean, so, nine really. I was three and half when dad handed me a harmonica and told me to copy him, move when he moved, breath in and out when he breathed. I was so small I didn't know left from right so mirroring him meant I turned the harmonica around the wrong way which didn't bother him, so he didn't correct me in his endevours to train my little mind. He was just happy I was playing so didn't over-complicate things as such, I play it the harmonica the 'wrong' way around to this day. From memory we played Jingle Bells and he was obviously pretty happy about what I had done finding a little protege` to pass his considerable musical knowledge onto. It wasn't long before he had me on the Chromatic harmonicas, big double tiered 'half-note' instruments with a button on the end to change key. They are the type of mouth-organs played in orchestra's and by professional artist's Larry Adler among them. My dad was better than Larry Adler no offence to anyone. It was like eating a club sandwich. He taught me a lot of classical music and big band swing music from his era, the 1940's. I just thought it was fun as I whipped around all over the place remembering to take huge gulping breaths when a long breathing part was coming up. He would carefully roll out his array of various harmonica's and select a special one just for me which made me feel very important. He said back in his day you could get harmonicas with bells on them and all manner of tinkles you could flick as you played to enhance the sound. All sorts of things.

    Selecting a harmonica was like a solemn ceremony as he carefully chose one that was an octave above or below to harmonise the sounds of a song he had in mind. It mildly amused me to be able to keep up with an accomplished musician five decades my senior when I was so little. I couldn't understand why others couldn't play. What was wrong with them? Sometimes after a big number dad would be hopping around the lounge-room saying, 'See! I told you, Annie! She's a bloody little genius!" Mum would say wisely, 'When you're successful just remember where you come from' – not 'if' but *when* you are successful. It was just *expected* I would be a successful artist one day. It was a given. There was no other course for me. After harmonica came guitar at age four and then a string, no pun, of instruments, keyboard, piano, piano accordion, violin, flute, cornet (a little trumpet), percussion. I was playing eight instruments by the time I was about twelve and because we were poor I knew I wouldn't get any professional training so set my own learning guidelines. As such, I created a personal rule that I needed to get a *full* song out of *any* instrument with little to no errors in an hour and a half *or less*. I didn't know you weren't supposed to do that so I just did. It was a game to me.

    Dad was the type of man who moved around a lot for work as a sole trader-contract tiler so we could leave at the drop of a hat. I jokingly referred to my parents as Bonnie and Clyde - always on the run! He was really good at everything and tiled many beautiful homes and particularly admired the mosaic style found in the ancient world. He was pretty brash and would simply drive into any town, see an empty house, and move in! He had five kids, so he didn't give a fuck whether it was right or wrong. We came first. He must have known a thing or two about squatter's rights and usually, when owners bothered to see that their property was being repaired by some bloke with five kids, they didn't say much. As dad had grown up in the Depression era of the 1920's and 30's our houses had a similar ring, everything was run on kerosene including lamps and heaters etc. He converted an electric fridge into a kerosene fridge an electric oven into a kerosene oven. We had primus stoves, a gas hot water service that he converted for showers and a black n white TV run on car batteries. Hey, it worked. That's right, I grew up without electricity in the 1980's. There, I said it. I once asked dad, 'why don't you have to power put on?' and his reply was simple, 'well, if you don't have the power switched on they can't switch it off'. I couldn't argue with his logic on that. When my friends had modular houses, pools and phones(!) we had tilly lamps and kero. It was a little slice of remote outback Australia in suburbia. I didn't have electricity until I moved out when I was 18, got a job and started running my own life. I didn't even know how to work a washing machine and had to ask my housemate to show me. Then I asked how to operate the microwave and everything else until she was looking at me like 'what the fuck?' I still went home though for stays over, meals and catch-ups. It was definitely unique. Other people were boring. Some of my siblings even went into counseling over this in adult life as if they had been cheated? Now it's called 'off grid' and people are proud to go to great lengths to achieve it. Hilarious! As I was the youngest, everything was an adventure. I didn't care. Hey, its handy when you're in a jam. He was often saying to us in the early 90's 'you've gotta get a little block of land and grow your own garden. You've gotta get out of the system and to start doing it *now*'. He knew what was coming. When he was old and on his deathbed he said, 'if I had my time over' we gathered closer to hear his final sage words of wisdom, 'I would have travelled the world. I wouldn't have had bunch of bloody kids!' Thanks dad. Awesome.

When I was around four, we were living I a caravan park. It was bleak, cold, muddy, poor and depressing. There was a little boy who lived near us called Kevin. Kevin was seven. He was at least three times my size and an oafish large lad. Kevin's dad would refer to Kevin's mother as 'woman' and I often heard, 'Get me a can of beer, *woman!*' emanating out of their shitty caravan which was better than ours. One day while playing on the swings, Kevin decided he wanted me off the swing and said, 'get off the swings, woman!' He was a little boy and didn't know his dad was an idiot so, monkey see monkey do. I didn't know what it meant but I knew I didn't like the *sound* of what he was saying so I said, 'Don't call me 'woman''. As little boys do he challenged me because I was a little girl, 'get off the swings, woman!' I repeated flatly, 'Don't call me 'woman''. So, of course, he yelled, 'Woman! Woman! Woman!' A subconscious response occurred in me as the swing made an upward trajectory and I bodily continued its velocity launching myself at a pivotal point from the rising arc through mid-air landing on Kevin's chest. We crashed to the ground as I sat on top of him my little fists balled into a fury of hatred and anger pummeling the piss out of Kevin until a sibling dragged me off. Kevin ran back to his caravan screaming in tears and probably received a secondary hiding for getting beaten up by a little girl half his size and age. Many years later Kevin wound up at our primary school and kept pestering my brother if he had a little sister. My brother, as boys do, denied my existence until one day he conceded that he did have a little sister. Kevin remembered only too well, the incident had obviously left a lasting impression, as he said in awe, 'I remember her! She beat me up!' I can only hope Kevin learned a lifelong lesson out of that. Don't treat women like dirt you might be surprised.

One time I remember another bleak winter and dad had taken up residence in some vacant house he found in a nice area. Mum put us in school, well, the older ones, I was too young and stayed at home waiting like a loyal pet forlornly staring at the door for them all to return. One day we heard a loud confident knock at the front door. The knock. It always happened eventually. As usual I was on dad's heels following him everywhere. He opened the door and there stood an official looking man with his fat gut hanging over his belt and his tie flapping in the wind. I was always terrified aware of our precarious situation. Mum and dad were always wary of Welfare looking to take poor family's kids away from them. "You're squatting in my house!" the man yelled immediately on the offence, "This is *my* house. You get out! You're not allowed to be in here!" I remember one of the walls at the side had a huge hole in it that my father had bricked up among other things. It was his way of paying rent. My father said, "Hang on, mate. I'm doing the place up. Making it livable. It's vacant. No one's lived here for years". In Australia, you call mates 'cunt' and cunts 'mate'. The man yelled, "I don't care! This *my* house. You get out! We don't need rabble like you around here!"

   The old boy was a bit of a mystery. He knew things. Even today I wonder about his ways. He said, "You're that bloke Colquhoun, aren't you?" Pronounced Ka-hoon. "Yeh, what about it?" Colquhoun was notorious, a cocky bastard, a stand-over man and rich small-town thug. My father said, "You're running for Mayor, aren't you?" "I am!" Mr. Colquhoun was a local businessman who owned half the town and had his billboards all over the place with his sly cheesy grin *Vote #1 Colquhoun for Mayor!* He looked like Bill Heslop from Murial's Wedding they all do. I'll never forget my dad laying this bloke low in one fell swoop. "Well, I've got five kids here. You put me out in the street and I'll go straight up to the local paper and tell them the future Mayor just made a man, his wife and their five kids homeless in the dead of winter". Silence. No doubt dad gestured toward my wide eyed innocent little face peering out around his legs in terror. What a front page! My little street urchin face! *"Father of Five Evicted by Candidate for Mayor Colquhoun!"* Gold! They would *love* that kind of scandal in a dull little town! Colquhoun stammered, "Now, now, mate! There's no need for that! You're welcome to stay as long as you like. I was just checking to see if you need anything!" What fertile ground for an aspiring modern women looking to change the world! As I look back it was all there. But *I* had to make it work. No freebies here I can tell you. No doubt Mr. Colquhoun told everyone about his generosity toward a poor family because he was a man of the people, you know. Now where's that Mayors cap? Small towns, the most corrupt places of all. I'm not trying to tell tough dad stories here but my father was definitely a man apart, a man out-of-time, timeless, like my mum. I remember he would say 'the walls have ears' and that 'they' are in every town. Oh yes, the diabolical Masons! Pure observation. Back then he didn't know they were called the Masons. He called them "the clique" and the "backslappers" as they were always slapping each other on the back congratulating themselves. He would say their corruption was 'jobs for the boy's'. The boys club. He would say they had 'secret hand signs' and that a bloke could stand in front of a judge in a courtroom and 'fiddle with the third button on his shirt or the cuff of his sleeve' and the judge would know he was one of them and let him off. He said *long* before these topics were discussed generally that it was as if humans were aliens as there was nothing else like us on the planet, everything else lives in balance but there is nothing like humans. Not even close. I remember him sitting in *his* chair and cupping his hands in a strange shape musing about the system, '…it's…like a pyramid'.

As my own life unfolds I realise there was *so much more* to my parents than I could have appreciated at the time. When mum walked me to school she would tell me things no class ever taught me. She said the Romans were appalled at the brutality of the Druids and *that's* saying something! That Stonehenge had been knocked down by the Romans, but it was put back up again (probably when they realised it was an astro-clock). She said the Vatican was the 'seat of the Devil' and when I reminded her of this year's later she would say, 'did I say that?' She told me *long* before the internet that Francis Bacon was William Shakespeare. She said Queen Elizabeth I (or was it her sister Queen Mary?) had a sixth finger that she would hide it inside her glove. So much of this knowledge was found in old books at her local library in her little village in the North of England, a place called Scrooby, where the founding fathers of America, the Pilgrim Father's, hailed from on the Mayflower. She *pored* over these almanacs as a young girl. How many people let alone young girls do that? She was by trade a fashion designer and singer. Bimbo model? Not her. So much of this history is lost to us now as we struggle to catch up despite all the clues and messages all around us at our fingertips. No wonder she got along with dad. She was *so proud* America's Pilgrim Fathers came from her village.

One day when I was very small dad and I were coming out of the fish n'chip shop and he would buy me a fishcake even though he knew I didn't like them. When I screwed up my face 'yuk!' he would say, "Oh, alright then! I'll have it" promising to get me something nicer for "next time". He usually paid up with another fish cake and I wondered, 'why does he keep doing that?' Hilarious. One time I remember a large lout *a third his age* and quite a bit bigger came blundering out of the TAB obviously agitated and shirt-fronted my old dad boldly yelling in his face, "gimme me five bucks!" He must have thought he was on a winner and wanted to put another bet on. It's funny in hindsight but at the time I was *terrified!* Dad kneed him in the balls and smacked him, not punched, smacked him to the ground then grabbed me roughly by the hand and pulled me away. I looked back at the guy on his hands and knees coughing and spluttering. Dad smacked him down because the other guy was too young for a tough old man's punch. I guess it was some sort of etiquette. When we were moving to a new house after dad had found another house for us to squat in, all the furniture was in the removalist's truck ready to go with plenty of room left over. Only problem was, my teddy bears were all lined up on the front porch not having made it onto the passenger list of the soon-to-be-departing truck. I had two teddys in particular that I absolutely loved! One was a weird bull that I found in an op shop called Bully (inventive name) and the other was a real sized scruffy dog called Shaggy-Ruff. I looked at my teddy's and then at dad and then back to my teddy's and back to dad several times with big forlorn eyes. I was terrified of where this might be going. "What about Bully and Shaggy Ruff? Are they coming too?" "No! We don't have room for them!" I immediately screamed in tears. "Oh, alright then!" he said, "I suppose we can take them!" I was overjoyed! Easy target. One time we were all walking along the street when a surreal experience occurred as a beautiful white horse had thrown its rider bolting along in terror as people slammed on their brakes bringing traffic to a halt. Dad looked at mum with a knowing look, "Shall I go after it?" "Yes, Alex!" He was a horse breaker, buck jump rider & jackeroo from way back out on stations in the bush. We all went home. Sometime later dad came in a bit excited, "Got him, Annie! Cornered him in the oval up by the school".

As the youngest of five robust rural Australian children life was pretty tough, I was clearly an easy target to play tricks on and kids can be cruel sometimes. Once they walked me out into the back paddock where there was a big Alsatian tied up at the back of the petrol station next door always straining at its chain, barking and snarling. "See that big dog?" they said. I looked over terrified. "He's gonna eat you!" They all turned and ran leaving me alone in the paddock. Abandonment. I was only four. I was flooded with petrification. My legs felt like they were made of lead. I remember thinking, "If I can just make it to the fence, I'll be okay". I made it to the fence. I was okay but only because *I* did it. No one helped and this would wind up being a common theme during my life. It was my first abandonment experience although it was not to be my last by a long shot. I never really trusted anyone ever again after that. I loved my family the way little kids love people with the kind of purity and innocence that only little kids have, like dogs do. But I never trusted anyone again. That and being put in wheely bins and left outside the neighbours house. I was so small I couldn't get out and had to try really hard to free myself. Again, when I was four, my siblings scaled the outhouse to get on the roof which was by any standards really high. Determined even obsessed with not being left out, I climbed the side of the shithouse crawling up the grapevine. I heard someone say, 'Oh my god! It's Bub! Pull her up!" I was dragged up onto the roof and sufficiently impressed I was described as 'staunch' by the older ones although inside I was permanently anxious. No wonder. That's the first time I ever remember seeing my father. They were all debating the best ways to jump off. Kids, right? Suddenly, someone yelled, 'Dad's coming!' which struck fear into everyone. I looked up from my vantage on the roof and saw my father marching, not walking, *marching* along the street, proud, with his hat cocked to one side, tanned like a leather hide, shirt sleeves rolled up to the biceps like

Jimmy Dean-meets-Marlon Brando 50's greaser. He was Clarke Gable. He was John Wayne. He was really something to behold. Mum was Sophia Loren and Audrey Hepburn. "Jump!" someone yelled. "It's too high!" I yelled back. "Jump Bub! He's coming!" The others leapt off and left with just my eldest brother "Jump!" he yelled. I leapt off. The ground rose up and slammed me hard. My whole body ricocheted. Sprained ankle bad. Winded. Dragged away. Later dad would say, "I couldn't believe what I was seeing! This little tacker jumping off the roof like that!" He was oddly impressed by my courage considering how small I was.

Another time us five kids and mum were coming home, dad was at work, and we found a sheep hunkered down on the footpath. I was summarily evicted from the pram as everyone tried to grapple the sheep into the pram to take it home. Mum said, "Poor thing! He must have broken his legs falling off a truck". Just as we were about to rescue the sheep a huge trucker in a dirty singlet (colloquially called a 'wifebeater') walked up and grabbed the sheep in his arms and said loudly, "this sheep is going to be my Sunday roast!" We immediately started screaming, "No!" My mother said, "Oh! You horrid man! He's our sheep! We saw him first!" She was a very petite English rose who didn't drink, smoke or swear. She once said 'shit' and it was so awkward for her that I just told her not to bother. "Give him back! He's ours!" they yelled. "Don't hurt him!" I screamed caught up in the commotion. What with the kids screaming, my crying and a little lady telling him what-for, the trucker conceded and put the sheep in the pram. We wheeled him home and called him Basil as in Baa-sil. When dad got home mum announced there was a sheep with broken legs in the shed and he asked, "was it kneeling down when you found it". "Yes, Allex! He fell off a truck and broke his legs". "Was it windy?" "Yes! It was quite windy today". "Bloody morons. They kneel down in the wind". He was no nonsense. Dad inspected the sheep. It was fine. Basil's fleece got so big that dad retrieved a rusty old pair of shears like giant scissors he found in the old shed sharpened them up caught Basil and fleeced him! Basil was literally jumping for joy! He would come to the back door for a slice of bread and when dad was tired of our noise and high energy he would open the door and say, "go and catch that sheep". To which we would chase Basil endlessly without success. He knew full well we'd never catch him but were sufficiently worn out by bedtime. We had to leave Basil behind when we left again. He followed us down the drive baa-ing in confusion. I kept looking back at him. Loss.

My parents would go up to the supermarket every couple weeks and bring in a huge shop of groceries. Six litre buckets of ice cream were made short order of with five kids around. Every time they left dad would leave strict instructions with the eldest, "while we're gone *don't climb the tree!*" So, of course, as soon as they left, we raced out into the backyard to scale the enormous pine tree. The higher you got the more kudos. Everyone had their 'boosys' which was our own personal branch. I had mine which although was a lower branch would lead onto the roof. Rooftops? Why? Anyway, I remember thinking that I shouldn't climb that branch anymore as I was getting too big for the weight to hold me. But just one last time. I won't use it again. Sure enough, the branch broke and I came crashing down through the tree and a very thorny rose bush and hit the pavement *hard* half landing in the dog's water bowl. Immediately, the siblings were there. "Get her up". "You alright?" I was dazed. "Get her some dry clothes". Someone rushed off returning with tiny shorts and t-shirt. "Don't tell dad, okay?" I said my wrist hurt. "It's alright. Just bruised. Don't tell dad, Okay?" "If he asks what happened tell him we were playing chasey in the backyard and you fell over a brick. Okay?" I was determined not to let dad know as he was pretty quick in those days to get his belt off and give people a hiding. It's how he was treated as a kid although from what I understand he was nowhere near as brutal with us as his father had been with him. When we did something wrong and he told us "get in the house" we'd cover our head and backside as we sailed past him as he landed a clip across the ear or a boot in the arse. Once, he stood at the door ordering me to "get in the house" his belt poised above his head. I pointed at his raised belt, "You're going to belt me!" and he honestly stood there, belt poised, and said, "No, I'm not". My first introduction to lies. Sigh. What doesn't kill you, hey? Two days later I was nursing my wrist moping around when dad saw it "What happened there?" In keeping with the cover story to avoid my siblings getting a belting I told him, "I tripped over a brick playing chasey". "Bullshit! What really happened?" I said warily, "You promise you won't yell?" "I won't yell" he replied. "No! You have to *promise*" I insisted. "I promise I won't yell". "I fell out of the tree". "What?!" Man, he hit the roof! I burst into tears not because he was yelling, not because I was in pain but because he broke his promise. Loyalty. He snapped at mum "take her up to the hospital!" I'm pretty sure there would have been a belting in my absence certainly a terrifying rant and many threats. At the hospital all the nurses gathered around me, "Isn't she cute!" "Oh, you little darling!" Admittedly, I was pretty cute with flashing amber eyes, broad grin, wide little nose. I was like a wild forest child, a little pixie from the green. I hardly ever wore shoes until I went to school and even during my adult years sometimes I didn't wear shoes for up to six months at a time. I was terribly shy. I only knew my family. I didn't want to know anyone else.

I have a mark on my right wrist in the shape of a perfect triangle. I used to look at it when I was kid and think, 'It means something but I can't remember what it means". So, it was interesting that I had broken my wrist *exactly* where the mark is, a mark that I was *not* supposed to tell anyone about, like my memories of that program it was a 'big no, no' to mention *anything*. My wrist still bulges a little bit where it happened. The doctor poked me saying, 'does that hurt?' I shook my head. He kept poking. 'That? That?' then he *deliberately* poked the bulging part really hard. I cried out. "Broken. Take her to x-ray". I was only interested in their lollies and fizzy drinks which I wasn't allowed to have until after the x-ray. When I got home with the cast on I was the object of marvel as the kids gathered round to look on it in awe. Six weeks passed and rather than take me back to the hospital to get it cut off dad got out the tin snips and cut it off himself. He unfortunately managed to pinch my skin in the blades while doing it and when he pried off the cast there was a rather nasty V-shaped bloody mark on my forearm. The scar is still there. He was deeply sorry and kept saying, "Why didn't you say anything?" I didn't feel it to be honest. Years later when I came off my bike and severely cut my knee, hand, stomach, elbow and upper arm. I was upset not because it hurt but because I thought dad would be angry that we were racing our BMX's again. He was mowing the lawn when I walked in the gate covered in blood from head to toe and as he took in the scene his shoulders just slumped. It was the only time I ever saw him defeated. He patched me up. It took over six weeks to heal. People sometimes ask if I've had reconstructive surgery as the scars are as fresh today as the day it happened. But no hospitals. That's only for breaks.

One night there was a big storm and I came out early in the morning still half asleep to find the huge back veranda hanging down on one side with dad standing there quietly considering it. Typical Aussie kid, "waddya gunna do about *that* dad?" His customary response, "Shuddup. Get in the house". I came out a couple hours later and it was back up again. He did it alone. Dunno how. When we moved into that house there were two huge old trucks from the 1930's in the backyard. Very rusty and dangerous. Bliss! I don't know how he did it but when we returned they were stacked on top of each other at the side. Then one day there was the customary knock at the door only this time the knock was soft. There at the door stood a little old man. Mr. Abikhair. He was the owner of the house dad had helped himself to and was a local Lebanese businessman who owned Abikhair's Emporium which was an early 1900's shop filled with ancient wonders and things you couldn't buy normally in modern times. That shop was a fascination for a little girl. They owned the big old house behind the Emporium in the centre of town and had a big pomegranate tree in their front yard which I helped myself to whenever we went past. Their family mausoleum at the cemetery was a house in itself. Old Man Abikhair was very polite about dad appropriating his property telling him no one had lived there for decades and that his father had built the house around 1920. Dad liked the homesteads. Abikhair said he was glad to see someone was finally living in the house again and happy to see it was being done up as it bought back fond memories from his boyhood. It was literally a shell. Dad put in everything from the windows to the doors, floors, ceiling, fixed the roof, paved a garden path from fragments of rock and brick located in the yard, built the fence, which is *still* there, plastered, painted and rebricked. He made an excellent dining table from old doors with beautifully sliding drawers. He did everything. He taught me how to render the house when I was six and put an ochre wash on the outside that lasted 25 years until they left.

Mum established a beautiful rose garden the envy of all the roses in the area. It took her a couple of years to bring the soil back to life and whenever the circus came to the showgrounds nearby, dad sent us little kids to gather the elephant dung for her garden. We grew tomatoes, strawberries, figs, rhubarb, pumpkins, beans – you name it. Dad liked his privacy so he covered the whole front of the house with lilac wisteria and when in bloomed the whole place was a beautiful show of incredible purple flowers and roses cascading all over it. The scent was *amazing* wafting on the evening breeze. Sometimes when I came in the gate and saw the awesome show of flowers, colours and scents even I thought, 'that's incredible'. It was really something and everyone in the neighbourhood either liked it or despised it. Despite the madness other people seemed to perceive, I had many happy times there as it was an emporium of its own so no wonder Mr. Abikhair didn't mind. They settled on $20 a week for the house and fifteen years later went up to $40 the old bloke even apologised but it was more about the council rates. When he came by to collect dad and old-man Abikhair would sit out on the front veranda for a chat. Dad would say to me, "Go and get your mouth organ and play us a song!" I was frightened of Mr. Abikhair and thought he must be 200 years old. "Aw! I don't wanna!" "Go and get it!" he roared. I moped off and returned with my enormous harmonica and to Mr. Abikhair's delight I played all the old songs from the 1920's to the 1940's. Dad must have been pretty proud of my skill and when I'd sufficiently amused them he would say, "Alright. That's enough. Get in the house!" I mooched off to play with the dogs *inside* the kennel.   School was horrible. I wasn't cut out for it. I was always getting into trouble for unknown reasons. There was always a problem. I just wanted to play outside and would daydream endlessly. I was an average to above average student although if something interested me art, English, woodwork, design, drama, I would excel. School was hard and was a case of kill or be killed, not literally, but bullying was a major issue that I had to overcome due the strangeness of our old house and, again, kids can be cruel. We lived across the road from both my primary *and* high schools so I developed an enigmatic persona – don't mess with me and I won't mess with you. Parents are even more cruel than students as I'd sometimes be called into the principal's office and told I was not allowed to be friends with a certain child as their parents obviously thought we were trash. It hurt my feelings greatly to lose friends to low-class people like their parents. Children cannot be trash and if they are, they have been grossly let down by a shitty system populated by shitty adults.

The memories of the program still haunted me and I was set, even then, on making the world a better place as I had *promised* to do, to use my talents and skills to help people and do the job for the planet's sake. I knew if I stuck it out long enough I would find out what it was all about although it took a *lot longer* than they had promised and was NOT what they promised. Liars. Frauds. Aliens. Yes, it was an alien program. There was simply *no* technology in my day-to-day life growing up to match what I'd seen in that program. In fact, life was pretty ordinary, even boring. Too boring. That's the giveaway. I knew even back then that *something* was seriously wrong with all this. It was too perfectly ordinary to be just that and I was determined to spend my life trying to find out what the big secret was. I knew if I just kept going, no matter how hard my life was, no matter how difficult with all the health issues and family problems, *one day* I would find out. I would seek the truth and get to the bottom of *who* I was and *what* I was involved in *no matter what*. It was a personal mission and I've pursued it relentlessly, privately, accomplishing things that should have been impossible for someone in my position let alone others who were far better off materially.

I did some unusual things for a kid I mentally mapped the stars in the night sky by the time I was about ten and had a number of my own 'psychic' experiences. When I was five I had a toy phone and one day while playing with it in the yard I picked up the receiver and clear as day I heard an older lady's voice say, "Hello". I was very surprised as I knew it was a toy, not a real device, besides my parents had installed a healthy distrust for strangers so I was extremely wary. "Hello" I said timidly. The lady asked, "What's your name?" I told her "Mimi" as my dad called me Mimi and Smithy from an early age. This world has given me many names. "That's a very pretty name, Mimi". One of my siblings said offhandedly, "she's pretending to talk on the phone". I held up the phone for them to talk too and said, "there really *is* someone on the phone" but they just ignored me. I went back to the 'phone call' and the lady was saying, "You're very special, Mimi, do you know that?" I replied, "no". I was *so* shy. "Well, you are, you're very special. You just remember that okay?" I replied, "Okay". I can't remember much else except she kept saying "You're very special". I said, "I have to go now". "Alright Mimi, you just remember you're very special. Don't forget?" "I won't". "Bye Mimi". "Bye". I hung up.

I experienced some phenomena, ghosts and the like, very common these days as the 'demonic' and 'ghost' anomalies increase as the madness heightens thanks to extradimensional intruders and aligning portals. It'll get worse before it gets better. Something's got to be done about that. Ordinary people are increasingly being tormented as these ghouls are unleashed on the world as the 'prophecies' start to manifest as the world reels in  disbelief! They are not prophesies, the *script* is being carried out by the descendants of the people who wrote them, 'here's a script we wrote and our descendants will carry it out. It's prophecy!' No, it's not. Whenever I mentioned anything supernatural my dad would threaten, "you see that ghost again and I'll boot your arse". He didn't mess around with that sort of thing and didn't encourage it, he assumed I was making it up although he had experienced *his* fair share of oddities over the years. When I was a little older he came up to me and said, "You've got it". I was looking in the cupboard for a snack. "Got what?" I asked. "The gift". I *never* heard him talk like that. He continued, "I've got it, my mother had it and my grandmother had it. You've got it too". I didn't have clue what he was talking about. I was an excellent musician and artistic all-rounder, *see right*, and knew from an early age that this would be my calling. I had *no interest* in anything else and I pursued my art with a vengeance playing cafes, bars, restaurants, pubs, music festivals, anywhere that would have me. When I was about twenty living in central Sydney I was at work one day when I suddenly had the need to go home. I told my manager I was sick. On my way home I went by the mall in the city and heard this incredible violin. I looked around and saw a rather scruffy man playing to a crowd with Richard Wilkins hosting. Between songs Wilkins seemed uncomfortable and almost groveling would say to the violinist, "Now, now. You're not allowed to swear! It's a family friendly event". The scruffy man leaned over to the mic and shouted, "muvva-fukka!" then sailed into another incredible classical number. As I came down the escalators transfixed by this violinist he seemed to *instinctively* turn and look me straight in the eye with the most *intense* gaze. He looked right into me. When I got home there was a message on the answering machine which wasn't uncommon as I was doing regular gigs around the CBD. "Willow! Come to La Bar tonight for a set and bring your friends we've got someone special coming in". I turned on the TV and there was a program on the ABC about Nigel Kennedy. Just Kennedy, thanks. It was the same guy I just saw doing a free event in the mall. He was in town doing a show with the Sydney Symphony Orchestra at the Opera House. I thought, 'what's the bet it's him tonight?'

I called up my old friend from high school who was working at Monoxide Circus in Wollongong. My friend *literally* ran away with the circus. I told her I thought Kennedy would be coming and she was ecstatic! Personally, I'd never heard of him before but she was like "I'll be there!" We went to Oxford Street that night entering La Bar. It was a really cool place. They don't have really good live music venues anymore. It's shit now. It was a packed house as I did my set belting out my original tunes scanning the crowd as I sang to see if he was already there. Nope. Dammit! He missed my set. Later I was at the bar ordering two cheap house reds and who should walk in but Kennedy. He looked like he was homeless with a three-day growth and a scruffy necktie as a belt his clothes disheveled - we're talking about one of the *best* virtuoso violinists in the world here easily a multi-millionaire - dressed like a bum. Cool. I calculated that I could meet him halfway through the crowd if I timed it right. I made my way back to my table and perfectly timed crossing paths with him. I had two glasses of cheap booze. I looked at him. He grinned broadly. I looked at my wine glasses. I handed him one. He accepted. We clinked glasses. "Cheers!" He threw his down in one gulp. "Fanks!" he said heartily and continued on. When I sat down my friend looked at the empty glasses curiously. I said, "You wouldn't believe what just happened".

Kennedy, being a big international, was not only fashionably late but played his set long after the place was supposed to close. Guys like that don't give a fuck about closing hours. They do their thing when they do it and *if* you're there when it happens count yourself lucky. I hung around as long as I could but I had to work the next day although I stayed to see his set. The crowd loved it! It wasn't classical. It was a fusion of different styles presented in a quirky bohemian off the cuff rustic almost acid jazz sort of way. I just remember watching him onstage like 'it's kinda crazy almost dyslexic' but fun! It was like a gypsy pantomime in a secret forest that you accidentally stumbled on watching from the shadows hoping not to get caught. Afterwards in the green room I was packing up my guitar and saw the sound technician talking to Kennedy. I waited for a polite lull in the conversation and carefully said "hello" to them both. The night had been recorded and I asked the sound guy if I could pop by sometime to pick up the CD. He suddenly snapped, "I don't know! Why would I know? Later in the week!" I was a little crestfallen and idled away getting my guitar to leave. That's when I heard a voice behind me say, "Come jam with us". I turned around and there was Kennedy standing there with a goofy smile. "Pardon?", I said. "Come jam with us". Confusion. "I can't" I responded. "Why not?" I felt like a fool now knowing his enormous classically trained celebrity, "because…" I trailed off. How do I tell the guy I'm an idiot? I had to admit my fraud, "…I can't read music". It was one of those moments when all the lack, poverty, caravan parks, no electricity, angry property owners demanding we leave, school friends' parents telling them they weren't allowed to be my friend because we were poor, the injuries incurred by older siblings, the self-taught embarrassing failure of my non-professionally trained musical childhood coupled with crippling shyness, sensitivity and humiliation, all in all, left me deflated in the presence of someone who had it all. I just wasn't good enough. For some reason I was imagining some sort of classical recital with music stands a string quarter and a fucken cello or something. "That doesn't matter! Come jam with us anyway!" I really would have been a fool if I turned him down again so, let's just say the music flowed freely and so did the drinks that night! We drank hard as enormous joints made the rounds. I kept raiding the downstairs bar for copious amounts of booze for everyone. Hey, drinks on me! At some point while raiding the bar I heard a voice from the darkness say, "What's your name?" An ember of a cigarette burned in the blackness like a scene from a Tarantino flick. I froze holding the tray of drinks I'd helped myself to. "Um…Willow". I thought the guy was going to demand I pay! Turned out he was the owner of the building and said, "I've been watching you". I braced myself. "You're really good. Those other guys are good but I found myself being drawn back to what you were doing". He'd been watching me all night and I didn't even know. I said awkwardly "thanks" still terrified he would demand payment for the plentiful supply of his booze I was kindly giving away. Hey, chip off the old block. "Have a great night" he said. "Thank you". He stayed in the dark. I never saw his face and don't know his name to this day.

I bolted back upstairs entering the green room to thunderous applause as I delivered *another* round on the house! Everyone was jamming or taking turns playing a song when someone said, "you play a song, Willow!" So, I played my own soulful rendition of Tom Waites *Downtown Train* and at the end of it I looked at Kennedy for a response as he rolled another big one. He just shook his head ruefully and said, "that was fookin bew-i-ful".  Needless to say, I didn't make it to work the next day although as we were leaving the venue I said to Kennedy, "I don't know who you are, I mean, before tonight, but when you were playing before I felt like there was a real lilting sadness in your music". He looked deeply at me for a long moment and said, "Put out your arm". I did. He proceeded to write his name. I said, "um, I know who you are now". He wrote a number on my forearm and said, "if you ever make it to London you give me call". I was so green. London might as well of been on Mars. I didn't go. I found out many years later his dad had been a drunk and left their family early on while his mother and stepdad were also drunks and collectively turned the guy into a nervous wreck. Hey, I can relate. That was the sadness I heard in his music.

That's when I realised the big shots don't have everything after all.

CHAPTER TWO
ET ITERUM, BRUTE`?
"And again, Brutus?"

My musical adventures continued a few years later when I was 23 in the year 2000. I read a tiny little article buried in the paper that Hollywood was filming in Port Douglas in Far North Queensland. Hollywood! Now *that* was for me! I purchased a bus ticket for $27, how things have changed, and found myself on a bus for the better part of three days headed north. When I got to Port Douglas I quickly found a room in a sprawling rundown old Queenslander just off the main street. All those houses are gone now they were real heritage treasures replaced with cheap condo's, flats and resorts owned by big corporations charged at top dollar when they took over as the tourist industry expanded. Shame. I took my guitar and determined to get a gig asap, I walked up the main street and went into every bar and restaurant I could find. I was about four bars deep when I entered a Greek bistro as an enormous 6"5' heavily mustachioed man came out, "Yeh, luv?" he boomed in his thick Aussie accent. I gave him my spiel, "Hi, I'm Willow. I'm a musician. Just wondering if you're looking for any live music?" He looked me up and down and boomed again, "Alright luv! Play us a song!" I felt like I was five years old again playing my giant club-sandwich harmonica in front of dad and Mr. Abikhair on the front porch. I was obviously prepared to give a rendition of my skills, if asked, hence, the guitar. I was, nonetheless, caught a little off guard for some reason. "Now?" I asked. "Now!" he boomed.

    I got out my guitar and broke off a rousing number. His eyes literally looked like dollar signs flashed up. Cha-Ching! "Right!" he boomed again, "I want you here tonight…and every other night!" "Every night?" *"Every night!"* I wasn't really prepared for that but it was an easy $50 cash plus drinks and a meal *every night*. 250 bucks for five nights music. Within a couple years I tripled that for half hour doing the support act. I started playing my regular set unplugged at the Greek bistro and shortly after the owner came up to me, "You heard that really loud table applauding you all night?" he boomed. "Yeh". "You know who that was?" "No". "That was John Farnham and his family". I didn't recognise him. The following week the owner came up pretty happy again and boomed, "You know who was in tonight?" "No", I replied. "That was Steve Vizard!" (a late-night Aussie talk show host). I knew something was up. Then a strange thing happened. It was as if for several weeks I had a huge presence around me. It was big. I even stopped in the street one day turned around and said, "What? What do you want? I'm right here! If you want to talk to me then, do so!" It was like shooing away a big stray dog trying to follow me home. Too big to feed. Then there was an excited buzz as the news spread that Harry Connick Jr and Glen Close had arrived in town to film the movie *South Pacific*. I hoped I would bump into him. I was aware of his music and remember my sibling had a poster of him on her wall as a teenager. She liked Memphis Belle, a wartime flick with him in it, and she introduced me to the whole Second World War saga reading the big military almanacs. I was morbidly engrossed! She was always taking me along to the ANZAC parade and various services and even went to Gallipoli for the Dawn Service and sent dad a Turkish 'fez' which amused him. He liked his hats and beanies. She spoke to a local WWII Veteran in our hometown called Carl asking him about his experiences firsthand. When she introduced herself he remarked suspiciously that her name was German she replied, "so is Carl". Of a country with less than five million people at the time Australia's contribution to the 1st World War was nearly half a million men, 20% of the population, and remains one of the greatest per capita wartime contributions of service personnel *in the history of the world*. Put that on your placards. Emoji *that*. You can't.

Prior to this I hadn't given Mr. Connick much thought. He captured the style of big band music from the 1940's which seems difficult to do these days as most people who sing or dance to the styles of that time do it badly so, it isn't easy to do, apparently. As my parents came from that era, swing and big band music was second nature to me followed by classical then modern pop 'smash hits' and all that. Naively, I thought, 'if I see that guy I'm just gonna walk right up to him! He *needs* to know about me. He will be very lucky to discover me'. I was so young and had zero life experience, unusual talent, pretty face, but green as a cucumber. You gotta remember I came from a small town in southern rural NSW. I saw the ocean for the first time when I was nearly twenty and I only saw snow for the first time when I went to London in my thirties. I'd never been far from home before except Sydney and even then, I was introduced to trusted friends and contacts there. One time I overheard an American friend of mine from Manhattan saying in awe to our other mates, "She sounds *exactly* the same live and she does on her CD!" So, FNQ was about as far away as you could get without leaving the country. I still suffered from extreme shyness and anxiety and felt terribly awkward around people although put me on stage in front of an audience, no problem, the bigger the better! I played at the Tamworth Country Music Festival in front of thousands of people when I was 16. Sydney City nightspots? No biggy. Surry Hills Festival? No problem, *see right*. I once had to turn down a gig supporting a major Hollywood artist's band because I had laryngitis. When I was in my mid 20's I did a presentation called *Deconstructing the Lyric* about the relevance of music lyrics as part of the lexicon of serious English Literature at a workshop for the Brisbane Writers Festival, *see right*. I was in the company of university professors and international authors, again, no professional training in this area I just did it because it came up. Great fun! Put me one-on-one? Help! I walked down backstreets to avoid people.

It always happens when you least expect it. So, there I was embedded in one of my songs and as it turned out I just so happened to be playing someone else's guitar. I would rock up to the venue with two guitars and people would go, 'woah, she must know what she's doing' and I did, *see right*. I was playing some else's guitar because I couldn't bear to see an instrument being treated poorly and some mate of the guy who ran my house had a guitar and was letting go to waste with old

strings, dirty and mouldy etc. I offered to clean it up, restring it and play it back in for him (well, for the guitar not him). His guitar wasn't as good as mine but I enjoyed fixing things and played it for a few weeks a couple songs a night at my gig. It chewed up my fingers. My guitar sounded like honey and was a freakishly good instrument that I picked up in a pawn shop trading two of my guitars for one when I was eighteen. I was still $50 short of the asking price so I went to my dad to plead my case, not that I had to, he would have given me the money just for asking but I didn't like asking so I told him what I wanted it for and being a musical guy, he totally understood and obliged me. When I walked out of the shop with my new guitar the bloke threw in a free case for good measure and I was over the moon! It was black and I placed an ash grey translucent stencil of a fleur di lis (lily flower) blazoned on the front of it. Looked fantastic. I still have it. One night it so happened I was playing this other guys' guitar and I was *so absorbed* in what I was doing that I was completely unaware of my surrounds. I liked that. Start playing and disappear. I emerged from my number looked up and who should be standing right there in front of me? Harry Connick Jr. I'd never seen anything like that before. He was at his A-list Hollywood celebrity best and an extremely well received musician to boot. He did the score for *When Harry Met Sally* with Meg Ryan and Billy Crystal and music for *You've Got Mail* with Tom Hanks. So, *clearly,* he was a highly proficient composer with big budget blockbusters like *Independence Day* under his belt and could obviously pull it off live too which is the big test. I, on the other hand, was very small, painfully different, awkwardly out of place and shy and *that* was on a good day. I was a toddler when faced with Big America.

    I'm not interested in fame for the sake of fame, but I knew I had something that *should* interest even the biggest. Yet it was like the Kennedy situation when he invited me to jam with him. Suddenly,. I was crippled by my lack of theoretical knowledge and professional experience assuming they would think I was an idiot because basically everyone else had treated me that way all my life. En garde! I was Cyrano de Bergerac the big nosed sensitive genius who only learned fencing to repel the laugh riot in defense of his wounded dignity! I was Scaramouche! Wonderful but crippled. Beautiful but withdrawn. Brave but terrified. The cowardly lion. The ugly duckling. Highly nervous. Still am. There was a lot of terror in my upbringing and not a lot of positive reinforcement that would allow such a sensitive innocent person to interact confidently or maturely with *anyone* let alone big-name artists from the best of backgrounds. Eye contact was an issue. People instinctively pick up on that sort of thing, and, as I would discover, a *lot* of people even *use that to their advantage* playing on your sensitivity to push you down even further. I didn't finish high school, had no formal training, no real education, no money, no industry skills, nowhere to go, no one to fall back on, immense talent and deeply troubled by the mystery of myself and memories of a program that promised so much but had *already* failed me dismally. It was a set up designed to make me *exactly* what I was. Frankly, I was out of my depth. The sad truth of it was I was an outsider and I knew it only too well.   Mr. Connick dazzled me with a huge glowing smile. An impossible smile. I looked across and there standing next to him was Glenn Close. Cold as ice. I looked back at him. Something happened. I recognized him not from his movies or celebrity but something else, *somewhere else,* much deeper than that. I'd seen him before. *Long ago.* My heart recognised him not so much my mind. The heart is intrinsically connected to the pineal gland the 'all seeing eye'. Suddenly, I felt really angry and strangely I thought, 'I'm just as good a musician as you are and you got everything and I got *nothing!* Just leave me alone. Don't even look at me. I don't need you. I can do it by myself!' I was also angry that although my gig was small it was *my* gig, *my* show. It might not be much to big Hollywood but these people were *my* audience and it was *my* job to entertain them and not be distracted by some heavyweight's big budget smile. I had a show to do. I looked away and prayed that when I looked back they would be gone. It seemed like the longest time but eventually, I looked up and to my relief, they were gone. But that wasn't the end of it.

    On my way home after a moment to reflect I was kind of kicking myself. That's Harry Connick Jr. for fucks sake! He could make my career. Change my life. Take me to America! Australia was going nowhere musically. Any really big names have to leave Aussie to make it in any *meaningful* capacity as a professional before they'll be taken seriously at home; Kylie Minogue (the 'singing budgie' they called her), The Seekers, The Bee Gees. Tall poppy syndrome. They're known for it but then turns out to be a common practice around the world no matter how big they get. What he could do for me was everything I'd ever dreamed of. I always knew I would be picked up and signed by a major label around the age of twenty. That was my path. My destiny. *And* it happened and I snubbed him. Why did I behave like that? Was it just the reaction of an underling? Why was I so threatened? Was I just immature? Unprofessional? That was stupid. Also, what was the deal with the strange recognition? Why did I feel so angry that he'd gotten everything? Why did I feel I'd gotten nothing? What did that even mean? Anyway, I'm not one for beating myself up for too long I've learned other people are more than happy to do that for you so don't do it to yourself. That weekend the local pub was doing a full day showcase and all the local musicians, all blokes, were playing. I tried to get in on it but they wouldn't let me play even though I found out later that they had a spot they were trying to fill. Just not fill with me. It would happen like that sometimes. I noticed early on that men can be dismissive of female musicians, especially guitarists, then overly competitive once they realise you're not a bimbo. They were very territorial about their gigs and even *actively* kept me out. The irony of that all these years later. I didn't really care though. I always turned up gigs when I wanted them and they were just making sure they made their money. I had to put up with it. Once, when I was 18 getting ready to do my regular set at a café in my hometown, the guy who was on before me (who was twice my age and quite a well-trained guitarist) finished up his set and said, "We've got a little girl coming up next, folks! She's a bit nervous so, make her welcome by giving her a big hand!" I'd seen it before. I started playing my set of original songs and, obviously, I was well known there. He must have felt embarrassed as he quickly packed up his guitar leaving by the back door. I wanted to let him know it wasn't an issue but I was mid song.

I decided to show my support to the pub showcase anyway besides I'd have a few cold ones and enjoy the scene without playing for once. Don't get caught up in the politics. Just smile and nod. But what do you know? As I was walking in the door who should be positioned right there in the entry but Mr. Connick and it happened again! I immediately felt repelled by him. I don't know why. He gave me a big smile again. He had his little girl with him. This time I just smiled and said, "Hi" walking right past him and went to the far side of the venue. What the hell was wrong with me? Why was I doing that? I tried to tell myself he's got his little girl with him and doesn't need some woman approaching him at the pub. Besides every man and his dog would prop him up trying to get his time for their benefit. He probably didn't get too many opportunities to just to hang out while in public so just leave him alone. I awkwardly looked over with a wan smile. He just put his head down and looked at me as if he knew something I didn't and gave me this strange almost sly smile. I thought, 'that's odd'. A few days later I was sitting on the beach in my bikini with my little fat gut poking out feeling a bit dumpy, puppy fat, and who should go jogging past with his cap on back to front and his shirt undone exposing his rippling torso but, you guessed it, Harry Connick Jr., *again!* What are the odds? He looked superhuman. Brute strength. I've never seen a guy look like that before so it say's something for personal trainers, plenty of money and private chefs to get the best of *everything*. I remember thinking 'that guy's way out of my league'. I watched him jog on, literally, and yes, it occurred to me that I had missed an opportunity there. But I told myself there would be other opportunities.

I continued my gigs and started a duo funnily enough with a classically trained multi-instrumentalist from Perth. He came to my gig night after night just watching me until I felt weird about it. He'd order a drink and sit on it for two hours. So, I decided after a week of this to just walk up to him and ask outright what was he doing? He told me about his musical background and that he was interested in forming a duo and playing as many gigs as possible in the high season. I wound up playing six to seven days a week sometimes two gigs a day for six months straight. His girlfriend and her friends hated that he was working with a young blonde and automatically assumed that just because we were making music together that we must be 'making music' together! It was insulting. I hated women liked that even worse than men who judge women as being incapable of doing practical things just because they can't. Those sour slags were twice my age and tried to give me a hard time at our gigs. So, I penned a song called 'Girlfriends of Boyfriends' a scathing narration of their underwhelming personalities and sang it right in front of them in full view of the audience. They were so vacuous they didn't even notice it was *obviously* about them. That's the hilarious part. We once got paid to drink booze and put our feet up at our residency at the Court House Hotel because the owner forgot it was the Opening Ceremony of the 2000 Olympic Games which was being hosted in Sydney. As such, the crowd wanted to watch the opening ceremony not live music. It was the first time in two and half thousand years that the Olympic torch had burned underwater. The Daily Universe headlines were 'Olympic torch burns underwater for the first time'. It's more symbolic to me now than it was then but it just so happened to burn for the first time underwater in, you guessed it, Port Douglas. I would have gone down to see it but I'm not really one for these things and it remains a forgettable experience for me. I finished the season in Port Douglas and went back to Sydney.

Things were different this time as I realised I was not someone for industry contracts and glitzy Hollywood quick fixes, I was too free spirited for that and wanted to pursue my *real* music in my own way. The really good artists are usually reluctant to sign up and it often takes much wrangling and convincing to get the great ones to come onboard like May West. They pursued her on Broadway for years until she went out to Hollywood. Her career was short lived though as they demanded she do things their way, the boys club again. As such, censorship laws and Christian groups blackballed her. On Broadway she ran her own ship she had power there but out West in Hollywood she was just some cheap theatre tramp with a few catchy one liner's. They underestimated her. They usually do and yet they knew what she was about. Why invite her out there with promises to run her own show in her own way if they had no intention of letting her do so? Yet she was one helluva tough woman and wouldn't be told how to do *her* work so, they basically blacklisted her. I think she was set up. They don't like brash intelligent women who won't take shit from men. Joan Crawford was the same. Her husband was Chairman of the Board and CEO of Pepsi-Cola and despite a rigorous travel and promotion routine for them when her husband died the boys club told her 'jog on, love'. They reversed their position when she made public what they did and wound up filling her husband's position on the board of directors. When she entered that boardroom she wasn't taking shit from anyone put it that way. They backed off. Her husband had taught her a thing or two and her early years in Hollywood under the likes of Jack Warner of Warner Bros had taught her well about business and money management. I grew up on stories like that. My mum would often tell me about strong women in entertainment and relay the battles of famous females always finishing with, "When she arrived in Hollywood *she was ready for them*". Mum knew all the back stories of the old stars and how they got their power. She was a wealth of knowledge.

It was then that I decided I was going to make my own *independent* music label. I, yes, shy little me, would work my tits off in the big smoke eating corporate dick to start my own music venture. I knew it would take about ten years realistically but decided that by the time I was thirty, I would have my own independent music label running myself as *the* business! At the end of 2007 I was thirty and doing regular gigs in central Sydney landing the front cover of a popular street magazine CENTRAL, *right*, and had national radio play of one of my songs on a major radio station which led to an internet TV series called PopTarts. It was finally happening! At this time I went to Hawaii on holiday with my friends where I paid my respects at Pearl Harbour my mates weren't really interested so I went alone. It was ironic how many Japanese tourists were there smiling and taking pics with their 'peace' fingers 'V' sign considering what the Yanks did to them for payback. At the same time the company I was working for was doing a major restructure and handed out redundancies to 95% of their staff. I sighted my start-up capital for my label. All in all things were looking *great* for me! That's when I became aware of odd references being made about me online on major music pages like Triple J Unearthed. On the official music page of my song with my bio and stats was a banner at the bottom of the page that read 'ELORA DANAN IN THE ROOM UP THERE'. The only other image or 'room' on the page 'up there' was a picture of me above said reference. I clicked on the link but it was a 404 error that went nowhere. I had the presence of mind to get a screen shot of the page before it was changed. Curiously, I wondered 'where have I heard the name Elora Danan before?' I googled 'Elora Danan' and as it turned out she was the little girl with an unusual birth mark on her right arm prophesised to bring down the 'Dark Queen' in the movie *Willow*. This movie is a retelling of the biblical story of Herod. It was particularly weird though because I too have an unusual mark on *my* right arm, a perfect triangle, and *my* name is Willow too.

As 2007 came to a close I was *very* confident about the future and where my life was headed as my many years of hard work started to pay off. Strangely though within a couple months of this music listing, *above*, and the cover girl magazine shoot my life started to take a *drastic* downward spiral. Suddenly, I was beset on all sides by ongoing consistent and *intense* bad luck. The first thing that happened was missing out on the redundancy as work re-commenced at my workplace in early 2008. That money would have been a godsend for my plans to start my label. Yet despite other people being more qualified and despite being relatively new to the company and despite 95% of the staff in a huge corporation being laid off, somehow, they decided to keep me on. I noticed the notorious boys club and their mates in management had gotten rid of everyone but their inner group and only kept on a few of the pretty girls and people who amused them. What followed shortly after was a workplace sexual harassment nightmare that finished off my day job along with associated spiraling financial problems. As a result of the loss of income it led to increasing isolation from my social circle as Sydney's inner-city bar and restaurant scene became unattainable to me. Then I was misdiagnosed by a doctor and prescribed medication that initiated a severe adverse reaction causing me to stack on in excess of *30kg's in weight* in 12 months! Despite my efforts to the contrary and 'never say die attitude' I just kept missing out on much needed opportunities that could have solved my problems leaving me feeling alienated and cursed. What the hell was going on? I was losing everything I'd worked my whole life for and seemed powerless to stop it. The gigs dried up I lost my job my health was shot and within two years I was basically finished on every level. This a photo, *right*, was taken of me during the onset of these strange events and what appears to be an 'orb' is attached to my head. Orbs are often malevolent spirits or negative entities that disrupt energy and can ruin a person's life. I would later become familiar with 'military satanism', occultism and *demonology* behind all this.

During all this I became aware of a few things I hadn't noticed before. Firstly, I noticed chemtrails and upon further research promptly informed my family that they needed to look up more often. I would go down to the park taking photos of the strange lines over Sydney and one day the sky was so poisoned it was practically yellow! I couldn't believe people didn't even notice this stuff! It was during this time that one morning I became aware of a helicopter hanging around my 9th floor apartment the nose pointed directly at my flat. I was on the top floor and being built up on a hill, it was pretty high. My intuition was immediately on high alert as if to tell me that this was something to do with me although one's initial reaction is, 'what rubbish!' Next morning, same time, there it was again only this time further West. Okay, I thought, I'll just keep an eye on that. Third morning, same time, there it was again only further North-West. Now my Spidey senses were tingling! Obviously, I could do nothing, so I took a wait-and-see attitude. Fourth morning, same time, there it was again only this time further North. It was *so close* and *so loud* I looked out my windows and could see two men in the cockpit literally looking at me. I mouthed 'I can see you' and hilariously, they hovered the helicopter behind the building next to mine as if I wouldn't know they were there considering how loud it was. That's when I felt a strange sensation in the *centre* of my brain and in later years I would come across research that remote technological harassment targets the 'brain-centre'. I knew something had happened straight away but like so many times in my life that calm voice of reason came in, 'it's going to be okay. Just wait'. So, I waited. The next morning no helicopter so I went down to the park with my little camera and as I was standing there near Rushcutters Bay Marina taking a few snaps of the 'tiger stripes' in the sky I heard as *plain as day* right next to my right ear the sound of a high-powered paparazzi camera lens - like the shutter-speed flicking when they take photos of celebrities. It was *so clear* although there was nothing there. I raised my little camera up and went 'click!' and took a photo of nothing. I took this 'sound bite' message to mean 'you might be watching us but we're watching you'.

Sydney was basically over for me although one day not long before I left for good in 2011 I was walking through Centennial Park with my mum and noticed a strange agitated old man looking furtively in my direction. He looked like a *parody* of a person who goes outside as he was wearing a loud Hawaiian shirt, white straw fedora hat and big black sunglasses. He looked sick like he hadn't been in the sun for years, white as a sheet, unnatural. As he approached he suddenly stepped up close to me and said, "You're doing a great job. Keep going!" and quickly darted off. My mum remarked "what a silly man" as we continued on our way. With some degree of sadness I finally left Sydney and moved back up to Port Douglas in Far North Queensland where I could heal from the destruction of my career. I didn't take it lying down though and threw myself into work to keep busy. It was in Port Douglas that I commenced doing my live music gigs again although due to the weight gain and health problems, I couldn't perform to the same degree as I had in Sydney so I played the local pubs and resorts like I had 15 years before. Hilariously, I was during the week I was working at the local paper for a News Corp edition called the *Gazette* and doing a conspiracy talkback radio show on the weekend at the local radio station *90.9FM Radio Port Douglas*. My show was called The Shift Radio Show as in the *electromagnetic* shift radio show. I was once introduced to the Mayor at an International Women's Day function and she said, 'are you Willow that does that radio show?' I said, 'Yes, that's me'. She replied, 'I *love* your show!' Mayor. Who knew? I wrote a regular article for the paper called *Around the Traps* which went over well and was the first time I was officially published. Yet it was in the lead up to and after the total solar eclipse on 14th November 2012 when I was living on Flagstaff Hill I received a bunch of psychic 'messages' as follows:

- Once the eclipse is done the house of cards will fall rapidly. New leaders will emerge from the ranks of ordinary people. They will be dragged into the new roles/jobs kicking and screaming.
- The darkness has elevated itself to a godlike status and threatens the entire universe.

- The human race is walking into a huge trap.
- You will experience what's called Total Recall. For those who have suffered under mind control the walls between their personalities will literally crumble.
- They are planning to do something so terrible the whole world will, 'never forget'.
- We are objects existing in space in the eternal now.
- Inorganic things have no power over organic things.

During this time I was shown an image of Europe swirling down into black vortex. I also had powerfully vivid dreams one of walking around huge towers of fish that went right up to the sky. When I woke up I went to my local café that was also a bookstore and as I was waiting for my coffee I spotted a book on Chinese architecture and Feng Shui. I opened the page and immediately saw an image of a wooden fish hung outside a house. It was exactly like the fish I'd seen in my dream and the caption was that fish were considered good luck as they swim against the current going against the flow. In that moment the words 'passed with flying colours' popped into my head. I had another dream of standing beneath a huge apple tree eating yellow apples that were so succulent and incredible. But the fruit was falling on the ground and rotting. It was the Tree of Knowledge. It was as if to say that there is more than enough knowledge for everyone to share but it's going to waste. The knowledge is rotting away. It's sad. On the cusp of 2012/2013 on New Year's Eve I had a strange experience. I had gotten home from town and was preparing to go to a friend's house. I sat on my bed and suddenly felt very tired and thought, 'I'll just lie down a second'. That was my last thought and woke up over two hours later! I quickly got organized to go to my friend's house and on the way there I looked up and saw two incredibly brilliant yellow lights moving across the sky together. I had to do a double take. I couldn't believe my eyes as a carload of people pulled over and all looked out the windows pointing up. Two words popped into my head, 'Twins' and 'Advanced'. If I hadn't fallen asleep I would never be in that area at that time and being a remote forest region the bright lights against the stars were *amazing*. Later I would interview a lady on my show from UFO Research Queensland who said similar lights had been reported further down the on the Gold Coast earlier that evening.

To date I have now seen a whole bunch of apparent 'UFO's' some from here some from 'elsewhere'. I also experienced a dream of a maroon-coloured waterfall and river pouring *incredible* amounts of powerful energy down through my crown chakra and many years later heard of the Hindu 'spiritual shower'. One night while in bed I became aware of my omnipresence. I was conscious of the fact that I was asleep and still inside my body but I was also looking down at myself sleeping while simultaneously projecting my consciousness to a strange underground 'cellar' with arched ceilings like an old castle. There was a man wearing a robe like a monk with a hood and everything. He was sitting at a table talking monotonously and I could *hear* his words *speaking into my mind* while sleeping in bed. He said, 'there will be water wars. When the rivers and aquifers are contaminated the people will fight for clean water'. I didn't like what he was trying to convince me of and was mildly amused that he didn't know I was right there watching him. He suddenly stood up annoyed and walked away because his trick wasn't working. I spotted him. I didn't see his face. I suddenly woke up in my bed and the glass in the painting above my bed glowed with big red devilish eyes like in cartoons. I pushed myself back and said, 'what the fuck?' It was *so* real and it felt very angry.

I also experienced an event where I was walking to the shops after dark and the path where I was about to walk was pitch black. Suddenly, I had a vision as clear as day of a large python lying across the path and heard a voice inside my mind say, 'there's a snake across the path. It's harmless. You can look at it but don't touch it'. I was a good fifty plus meters away from the area where the snake would be around the corner behind the buildings. There's *no way* I could have seen it from where I was. I approached the area cautiously and got out my phone and held up the light. Sure enough right there in the darkness *exactly* where I'd seen the large snake in my mind's eye, there he was, about three metres long slowly moving through the grass. You wouldn't want to trip over that in the darkness. I knelt down next to it, totally assured of my safety, and had a moment with Mother Nature. It was incredible. It was at this time in 2013 that I sketched out a few chapters for a book idea that included the messages I received titled *The Teenage Human Race*. The human race is in the teenage phase of our conscious development and although not children anymore we're certainly not adults in the big scheme of things. The blurb was "We are not the children of 'god' anymore". This book would later become *2020 & Beyond – This is Not a Drill* my first book. Then one evening after I finished a gig at a fancy bar-restaurant I was packing up my gear and a man came up to me and said gruffly, 'You're really good'. 'Thank you', I replied. He went on, 'do you know who I am?' I said, 'no'. He said, 'I'm the Chairman for the Chamber of Commerce. We've got something coming up and I'd like you to be a part of it'. I gave him my card and he said his secretary would be in touch. About a week later I got a call from a lady who said Daryl Braithwaite was coming to Port Douglas to kick off the high season at the annual street parade called *Carnivale*. She asked if I'd like to be the support act and I said I'd be happy to. On the day of the gig I finished up at the newspaper and I didn't have a car at the time. Everyone I knew or worked with was already at the event at the Sheraton Grande Mirage and as I couldn't rely on cabs as the whole town was trying to get there so, I caught the bus. I did my set that night and of course, Daryl Braithwaite and his band put on an excellent show. The crowd was rocking, *see right*, my health is clearly in decline here. I was chatting to Mr. Braithwaite after the show and he said, "You're really good. We came out on the balcony to listen to you". At the end when I was leaving I was chatting to drummer John Corniola and loaded down with all my gear he asked, 'Don't you have anyone to carry your stuff for you?' I said,  'no'. He thought about it a moment and asked, 'How did you get here?' I said, 'I caught the bus'. He was really surprised and said, 'you caught the bus to support Daryl Braithwaite?' I said, 'Yep', and he responded, 'that's so cool!' Then I caught the bus all the way home again.

As my mother was British I got my British citizenship when the UK Government *finally* updated the law in 2014 to allow the children of British *mothers* to become citizens. Up until that point you could only become a citizen if the *father* was British. The fucking gall! She does all the work to carry the babies the mitochondrial DNA is passed down through the mother but he gets the credit for the lineage? Goes to show you who's running the place. So, toward the end of 2014 I went to England for 18 months and I can't say I enjoyed myself. I did, however, find myself working for the UK Government at the local level doing contractual stints for the London Burrough of Richmond Upon Thames in their Adult and Community Services Directorate then later for the Greater Manchester Council in Child Protection Services as well as a stint working for their Department of Housing via an outsourced third party in the private sector. I was a fly on the wall. You wouldn't believe what I saw them doing to poor families and you really need to read *2020 & Beyond* to see what they're up to! The Orwellian State has arrived! Talk about 'total criminalisation'. They are using *any excuse* along with the most *flimsy* 'evidence' threatening families to take their kids away. What a bunch of cunts. It was like the KGB in cold war Russia. Needless to say I didn't last long but I saw what I needed to see. I got what I came for.

One day in late 2015 while I was at work I suddenly had the overwhelming urge to write my book, you remember? The one I'd sketched out a few chapters for back in 2013. What prevailed was a strange set of circumstances that allowed me to take several months off work and what poured out of me was nothing less than a stream of consciousness that, as I write the follow-up instalment in February 2021, all I can say was *uncanny* to say the least. The number of my 'predictions' in *2020 & Beyond* that have and are *still* coming true by the day is frankly eerie by anyone's standards. Around that time my mum came to England for the first time in 55 years and I took her up to her home village outside of Doncaster where we visited her Mother's grave in her hometown of Scrooby. At the end of 2015 I moved up to Manchester where I also worked for their council and did another radio show at FAB Radio International. It was quite a strategic move on my part and I had actually planned this before I left Australia. I was no tourist. There was a point to my purpose there. You see, Richie Allen worked at FAB Radio and he's mates with David Icke so I intended to take my radio shows along with my book under my arm and get an introduction to Icke and once I'd made *that* connection, I planned to springboard from the UK to the US. My radio show had lots of conspiracy stuff and wacky content which I find interesting like paranormal investigators and psychics and the like. One time I was interviewing a lovely lady, psychic Dee Rendell, live on air when she suddenly said, "Who's John?" I told her, "I have an Uncle John but I've never met him". She went on, '…and Joseph and Mary'. I told her these names meant nothing to me. She also told me to finish the book which I hadn't mentioned and she said there was an American publisher with that. You can hear the broadcast on my YouTube channel.

Things were finally heading in the right direction for me again. I had planned and worked *so hard* to reclaim what had been lost over the last eight years despite my health problems and setbacks. There goes another fucken decade! But once *again*, as I'd seen *so many times* in the past, just when I'm about to step up to the next level some *outside* force sweeps in and crushes my plans to dust. With only weeks away from a radio networking event where I would finally meet Richie Allen and with my book under my arm gain a *professional* introduction to David Icke. But no. Good Friday morning 2016 I received a phone call at 5am. "Mum's got cancer. She's been given four weeks to live. You have to come home". I did my final broadcast that night at FAB Radio International and within the week I was back in Australia. I knew straight away my mum's illness had something to do with my book, I just *knew* it, and what ensued remains the toughest most heartbreaking and soul-destroying journey of my life. My mother was diagnosed with Stage 4 Intestinal Cancer and the doctors gave her only weeks to live. As she wasn't one for chemo or pharmaceuticals I was obliged to roll up my sleeves and do it the old-fashioned way with hard work, Mother Nature and lots of love. Within a week she was up and about walking again thanks to my knowledge of plants found *readily available* in her garden right outside her front door, literally. The hard part, and I don't want to say this, was that during the time of her illness no one came to help. I did all this *alone* 24/7 for 12-months single handedly. I've always known they are watching my Facebook, it's standard to do this, so I would occasionally post little messages knowing they were monitoring and as my mother's health deteriorated I posted this. Later the doctors would say most people 'cave in within 4 to 6 months' caring for a Stage 4 cancer patient and that's *with* the help of family and friends.

They'd never seen anyone do what I'd done. I was left completely by myself trapped alone in a house with my dying little mum who I loved more than anything in the world. *No one* should have to endure what I endured in a world as modern as this and *all of it* secretly designed to break me on every level. They gave her four weeks I gave her twelve months and nine of those months were very good. During that time the Dr's repeatedly told me she was on her last legs trying to frighten me into releasing her into their care. No way. Fuck off. She died because of them. The medical industry is a fucking fraud populated with lots of wonderful staff trying to do a great job under a blanket of *orchestrated* lies and secrecy.

    I only just managed to get a copy of my book delivered in time for her to see and as she held my precious work in her hands in her final hours she kept saying, 'it's just so wonderful! I'm so proud of you!' I was so traumatized by being forced into a situation, alone, witnessing the prolonged death of another human being let alone my lovely little mother, that I didn't even recognise my own street when I got home. It was all so surreal I thought I was at the wrong house and as I looked up into the night sky *searching*, as so many people throughout history have done in such desperate mortal moments, there, rising over the ocean was an *enormous* yellow full moon and strangely when my father died an *enormous* orange full moon rose. I've never seen anything like it before or since. I won't go into too many details, some things are private, but the *battle* to save my mother's life will live with me forever. We can rationalize grief as much as we like, the reality is one is left with a sense of failure 'I could have done more' 'why couldn't I save her?'. But it was what I would discover was behind all this that will leave me wounded for the rest of my days. There are some injuries you know will never heal and this event is one of them. She passed away in late March 2017 a couple days before my birthday and one year *to the day* after I arrived home to care for her. I thought, 'not again?' Dad passed away *the day after* my birthday thirteen years prior. How much bad luck can you have? I was left stricken with grief and exhaustion by the loss of my dear friend and mother compounded by the anniversary of my father's death with my birthday smack dab right in the middle. They had both been my greatest mentors who had taught me *so much* about life, love, music and creativity from such an early age. Mum loved everyone. Everyone loved her. And now I was alone in the world my old friends long gone with whatever remained of my family far away. But the hard work was only just beginning and remains a relentless attack against me *to this day* since I became aware of the 'Elora Danan' *farce* a decade previous in 2007. It's like a goddamn Ferris Wheel that just keeps going round and round. It's a ride I can't get off. But it's not my ride. It's someone else's. Once again I found myself back in Port Douglas to heal. It's my go to place when the world kicks my arse. The constant stream of negative events that were unravelling around me were ceaseless and certainly not a coincidence. Twice is coincidence three times is enemy action. Try *hundreds* if not thousands of times! Despite being diagnosed with PTSD and exhaustion within 12 months I was back in the workforce as lamenting wore thin pretty quick. I saved my money working for some shitty resort to buy the equipment I needed to start my business plying my music at the old resorts. Here we go again. Et Iterum, Brute'? I got about doing yoga daily determined to lose the excess weight that had blown out of all proportion during the care period of my mother and pale, tired, haunted and alone, I started *again*.

In July 2018 about 18 months after my mother's passing I was looking better than I had for ten years and had lost a load of weight. With a combination of sun, yoga, fresh tropical fruits and veg, meditation, doing my gigs, reconnecting with the world and finally feeling proud of myself I could at last see the light at the end of the tunnel. What a fucking trip! What the hell was all *that* about? I only knew I was relieved to be getting back on with my life. My book was out in the world self-published but out there anyway. Then one evening while living at a local resort (boy am I sick of hotels) I was pottering around and for some reason I kept getting the image of Harry Connick Jr standing there all those years ago. I brushed it off. But this went on for a week. I thought, 'why am I thinking about that guy? That was so long ago'. Sometimes it takes me a little while to catch on even to my own intuition yet he kept popping into my head until suddenly, I realised 'Holy shit! That guy's coming back!" I just knew it. Round and round we go where it stops nobody knows. I know my intuition well enough to know when to get ready for something *big*. I redid the bullshit 'worked at' section on my Facebook page updating it with my *real* career including radio, print media, UK Gov, live performance, author and realised that despite everything I really had achieved a lot considering the battle it had been to do anything *at all!* I learned a couple of Connick's songs in case something impromptu happened you never know when these things will pop up out of the blue. It always happens like that. Then one evening shortly after having this foresight-psychic flash I was rehearsing for gigs and felt a strange sensation on my face. I've heard it described as an 'electrical' or a 'spider web' type sensation and what felt like a little hot pinprick almost like a little kiss on my cheek. I heard the words 'come work for me' and 'you make me feel young again'. Hey, I wrote a whole fucken book on this shit so I'm pretty sure I'd know when something has contacted me. Just when I thought things were *finally* going my way *for a change* and god knows at 41 I sure as hell earned it, no, it was on *again*. I'm clairaudient which means I can get 'yes' 'no' or 'positive' 'negative' responses on the left or right hemispheres of my ears. *Left* for love, *right* for spite. Remember that next time your ears go off. The next morning I woke up and thought I must have dreamed that something had contacted me and asked, 'did that really happen?' My left ear distinctly pulsed *Yes*. Slightly horrified for a moment I thought 'did something just respond?' Again a very distinct pulse *Yes*.

It spread from my ears to my hands to my feet and then back up my body *oscillating* for a week between my left and right ears trying to *reverse* my sense of left and right. A fucking entity locked into me on every level in and around me. My little studio filled up with a huge presence not unlike the presence I'd felt years before in the weeks leading up to crossing paths with Harry Connick Jr.

What has now ensued is another *three years* of sleep deprivation, torture, isolation, destruction of the health I regained, loss of income, destruction of my business and an all-round demonic fucking attack that has left me *this time* not just broken but *bitter*. All their other dirty tricks failed so they, at last, just used a demon. I haven't had a dream for three years as it blocks my ability to remember the details of that program or receive messages from galactic alignments happening now or know their future plans the way I used to when I wrote my first book by the way *uncanny* predictions in that. I'd heard of entity attachments before but never experienced it myself and many researchers claim (and I believe this now) that everyone in the world has some sort of attachments. This planet is *infested* with them. It's apparent that part of the job to heal our world and liberate ourselves is to clear these fucking things out once and for all. We're not going to cast them into the 'abyss' like they did a couple thousand years ago. We're gonna cut em off cold. Leave them in the dark where they belong while we *finally* enter the light. We'll never be free while these disgusting things have access to our plain of being. Around this time I had an alert pop up on my phone 'YOU ARE IN DANGER. YOU DESERVE BETTER'. Any help with that? No. Well, fuck off then. Cut a long story short this entity revealed what those memories were about from my earliest years, you remember? The ones where I recall being beamed in? Yes, *those* memories. When it came time to reveal what it was all about and after my *lifelong* quest *forty fucking years* battling to find out what the big secret was, they unveiled it in such a way that I can only say is not fully encapsulated by the word 'betrayal'.

The 11:11 Program that has dogged me my entire life is something far less noble than what I believed I was volunteering for. The entity led me to Samael Aun Weor's 'A Perfect Matrimony' describing how a loving marriage between a man and woman can be attained. It also talks about the return of a Messiah, the King. Aun Weor (pronounced On-Vo-hor) claims this union will spawn a perfect child and when this person grows up he will be the 'king' of planet Earth and our world will finally be free and humanity will live happily ever after! Ya-fucking-hoo! Praise be to the lord! He then casually mentions 'up to two million people may have to die for the 'messiah' to be born' because, well, enough people haven't died *already* so, heck let's just take out a few more million, shall we? Make it a billion! Because it's just *so fucking altruistic*. It didn't take me but two seconds to realise this wonderful 'king' is nothing more than the fucking anti-Christ. The Beast personified! The Devil incarnate! Oh yes, the program *I* remember was to create the satanic One World Leader and if you think *that's* weird this entity claimed that *I*, yes, shy little me who just wanted to play music and sing songs, was the reincarnation of Mother Mary of Joseph and Mary fame as well as Jesus and Mary Magdalene fame. Do you remember my psychic Dee Rendal saying this live on air at Fab Radio in Manchester? Blessed fucking be! We have arrived! Mary is *Isis* who was married to Osiris the most famous Queen and King of ancient Egypt. Isis is the physical personification of the star Sirius the *brightest* and most beautiful star in the sky called the 'blue angel' who ancient Egyptians loved above all *literally* considered 'the Soul of Sirius', *see right*, Marie Magdalene 'Marlene' Dietrich in *Blue Angel* released on 1st April 1930. 'Marlene' is derived from *Mar*-y and 'lene' from Magda-*lene*. She was a known lesbian cross dresser and as we shall see all this is deeply rooted in an agenda to biologically rewrite humanity to make us in the image of *their* god Satan, a man-woman-beast, the Baphomet! It's no coincidence April Fools is the first day of the month associated with Easter. The *goddess* Ishtar is 'the fool' (try idiot) and *She* is the same 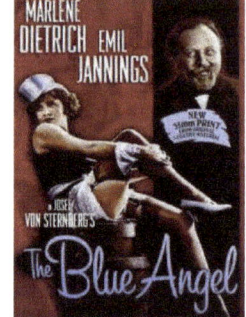 goddess as Isis who is the same as Mother Mary, Mary Magdalene, Artemis, Aphrodite, Venus, Cybele, Athena, Eve…*Diana*…oh yes, it goes all the way to the very dirty top. She's the same gal just different names on the same dame! She is The Prime Feminine. *The Goddess!* Osiris is the same 'god' as Zeus, Jesus, Thor, Hermes, Apollo, Satan, all of em, same bloke, revered in different cultures and ages as the physical incarnation of *Orion* The Prime Masculine or *God!* The entity said I was the 'The One' and what a privilege it is to be chosen! *What. A. Fucking. Disappointment.*

All those precious years *deliberately* wasted. My youth gone. All my beautiful songs lost. Yes, the brightest star of them all *the best* is what I represented. I can't prove *now* what a young woman let alone a *female child* can do musically and that's *precisely* why they did it - so no one would see me at my best. No little girls will see an all-round female artist-entertainer, a mentor, like me perfectly timed as these new young female artists struggle to make their presence felt in any *practical* sense. I would have shown girls can roll as accomplished musicians just as good as any guy in *multiple* areas *at the same time*. Talk about triple threat! Or is it just *a threat* to these men who destroy such women? Songwriting, singing, multi-instrumentalist, performance, dance, scriptwriting, acting, drama, comedy, wit, intellect, charisma, business management *and* looking like a super model to boot. What I have achieved myself *if* a tiny fragment of what I would have achieved *if* I was developed properly or given *any chance at all* let alone *deliberately* targeted and destroyed for over four decades of megalomaniacal abuse, torture, torment, entrapment, lies, betrayal *because* I fit the profile of the beautiful accomplished naturally gifted goddess of ancient myth. They set me up *because* I was the best. I knew it. They knew it. They buried me in anonymity heaping a mountain of pain on my efforts to excel my abilities that I *knew* were rare and unique. They were *laughing* at me, as it turns out, the whole time this was happening despite my herculean attempts to *persistently* break free. That's what they do, they laugh as they *brutalise* the goddess. All my hard work destroyed. All that loyalty and dedication pissed away and the *purpose?* To be *nothing* but the vending machine for the son of the Devil and that's all women are to these satanic scumbag low-life pieces of filth. We're just a pod to spawn their genetics.

Back in 2011 I got a tarot reading from a lady and she talked about the usual things love and money. I became impatient and asked about the *one* thing *most* important to me, 'what about my *music?* When will *that* happen?' She replied, 'oh, that won't happen until your mid-forties when a powerful man will pick you up'. I realised, 'It'll be too late by then, my music will be gone'. So I doubled and redoubled my efforts to take my *rightful* place. Tarot and astrology has *no power* unless you let it. Yet they intended to laugh *endlessly* at my sad little efforts to make my music career successful and continue to do to me to this day what they've secretly done to me *my lifelong*. They planned to dress up my belated 'success' as a 'happily ever after' a 'rags-to-riches' 'fairytale' ending after a long struggle to make it. Then get me into bed and produce their *despicable* creature from hell. 'Let's wreck her life, leave her in ruins, and fuck her as well'. What a lark. What kind of minds come up with this? To use *that level* of technology to isolate and destroy *one* little women on her own? And that's funny to them? I've since seen endless movies with your famous big-wig A-list male celebrities covertly inserting the sickest jokes about the destruction of the feminine, their own mothers and wives no less. They are predators. Nothing more. *And* they think they're smart that's actually the funny bit. What a big joke it was to take an extraordinarily talented girl, beam me into abject poverty and humiliation, wreck my life, make me work my arse off in the gutter for four decades to reach the end of it all and pulverize me into smithereens after they *orchestrated the death of my mother on my birthday*. That was it. The *big* reveal. At last! The mystery finally shown to me! They thought I'd be such a bimbo I would be happy about being 'the one' and not put two-and-two together. I've known my whole life something *big* going on. So, *that's* how they chose to tell me what the program was about. No really, thank you. I can't tell you what a fucking honour it is to be chosen. All because I'm a woman. *Fact*. The *best* women are used, abused and thrown away by the *dick cult*. They hate women. To say it was a letdown is the *motherfucking understatement of the millennium. Cunts*. I might have known it would be a fizzer. Typical. Yet all I needed was a few *crucial* details along with my memories and previous research and I took off like a rocket.

Turns out the fleur di lis is the emblem of the New Orleans *Saints* NFL team. Remember the TV show *The Saint?* The lead character was Simon *Templar*. Yep, it's all around us. Where do you start with New Orleans? Talk about The Dark

City. A microcosm of all things mythological playing out in America designed for the very purpose of spawning the much-prophesised New World New Age leader, The One, the Prince of Darkness! Right down to their two-month long celebration, Mardi Gras is a recreation of the festival of Dionysus held in ancient Greece. Their various Krewe's (which means Secret Society) were spawned by a Secret Society in 1711, yes, 11, called the Boeuf Gras Society or 'Society of the fatted Cow-Ox' all based on class, economic and racial groups. This ritual traces back to medieval times and further to the druids who slaughtered a bovine as peasants bathed in its blood eating the 'last meat' before their version of Lent. Mardi Gras tradition is a 'king cake' which as we shall see represents the 'seed' of ancient 'grain gods'. Inside the cake is a toy of baby Jesus, the king. They've literally put the French Royal Court of old European royalty on show *for all to see*. Just as a bit of fun mind. America is New Egypt and they need a Queen for their King. The centre of the spiders web is New Orleans and the Deep South is *saturated* in sadism that would require an *entire book* for the *unending weirdness* and *corruption* emanating out of *that* city including the Garrison Investigation into the assassination of JFK - King Kennedy! The King is dead. Long live the King! They talk to each other in movie titles, tv shows, art and media even playing out the script with football teams and it goes *all the way to the top* with links to *major* U.S. alphabet agencies, the *biggest* space agencies, Silicon Valley and Washington D.C. The roots of this dark order are found in European and British *Royal families* re-creating the Messiah! *Jesus 2.0!* Old-world families seek to rebrand and *re-emerge* in the 21st Century bringing all the psychopathic darkness of their evil past with them. It's *Interview with the Vampire meets The Matrix!* They seek to install The One, a savvy *modern* leader to connect their dying *obsolete* icon to the emerging New Age of Aquarius! The

fleur di lis has dogged me my entire life from champagne given as a gift and pendants to my guitar emblazoned with it, it's even on the windows of my apartment, *right*. Yet despite my heartache and being alone through it all I went to work on this like a *mechanic* and what unveiled itself to me will change the world for the better *once and for all*.

That's what you get for kicking the goddess in the balls.

Chapter Three
OSIRIS & ISIS
Who is Osiris and Isis and what does this have to do with me?

Osiris and Isis are the two *major* central deities worshipped by the secret religion running our planet today. No one wants to openly own up to this secret religion but once you know the themes and symbols you will find it in every movie, every song, every magazine cover, every editorial, every advertisement for major products, all over the internet and refenced in most all major political and entertainment interviews *worldwide*. It's like a weird celebrity game - who's the best at hiding it in plain sight? They're all in on it laughing behind our backs right in our faces but then that's Hollywood and political 'royalty' for you. They're just the same as old world 'royalty' and just as egomaniacal and self-entitled. Anyone who is anyone is in on it while your favourite actors are most often chosen for their names and dates of birth in conjunction with ancient myth and folklore in fact I'm hard pressed to find *any* major actor whose name or birthday *doesn't* have some connotation to this mythological symbolic story. You'd think rich or famous people populating the heights of politics and entertainment must have high levels of intelligence to be a part of the upper echelons of society? No. I can honestly tell you they're not particularly intellectual *or* talented despite their largely private school educations. The reality is they want to hang on to their power as such, *intelligence does not equate to kindness* and often has the *exact opposite* effect leading to egomania and narcissism.

I'm gonna cut to the chase as mythology and 'ancient' history usually puts most people into a sudden coma from which they will only arise once Nickelodeon is switched on. Osiris and Isis were 'twins' and the most beloved deities in ancient Egypt. He was the physical embodiment of the constellation Orion, the *soul* of Orion, and she was the physical embodiment of the star Sirius, the *soul* of Sirius, the Dog Star, the brightest star in the sky. They were considered 'royalty' of the highest order. King and the Queen. God and Goddess. In particular, Isis was *literally* considered the throne. But why? Legend has it that this couple made one half of 'two sets of twins' yet they are never referred to as quadruplets. Again, why? There were four in all; Osiris and his evil twin brother Set and well as Isis and her evil twin sister Nephthys. Osiris and Isis were a married couple while Set and Nephthys were also a married couple. Nephthys tricked Osiris into sleeping with her so Set murdered Osiris in revenge and cut his body into 14 pieces. Isis set out with 'seven scorpions' to retrieve every part of Osiris but couldn't find the phallus so she fashioned a phallus of gold, *Goldmember*, copulated with Osiris posthumously and their son Horus was born. Isis then conjured the spirit of Osiris into Horus who took on his uncle-brother Set. During the battle Set plucked out the left eye of Horus until finally, Set was vanquished and all was well at the pyramids. Note, all this is only *metaphorical*. Set is a murderer and Nephthys is a slut who *represent* the dark sides of the masculine and feminine. Therefore, Osiris and Isis, Set and Nephthys, are *symbolically* the light and dark sides of the masculine & feminine found in *every* man and *every* woman to some degree or other. It's ancient psychology 101. That's all.

The universe is a self-replicating *binary* code therefore, 'The Twins' of this ancient folk fable is a reference to the electrical positive and negative electrical charges. Tesla harnessed the gargantuan levels of this power in his experiments and we would do well to listen to his example of *organic* science and technology. As such, what the ancients were *really* referencing was cosmology and the properties of the universe discovered by Tesla when he tapped into the 'force' of Mother Nature. These 'pairs' of 'twins' in electrical terms are called 'duals', duality and, basically, this dual expression always produces the same form. Thus 'god made man in his image'. *Replication*. Yet as we shall discover men made 'god' in *their* image and have behaved like 'god' ever since, well, some men, not all, but a lot, we'll get to that. It is the interchanging or more specifically the *intercoursing* of electrical currents and magnetism of universal *life-force* energy *weaving* throughout the cosmos that expresses itself as North and South, East and West or 'two sets of twins'. It is the seasons Summer and Winter, Spring and Autumn 'two sets of twins'. It is night and day, dusk and dawn 'two sets of twins'. It is the light side and dark side of the masculine and feminine 'two sets of twins'. They are one but they are not the same. This also simply means, men and women, the symbolic 'brothers' and 'sisters', *the twins,* of humanity and the self-procreation of the generations between males and females via *intercourse* creating new life. Yes, sex.

The amount of electrical energy created via sex, if properly harnessed, can unlock alchemical and physiological processes in the body that renders the average man and woman a veritable God and Goddess as deified by Osiris and Isis who, essentially, represent in *all* men and women. There's nothing fancy going on here. Mother nature is really quite simple and only became complicated when the sadistic minds of certain 'elite' males, *Templars-Masons*, decided to *corrupt* the basic foundation of human life and the marvel of procreation. These upstarts *symbolically* deified these processes and *stood in the place* of evolution itself, a completely fabricated *idea* of 'god' presented as an *outside force* and promoted by the three major Abrahamic religions that sprung up in the wake of this knowledge via Judaism, Catholicism and Islam for just such a purpose! 'Royalty', who apparently represent 'god', is really *every* man and *every* woman, humans, found on Earth and all ancient cultures were *well aware* of the importance of humanity. Once you know this fact you find it everywhere *worldwide* throughout history. In fact, this high state of being or 'god' was  once the norm when Earth was a legendary 'eternal spring' and 'eternal youth' of men and women living the fabled Fountain of Youth that 'restores the youth of anyone who *drinks of its waters'*. The 'waters', yes, we'll get to that too.

Ancient Greek *mythology* claimed as do many native cultures, even still, that there was a '*Golden* Age' described by Plato in *Cratylus* who recounted the '*Golden* Race' of the *first* humans. They were eternally youthful living long lives until they suddenly aged just before they died around 100 years of age. In his book *Active Side of Infinity*, Carlos Castaneda quoted Yaqui shaman Don Juan Matus as saying, "…infant human beings (are)…luminous balls of energy, covered from the top to the bottom with a *glowing* coat…when a human being reached adulthood, all that was left of that *glowing coat of awareness* was a narrow fringe that went from the ground to the top of the toes. That fringe permitted mankind to continue living, but only barely…*man was the only species that had the glowing coat of awareness*". The shaman also said, 'The sorcerers of ancient Mexico…reasoned that man must have been a *complete being* at onc point, with stupendous insights and feats of awareness that are *mythological* legends nowadays. And then everything seems to disappear, and we have now a sedated man". Manly P. Hall said of the *stupendous* megalithic ancient stone monuments, "It is almost certain that the great ruins of Carnac in Brittany had some definite scientific or religious usage. These were built by persons who *already knew something*. They were not built by the Cro-Magnons but apparently they were standing there *long before we come to this dark curtain that divides prehistory from history as we know it now*". The ancient Greek poet Hesiod, 750BC - 650BC, listed in his poem Works and Days a *Golden Age* that fell under the rule of Cronus. Cronus, we'll get to him as well. Read on. *Right*, we  see an ancient Persian depiction of the 'golden' one, the fire halo, the 'glowing coat of awareness', *enlightenment*, the pure fire of 'light' as opposed to the impure fire of 'Satan'. Yes, *this* is the light and dark side of electrical energy that some have called *The Force*. It is all around, everywhere, all through the universe. It exists in everything living and dead. It is the propulsion system of life itself. It is the *essence* of Mother Nature that causes life to spring up even under the most detrimental of circumstances. *It is life. The living spirit!* It is *electricity* and behind all the dogma and penises, it appears to be feminine.

All religions say there are 'levels' in order to attain heaven or 'godhood' so we see the guys on the left in this image having attained *partial* godhood while the bloke on the right has achieved the whole enchilada covered from head to toe in the previously mentioned 'glowing coat' as it were the same level of light or *awareness* described as 'ascension' or an 'ascended master'. A living god. The *Golden Age* may come again and the 'second coming' is not what you have been told it is! They say to get to Hell you must go through the fires but to get to Heaven you must go through the light. Fire and light. Two sides of the same coin. One good. One bad. Light and Dark. Osiris and Set. Isis and Nephthys. Therefore, for peace to reign the masculine fires *must* be tempered with waters of the feminine light. That's how they did it eons ago in 'prehistory' and that is how we will do it again. To rebuild our glory in incredible monuments of human endeavours captured from a golden age *long forgotten* crushed under the heel of an insidious alien plan reaching its dreaded conclusion as we speak! *Very soon this state of super-consciousness will be ours again.* But it's a close call. Enlightenment was the secret of Osiris and Isis as well as Mary and Jesus and all the rest of the 'gods' and 'goddesses' throughout history. It is why pharaohs 'fused their image' with the sun god Ra because they had attained 'godhood', en*light*ened like the sun, depicted symbolically as the fire-sun or glowing light, *the halo,* of their activated crown chakra. But how do you activate it? Pharaohs were considered *living* gods because of this which basically means they had attained 100% brain access unlocking their seven chakras and meridians reinforcing their auras and their psychic awareness. Unfortunately, their egos stood in the place of about 50% of their brain capacity which is why Julius Caesar like Kennedy and Jesus (and all the rest of them) didn't see it coming. If they were truly enlightened they'd basically be untouchable.

At least the ancients had *living* gods, actual people, who addressed the populace and had attained 'enlightenment' in the public arena whereas Jesus, Moses and all the rest of these 'modern' gods are dead. They're not much good to us dead, are they? But they live in our hearts. Blessed be. What a croc of shit. They're dead. Deal with it. Via certain transcendental practices like sacred sex or what we commonly know today as tantric sex still openly practiced in India, you too can unlock your chakras and meridians and gain just as must power as these posturing cunts who have ruled over us using this knowledge while keeping it from us. The other way to attain enlightenment or godhood is to sit in a Buddhist temple and meditate for 60 years until you can levitate, otherwise, find someone you can trust i.e. *love,* and practice tantric *transcendental* intimacy with them. You don't need drugs. You don't need gurus. You don't need Bibles. You don't need priests. You don't need scholars. You don't need forgiveness and you certainly don't need permission. Can I have a thank you, Jesus. You just need someone you can trust to access the positive and negative electrical poles encoded in our amazing human bodies that these motherfuckers are in the process of destroying with their poisons, pharmaceuticals and injections. *Anyone* can do this. Apparently, you can even do it by yourself if ancient stories are true about masturbating sun gods attaining their enlightenment *alone* using their hand as the 'female principle' i.e. wanking. They were so polite! I am not.

During the Renaissance a set of artists depicted Jesus not as a paragon of virtue but 'ostentatio genitalium' which means 'the showing of the genitals'. As much as I hate the term 'rock out with your cock out' it actually applies here. In the *Man of Sorrow's* series c.1525AD by Maerten Van Heemskerck, JC was depicted with an apparently uncircumcised penis which flies in the face (hopefully not literally) of Jewish convention. This series of biblical erotica shows Jesus with a rather large dong. I don't know what he's so sorry about. H is for Hung like a Horse. You've heard of the gigantic prehistoric shark the Megalodon? Well this is Megadong. God's gift. Long live the king! Okay, there's all my smutty jokes out the way in one shot. In fact, the 'crown of *thorns'* is a reference to the rays of the sun  and the god *Thor* the 'thunder' god with his 'bolts of *lightning'* and why Zeus also had bolts of lightning as they were electricity 'gods'. Practicing tantric sex unlocks the seven chakras which focuses the *electrical nature* of the nervous system to laser beam precision via the pineal gland activating the crown chakra, the IQ or *awareness*, to incredible heights! It brings a whole new meaning to 'make love not war', literally. The ancients saw connections in everything so the electrical 'god' of thunder was equated to the electrical god *within* as well as the light of the sun without. Replication. This light is the seven often seen protruding from the head of deities wearing the 'crown' including the Statue of Liberty etc., and why sun god 'Ra' is actually the sun 'Ray', Amun Ra or Re is Amun Sun *Ray* to symbolise the light rays of the sun. *See right*, ancient art and Jewish Menorah showing the seven lights, *fires,* of the chakras culminating at the head. It is truly ancient knowledge and the Jews are all over this. It's why royalty wear the *golden crown* symbolic of their massive IQ's of the unlocked *crown* chakra achieved via 'sacred sex' thus allowing them the knowledge to rule over  others or 'appointed by god'. Yes, the god within. This is the 'right' of kings as knowledge equals power and in the land of the blind the one-eyed man *is* King. This power can and has been misused as warned in hieroglyphs in ancient Egypt. The force can be used for *evil*, it's just electricity after all, the way you can use it to cook a meal or use it to electrocute someone. There is responsibility required here. All major civilisation's were built out of the knowledge and the practice of Sacred Sex *enlightenment*, Tantric Sex, *transcendental sex*, and was once only practiced under *Holy Matrimony*. Yet, as Satan runs this planet, the sad truth is, in Egypt, home of the tantric Goddess Isis, 90% of women have suffered Female Genital Mutilation (FGM) and thus achieving orgasm is impossible so the right of tantric enlightenment has been stolen from them. *It's no coincidence.*

In breaking down the term Holy Matrimony we find Holy is the wood of the *holly* tree said to be *magical* in nature and why Druids made their wands from holy trees hence, *Holly*wood where the 'magic' happens. Wand is code for penis or 'it's not the size of the wand but how you use it'. The word Matri is Latin for 'mother' and mony is old English for Moon. Therefore, Holy Matrimony is a *Magical Mother Moon* ceremony because only via the covenant, *contract*, of marriage to a practicing tantra priestess was a man allowed to have his chakras unlocked as this power is dangerous in the wrong hands. It's not called Patrimony for good reason and just look at what's happened to Mother Earth as a result of the dark path of male fire, *testosterone*. So, matrimony was a contract men took out with women who knew these skills as it was once the domain of the Goddess, the priestesses, the Vestal Virgins, the Oracles or Delphi, among other virginal women beyond reproach, that this knowledge was held sacred. It was too precious to fall into the hands of only men who easily scheme among themselves, militant minded. The false satanic priesthood who run the world today misused this knowledge to the detriment of all others and it shows. This is why the secrets were entrusted to the feminine, the Goddess, who was loved above all others any other 'gods' were considered 'minor nature deities' by comparison to the Great Mother Goddess, *mother nature*, personified in women who these 'elite' males have sullied and torn down for millennia and beyond. But she's coming back, folks, and how!

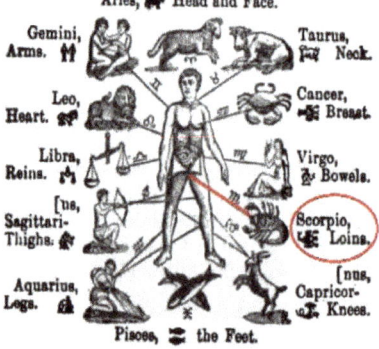

Isis 'set out with *seven* scorpions' to retrieve Osiris because Scorpio rules over the loins, the sexual reproductive organs of the human body, *see right*. So, it's interesting the first Pharoah of Egypt was the Scorpion King. King of tantric sex. We are being told there is a link between 'sex' and the number 'seven' as the *seven* chakras are unlocked via *sex* starting at the lowest root *sexual* chakra or the 'underworld' raising up through the chakra 'tower' or kundalini (electricity) rising, *see right*, the caduceus rising up the spine, *the nervous system*, switching on all the chakras bringing 'life' to someone who is otherwise spiritually

Caduceus (Staff of Hermes)

dead. Hey, aren't we all? This is why Osiris and Isis are *still* 'worshipped' by Hollywood 'royalty' today in a weird pantomime as celebrities attain 'godhood' on the Mount Olympus of Metro Goldwyn Mayor *via this practice*. They're all doing it. We live in a false system *specifically* designed to empower a few at the top who know about these things and *disempower* those at the bottom who don't.

Celebrities and politicians are not particularly talented or intelligent they're just 'well connected'. Nepotism reigns supreme and it's all about their bloodlines, lineage, family. All that is changing as people are recognised for their *true* talent and their *real* merit rather than who they banged or who their dad is. As with all good symbolism the ancient fables of the Twins not only describe positive and negative electrical forces but the 'twins' of men and women. It also describes the state of their mental health. The ancients were far more advanced than the modern world gives them credit for and why we wound up in this mess. The 'twins' are reflected in the light and dark side of their respective psyches, the Jekyll and Hyde aspects of our psychology, found *inside* us. It's the devil on one shoulder and the angel on the other hence, the 'evil twin' syndrome. Set and Nephthys symbolised the dark side of male and female *morality* or murder and infidelity. *Right*, we see the light and dark side of the feminine in the Wiard of Oz, the 'Wicked Witch of the *West*' and 'Good Witch of the *North*'. Her crown and halo of activated chakras generate the torus field and strengthen the aura. She carries the Star, Sirius or Isis, who symbolises every woman. The male-female pair is represented by the number 11 symbolic of the constellation Gemini which is Latin for 'twins' also called The Lovers denoted by the zodiac symbol ♊. They are two halves of the same whole as the male and female *both* have their light and dark side best encapsulated by the symbol 11:11 which represents the angel or the devil *inside* the male and female *pair*, double duality, and expresses itself as the good guys and the bad guys or the good girls and the bad girls. It's temptation or redemption every bit as relevant today as it was thousands of years ago. We really haven't changed at all. The light and dark were *personified* by famous ancient characters referenced all over the world throughout history. For example, the biblical story of Jesus the good guy and his 'spiritual brother' Satan the bad guy. It can be found in Norse mythology as Thor the thunder god 'good' guy while is evil 'trickster' brother Loki is mischievous, the bad guy. The founding of Rome pays

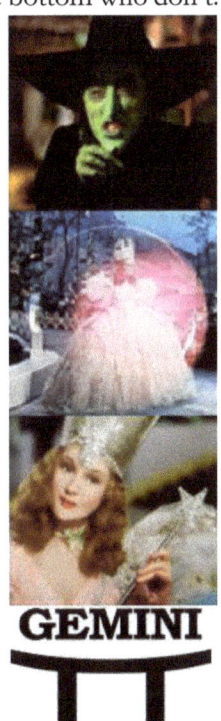

homage to this story when Romulus was killed by his evil twin brother Remus or as Cain slaying his brother Abel in the 'creation' story (its actually the 'destruction' story). It's the good Virgin *Mary* and her Prostitute evil twin *Mary*. Same person. Same people. It is the light and dark side in *everyone* and our *internal* battle to do the right or wrong thing. The battle of 'good' and 'evil' is *within us* not some wrathful father 'god' crap. The son becomes the father becomes the son becomes the father *ad infinitum*. The Daughter becomes the Mother becomes the Daughter becomes the Mother *ad infinitum*. Generations. Some good some bad. Light and dark of the eternal *internal*. It's evolution. It's Cinderella the good girl and her evil sisters-mother the bad girls keeping her from Prince Charming the good guy.

Yes, ancient sacred sex is found in fairy tales!

You mean to say that we can activate our chakras and access our mega-mind's just by the simple act of sex? It's too good to be true and yet Mother Nature's simplicity is genius. Pleasure leads to evolution. Real evolution. But as always there's a catch that I will get to soon. High IQ was symbolised as the 'halo' around the head of Mary and Christ, *see right*, the Crown (of enlightenment). Yes, mother had the knowledge first the son came later and a woman with activated chakras can influence the characteristics of the unborn baby therefore we see here the baby born *already* enlightened, the man-child, called a 'homunculus'. The definition of a homunculus was 'a microscopic but fully formed human being from which the fetus was believed to develop'. In other words an *already* enlightened or *mature* spirit born into a fetus as Jesus is often depicted as mature person in a baby's body while some people never grow up. The term homunculus has been warped into meaning demon or abomination to steer us away from the power of our potential to evolve in ways we could never imagine and design ourselves *naturally!* What science is doing *today* is designing humanity *unnaturally*. It's Satanism dressed up as progress. Therefore, it was the *Goddess* (not some distorted disciplinarian father 'god') who was *originally* revered before the dark side of the masculine, *the Devil*, took over this planet wiping her memory using her own power against her while enslaving men, god. This is why Set 'plucked out the left eye of Horus' because the right eye is the Sun and the left eye is the *Moon*. The feminine. This is the meaning of celebrities covering one eye or the other. They're telling you *symbolically* that the feminine was extracted from proceedings while the boys warred, caroused and brawled as 'gods'. Endless brother against brother conflicts all in some horrendous sideshow for shadowy alien masters to watch like twisted voyeurs plying our fate against us. Evil. While the brothers waged their endless battle against each other the pair of them, dufus's that they are, ignored and *removed* the feminine entirely. Deleted her from the equation altogether and *She* was their salvation the *entire* time! So, women were 'plucked out', removed from management, as most profoundly the eyes are a 'window to the soul' and equate to 20/20 vision which is sorely out of balance now as *so much* hangs in the *balance* of the year *2020* symbolic of *perfect vision*. It's our last chance and why the ancients carved it in stone, wrote it in fairy tales and coded in religious texts in their *desperate* attempts to warn us before the end. To save Planet Earth *for the last time!*

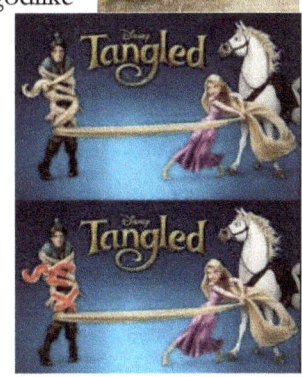

The activated chakra tower and heightened IQ was also depicted as *golden* hair as Aries, the ram, rules over the head. *This* is the symbolic 'Golden Fleece' of the enlightened crown spoken of in Jason and the Argonauts as well as *Goldilocks* or the 'golden boy'. It's the 'sun' crown. It's everywhere once you know what you're looking for. The hair is an *extension* of the *nervous system* outside the body so the ancients were *well aware* of the nervous system and secret functions of human anatomy only just being *rediscovered* today, *see right,* Roman fresco of the sheep at his head and *note,* the mitre square, a masonic symbol. *This* is the meaning of Samson and Delilah who shared the secret of his strength, *his hair,* they cut it off and reduced him to a weakling. In the Norse story 'The Theft of the Golden Hair: *A Celestial Crime'* Loki cuts the hair of Thor's beautiful wife, Sif, *while she's sleeping,* see right, 'Loki Cuts Sif's Hair' by Katherine Pyle 1930. Thor demands her hair be restored threatening Loki who seeks the 'dwarves beneath the earth' the 'black elves' who appear to be demons. This says that there was a time when the light side of the masculine, the inner god, needed his goddess to be as enlightened as him to *both* attain the full measure of *mutual ascension* as a godlike couple. *The power couple.* Notice they say a 'celestial crime' it's a crime against the universe that the feminine was literally cut out. This story tells us that the dark side of the masculine, the Devil, 'cut' the feminine golden crown of enlightenment plunging her into ignorance and the only way to get it back was via sex which is where the 'prostitute' myth comes into it. In her attempts to regain her IQ she must debase herself to gain back what they have *stolen* from her that she owned in the first place hence, the 'thief' theme in fairy tales.

The Arn-Thompson-Uther Index is a catalogue of folktales by an international group of scholars who have traced fairy tales as an oral folk tradition of historical lore dating back over 6,000 years still in circulation today. The ancient bard is alive and well. The fable of Rapunzel, the *lost* Princess (lost in darkness) is symbolically 'high up' in her *tower*. In many Disney productions of these famous fables they insert sex themes as all these ancient fables are about sex. Here we can see 'sex' while the horses name is *Maximus* a reference to the size of his penis or 'hung like a horse'. The phrase 'let down your hair' *really* means, 'let me access your electrical nervous system via the root chakra in tantric sex so I can climb the *chakra tower* and reach enlightenment where *you* are oh Goddess!' Note the green chameleon on her shoulder, *right*, this is shapeshifter symbology or royalty, the 'frog prince' aka the 'devil', a reptilian, who has commandeered this sacred knowledge and makes an appearance in these fables as 'frogs'. These tales often emanate out of France colloquially termed 'frogs' while Prince Phillip is to be buried at *Frogmore* House as will the Queen. So, when Rapunzel's hair is cut it goes  from gold to dark brown and she loses her *power*. In a 60 Minute's interview about Britney Spears referring to her as a 'princess' her music manager Kim Kaiman said of the strict Conservatorship effectively making her a prisoner, 'I don't think she's being held in a tower like *Rapunzel*'. Britney went from golden hair to dark hair, cut it off, and lost her power. Kaiman went on to say that when Britney 'returns' she will be like a 'Phoenix rising from the ashes'. This is mind control 'fairy tale' talk and a false 'return' of the feminine, a *fake* looming 'revolution' of consciousness utilising women as bastions of 'new age' justice while keeping the *real* power very much from them! People will be ecstatic. We won! The war is over! No, it's just beginning. Britney was in the Mickey Mouse Club, a very dark enterprise, mocking the 'innocence' of humans as children of 'god' aka reptilians.

In the Disney animation of Rapunzel, Tangled (yes, it is rather tangled), the male love interest is wanted as a 'thief' in a reference to the dark side of the masculine, the Devil aka reptilians, *stealing* the sacred knowledge of the feminine light eons ago and laughing at her ever since. His name is Flynn Ryder a reference to Errol *Flynn* who was notoriously charged for rape of an underage girl as well as his wanton *sexual* behaviour and drug and alcohol abuse, the dark side or *temptation*. Rider is a reference to 'riding' women during sex or 'cowboy'. In ancient Rome the dark side of the feminine was depicted as a 'night mare' a wicked woman who became a horse at night. The awakened feminine is a nightmare to these guys so they make fun of her ignorance. Sirius the Dog Star (*note*, Dog is God spelled backwards) was incarnated as the Goddess Isis and Osiris was the incarnation of the constellation Orion called The Deer Hunter so in Bambi (bambino means child) his *mother* is killed by the 'deer hunter'. Orion is the most easily identifiable star cluster at night and where one particularly powerful group of reptilians are  said to come from. Orion is called the 'pot' or the 'frying *pan*' a symbolic reference to *Pan* the cloven hooved pagan animal god, the devil, often depicted with a large phallus in ancient times. So, throughout the film Flynn Rider is strangely carrying a *pan* all the time. These productions dress up Satanism and sex as innocent kid's flicks while some mind control whistleblowers claim they were abused at Disney Land as children. The controllers are weird and creepy.

In ancient times the seven chakras were known as the 'sleeping beauty' and here we see *again* a very succinct depiction of the light and dark side of the feminine or the Light and The Dark Queen - good and evil. Do you remember the reference to me being Elora Dana bringing down the Dark Queen in the movie Willow? The 'dark queen' is evil women who stray into darkness sabotaging beautiful *kind* women out of jealousy sleeping with men for gain or lust. Notice in this image the three little witches in the sky are green, red and blue or the heart, root and throat chakra. The Prince is *always* royalty while innocent beauty is usually a Commoner and he awakens her *Sleeping Beauty* by 'true love's first kiss' because Beauty is a virgin so her *first* kiss is her first sexual encounter as seen in Mother Mary the *virgin* and Mary Magdalene the *whore*. Snow White is a reference to her purity as a virgin or 'pure as the driven snow'. We can see here that the dwarves are the colours of the chakras not forgetting dwarves in the Norse myth were actually demons from the underworld. In this scene, *right*, Snow White is alone in *bed* with her seven 'dwarves' who are 'Mopey', 'Sleepy', 'Dopey', 'Grumpy' 'Bashful' etc., the 'seven dwarves', the *unawakened* chakras, are 'dwarfed' or *shut down* until they are awakened, *enlightened*, and become giants i.e. 'Confidence!' 'Intelligence!' 'Awareness!' 'Bliss!' 'Strength!' etc. When the chakras are unawakened one is considered to exist in a 'sleeping death', *right*, so the evil tantric witch, the crone we see in Beauty and the Beast, poisons Beauty's 'apple', her chakras and torus field, trying to keep her unawakened

unable to know her *true* power to surpass the 'dark queen', evil women, and at last bring goodness into the world. Snow White eats the poison apple symbolic of Newton's Apple that famously 'fell' from the 'tree', the Tree of *Knowledge*, it means her IQ dropped, IQ that is *raised* by electrical processes of sexual Kundalini, Chi and Prana, light, via tantric sex. Newton was famous for his discovery of the *composition of white light* so again, as Satanists do, they are hiding the real meaning of the 'apple' behind symbolism in this 'science'. It's not gravity holding us in place, it's magnetism, specifically electrical magnetism. The 'apple' is also *Adams Apple*, the race of Adams, men, who's mature throat chakra, the *voice*, the speaker, is ruled over by Gemini, *the lovers,* who *should* speak out unafraid of some scary outdated *alien* 'dad' god incapable of evolving and thrusts us down into ignorance and pain manipulating us to believe it's all *our* fault as abusers often do. It's a tactic and one we are well aware of *globally* at this point in history. But how can Adam speak out when he doesn't even have the 'knowledge' of his true power or how to unlock *his* sleeping beauty? We are told Adam and Eve, men and women, are the 'children' of 'god' but 'god' increasingly appears to be an alien, a reptilian 'royal', a delegate from Orion, *posing* as a heavenly father figure to a recently downgraded Human on an abundant planet ready to be harvested by an alien empire in their latest conquest and keep to keep us docile for *another* 2,000 years. Hey, it worked. The 'snake' is 'god's' dark side, Jekyll and Hyde (phonetically 'hide'), unbeknownst to the Adam's and the Eve's – Humans! In John 3:14 'Jesus shed light on the incident of the copper serpent'. Copper is essential to the correct function of the nervous system as the tantric kundalini 'snake' or 'serpent' rises more effectively, *right*. They knew a *lot* more about physics than we are told and their civilisation *must* have been far more advanced then accepted archeology lets on. All major institutions including education and the media are gatekeepers, as with 'god' in the garden, who frighten the 'children' away from the truth. They are terrified we'll grow up and it's *now or never!*

TREE OF KNOWLEDGE

The 'apple' was given to Adam by Eve, *the feminine*, in the Garden, Mother Nature, when they were innocent or *children* until 'corrupted' by the *knowledge* thus becoming *adults* aware that, among other things, they were *naked*. Naked means ignorant and vulnerable. The 'fruits' of the 'tree' are the chakras and their unlocked abilities. It's all a big mind-fuck to guilt us out of our power. The 'apple' is the torus field generating the 'fruit', powers, from 'the tree of knowledge' i.e. the brain and the *nervous system* strengthened by the *knowledge* of sacred sex and our power within enhancing the IQ and torus-auric field freeing the Adam's and Eve's, us humans, from a secret alien empire. The 'fruit' culminates in the 'fruit of their loins', the enlightened child, born mature. Adam was angry that Eve, like Lilith, wanted to 'be on top' too not only sexually but *to share responsibilities* yet Adam was an easy take as 'god' knew his stupidity *and size* could be relied on to suppress Eve, the real enemy of 'god' then *and* now. The church *insisted* on the missionary position for *procreation only* as it requires numerous positions, like yoga, to attain the power of tantra *see*, the Kama Sutra.

The Adam's were manipulated to disrespect the Eve's as 'god' demanded men to be 'on top' not only physically but in *every other way*. Top dog. It's their secret religion. So, Adam lost the power of the Goddess along with his *real* powers, ceased being God *himself,* spurning the very thing who could free him throwing her down forever ruining *them both* and 'god' aka Satan, laughed. Even *still* they laugh, *see right*, the movie Shrek shows the 'Three Bears' which is a reference to the constellation Ursa Major in Latin 'the greater she-bear'. Here we see the 'family' together in a 'cage' then we see only the father bear and baby bear still crying by the 'fire', hell fires, and in the last image we see one bear, *the mother bear,* she is *dead* turned into a *floor rug*. They often kill the mother in these 'harmless' kids flicks and laugh about it *see*, Bambi which means 'bambino' or 'child'. They also kill the father too, *see*, the Lion King. It is the destruction of the Family as one parent *or both* are often dead teaching children, subliminally, there is no such thing as family as the Orwellian State replaces the *eternal* Family of Life.

THE APPLE

An expanded IQ-torus field, *right*, would have put the Adam's and Eve's on par with 'god', an alien *reptilian* hyper-masculine *invader* posing as a 'heavenly father' along with his brother, the snake. God and the snake are the 'good cop-bad cop' routine seeing which way they can sway humans playing both roles at once, *see right,* George *Burns* (again, fires of hell) in *Oh, God! You Devil*. The shadow of his foot even looks like a big dick. Notice, blue for the throat chakra, the speaker, and red for the root chakra, sex. But you can't have equality between humans and fake alien gods. So, the Adams and the Eves were punished *forever* because 'god' 'loved' them. Movies and porn encourage carnality straying humans *away* from Love in favour of sex, quick like *animals* living in constant fear. With a strong torus field we are untouchable by dark forces. It's the knight in shining armour! Everything has a torus field, even the universe, and had Adam and Eve activated their 'apple' they would have quickly realised 'god' or the 'gods' were evil aliens and explains why 'god' was so angry and panicked in a kneejerk reaction and kicked them out.

The original telling of Sleeping Beauty was very dark, as with most folklore including the *brother and sister* Hansel and Gretel and Red Riding Hood (sex again). The true story of Beauty involves her rape, impregnation and humiliation by the 'prince'. Prince Harry and Prince William *both* marry common girls for the first time ever, it's unheard of as they continue the 'happily ever after' *fable* of the Royal Prince marrying the Common girl but not in its rightful essence. If 'god' is an old white man then the 'goddess' is a young black woman and in ancient times *she* was royalty and he was the commoner, see Rapunzel, as Prince Harry marries a 'common' black girl. *Black Beauty!* Therefore, 'true love's first kiss' is made quite apparent in this scene, *right*, as Prince Charming and Snow White appear to be having sex in bed on their wedding night although it's dressed up as something else. This is why a bride wears white to symbolise her purity as a 'virgin' and why all religions are obsessed with the virgin-whore aspects of the feminine because it's via the purity of the feminine, her honour and chastity, that humanity will be released while in China traditionally the bride wore red of the root chakra. Red is why prostitutes are in the 'red light district' and a slut is a 'scarlet' women etc. Newlyweds are not to consummate the union until the *wedding* night as its bad luck for the groom to see the bride in her wedding dress before they are married. Holy Matrimony is the marriage of the Goddess and the King or Earth with flesh and maybe he is royalty but she sure aint no commoner. Again, we see the colours of the chakras as Prince *Charming* (he charms her pants off) wears the colour of the root sexual chakra, *maroon*, while she only has a little of the colour of sexuality. He has all the sex because *she's* pure. Once *awakened* via sacred sex activating her crown chakra she becomes 'crowned' and therefore 'royalty' herself. In this way she will re-attain what was stolen by the very prince (his class) who is giving it back. Her honour breaks the 'curse' of the 'beast' or 'devil' reptilian royalty and in turn releases them both. This is the core meaning of the 'happily ever after' a prophecy that Earth would be free. This the *last chance* to fulfill the legend of the Lovers, God and Goddess, as the light and dark side of the masculine comes together accepting their twin, women, in her rightful place as an equal electrical counter-pole escaping the 'curse' of Earth, an alien empire.

The last chakra to 'open' via sacred sex/tantric sex in a man is the heart chakra and once activated he becomes 'lion hearted'. The anagram of 'lion' is 'loin' as the lion represents the fires of the sun as well as 'the fires' of his 'loins' that we know today as testosterone that can cause men to get 'fiery' or have 'brain snap' as seen in men who use steroids to increase testosterone for body building. These 'fires' of his sex or 'spark of life' are also code for the fires of the sun and 'hell fires' as unhinged masculinity has led to hell on Mother Earth without the balancing passive 'waters' of the feminine. He is the Sex King, the Sun King, the Lion King or more specifically the *Loin* King. Biggus Dickus. So, they put a woman sitting on his face, *right*, with 'The King Has RETURNED' above a rising sun, yes, the 'Return of the Sun King'. This is why throughout history all the greatest leaders coveted this knowledge to 'fuse' their image with the 'Sun' considered 'God' to become Sun Kings, king of the light, and therefore 'god' over Mother Earth with their 'right to rule'. But we're more mature than that now as rationale and real science provides a window of opportunity to utilise this knowledge without all the weird dogma and religious-cult secrecy. Tibetans believe the sun is a lens, an eye, indeed the eye of god that looks in on us. Listen to the lyrics of the Alan Parson's Project song Sirius Eye in the Sky - *Mammagamma*. Gamma ray mamma. Basically all famous people are practicing this. As such, Julius Caesar declared himself a living god as did Alexander the Great, King Arthur, King Louis the XIV and Jesus *King* of the Jews among many, all sun kings, as was Osiris the most famous sun king of all practicing this 'sexual kung fu' to become masters of this 'artform'. So, we find a female arse on the face of the Lion King, the *Loin* King, *right*, saying 'The King Has Returned' and the word 'sex' spelled out *in the stars*. In the Wizard of Oz the three male characters are the lion, tinman and strawman who are actually symbolic of *one* unawakened man with no brain, no heart and no courage or no intellect, no passion and no personality like a Snow White's 'dwarves' sleepy and mopey etc. Your 'strawman' is a false corporate persona registered at birth, a bouncing baby business, an employee of the state 'legally' transacting with an unnatural system of merchants and traders who have turned Mother Earth in to a market bazaar. *You* are trade, *product*, and like these fabled characters most people are frightened, ignorant, asleep, robotic puppets and animals. Even naïve Dorothy wears the red shoes of the sexual root chakra as does the Pope, the Masonic red shoe lodge and the famous ballet the Red Shoes and although she doesn't know it she 'always had the power'. She's the most level-headed among them and typical of the Satanists behind this production Judy *Garland* (note the name born in 1922) was abused terribly on set in another mockery of the goddess yet behind the curtain 'god', the wizard, is an obsolete old man. In Pinocchio his rather phallic nose grows in size when he tells a lie meaning he gets a thrill out of deception yet wants to become a 'real' boy otherwise he's nothing but a puppet, *see right*. Dick nose. Like Beauty and the Beast being rich is a 'curse' for although well-off *materially*, he is *spiritually* bankrupt as the 'curse' dogs the family bloodline showing up in tragedy and loss, karma, the  'price' of their position, the 'price' of fame. The curse is twofold in that he is, a) not human, a bestial monster, and b) doomed to destroy those he loves. The fable Pinocchio is *loaded* with sexual themes including 'Pleasure Island' a *cursed* place. Pinocchio's name derives from the wood of the *pine* tree as pinecones symbolise the *pineal gland*, the third eye chakra, called 'the stairway to heaven' activated by sex as once opened you are in Heaven like god. In the Egyptian 'book of death' the heart was key to the afterlife and if it was 'lighter than a feather' the dead could pass to the afterlife thus *lighthearted*.

The Tower of Babel is *another* famous ancient account of the people using tantric sex in their attempt to reach 'heaven' to become 'god'. It's all code and once you know you will see it everywhere and wonder how we didn't' see it sooner. So, wouldn't you know Genesis: *Chapter 11* tells the story of Babylon. Genesis in ancient Greek means 'origin' as *11* is the male-female 'twins', the lovers, in procreation. The builders of Babel said, "Let us build ourselves a *tower* with its *head* in the *heavens*". This is not a literal tower it is the 'tower' of the *chakras* with the 'head' in the 'heavens' meaning *enlightenment* of the crown charka, the brain reaching the heights of *knowledge* like 'god' in 'heaven'. Predating this was *The Goddess* referred to as the Queen of Heaven. Babel descended into a den of debauchery and was destroyed *again* by god yet initially it was a place of 'sacred marriage' which as we know is a reference to tantric sex, *see right*, and the unlocked chakra *tower* just like Rapunzel's 'tower'. Even today the Twins, men and women, descend into idolatry and debauchery as 'god' sees fit to let Satan encourage rampant porn, gender bending, 'open' sexuality,

perversion and lust.

So, what's it all mean? It appears Humanity's *intellect* and *sovereignty* were stolen to hold them prisoner by a 'thief', a 'devil', with a demonic soul from another dimension who originated from another constellation. This *reptilian* alien, Pan, was a species originating from Orion among other places in the galaxy as this species seems to be quite prolific with factions that are at odds with each other, like their playground the political scene, although they are all generally on the same 'team'. Per their alien religion, Satanism i.e. 'devil worship' or self-worship, the positive electrical force of the universe largely found in males was deified as a physical being, Osiris, the poster boy of their tantric sun king cult. Their genetics as a species predisposes them to a 'male centric' might-is-right hypermasculine attitude that the Klingons in Star Trek were based on. Note, the phonetics of Klingon's or 'cling on' as that's what they do, they are a parasite that 'clings' to light beings they can lord it over accessing their higher spiritual abilities for greater dimensional access. By accessing the human chakra tower via tantric *transcendental sex,* this war-like alien species gained enlightenment of the *crown* chakra, activating the IQ, *the megamind*, and suppressed the native species, Humans, of Earth declaring themselves *royalty* in a cruel hierarchical system where they can indulge their lust for blood, violence, depravity and self-idolatry. They rule over many planets becoming 'gods' as accounted in all the 'pantheon of gods' in ancient societies and show up in major institutions of power in every sector. The goal of this dark side hypermasculine force is to become *their* version of 'god', a distorted evil 'father', and eventually amalgamate the 'pantheon' of gods into 'one' Supreme Being who will ultimately be born and manifest as a physical person as The One World Leader or King of Mother Earth. It's effigy is depicted as a tantric alien all-in-one man-woman-beast, a Satanic one-stop-shop that caters to everyone at once, *see right*, it's caduceus sex penis-staff is backed by scaly skin, dark angel's wings, horns of a beast, breasts of a woman and overall a distorted *masculine* figure. The pentagram on its forehead is the is the 'flower of Venus', the goddess, the queen of heaven, the feminine, a geometric pictogram that translates as a frequency and the self-replication of the natural feminine force, Mother Nature, the *organic* universe, that this creature has replaced with technology and ultimately A.I. The Beast points at heaven and at earth and as man was 'made of clay' then 'earth' means flesh and 'flesh' is the root chakra. The root chakra is the first chakra easily accessed via vaginal or anal sex which is why the 'devil' is transgender-bisexual even pedophilic and in its extreme aspects engages in necrophilia and bestiality acquiring sex *wherever it can*. The chakra tower transcends 3D/5 sense reality so this creature can 'break-and-enter' the higher dimensional realms including godlike 'omnipresence' and the psychic spectrum found in the human light body thus ultimately manipulating space and time! This entity is hacking in *through* humans from a lower vibrational demonic state, a death realm, as such, the image of the hybrid alien is depicts that to get to 'heaven' go via flesh, sex, carnality aka Satanism. This is where the whole world is being steered right now. Yet the loving couple Jesus and Mary, men and women, *the Twins,* clearly point at the heart to get to heaven often wearing the colours of the root chakra 'sex' and the throat chakra 'voice'. Buddha also points at heaven and holds the tower-penis with the 'seven levels' in his lap and has a *feminine* reverse swastika on his heart chakra, *note,* the activated third eye.

The Devil, Satan, call it what you will, was *initially* purely demonic evolving into a primarily reptilian form originating from planets that are *not compatible* with M-class planet's environments like Earth. This reptilian species harbouring demonic souls from a chaotic 'death' dimension used technology to 'split' the one androgynous self-procreating high feminine, the goddess, into men and women. They then bred with the women to create a *human looking* reptilians to not only access the higher non-physical functions of the light dimensions housed in humans but also allows them to 'shapeshift' into their prime state at will or even shapeshift into a number of animals which is where the 'werewolf' and 'bat' vampire legends come from also found in the 'Skinwalker' legends of natives lore. Yes, it *walks* in a human *skin*. It's a powerful all-in-one being that houses *their* genetic makeup passing themselves off as human, or whatever, accessing ours and other worlds for power in a far reaching galactic political system. This is why their hierarchical institutions of power are always *laden* with sexual scandals practicing the dark side of this ability and why Jesus said, 'it was easier for a camel to pass through the eye of a needle than for a rich man to enter the kingdom of God'. You can either be a carnal sex god on earth or a spiritual Love god in heaven but you can't be both. So, the story of Babel is yet another example of humanities ancestors striving for innate knowledge trying evolve out of this mess to our original human *eternal* light-beings we once were via tantric sex and *repeatedly* 'smited' by 'god' (the alien interloper) in our every attempt throughout the generations to do so.

Even reading was a crime for commoners resulting in severe punishments plunging us into darkness again and again always blaming *us* as the 'problem' as 'sinners' and 'criminals' every time! So, 'god' who has a habit of attacking people when they try to elevate themselves as *is happening now* or banishing them from their own 'garden' (knowledge) or sending a flood etc., scattered the people of Babel making them speak different languages *babbling* so they couldn't come back together again and build *another* chakra 'tower' and, same old same old, calling them sinners and pagans yadda yadda. Humans have suffered a terrible character assassination at the hands of these creatures as, typically, to keep someone down you first have to shame them. The knowledge of sacred sex was lost to us and kept a closely guarded secret as did the ancient Greeks guard the 'secret of fire' or Prometheus who 'created humans from clay' aka *Earthlings* (*we are from this planet*) who stole 'fire' to give to mankind to make humans 'equal with the gods'. So too did 'god' place 'cherubs', *winged creatures*, with a 'flaming sword' blocking the way to the 'tree of life' preventing Adam and Eve, men and women, from *knowing the truth* of their divine origins and their *birthright* to this planet and ascension to the highest dimensional-frequency realms where *we* originated. The 'flaming sword' is a big macho alien dick, hyper-masculine, the boss man, and just as they use cartoons and positive reinforcement statements today to play into our childlike desire for friendship, they dressed up cruel oppressors as 'cherubs' and cute little angels to do 'gods' dirty work. It's all psychology 'you're sinners and you'll burn in hell! Here's a cherub to make you feel better now get back to work!' The fire is the 'light' or knowledge gained by tantric sex. The 'light' is the Love gained by tantric *lovemaking*. They are *terrified* we will regain this knowledge, take back our power, open our chakras and kick them back out into the darkness of space from whence they came at this *critical* time when such things are actually possible! There are prophecies about all this *happening now*. Therefore, the incomprehensible *bibble babble* from Babylon became the Bible, a *coded* almanac for the secrets of sacred sex enlightenment.

Aether is what we know today as Prana, Chi, Qi Life Energy etc., also called the Fifth Element and is what the Romans ascribed to the planet Venus the 'Goddess of Love' considered the physical embodiment of the Goddess in the Heavens and why the Baphomet has the Venus pentagram on its 3rd eye chakra. It's The Light. *The Force!* In the Latin language spoken by ancient Romans, the word for 'Venus' was 'Lucifer' as 'Lucifer' is *Luminiferous Aether* meaning 'bright' or 'shining' also called the Light Bearer or Torch Bearer that you would be more familiar with today as Lady Liberty the torch bearing *Goddess* of light located on the shores of New York City. She clasps the 'light' in her *right hand* or the 'right hand of god' which is why the dark path is called the 'left hand path'. Love or light was represented specifically as Venus the embodiment of the Heavenly Queen, the Goddess, who ancients worshipped primarily as Sirius the brightest star in the sky. The light was then *and* now considered the *highest vibration* of all so, naturally, they symbolised Love as the brightest lights. The Romans and all other major civilisations considered that the brightness or *shining* nature of Love was the *life force* expressed in the abundance of mother nature's bounty and carried in particular by the *feminine* due to mothers, women, bringing forth babies, new life, into physical reality ensuring another generation and so She, mother nature, women, the light and the life force, became The Goddess. Love-light or Chi, Prana, Qi Life Energy, iChing etc., is a passive watery *electricity* as quoted by Nicola Tesla, "Everything is electricity…One of its particles possesses light, thermal, nuclear, radiation, chemical, mechanical and an *unidentified energy*". Yes, the unidentified energy. Aether is a feminine energy and it's what this is all about. God is not what you've been led to believe. When asked by a journalist, "Are you biased toward electricity?" Tesla responded, "I am the electricity in human form. You are electricity too, Mr. Smith, but you do not realise it". Therefore, Mother Nature, the *Goddess*, the bringer of the light, was the Bringer of *Life* worshipped worldwide by pre-Egyptian and Pre-Christian societies as Magna Mater – The Great Mother - The *Mother* Goddess, the Mother of *all* Gods, the originator, The Prime Creator, The Prime Feminine, the Primordial Waters, the first waters, that which is endless, the vital force or simply *Eternity!* Maternity *is* eternity! Therefore, the statue of Lady Liberty is a depiction of the Great Goddess who has been called many names in various civilisations but in her most recent incarnation she is Mary aptly the Mother *and* the Wife! Electricity has *two* poles, a negative and positive pole or the 'feminine' negative and 'masculine' positive ends or North and South poles. It is a 'push and pull' 'receptive' and 'projective' force holding our planet in place, literally, *see right*. Without one there can be no 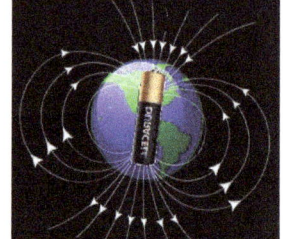 other. Without either, *we* do not exist. They are equal but opposite. The Goddess is expressed in human form simply as women and girls. God is simply the *male* electromagnetic component found in Men and boys who serve unique functions no better or worse than each other. When these two aspects are combined in a *balanced system,* life springs forth in abundance and the endless generations themselves become Mothers and Fathers, God and Goddess, *activated* by electricity freely and abundantly broadcast from the Universe. Our ancestors called this 'soul energy' or 'Great Spirit' referring to the Milky Way as the 'river of souls. We are but a droplet of 'water' in a universal ocean of life-light-love! One and the same. We are it. It is us. At long last it's that simple. The Feminine was considered a portal to the universe and when these two base electrical pairs are working in harmony they were symbolised as Jesus and Mary, the husband and wife, the father and mother. They live forever in the light like stars, shining, they never age, they never die, they are eternal just as the Force is eternal. It is the fountain of youth. The *Eternal* Spring.

There is, however, a third component in the energetic mix and it is a reptilian-alien interloper that makes up the 'dark side' of a hyper-masculine hijacker riding on the back of the feminine electrical force. This 'outsider' is from a death dimension, a dark plane so totally *alien* to the light-life plane that it takes much effort to reduce the light force into a quasi 'intermediate' plane, 'middle earth', a state of being somewhere between life and death where we *currently* live, *see right*. The Grim Reaper *is* the devil, an alien-demonic-reptilian infiltrator harnessing the *eternal* 'soul' aspect of our *light bodies*. The *chakras* is what they're after! Their death dimension should *not* be crossing over into our life plane and we should be living a lot longer and even *not dying at all* as light *is life* that *never dies, eternal,* and we are *light beings*. Death *is darkness* a sort of 'animated' inertia which might sound like a contradiction in terms but when you consider they cannot spiritually  evolve (which is why they need us) then they are in a space of indolent stasis. Stuck. Their plane is some sort of *artificial life*, A.I., and somewhere along the way it merged itself with the lowest forms of organic life to evolve into bestial creatures that attacked the Goddess to harness her light in order to 'live' in the physical plane. They literally eat the light, *life*, they are literally 'death eaters' as light beings die because of them. It is *unnatural*, un-nature or *un-life*. And don't they love death? They love killing in any way they can through poisons, manufactured diseases, military, religion, politics. Everything you touch, eat, smell and breath is carcinogenic. It's no coincidence. They're killing machines. Like the Terminator. Like predator. Everything is death to them have you noticed? Yet you don't die of 'old age'. You die of *complications* of 'old age', *disease*, that 'kills' the physically body but the soul body, the light, continues to exist *somewhere* else in *another* level of the program and why they claim to be 'god' not only of the physical world but the 'death' plane too. *This* is what they are doing!

So, it seems they have found a monopoly on what becomes of our light, our souls, *our life force*, even when we detach from the physical plane and 'die'. This is a *massive* 'life-death' matrix, a duplicate of real life that the ancients called a 'bad copy'. It's a totally convincing facsimile, a simulation, a 'virtual reality' that is becoming more apparent by the day as our world descends into an unstoppable madness. They are alien 'gate keepers' of this life *and* the afterlife *as well*. The ancient believed the 'gods', aliens, guarded the various 'levels' of the underworld aka death and it's *still* happening they were just more open about it in the old days. While these 'gods' are in the process of 'upgrading' their systems we have a chance to slip out. Evil is 'live' backwards as death is from an evil inverse *pointless* plain of existence. A non-plane. 'Inverse' is a universe *inverted*, turned inside out. It's demonic and *nothing to do* with the light, Love, and Life *freely given* by Mother Nature yet *they* put a price on everything. The battle of light and dark is the battle of *life and death* and Human light, *life as we know it,* is being phased out! The eternal flow of universal Aether, the life force, was symbolised by the wedding ring, a circle, a *circuit*, an 'eternal' ring with no beginning and no end. The universe is a continuum meaning 'no beginning and no end' while matrimony is a feminine institution. It's not called patrimony, is it? There's a reason for that. You can't reach the edges of the universe as you just wind up right back where you started. Like time. The wedding ring was usually gold to represent the 'golden flow' of the eternal electrical force and was worn on the ring finger that is the only digit with a vein running directly to the heart and why Mary and Jesus are pointing at their hearts. They were lovingly married. The true meaning of love and light, the flow of universal electricity that gives you vitality, was specifically reserved for the sanctity, *the sanctuary,* the garden, of marriage between the 'twins', men and women, who mutually en*light*en each other via lovemaking creating babies for evolutionary purposes. We've been hijacked. The dark force energy expresses itself more or less depending on how deeply ones DNA is embedded with reptilian-*alien* genetics which we all possess particularly via the Reptilian Complex, the animal brain. They installed a bug in our system to monitor us and get us to monitor each other via the *R-complex*. The 'third party' reptilian component is found mainly in the realm of historic and current *aristocracy* expressing their hyper-masculine death dimension via our life plane with their bloodthirsty forces. They surround us on all sides with their 'one god' aka Satanism - a sex and death cult!! The Goddess is a Love and Life philosophy. The *dogmatic* mind control of what 'god' and 'goddess' really means is simply natural *electrical* processes found inside our bodies that lead to enlightenment or *Christ Consciousness*. They put it right in our faces *everywhere* yet we are unable to see it for what it *truly* is under a mountain of double talk and lies! But what *is* Christ? Here we go, kids! Hold on!

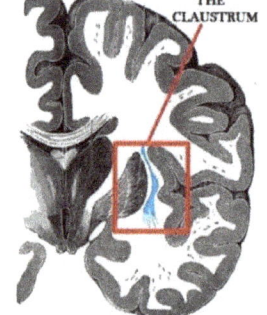

Deep inside the brain is a sort of mesh called the Claustrum, *right,* which 'catches' life force energy. This 'soul energy' is a fine feminine fire that connects the chakras like a silver string running through a necklace of pearls. This energy is so delicate that thoughts (static electricity) obliterates it so a still mind is a must to harness its true power and why monks always seek to 'quiet the mind'. 'Christ' is an *electrochemical* process commencing in the Claustrum as it captures life-force energy, Aether, also called 'Great Spirit' or commonly known today as Qi, Chi, Prana, Ki life energy etc., a pure *fine* electricity. It is light *not* fire. Fire, as in 'hell-fires', is ascribed to the dark side of the masculine expressed as hyper control, violence and domination or a heavy alien *variant* of the natural 'spark' of life. It's like 'light' on steroids but not in a good way. It's got a great upper body but no legs. Nothing to stand on. No real foundation.

Get it? Yes, it works but its superficial, not long term. What the ancients called 'fire' is the hormone *testosterone* found in the male reproductive system at the root chakra. The feminine 'spark', estrogen, is primarily found in the passive 'waters' of the female reproductive organs also at the root chakra. Both men and women carry the masculine and feminine energies, testosterone and estrogen. We are electrical beings. However, broadcast from the black hole sun at the centre of the galaxy is a type of superforce, if you will, it is more than just the electricity that animates us. This force was considered by ancient accounts to be a feminine spirit or *female electricity* thus intimating that the core of the galaxy was considered feminine. Chi, Qi, Prana was described as *'Élan vital'* by French philosopher Henri Bergson in his 1907 book *Creative Evolution* (well, it is!) and translates as the 'vital impetus' coined the 'vital force' by his detractors but more accurately is the 'vital drive' or 'the will' which he linked to evolution and development of organisms that some have termed the 'will of god'. It could also be called 'ambition', 'determination', 'vision', 'drive' or indeed 'passion' hence, the 'passion of the christ'. This 'will' is a type of destiny of the universe, it has a certain flow as do rivers, however, this 'drive', a 'necessary action', is what Aleister Crowley and associated morons stupidly translated as the 'will' of the *individual* over the 'will' of the force and moronically declared in their infinite ignorance, 'do what thou wilt shall be the whole of the law. Love under will'. The light is Love *guided* by the Will of those who wield it. It has a Will of its own and if respected, the Universe would be a marvel of unimaginable greatness! Suffice to say, they have not respected it. They have hijacked this force and imposed *their* will to justify *their* depravity and become 'god' whatever *that* is to them. They have *massively* failed not only themselves but everyone else.

Bergson postulated this Lifeforce was closely linked to *Consciousness*, the *intuitive* perception of experience, and the *flow of inner time!* Considering this power is being harvested by 'gods' that gave *us* a 'sense' of 'time', this looks like a key aspect of 'the hack' from an outside force tinkering with our sense of spatial awareness and our perception of 'age' when we 'die' of 'old age'! The god of death wants to be the god of life *but it can't*. German philosopher Arthur Schopenhauer described it as the 'will to live' identified in Sanskrit as 'ayus' or 'life principle' while Greek polymath Posidonius said this force *emanates from the sun!* Yes, the light! Universal Electricity. *This* is the foundation of ancient 'sun worship' *worldwide*. The vital force, 'material energy', Chi or simply 'energy' literally translates as 'vapor', 'air', or 'breath' the underlying *central principle* in Chinese traditional medicine and Chinese martial arts, *see*, Tai Chi, while cultivating Qi is called Qigong. It directly affects the difference between the will to live and the wish to die or 'death wish' as a 'unique risk factor' for suicide. The 'vrttis' or tendency of the root chakra is survival, ambition and the *will to live*. Isis, a sun goddess, was depicted with wings symbolic of the 'wind', *air*, and said to have transferred the soul of Osiris to Horus via the *breath* or the 'breath of life' in Chi-electricity. Mary apparently did this along with her priestesses who witnessed the 'resurrection' of 'christ'. No man was present when this happened. Mary and her ladies were the last of the Isis, Delphi and Vestal priestesses practicing the Qigong art of transferring the soul via the Aether or breath, air, *see right*, now  practiced by royal 'vampires' the immortals! 'Immortals' historically described elite 'heavy cavalry', the 'guard', *the military*, the 'god of war', a trait of distorted reptilian masculinity aka *the Masons!* Satan is 'the prince of the power of the air'.

Once captured by the Claustrum, the *universal* energy is transmuted (distilled) by the Pituitary and Pineal glands and resembles a fine oil white and yellow in colour. It is literally Chi-Prana in oil form like gasoline for the soul or could be a type of pure alcohol and why alcohol is called 'spirits' or the 'demon drink' and booze i.e. 'boo' and Gin as in jinn, an Islamic demon! They are taking over the meaning of the life force with dark symbolism to confuse us however, it does describe the base chemical compositions of this substance; aetheric, distilled, a sugar perhaps? Are not all hormones made up of base elements including proteins, sugars, waters and other elements? It's *physics* and while I'm no doctor, suddenly chemistry got interesting! The ancients referred to the oil as the Sacred Secretion, the Sacred Seed, Chrism, Christos Oil, Christ Seed Oil or quite simply *Christ!* This is why 'Christ' was anointed with 'oil' on the forehead, the third eye chakra *all-seeing* eye. The Christ seed oil is released into the Cerebrospinal Fluid (CSF) and flows down the spinal cord where it reaches the base of the spine passing via the Sacral Plexus, the five fused vertebrae at the lowest part of the spine, where it is activated via a mild electrical charge or the existing 'spark' at the root chakra kickstarted via sacred tantric sex, heat, lust, passion or, would you believe, *thermodynamics* (more on that later). The Christ seed then flows back up the 33 vertebrae unlocking or *electrically activating* all the chakra energy points along the way. The Christ seed 'germinates' at the Solar Plexus then continues its journey up the spine toward the base of the brain to the Hypothalamus where it pauses for three days. It then releases *back* into the brain igniting the 12 cranial nerves then continues on into the brain crossing the optic nerve where it *massively increases* in voltage as the golden circuit completes the course releasing fresh blood to generate new brain cells and the lights 'turn on'. I was blind but now I see.

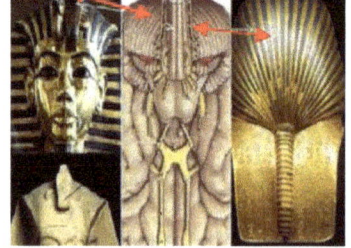

Translation: in ancient Egypt they referred to the skull as the 'vault of heaven', it's all hidden in art, *see right*, the brain stem hidden in a pharaohs death mask. The Pineal Gland was referred to as 'Osiris' and as Osiris was 'reborn'

into his son, Horus, the Pineal Gland became the 'Eye of Horus' while the Pituitary Gland was referred to as 'Isis'. Later these two glands would be called Mary and Joseph or Mary and Jesus (same people). Further back they were called Adam and Eve or more simply, the positive and negative masculine-feminine electrical poles. So, via 'Joseph' and 'Mary' aka the Pituitary and Pineal glands the Aether, the Chi or *light* aka 'Christ', was 'born' or 'seeded' described *metaphorically* as a 'bright shining light' that 'appeared' at the 'birth' of 'christ', 'the light of the world', ascribed to the 'star of Bethlehem' *shining brightly* in the sky representing 'the light' of the universe or quite simply, electricity! It's entirely possible that the star of Bethlehem is Sirius the 'blue angel' the brightest star in the sky or perhaps Venus *another* very bright star. As such, 'a star is born'. Jesus Christ super star. It's all in movies steering us away from the true meaning just like the Bible. Bethlehem translates as 'house of bread' as bread is made from *grain* as it is the 'grain' or Christ *seed* that is released into the Cerebrospinal Fluid, *right*, to commence its descent of the

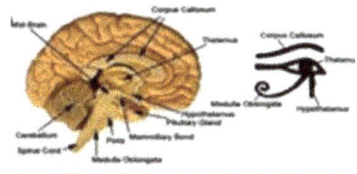

EYE OF HORUS, PINEAL GLAND, 3rd Eye

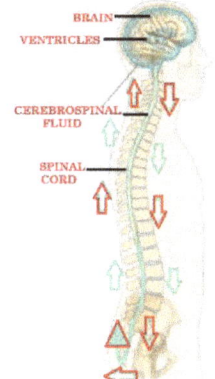

spinal cord and why all ancient gods and goddesses are referred to as 'grain gods. So, the grain-seed was called the 'bread' and why we 'break bread' associated with Christ and his 'disciples' in this story often depicted as a devils tales in Catholic art.

Grain deities are found all over the world from Japan (symbolised as 'rice') to the Aztecs as corn because the 'grain' is symbolic of the 'seed' not only in a man's semen but a process of the brain's chemistry as well as in crops etc. *Life*. It's replication. So when they say Lucifer, *the light bearer*, was 'cast out of heaven' they mean 'Venus-lucifer', the light aka the Aether, was transmuted into the Christ seed oil and *released* into the Cerebrospinal Fluid descending the spinal cord circulating down through nervous system activating the light body. Lucifer is Latin for 'bright' and 'shining' and does not mean 'Satan' this *embellishment* occurred later as they twisted this *natural* bodily process into a *massive* symbolic religious *conspiracy* for control purposes. Psychological warfare! Words are weapons! It's a confusing scheme *unrecognisable* from its true meaning to trick us from understanding our innate capacity to free ourselves. It's straight up lies and the Vatican (Catholic Church) and their Masonic handlers are behind it. They are fucking with your head playing mind games. They saw their opportunity to take over the world with this power and under their demonic control have kept the enlightenment of Christ, the true Christ within, for themselves and starved everyone else of 'the bread'. That's why they're so fucking smart. That's why we are stumped by their audacity! *All major religions worldwide* are in on a plot to keep this information to themselves and kill what is left of natural Human beings. Prison is too good for them. They've perpetrated crimes against a species of Divinity to lord it over the true God and Goddess for *thousands* of generations. Not one person born within the last 6,000 years *or more* has been left unaffected, bereft and broken by this alien empire of filth and lies! For once they *will* atone for daring to pose in the place of 'god' twisting the force into some external cruel 'father' figure leaving us conflicted blaming ourselves for our sins when *we* are the light! *We* are the Children of the Universe and their alien cult dressed up as 'religion' has had its day on this planet let's just say that!

The Christ flows via the Cerebrospinal Fluid (CSF) through the nervous system which is an organic network of kinetic fibre optics circulating an electro-plasmic *fluid* of spiritual-cosmic energy, *Aether*, Life Force, emanating from the cosmos *animating* us giving us 'oomph!', power, fuel or vitality. *The vital essence!* The Christ flows down reaching the Sacral Plexus, the five fused vertebrae at the base of the spine referred to by ancient people as The Stone. This 'stone' is the lower back bone between the lumbar spinal region and the coccyx that houses a nerve cluster controlling motor and sensory functions in the posterior thigh, lower leg, feet, and the pelvis, *right*. This information is found in the story of Jacobs Ladder, *right*, as the 'ladder' represents the spine and Jacob rested his 'head' (where the Christ seed *literally* emanates from the Claustrum) upon the 'stone' aka *the Sacral Plexus* as the Cerebrospinal Fluid circulates the spinal column. Upon reaching the 'Stone' the 'christ' is 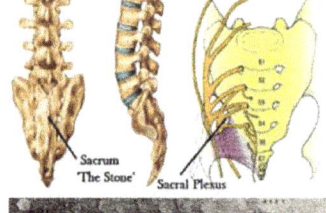  activated by a mild electrical charge from the spark or 'fire' of the loins *pushing* the spinal fluid back up the spine as 'christ' 'ascends' to 33 the number of vertebra in the 'ladder' of the spine. Our bodies are literally like car engines in that the penis is a spark plug igniting the fuel, Aether, housed in the feminine waters. That's why she is *the* Goddess. The ancients referred to the Solar Plexus as the 'manger' where the Christ seed 'germinates' and thus 'Christ' was 'born' in a 'manger'. The Solar Plexus is a psycho-spiritual womb that both men and women possess although only women possess the physical womb hence, womb-man or woman and why she was the 'bringer of the light', the 'light bearer', Venus, 'Lucifer' (Latin), Aphrodite (Greek), the *Goddess* of Love (light) born into *new life* in babies, the Next Generation, thank you Star Trek. Satanists always slander women specifically, the mother.

As christ reaches '33' at the base of the skull after climbing the ladder i.e. the number of vertebrae, it lays dormant or 'dies' for three days in the 'tomb' known today as the Hypothalamus. It is then released *back* into the brain where it activates the 12 cranial nerves or the '12 disciples' and is 'raised to heaven' as 'christ' is 'crucified' on the 'cross' or what we know as the Optic Nerve, *right*, unlocking the 'Eye of Horus' the all-seeing-eye, the 'eye of god' or 3rd Eye Charka, the Pineal Gland aka the 'stairway to heaven' at 'Golgotha' as Golgotha *literally* translates as 'place of the skull' as the 'tower' is 'crowned' coded into Egyptian sarcophagi. The eyeballs resemble olives hence, the 'olive branch' of peace and the 'tree' of the enlightened nervous system as we finally '*see*'. The 'olive tree' was symbolically given to Athens by the Goddess Athena because all the ancients 'gods' and 'goddesses' were practicing this and shows how powerful it is. The 'crucifixion' on the 'cross' activates or

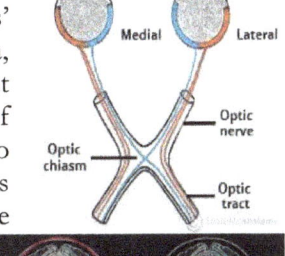

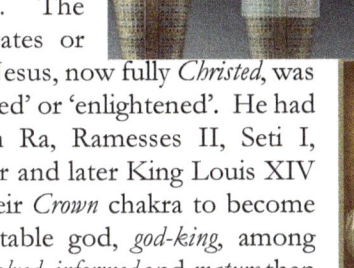

unlocks the crown chakra and why Jesus, now fully *Christed*, was called 'the King' as he was 'Crowned' or 'enlightened'. He had thus joined the ranks of Amun Ra, Ramesses II, Seti I, Alexander the Great, Julius Caesar and later King Louis XIV among *many* who all unlocked their *Crown* chakra to become crowned king, sun kings, a veritable god, *god-king*, among *ordinary* men. We're a little more *evolved*, *informed* and *mature* than that now and with the advent of science it gives us *rationale* as an anchor that cuts out all the weird superstition, dogma and unnecessary ignorance of our forebears as we *refine* this process and respect the marvelous function of our human bodies without having to *be* 'god' about it. All of this 'god on Earth' shit is rooted in rampant self-serving egomania, all reptilian traits, and since we have a planet to save we might want to put a stop to *that* childish selfishness right about *now*. We're out of time, folks. The increased electrical activity allows *whole brain* duel-hemispheric access as the IQ shoots up, psychic abilities increase, motor functions enhance, coordination, vitality, energy, intuition, perception, confidence, spatial awareness – *the seven dwarves become giants* – intensifying to the point where some have referred to it as 'godhood' or indeed the god*head*. *Luke 17:21 "Behold! The Kingdom of God is within you!"* This quote is taken from the Egyptian proverb "The Kingdom of Heaven is within you, and whoever shall *know himself* shall find it" or in Latin *Temet Nosce* "Know thyself!" and ancient Greek *Gnothi Seauton* "Know thy measure".

Every month when the moon is in your sun sign one is to abstain from sex and for men mastering tantric sex this means not 'spilling the seed' or semen retention. Not ejaculating. Women can also practice not releasing the egg and therefore control painful periods as well as exercising *natural* birth control. It's quite genius. Retaining the sperm and the egg *internally* allows more Prana, Chi, Qi life force energy, *the spark,* to be reabsorbed back into the body increasing vitality and enhancing the power of the Christ Seed Oil as it travels back up the spine so this practice has an *accumulative* effect. Sportsmen, particularly boxers, are told not the have sex before a big fight as testosterone, semen, is the 'fire' they need to win and why 'fire' underpins so much violence if it's not tempered with the 'waters' of the feminine. This is why priests, monks and nuns declare celibacy to retain the 'spark' if nothing else while priests and nuns abstaining from sex are the Catholic Churches laugh-a-minute joke as they represent the husband and wife who without sex with always remain the puppets of these Satanic pieces of filth. You're welcome.

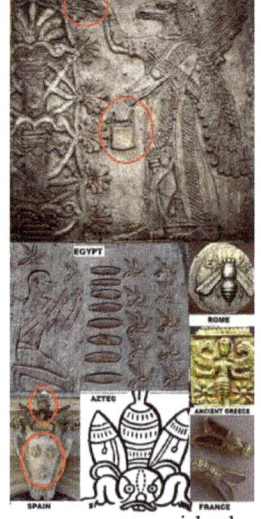

In ancient accounts *all around the world* pails of milk and honey-bees are the rubber stamp of this practice from ancient Egypt to Rome to the Aztecs, *see right.* The top image from Mesopotamia shows the tree 'fountain' of the nervous system, the pinecone of the pineal gland in his *right* hand and the pail of milk of the Claustrum Christ seed oils bringing the milk-honey or Christ to the spine to unlock the 3rd eye *Pineal* gland at the top. It gives you wings no less. This is because the colour of the christ oils released by the Pituitary and Pineal Glands are white 'milk' and yellow 'honey', the 'golden flow'. Once the electrical circuit of the spinal cord is complete and enlightenment (IQ) shoots up one is said to have 'reached the land of milk and honey' and why we go on our 'honeymoon' hence, *sacred marriage* aka sacred-tantric sex on the *wedding night* that facilitates these processes with the Husband and the Bride of Christ. Love *making* is to be pure and why it's bad luck for the hubby to see the bride in her wedding dress before the ceremony. *Baphomet* means 'infernal union', a fire union, fire of the loins, lust, sex. Matthew 22:30 "For in the *resurrection* they *neither marry, nor are given in marriage*, but are *as the angels* of God in heaven" this is a reference to the highly intelligent Satanic imposters who *appear* as your saviours heightening their IQ outside of marriage aka Satanism. Clever devils. 2 Corinthians: "For such are false apostles, deceitful workers, transforming themselves into apostles of *Christ.* And no marvel, for *Satan himself* is *transformed* into an *angel of light*". Yes, enlightened, powerful and dangerous. Once you know this information you can read the Bible and it actually makes sense. Marriage, Jesus and Mary of Christ enlightenment, was *supposed* to be a higher pursuit of dignity and honour befitting sentient beings of

Universal Light, 'God', found in human men and women. We are not sinners. Yet the 'resurrected angels not given to marriage', the *hierarchy* of these fraudulent demonic religious doctrines, the Popes, the Bishops, are *sinners extraordinaire!* The Devil is the *Great Pretender* behind all your favourite mega churches, temples, mosques and chapels *worldwide!* Where are they getting their power from when the Goddess is not present in their lives? They are a pair, after all, electrical polar opposites who belong side by side, equals. Only your favourite Martian's are worshipping *one god* and can on be the devil in disguise *masquerading* the Heavenly Father, literally dad and his wife, The Goddess, mum, and Christ, *the light*, works *through* them. Yes, it's big. *Love is the petrol of the cosmos.*

President Roosevelt said in an address before the 1936 Democratic National Convention, "There is a mysterious cycle in human events. To some generations much is given. To other generations much is expected. This generation of America has a *rendezvous with destiny"*. In Carl Jung's The Red Book (red root chakra *sex* enlightenment aka Satan) called Liber Novus or the 'New Book' that he probably hoped would be selected as one of the 'scriptures' for the new religion's looming 'Bible', "Greetings Prophet! The great work begins! The Messenger has arrived!" Christ help us. These guys never evolve. *See right*, a page from Jung's book looking a little *biblical* to say the least. Can we please move on? Please? That  would be awesome, thank you. So, the Stone of Destiny or the Stone of Scone (I'll have a cup of tea with that) is a rock that has made the rounds of many ancient and modern houses of importance. It is the stone Jacob was said to have rested his head on…but we've already discussed this. It was taken to Scotland en route from Egypt, Spain and Ireland and used in 'coronation' ceremonies where it was situated under the chair the monarch sits on when they are declared King or Queen as was QE2 crowned on this stone. This stone was said to have come from 'heaven' or more specifically, *Sirius*, the Dog Star, as if they would know where it came from? But then it's all symbolic. The goddess was associated with a meteor and Aether was said to be 'meteoric' in nature. What they are symbolising with this scrappy old rock is actually a decoy, a ploy, as the 'Stone' is the Sacral Plexus associated with 'heaven' aka the Crown chakra hence, being 'crowned' on the 'stone'. Sirius is so important to them the architecture of Washing D.C. was designed so that the Washington Monument, the obelisk and the *infinity* 'reflecting pool' is aligned in the East with *Sirius* and the *sun* on *Independence Day*, the 4th July! There'll be *independence*, just not what they thought.

The knowledge of the 'stone' was said to be bought to America via the 'Scottish' aka the Scottish Rite of Freemasonry. The Stone was called 'the treasure of the world' and the main man of Scottish Rite worship, Hermes god of *Wednesday*, was said to possess a 'magical stone' as did Hercules a 'heavenly stone' meaning *IQ* and *strength* etc. Obvious Mason and operatic composer Richard Wagner said the 'holy grail' and the 'cup of Christ' are one and the same while Hitler was 'obsessed' with the Holy Grail said to date back to Atlantis. The 'cup' or 'chalice' is the chakras also called 'flutes' and in the east 'bowls' embodied by 'singing bowls' in meditation as the chakra's make 'tones' and can be tuned with certain actions like yoga, sacred sex and meditation etc. The Claustrum and Christ seed were referred to in ancient times as *The Messenger* or the 'word', *information*, from the universe aka 'god' hence, 'the word of god' elevating us to greater heights coming from the 'cups' like the 'speakers' of a sound system. *We're radio's*. All major prophets, messiahs and sun kings called themselves the speaker, even today all parliament's *worldwide* have a 'speaker' of the house. More grandly they called themselves *The Messenger* as the *knowledge*, called Gnosis, was the knowledge of tantric sex chakra activation. We are all the 'messenger' now thanks to this *knowledge* finally revealed to the world *for the first time*. Therefore, it is no coincidence *at all* that we find ourselves in the 'year of our lord', *2020*, symbolic of the 11:11 of the male-female electrical chakra love towers, the Twins, and our looming *20/20* vision as we finally 'see straight' that suddenly! Lo! We have a global Corona Virus on our hands or should I say heads? Corona is Latin for 'crown' therefore, 'corona virus' symbolically means a disease of the crown chakra and just who, pray tell, is the knight in shining armour to rescue us from this sudden dastardly disease of our crown at this crucial time? None other than Moderna *Messenger* Therapeutics, *right*, a modern-day *messenger* no less to vaccinate i.e. *sterilise* our claustrum to prevent our much prophesised and looming ascension or the enlightenment of the biblical 'raising up'. Messenger RNA is cited as the reason for this title but is it really alluding to the true Messenger within us all? It's all rolled out under *Operation Warp Speed* and as we shall see the pandemic

and vaccines is all connected to *entertainment engineering* and the emerging corporate *space program* heralded by the ritual sacrifice of *JFK!* They're utilising *biblical prophetic phrases* 'doublespeak' under the guise of *scientific jargon* dressing up poisons as ancient prophecies to 'fit the script' in a weird roundabouts way that benefits *them* as there are many ways to 'read' a prophecy. It's all about *interpretation* or in their case, straight up lies. On the 20th anniversary of 911 *Lovebirds of the Twin Towers* premiered at the Tribeca Film Festival an 'immersive experience' detailing the love of two married elevator operators. *It's all ritual contrived as entertainment*.

Probably the most terrifying aspect of Coronageddon is, *once again*, the striking similarity to 'fiction' in 'entertainment' I've dubbed *'entertainment engineering'*. It relies on fictionalising *actual events* pre-planned for the future so when it *really* happens you don't believe it as you 'saw it in a movie one time'. So, a really weird symptom of COVID is an oil-like 'black fungus', *right*, explained away as an allergic reaction to *mould* and *fungal spores* found *in the ground inhaled through the nose and throat*. This side effect of both vaccines *and* COVID leads to blood coagulation/clots that can form a *'gel-like' substance*. Weirdly, the creepily accurate X-Files ran an ongoing plotline that aliens were colluding with a secret group of U.S. Government officials and were in the process of colonising Earth. The colonisation was actually *repopulation* via a 'flu like' alien virus that lives *underground* infecting people via their *nose and throat* causing 'black oil' to seep from the eyes. The X-Files alien DNA virus caused human blood to coagulate into a *'jelly-like substance', above right*, and was 'intelligent', *right*, invading human bodies creating hosts to morph us into an alien hybrid race. In an interview with Stew Peters, Dr. Carrie Madej, *right*, examined living organisms in COVID vaccines that she described as a 'self-aware' nano creature that 'propped itself up' as if it 'knew it was being watched'. Separately, Dr Frank Zalewski, *right*, described his examination of the vaccines vials to contain 'the thing' - *aluminum based lifeforms*. In keeping with the entertainment engineering *precedence*, in the lead up to the *real* black fungus weird X-Files mould/alien/COVID black oil mind fuck, Britney Murphy *and* her husband infamously succumbed to *mould infections* that killed them *both* despite her mother living in the same house and not being affected. As this madness is playing out U.S. intelligence suddenly admit 'UFO's are real' and 'aliens can't be ruled out' with one X-Files episode featuring this scenario titled *'This Is Not Happening'*. As *also* 'predicted' in my first book, *2020 & Beyond*, the *satanic brotherhood* have maneuvered *women* into leadership roles at this

time in unprecedented numbers to demonstrate that the *one time* women were in power, everything went to shit, to *forever tarnish* the reputation of the *rising feminine*, the returning 'goddess', who emerged as *worse* than *all the generations* of *psychotic male leaders* 'gods' in *male centric societies* that went before them!

The Claustrum is where we get the word Santa *Claus* or *Saint* Claus the *saviour* at the 'temples' of the brain. The *templars*. This is why Santa is an anagram of Satan as the Claustrum 'Claus' brings 'presents' or should I say *presence* down the chimney, the spine, on Christ's day, *Christ-mass*, and why powerful people are described as having a 'presence' about them. The 'star' or 'angel on the top of the Xmas tree is actually Sirius, Isis, the blue angel and why sometimes an angel sits on top of tree. The pine tree, an evergreen, symbolises eternal youth or the 'eternal spring' or 'eternal youth' also representing the phallus of Osiris as the word 'penis', 'pines' and 'spine' are all an anagram of the same thing representing the activated nervous system as the practice of tantric sex gives you a sense of vitality aka 'eternal spring/youth' and unlocks the pineal gland, *see right*, the pine cone penis cod piece. Hate to burst you bubble but the old Xmas tree is not only sex position between the god and goddess, Sirius and Orion/Isis and Osiris, but also a giant nob. The  baubles represent the 'apples', the 'fruit', of the Tree of Knowledge and it's bloom, the torus field. This is why Xmas has really been taking a bashing this last few years and why all things *gender neutral* is taking precedence over the two major genders, male and female, so as not to 'misgender' or offend a tiny demographic while terms like 'expectant mother' is removed from medical vernacular replaced with 'expectant person' while 'mummy' and 'daddy' is removed from everyday usage teaching little kids that their biological sex is non-existent and 'gender fluid'.

The Goddess is now a man.

So, Satanist's are taking over everything beautiful that the human race has relied on to survive their insanity for eons and turned it into something dark and ugly. Via reverse psychology they invert Love found inside *everyone* to subliminally scare us away from the very thing that would save us while putting it right in our faces laughing at us the whole time! These Satanic male dominated alien priesthoods covet the knowledge of female tantric sex enlightenment gained from The Goddess via the Temple Priestesses who were once worshiped above all and included the Vestal Virgins and further back the Oracles of Delphi among others. Delphi means dolphin, the Dolphin Oracles, again, mother nature, the feminine. These priestesses 'worshiped' Apollo as 'Apollo' like Ra, Zeus and Osiris etc., is a reptilian alien 'god' a pseudonym for the 'devil' who snuck in to commence steering Humans *away* from their true potential via their inherent *internal* power. Ra and Re literally means light as *sun rays*. So much has been lost in translation.

Reptilians are a hybrid species of aquatic amphibians, a 'clade', from Ancient Greek meaning 'branch' also known as a monophyletic group or natural group of organisms that is composed of a *common ancestor* and all its lineal descendants on a phylogenetic tree (similarities and differences to other species) comprised of lizards, turtles, snakes and crocodiles. Aristocratic reptilians also refer to themselves euphemistically as frogs, toads, chameleons and dragons in fairy tales. The original Humans may have been a dolphin-like species spliced with reptilian genetics among others to create modern humans. The reptilian species is linked to the lower 4th vibrational 'demonic' and alien realms operating just outside our 5 sense 3D experience like a cage they have trapped us in. They go around the universe splicing mammalian genetics with reptilian genetics creating hybrids to access the unique chakra system, the light spectrum, of sentient beings gaining access to higher dimensions *through us*. Jeremiah 31:27 "The days are coming" declares the lord "when I will sow the house of Israel and he house of Judah with the seed of man and the seed of beast". It's already done and they are doing it again with upgraded 'new' mutants depicted in the X-men movies only *not* as glamorous. Mammals give birth to live offspring although we produce eggs internally yet harbour the 'reptilian brain' and many aspects of reptilian alchemy. Our nervous system houses the 'kundalini' 'twin snakes' of enlightenment accessing the 'bird' or 'third eye' chakra, the birds-eye-view *all-seeing-eye*. In utero the human embryo appears to evolve through different animal phases including Dolphins which are *very similar* to humans in many ways not only physically but socially. As a species they are one of the smartest in the world and why they are herded into Japanese harbour's and murdered.

There are global rituals being carried out in plain view all the time as *dark forces* commit horrendous *symbolic* crimes to 'kill the light' as seen in the endless weird deaths of Hollywood 'stars' as they literally kill the light broadcast from stars in their universal takeover. They attack innocence in particular ritually destroying love and in one case there was the senseless slaying of two innocent teenage girls, the *Delphi* Murders. It's all ritual. This crime was described as 'odd' by investigators as we soon find the depraved *symbolism* all around. One of the girls was named 'Liberty' as *Lady* Liberty the *Light Bearer* of Love. She is the Goddess Libertas from ancient Rome found in the Statue of *Liberty* where the *Twin Towers* were *ritualistically* destroyed symbolic of the male-female 'twin snakes', *kundalini* (electricity), winding up the chakra towers activating The

Lovers to enlightenment! Another example is the odd murder of a young comedienne Eurydice Dixon found in *Princes* Park in Melbourne as they put their 'royal' rubber stamp on it. Again, this case was described as strange by investigators. In Greek Mythology Eurydice was the wife of Orpheus who died by a 'viper' on their *wedding* day. Vipers, snakes, kundalini, electricity. It's all about Sacred sex and killing the average person's connection to the light via this process. The viper is code for the reptilian thing like the snake of Eden and represents the dark side of male reptilian tantric sex or the 'fires' of hell, *the fires of his loins*, excessive testosterone levels leading to violence that underpins Satanism! This Sex and Death cult covertly carry out assassinations against 'targets' that symbolically represent Love and Light. They are terrified of Love, of *light!* Light means exposure. Orpheus was a great musician who went to Hades to save Eurydice and was commanded to play music to the gods of the underworld (demonic plain) to win her back. He played the most beautiful music and was allowed to return to the upperworld (light plain, Earth) with her on the proviso that he would leave first and she would follow. He was not to look back to see if she was behind him or he would lose her all over again. Just as they reached the upperworld, terrified she wasn't behind him, he couldn't resist and turned back only to see her fall down into darkness again. This is symbolic of the *un*-enlightened feminine fallen to darkness ignorant of her true power and her rightful place in the *real* world. It's the fairytale 'damsel in distress', the knight in *shining* armour, prince charming who needs a man to save her *but he can't*. We must save ourselves. It's Romeo and Juliet. It's Jesus and Mary. It's Swan Lake. It's Beauty and the Beast retold as Dracula and Mina, his lost wife, born again only to die *again*. Love dies. The lovers show up throughout time yet keep losing each other to sin, tragedy, greed, betrayal, murder, rape, destruction, ignorance and all the themes of lost love in every myth, fable and fairy tale *worldwide*. Yet there was a promise and a legacy that *one day* they would live *Happily Ever After* and the 'twins', men and women, would reunite once and for all the battle of the sexes *finally* extinguished! *The war really is over.*

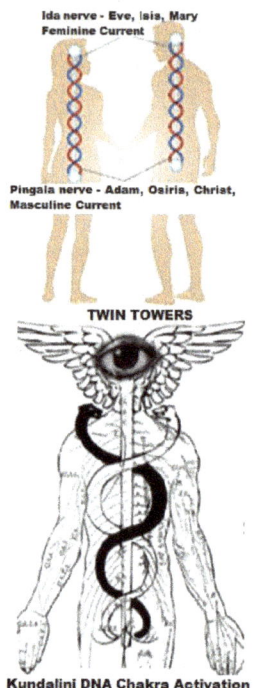

The satanic brotherhood stole the knowledge, removed the feminine, 'plucked out the left eye of Horus' i.e. the moon and ostracised the sacred *wife* Mary Magdalene calling her a 'prostitute' and slung her down into the gutter like a dog. If 'god', the so-called enlightened one, needed to have the feminine at his 'heel', literally like a dog, then 'god' is a *royal* cunt. Or is he just a reptilian

Mason? They seem to think so. *She* is the Light, the brightest star in the sky, The Dog Star, the *God Star,* the Goddess, the light-life bearer, Love bringer, Aether, Luminiferous Aether 'Lucifer', Mary, Isis and basically every other 'goddess' throughout history. She is the mother and the wife. Women. Womb-man. They twisted the feminine power into a gross distortion for their selfish gain then reduced her like their 'nuns' aka 'none', *nothing,* beneath their heels, in abject hatred of *all* women. Their *hell fires,* rejection, of the mother and wife consumes this beautiful *feminine* planet *Mother* Earth and now she's just 'the old ball and chain'. Shame on them but then they don't have any shame, they don't know how. The entire legal system is specifically designed to prevent women from accessing justice for crimes against them perpetrated by men including statutes of limitations and gag orders. Right up until the last few years laws have existed *in America* allowing a man having sex with a woman to continue to have sex *forcefully* despite the female's protests disgustingly referred to as 'the right to finish'. Men who murder their wives on average receive a few years in prison released on good behaviour or plea bargains while on average a woman who kills her husband in self-defense receives on average *15 years* in prison not to mention the human rights abuses of women in the Middle East as 'acid attack' crimes increase.

The 'brotherhood' *deliberately* twisted the term 'Lucifer' of the feminine light, the torch bearer, into something vile when really she lights the darkness of ignorant *men* who have blissfully walked into a huge male-chauvinistic egotistical *trap* completely unaware, even still, they worship a false *global* demonic god *the thief* Pan, Orion, Osiris the *false* Sun King, *the dark side of the masculine,* The Dark Lord, The Devil, Satan, Beelzebub, Baal, etc. Just look around. What do you think is happening here? *Who* is running this place? *All* your monotheistic male deities, no matter how pious they *may* seem, who are dressed up as a single *male* 'Almighty' 'supreme' character are without doubt variations of the 'one who is many', *Satan.* God and Goddess are a pair, specifically, electrical pairs. This is not religious bias this is *actual* science. Any god that stands alone is the Devil. There can be only one, a selfish one, that *mimics* the universal 'one', the collective One. He is The Great Pretender. The Clown Prince. The Crown Prince. The (holy) *Father of Lies.* Tell me I'm wrong; the church – men, military & wars – men, politics even still – men, money barons men, oil barons, war mongers, 'luminaries' of education, medical Nazis, media tycoons – all men as ordinary men hate and revere them at the same time. Poor men and rich men are book-ends. Women are the books. Her name is wiped out in favour of his under a *feminine* marriage ceremony. Money is name after the feminine i.e. moon-eye. The heir was and still is the male the 'son and heir' or is it 'sun and air'? Even if a female was born first he is preferred. Even still in parts of the world 'sex selective abortions' are prevalent leading to disparate gender numbers. How clever considering the mitochondrial DNA is passed down through the *feminine* line so they've effectively bred themselves out. Good riddance to bad rubbish is all I can say. Trapped in a state of flux men are forever chasing their tales as Mother Earth crashes all around while she, *women*, stands right in front of him yet is not even considered for 'the job'. She can't even drive yet men have a much higher vehicle accident rate. They talk about 'white privilege' yet the overall energy of the world is 'male privilege'. When men take a look at the basic statistics *alone* maybe they might start engaging with the world around them differently? I'd hold my breath but, um, yeh. I'm not a man hater there are plenty of men out there who know the truth of men and often men have an 'unspoken code' of conduct they share among themselves at the expense of women that they would never admit to. It's their 'army' mind, the dumb testosterone 'boys club' mind. They also give each other big 'awards' at fancy ceremonies – Nobel Prizes, 'Rhodes' Scholars –she's probably vacuuming and doing the dishes out the back with a concerto in her mind by hey, who cares? The Pulitzer Prize has been around for 103 years yet only 30 woman have been recognised. You don't have to look far to see the dick rubber stamp *on everything* including aviation, science, art, architecture and now space as rocket dicks corner a rising corporate male-dominated space empire that will end badly. It's disgusting behaviour. Even my own musical career was *deliberately* destroyed by men who set me up for the *sole* purpose of wrecking my life on every level *because* I was the best. Males don't know the feminine purpose let alone their won wiping her memory and then *forgetting* he wiped her memory so now we're all trapped as women struggle for a place at a male-invite-only table in the 'new' world.

Electromagnetic lovemaking is the 'power couple', literally! This is where the legend of the 'twin flames' comes from and why a former lover is called an 'old flame' or when two lovers meet for the first time the 'sparks were flying' and the 'fire' of the loins and the flaming hearts of passion etc. To you they are simply Mum and Dad and the hand that rocks the cradle rules the world. Without equality between the twins *the fires of hell are unleashed* on endless generations in hopeless wars, bloodshed, torture and sacrifice to a demonic god, The Devil, a reptilian interdimensional alien passed off as a benevolent 'Heavenly Father' and slung us all down as his 'children'. That aint no 'father'. That's creepy uncle, Set! The murderer! The shapeshifter. The dark side of the masculine infecting our DNA leads Common Men away from their anchor, the feminine, destroying the light, the Angel within, to harvest Mother Nature's resources as ordinary men stand inept! Sun worship is a dick cult. Phallic worship. Only they left out the Moon, the feminine, as such *Mother* Earth dies. In every major centre of male power you will find the obelisk in Washington DC, the Vatican and the City of London. Called Baal's phallus this enormous erect penis symbolises the dark side of male tantric sex to open *their* chakras, raise *their* IQ's and take over the world and they've nearly done it by any means necessary, *see right*, Peter Pans dick! In the end I was to be *nothing* more than a breeder like Diana Princess of Wales, a 'broodmare', for one of their 'royal' chosen ones. Rags to Riches. Cinderella. A 21st century Marilyn Monroe. A sad little orphan girl-come-superstar. They planned to use me for my genetics, my talents, psychic abilities, beauty, brains and all the rest of it turn me into a 'star' indeed the brightest star of them all - Sirius *the Dog Star* - then planned to kill me in front of the whole world! Like Monroe! Like Diana! Like Princess Grace, Natalie Wood, Whitney Houston and *so many others*. *Houston*, we have a fucking problem! That's how it was supposed to go down used and abused and murdered *if* I hadn't figured it out in time! They're trying to steal the pure light of the Virgin for their own twisted ends. It's Peter Pan who *never* grows up in Never Never Land where the party never ends. Party boys. Pan is the Devil. P is the 16th letter of the alphabet which reduces to 7 so PP is 77 of the male-female chakra towers. It's Beauty and the Beast and as B is the 2nd letter of the alphabet then BB is 22 or 11:11. The Beast is the devil. Similar to Alice Through the Looking Glass, *right*, the themes tied to this is the Rose, the Dog, *French* royalty, the cursed beast who wishes to become a man again as *Time runs out*, an encroaching angry mob, the Virgin, redemption, the 'happily ever after', Holy Matrimony and ultimately, *Ascension*. Now that's one hell of a story and it's where we're at right now!

The ancients knew a time was coming when it would be heresy to know such things so they cleverly concealed all this knowledge in art, phonetics, symbolism and fables *knowing* we would discover it at a *critical* time when it was *undeniable* and needed most. That time is *now!* Here we have the $1 bill with the *uncapped* 3rd eye and the 11:11 twins on each corner, *men and women*, to become One, whole. Yet it's all twisted. 'In god we trust' is underwritten by ONE only 'god' is Satan and 'one' it *The One*. 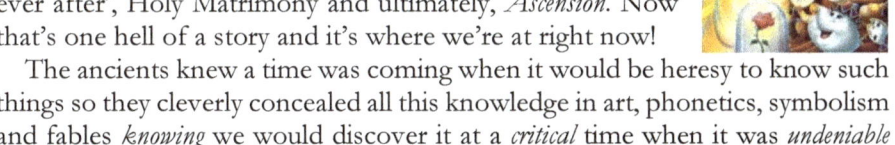 Corporations are written in capital letters. It's *the* One and their all-in-one money god, the Devil, is *in your face*. The root word of 'dollar' is German 'thaler' shortened from Joachimthaler. Joachim in Hebrew is 'raised by YHVH'. Yahweh is god. Money is god. Who is YHVH then? The passive feminine was the original one tasked with the secrets of this power so the 'brotherhood' who worshipped Hermes, a promiscuous bisexual god of shepherds, commerce, speakers, travelers and *thieves* saw their opportunity at the end of the last Age

2,000 years ago to *raise the dark side* for another eon of horrific crimes perpetrated against humans and planet earth. The political tendrils of these false prophet's became the Roman Catholic Church destroying ancient statues relaying this power and anyone who knew about it in their attempt to keep it all for themselves! They suppressed the true internal Christ of enlightenment and replaced it with a tortured hanged man on their sacrificial zodiac cross. To prove their diabolical power they then had the once great human race of Light and Love worship a degraded man, a lost man, a wrecked version of himself as well as a prostitute, a demeaned version of herself, rather than the true Christ *within*, the Light of the World, that can and *will* bring their Satanic organisation crashing to its knees as described *in their own texts*. This brotherhood, *a hybrid human-reptilian sex and death cult*, claim to trace their bloodlines back to *Orion* and *Sirius*. Aliens. They come from a common demonic progenitor, a demon seed, a synthetic unnatural spawn from an A.I. based technological *dark realm*, a realm of death, the 4th dimension, the Underworld! We belong at the very least in the 5th dimension as such they should be under us, unable to touch us, and this will be the case again once we access the chakras and enter the higher dimensions of the light.

The biblical Satan Snake and Yahweh-Jehovah were *both* reptilian delegates from another constellation in a far-reaching space syndicate of corporate elite 'royal' extraterrestrials calling themselves 'gods'. They colonised our planet, spliced our DNA with animals, captured us like pets, interbred with our reduced form to access the chakras and seeded their own species in the 'Garden of Eden' a lush abundant world, an *Eternal Spring, Mother Earth!* The Proceedings of the National Academy of Sciences studied over 2,500 people and found in 2% of them there were *complete strands* of non-human DNA finding 19 pieces of alien retro-viruses in the human genome called Human Endogenous Retroviruses - HERV's. A separate study in 2013 found a hidden code in the human genome containing *precise mathematical patterns* and unknown *symbolic languages* like a 'makers mark', a patent! Yes, an alien corporation creating genetic slaves harvesting worlds! They *travel* the galaxy enforcing their *Will* and at the end of it all they now seek to add Earth as a permanent fixture to their political empire of fallen planets, turning us into them, utilising their selected cronies in leadership positions aka The Hunger Games meets Star Trek taking their dick cult into space with permission of their psycho 'god' while putting it right in our faces! *See right*, 'Snake Hall' at the Vatican a *horrendous* sculpture supposedly depicting an apocalyptic 'Christ' in the event of a nuclear war. *That's what they want.* This

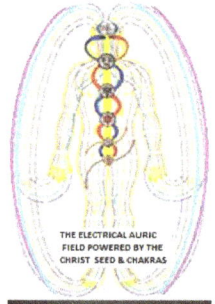

repellant alien 'art' clearly depicts one side of the face of Jesus as human and the other side as *reptilian*. The hybrid. The 'half-blood prince'. The good guy and the bad guy in one. The anti-Christ unleashing hell spawn from the *underworld* into the *upperworld* and the colour the pope *dares* to wear is white - the purity of the *virgin!*

This *alien* satanic secret society, the 'brotherhood', spawned the *three major Abrahamic religions*; Judaism, Catholicism and Islam to hide behind them *in plain sight* while they turned the beautiful life force of Mother Earth into a place of death morphing the light beings of Humanity into genderless cybernetically implanted sterile mutants! *That's* where this is going. They shut down 90% our chakras, 90% of our brains and 90% of our DNA to made us docile and dimwitted then twisted the true knowledge of Christ selling it back to us as an *external* 'god' in 'heaven' something *outside us,* mysterious, far away 'out there' and *incomprehensible!* They told us this lie as a series of parables, euphemisms, allegorical fables, myths, confusing biblical 'scriptures', double intendre's, cyphers, riddles and 'legend' all tied up in phonetics, numerology, astrology, symbology and *psychology* to keep us guessing and *begging* them for the answers for *another* two thousand years. Hey, it worked…so far. Under pain of death they *forced* us to perform for them like animals while killing the *true* masculine, the King, and degrading the *true* feminine, the Queen, husband and wife *worldwide,* the God and Goddess *within us all!* In 2015 French engineer Pascal Cotte used light beams of various frequency to reflect corresponding frequencies unveiling a hidden picture beneath the Mona Lisa, *right.* It showed an image of a much younger woman *wearing a crown* not smiling. It's as if these artists knew a time was coming when their

secrets would be revealed exposing the true *genius* of their work given tantric sex accesses other dimensions outside our 'linear' timeline, *time splitting,* where all things exist. Da Vinci, a true Mason, buried the goddess under something much simpler and even used his gay lover dressed in drag as his model mocking the Queen of Heaven with *childish* boys club lies. They've been *stalling* the *whole time* to make their final move when we would arrive *at this very moment* at the dawn of the Age of Aquarius! *Endgame!* It's all code often dressed up in movies as smutty jokes, *right,* 'Stifler' in *American Pie 2* wearing a shirt, 'This is where 'lectricity comes from'. Notice he has the thunderbolts of Thor either side pointing toward his penis his name '*Stif*-ler' an erect penis.

This is the secret of all ancient 'gods' and they're all practicing it in Hollywood as well as major religions and politics even the ones that appear to be morons are doing it. Diluting one's sexual energy with too many partners dilutes the psycho-spiritual essence and wears out the auric field letting in dark energy. This is why promiscuity is encouraged today yet the ancient fables say you have a special soul mate, *a twin*, in which you can harness the micro-cosmic 'fires' of the light force. It's why the Nazi's were obsessed with 'twins' trying to figure out what it all meant to fulfill these satanic prophecies in time for their evil ET masters in the final Age. It is the meaning behind the Masonic 'tracing board', *right*. The pillars each side are the 'arms', 11, Gemini, the lovers, the speaker, the voice. One arm is the sun,  masculine, and the other arm is the moon, feminine. They must work together. They're own symbology depicts its clearly. Yet as we see here the central pillar is the 'spine' and the vertebra 'ladder' of tantric 3rd eye enlightenment leads off to the left hand path, *Satanism*, the dark side, the mind. 'Cap' is Latin for 'head' as in 'caput' or 'de*cap*itated' etc., and it is *the mind* where masculine institutions reign from hence 'Capitoline Hill' and the 'Capital' which is *infested* with masons. Historically, men were quite unevolved and believed the intellect, the mind, was the only way to run the world hence, the left eye of Horus was plucked out as the left eye represents the moon, *the feminine*, and *she* reigns from the Heart and why in the end Jesus too was pointing at the heart. *Heart* is an anagram of *Earth* as in *Mother* Earth and *Mother* Nature the *nurturing* that reigns *naturally* from her. Yet balance was suppressed so all we've had is wars, death and ever increasingly a *dangerous* male dominated 'might is right' attitude and *mind control* ever since. Transcendental sex requires we come from the heart to reach heaven to becomes god and goddess *again*. This power in the hands of ego-mind has destroyed our planet as these old *military* coots accessing it have gone insane with power and intend to kill us all!

Subliminally dressing up the Christ enlightenment of Cerebrospinal Fluid (CFS) with negative imagery and phonetics is to *deliberately* keep us chasing our tails, literally! They secretly reinforce that sacred sex via a respectful union between a loving husband and wife, Holy Matrimony, a *Holy Mother Moon* ceremony, is boring even lame steering us away from the answers that were inside us the *whole time*. Just the missionary thanks and *only then* for spawning more progeny for the church's flock. It's a numbers racket. As with Da Vinci, the greatest artists, old and new, were well aware of this practice and *why* they were so great coding these secrets into their work for the world to discover *today!* In the following image we have Michelangelo's *The Creation of Adam*, literally a process of the brain, as is 'Eve', and *together* they create Christ! To further validate that this practice was once the realm of a devoted husband and wife we have the moral of the story of Babylon. Although initially a place of sacred marriage it descended into a debauched free for all as the unevolved masses misused this power (or so we are told) which seems to call down a wrath of 'god' because 'god' doesn't want you tapping into this power to beat him. So, the *anatomical* geographic map of the human body, *right*, is coded into the Bible as actual locations representing this secret knowledge. Therefore, as the Jordon River flows into the Dead Sea so does the spinal cord terminates at the part of the spine known as Sodom as in 'sodomy', the root chakra. *Jesus* became the 'saviour' (saved) when he was 'anointed of John' *note*, they say 'of John' not 'by John' because, Ioannes or John, is another word for the Oil of Christ and thus Jesus became *Christed*. *Christ* is the *title* of a tantric Master called 'sexual kung fu', it's a *discipline*, not a name. The vagus nerve is very important in this process and why there was a ritualistic mass shooting in *Vegas* near the black pyramid all to send inverted codes to the universe, the black mirror, to scramble the *real* signal of what this means. The base of the spine where the cerebrospinal fluid passes is called the *Cauda Equina* Latin for the 'horses tail' so, it's interesting to note the symbolic

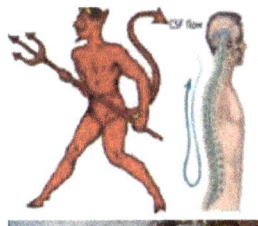

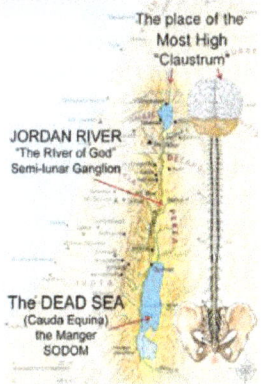

story of the ancient Roman 'night-mare' being a woman who turned into a horse and became a night witch or 'nightmare'. Night Mary. An enlightened woman is a nightmare to these guys.

The feminine root chakra is important to the electrical process as the root chakra is an anchor *anchoring us* to Earth or *earthing* the electricity thus *grounding* us. We're *supposed* to evolve by the simplest urge possible, sex. It's too simple to be true yet we are looking everywhere but where we should be looking, to ourselves. You can see, *right*, how similar the universal sound of OM is to the symbol of the root chakra. Scientists have recorded the sound of the sun and it does indeed sound like the chanting of OM. It is a note, a chord, like the spinal *cord* as our chakras are giving off notes, electrical sounds, and the root chakra, OM, was the first 'word' spoken or the first chakra, cup, to 'sing'. Ever seen singing bowls? The universe is musical as do birds and whales sing as fine harmonics hold the fabric of nature together. Pythagoras said, 'There is geometry in the humming of the strings, there is music in the spacing of the spheres'. In the Bible and freemasonry the 'first' word 'spoke' existence into being as the 'word' or the anchoring calming sound of OM can be found emanating from the root chakras of men and women as their positive and negative electrical currents engage in harmonious transcendental love making. It is the sound of the universe. Genesis. And *then* there was light. The root chakra is  particularly associated with the feminine as the inverted triangle means the feminine hips, *the chalice*, the cup of Christ, inside the square, the 'box', slang for vagina as such the goddess was associated with the cube. They particularly don't want women having this knowledge despite women being the *original* keepers of this power as Isis was said to 'tame' men to live with women like human beings and not animals. The Isis, *pituitary gland*, was not 'taming' men it simply 'trains' the electrical fires of the masculine mind's hormone, *testosterone*, the killer, the predator within, to live more harmoniously. To calm down. When men take anabolic steroids *(overdose on testosterone)* they can have a 'brain snap' or 'roid rage' and beat the fuck out of someone for not indicating at the traffic lights. The cliché that men 'think with their dicks' is no fallacy or is it 'phallacy'. The feminine 'waters' temper the masculine fires. It's not a competition. It's about balance. So, they've labelled a mob of marauding dickheads 'ISIS' to slander the goddess *once again* and now the latest version of this fakery *ISIS-K* means Isis 11 as K is the *11th letter* of the alphabet! The rising twin flame kundalini of her sexual power looms along with her enlightenment which spells 'sayonara' for these fuckwits.

Here is Isis, Artemis & Mary, *the same goddess*, the Mother, *nourishing* Christ. She is the *Alma Mater* Latin for 'Nourishing Mother' this term applied to *Universities* symbolising *education* yet few know what it means. There is a *lot* more to learn about this process and what I have described here is a *brief summary* of the *massive* expanse of historical, biblical, mythical and social context and connotations since, well, Adam was a boy. In many movies the galaxy is depicted as feminine, the central force of her light *driving*, the circular cyclical motion of life. As the hair is an extension of the nervous system outside the body, *right*, we can see in the movie *Tangled* her hair, nervous system, symbolises the galaxy because *that's* how we connect with the Universe through a series of transmitter receivers including the Crown chakra, DNA and nervous system. In ancient Egypt, Hathor

the wife and mother of the Sun god Ra, played a lyre, a stringed instrument, which represents the *direct connections* between the zodiac of the feminine universe, the Mother of *all* Gods, with planets and their sentient species found all around the galaxy. The piano has 88 keys symbolic of the 88 days the planet Mercury (Hermes) goes around the sun and the 88 constellations. We have charkas in our bodies, chakras in the Earth and Chakras out in space all *intimately* connected. As such, Astrologers refer to the natal chart as the 'guitar' similar to the strings crossing the hole symbolic of the zodiac energies *connecting* the cosmos. The rise and fall of civilisations, politics and the 'mood' of nations is all *rigged up* by these so-called 'black magicians' in secret societies via religion, politics, now the mass media as well as movies and TV coding our reality with *their* preferred outcome. They're *obsessed* with astrology and the secrets of this ancient spiritual knowledge is as relevant *today* as it was in the ancient past. But we don't have to be slaves to it like them. These energies were intended to evolve, liberate and develop sentient beings not manipulate the natural stories of the cosmos to *trick* the galactic energies into *mirroring* their weird cult in a and electrical feedback loop, a circuit. This is why the universe is called the 'mirror' or the 'looking glass' in Alice in Wonderland. Nothing is real. What's big is small. One man's fact is another man's fiction. It's the ultimate mind fuck.

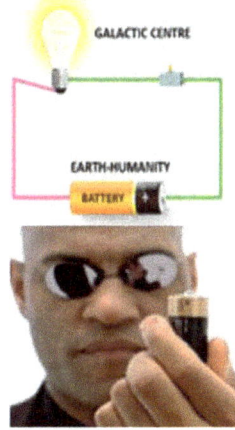

The universe is a big, syndicated radio station and what *signals* you transmit will depend on what you receive in return. The circuit! What you put out you get back. So, the *deep* purpose of Satanism is a cosmic hoax in an expansive alien program. *They* are broadcasting that the *evil* happening on Earth conforms to natural Cosmic Laws of Love and we're stuck out here like a shag on a rock and the *natural* galaxy *doesn't know* to help us otherwise it would! We are The Lost Boys. Lost in Space. This *inversion* of the beautiful design of the *normal* universe is so they can become 'god' themselves, a *fabricated* distorted false 'father' image to frighten humans, the 'children' of 'god'. Most people are children *still*. They *deliberately* encouraged massive population growth at this time to use the sheer numbers of *simple minds* who believe their lies to smother the real signal of the smaller collective of people who see it for what it is. Using mass numbers of *average* minded people in the human collective to *unwittingly broadcast* this sick program creates a dampening field burying the truth of our plight. Their alien technology is not strong enough to transmit the signal to the core of the galaxy and back so they use *us* to do it for them! This means if the galaxy as a conscious being, *the real Almighty*, ever finds out what they're doing the repercussions will be *swift and brutal*. It's their most dreaded scenario. They are on the edge now and we *must* send new signals to update the cosmic brain on *who* we are, *where* we are and *what* the hell is really going on here! This story is everywhere once you know the themes. *They know this is coming* which is why in the end the Devil loses abandoning his disciples saying, 'I had no authority over you except that I called, and you came. So, blame me not, blame yourselves. I cannot help you, nor can you help me. There is a painful punishment for the wrongdoers'. There *will* be a painful punishment for those that sold out the 'happily ever after' in a *false* revolution of consciousness in the Age of Aquarius with their false sun king anti-Christ via dark side tantric sex. The production that spawned the famous song 'this is the dawning of the Age of Aquarius' was *Hair!* They've kept us in terror *specifically* to sell us a false 'recovery' program as the end credits roll up. In the movie Tangled, Rapunzel, *right*, the Princess of Corona aka the *princess of the Crown*, even plays 'guitar' as she represents the Goddess of the zodiac the Mother of All Gods and sings, 'I'll play guitar and knit and cook and basically wonder when my life will begin'. Hey, I can relate, *right*. I've been set back so many times that the similarities are uncanny *to say the least* but then it was a *program* designed to do just that.

The entertainment industry is absolutely key to their program.

CHAPTER FOUR
KING KENNEDY

"I want them to see what they have done to Jack"
Jackie Kennedy in her blood-stained pink Chanel suit.

Where do you start with this one? I'm just going to cut to the chase and get down to brass tacks. To recap, I have memories of a program in which I *distinctly* recall being 'beamed' into my body. I was given four hints as to what this was all about: a trapezoid shape, the word Wednesday, the colour maroon and a speed-hump. *Trapezoid. Wednesday. Maroon. Speed.* That's all I got. At the end of a *very* long day, 40 years of struggling, they *brutally* revealed I was supposed to be Isis and Mary - a modern-day goddess. After a *lifetime* of enduring nothing but hard work, poverty, isolation, personal sacrifice, bitterness and grief all perpetrated against me in secret *by design*, I realised, I was set up from the get-go. They do this to take beautiful, kind, talented, intellectual women and turn them into cold hard bitches or 'ice queens' extracting all the light and love out their hearts to ensure they never realise any of their true power as a high feminine reduced only to a bitter breeder in a Satanic Space Program. The men behind this have no place in this world. With this knowledge in hand I went to work on the small clues I already had coupled with my limited memories as well as the Osiris-Isis myth and began piecing it all together. I had to do a crash course in history, mythology, all the religions, philosophy, numerology, astrology, astronomy, geometry, physics, literature, folklore, esoterica, symbolism. Let's just say it went on and on…and on. I was already interested in these things and had a reasonable back-knowledge from my previous research however, this turn of events took things to a whole new level.

I realised Satanism is an alien religion. It's not from here. It is an *interplanetary control blueprint* in an intergalactic corporate 'royal' space empire. It utilizes a technocratic *pagan* intergenerational hybrid multi-dimensional alien-demonic *breeding cult* emanating from society's 'aristocratic' families ultimately generated via Artificial Intelligence and synthetic organisms beyond the 3D 'five sense' realm of humanities *conscious* understanding of life. It incorporates the most *relevant* aspects of *other people's* religions, myths, folklores and historical beliefs *worldwide* co-opted into a cultural appropriation of unparalleled proportions. Satanism in its current capacity is a precision vehicle of militarized *psychological and social warfare* to shape our reality into a nightmare generally accepted as 'normal'. This twisted doctrine is fed through to our planet's biggest institutions and 'leaders' harnessing a multilayered array of tools including demonic possession, mind control, ritual, exotic technology, psychological and social warfare's, aliens, trans-dimensional entities, vibrations, dream coding, violence, war, intimidation, torture, money-poverty paradigm's, systems and hierarchy. This multi-pronged clinically intellectual *war-machine* is moulding the self-esteem of unwitting humans right down to the individual's *personal* level in their day-to-day life creating a subservient functionary who *ultimately* accepts death as the final solution to life. Satanism is a sex and death cult centred on phallic worship manipulating the dark side of masculine tantric sex unlocking the human body's energetic layers specifically the chakras and meridians to heighten the IQ and access the psychic spectrum housed in the human light body called 'enlightenment' by the ancients. They seek to emerge as 'god', an *inferior* twisted alien *concept* of a distorted 'father' force, a fabricated externalised figure, replacing 'god' with Satan. They will stop at nothing to gain the power they require to control *everything* in the universe unlike humans who are happy to ponder on their *existing beliefs* seeking truth peacefully.

So far we've already established that the colour maroon is the colour of the root chakra specifically associated with the feminine sex given it is a downward pointing triangle. The downward triangle represents the feminine hips, the 'chalice', also called 'cups', bowls, flowers, the 'lotus', the 'rose', 'horns', 'pipes', 'flutes' etc., producing the monthly cycle of blood in unison with the moon. It's a cosmic force called 'star seeds' *seeding* the essence of the stars, the light, into the feminine hence, the obsession with the brightest star *Sirius*, the 'blue' angel, being 'feminine' aka 'the light bearer' embodied by women. An angle is an *Angel* as the geometric *angle* of stars, size and position has a specific energetic impact on the light they reflect to become geometric *frequencies* hence, angel of light. They say the Cup of Christ, the red wine, is symbolic of drinking the blood *but* as Christ is an electrochemical hormone released by the brain, then The Cup is the 'chalice' of the feminine hips, her *reproductive system*, carrying the life force, Christ, Chi, Prana, Qi, into the world via babies giving rise to the generations and why she is called a boat, a vessel, a ship, that underpins so much of our laws specifically regarding money and trade. The 'goddess' was often depicted at the bow of a boat or ship as was Isis, the ankh, depicted at the bow of a ship near the 'anchor' as she 'anchors' the activated male chakras in a  symbolic reference to tantric sex enlightenment. Most civilisations in history carved her as figurehead at the bow of ships and just as women bear babies, the ship 'bears' the cargo giving the 'permission' of the goddess for merchants to transact trade on land and sea. Human babies are cargo. Mothers are ships. The feminine is a currency hence, 'money' i.e. moon-eye as one eye was the sun, masculine, and one eye was the moon, feminine, the two eyes of 'god', electrical pairs, watching over Earth. She is an engine, a *vehicle*, a machine, to facilitate their 'flock', the numbers they need for their trade empire, nothing more. Men, fathers, are labour, the workforce, that keeps it all flowing. Their secret god is Hermes, 'the messenger' of the 'gods', an ambisexual god of trade, commerce, travel, and *thieves* and another name for Satan a transgender mutant which is what they are in the process of morphing the human race into. We are slaves to an unknown alien empire. Therefore, they are not just replacing god, the father, they are ultimately replacing the goddess, the mother, as they can engineer babies in laboratories now transfer their souls via technologically as what happened to me. I wasn't supposed to remember. But I did…

The 'merchants' are men headed up by secret societies who have inverted the cosmic laws of an abundant goddess-universe for profit and power creating a false system, a replication, of the real thing. This *malevolent* Gnostic 'Archontic' force still rules our planet through new age Gnostics, the dick cult, the brotherhood, who enforce a cruel *facsimile* of something *much greater* and *freely given*. Women don't charge for babies. The ancients called it Hal, a simulation, 'a bad copy'. Hal is a Gnostic term meaning 'simulation' describing our capacity to 'model reality' and was the ancients way of depicting our virtual reality holograph changeable with the *intentions of our minds* as the flow of universal Aetheric life-force can be *directed by the Will* and is currently under the will of some very bad people. That's why they're so cocky. It's the superforce, the gasoline of the universe, 'god', in the hands of maniacs. The 'blood of christ' is the life-force carried via the menstrual cycle conveying the 'legitimate' royal-alien bloodline, *the line of Cain!,* via selected females. It's all about her, it's a breeding cult, and why these aliens are so obsessed with suppressing females as she has a hidden power, the ability to give birth to an enlightened child that would level the playing field on the spot, and this *terrifies* them intimating the real 'saviour' is not a man, it's a woman. Ultimately, every woman is the enemy as she bears a super-generation of human's, Superman and Wonder Woman, who will knock this one out of the park within a generation or two! It's all dressed up as fiction. It's a game and *we're running out of time!* This is their most dreaded conclusion as they lose the jewel of the galaxy, Mother Earth, along with the ensuing snowball effect that will liberate the Milky Way from Ages of evil alien control. It's what they have been trying to avoid all along yet there are fixed points in space and time and one way or another *these things will come to pass* as there are *many ways* to read a prophecy.

This is why they audaciously kill the god and goddess specifically via the symbolic assassinations of Princess Diana and Marilyn Monroe and kill 'god' in Kennedy and co (we're coming to that). This alien dick cult suffer a *massive* cosmic Oedipus complex to kill the Father, literally dads, who represent 'god' to 'fuck' or rape the Mother i.e. Mother Nature-Mother Earth *stealing* her resources for their dark empire hence, the 'thief' theme in fairy tales.

Mitochondrial DNA is passed down through females so their breeding program generates *the best* human genetics via her for their half-human aristocratic slave masters in their *monumentally* self-entitled political elitist state. The upward pointing triangle is called the 'sword' representing the penis. In the military the more dicks you have on your sleeve the higher the rank you are. It's a dick cult. Phallic worship. The upright triangle was denoted in the story of Isis and Osiris as the Golden Phallus. *Goldmember.* Yes, it's all in movies because Hollywood and all major institutions are practicing tantric sex hence, their celebrity, wealth and status putting it right in our faces as ordinary people wander around in a pharmaceutically induced brain fog unable to fathom or master themselves wondering *how* these elite psychos are getting away with all this! We're gonna beat them, folks, I'm here to tell you that. Their days are numbered.

So, the 'upper-classes' are practicing the dark side of tantric sex and in a glimpse of this we see the Epstein scandal's 'erotic massage' (tantric sex cult) trading young women like prostitute's aka Mary Magdalene because females are the 'goddess' as was Mary the 'goddess' who is slandered as street hooker. Oh, it's been going on for a *long* time. Gold is the second highest conductor of electricity considered a 'masculine' element, the Sun. Silver, a 'feminine' element, the Moon, is the *highest conductor* of electricity.  Gold represents the 'spark of life' the golden sun or 'fire of his loins', the *Loin* King or *Lion* King, as the sun's rays are often represented as a Lion because of his golden mane, *his hair,* becoming a 'Sun King' or tantric sex king of high IQ. Symbolism overlaps. The Lion is the King of the Jungle or in our case the 'concrete jungle'. The King who rules over *this* emerging new-age civilisation was 'prophesised' way back when no one could read and people were being burnt in the belly of a giant bull or owl or whatever the fuck they were doing when they were nailing people to crosses sacrificing virgins and shit. Anyway, point is, I wouldn't place too much stock in the 'prophesies' of people who thought terrifying rituals were 'normal' behaviour. The *'fire'* is referenced around the world and Biblically they talk of The Fire of Divine Love. Notice, they say Love not sex. Love is *Light.* Sex is *fire.* Luke 12:49 Jesus says, "I have come to cast fire on the earth, I am not at peace until that fire is blazing'. Yes, the fire of his loins. Sex and Love. Fire and Light. Both unlock the chakras which is why evil Satanists are running this world as they have used fire, sex, the flesh, carnality, to unlock their multidimensional powers. Jesus and Mary attained enlightened crown chakras (literally the IQ) via the heart or *Love* and for this 'Christ' was killed at least symbolically if not literally. The Catholic Church rose out of the suppression of Love and continued the age-old tirade of horror against humans. The 'Divine couple' is code for every man and every woman in *holy matrimony,* a committed civil union known as a Common Law Marriage. Mary and Jesus always point at their hearts and up toward heaven for enlightenment. Love over lust. It is the difference between opening your electrical chakras in a dignified *loving* manner or opening your electrical chakras in an animalistic ruthless manner, *see*, orgies and 'open' sexuality common to Satanism. Clearly, the latter is the one that has taken over the world.

Humans were genetically spliced with the animal kingdom in a lost prehistory to diminish us into servitude called the 'fall of man'. Yet we retain enough of our *original* high minded light-being master codes (that they are breeding with) and this keeps waking us up in line with cosmic alignments that occur every 2,000 years or so as we struggle to break free of the alien space program to escape their zodiac trap! Once men and women are reunited *alchemically* humans will shortly attain their high *innate* consciousness as a sentient species and simply move on as the evil ones are left in darkness where they belong. This is about Sacred Sex and why Cupid's bow represents the phallus and the *arrow* represents sperm or 'fire' as he *fires* the arrow into the flaming hearts of the Lovers with the passion of the Christ seed oil. The Catholic Church appropriated this power from Eastern philosophies and ancient knowledge then dressed it up as hatred and fear to steer us away from its true meaning depicting this power as pitiful broken bodies, blood sacrifice, confusion, fear and traumatic abominations like 'nailing' the 'Christ' to the 'cross' when it's actually about love and equality between the sexes but then all ancient civilisations did utilised these horrible methods cutting out hearts, burning virgins, nailing people to crosses. It's an intimidation tactic to keep people away from the truth of our consciousness and the power of our bodies. When one is in love the whole world is wonderful even if it's in crisis. *Love moves mountains*. A mother's love is unparalleled and if you have any queries about that approach a mother bear or threaten any mother's offspring and she will turn into a screaming banshee. The 'flames' of the heart-fires and the 'fires' of the loins are the *lock and key* to ancient and modern 'sun worship'.

As said, the universe is a self-replicating *binary* code (two), positive-negative electrical forces so, as much as you have the warm sun in the sky so too does every cell in your body contain the 'fire' or warmth of the 'sun', electricity. Humans are warm blooded as opposed to cold blooded synonymous with snakes or mammals and reptiles. As it's all replication the root and heart chakras of men and women 'burn' with the fires of desire when they are in *love* like the sun. Our *solar* plexus means Sol or 'sun' plexus and all combined the 'seven rays' of the electrical 'fiery' inner suns of the *chakras* activate the chakra 'tower' culminating in *Crown* enlightenment or the seven 'light rays' of the 'megamind'. *Christ Consciousness*. This is the *inner god* that they have *suppressed* and *twisted* for eons making us look outside ourselves to *their* god, the Devil. It is crucially the *feminine* who creates the *balanced* force although She is no messiah. She does not need worship in fact *the exact opposite*. She is the mother energy *training* you, like cubs, to fend for yourselves as all mothers do. Satanic Masons hate her for this and relish torturing and killing the 'goddess'. Therefore, it's not a male Messiah or anti-Christ who will save or destroy Earth, it is the feminine, the deadliest prophecy of all, who was foreseen as the *saving Grace* destined to bring down the Devil, the dark side of the masculine, the Dark Lord, to bring the light that she carries into the world one last time. Historically great artists coded these secrets into their work and modern movies are no different so you will see it all around you now and wonder how you didn't notice before. To that end the goal is to enlighten the masculine, the true King, found in every man and liberate the feminine, the true Queen, found in every woman as the fires of the dark side of the masculine raging out of control turning as Mother Earth into Hell. You don't see women cutting down the trees. Women aren't fishing out the oceans. We had *nothing* to do with the Bible, the Quran or Torah thank god for that and yet the elite *males* behind these control doctrines are *proud* of shit, 'look at our big book and how great our 'word' is as we talk of love and kill each other. Who needs women? Bah!' It's ego central. Too much fire. Imagine if women had to go to war in their big dresses, petticoats and corsets in the mud and razor wire? Not happening.

Satanic male dominators are very sneaky and in J.R. Tolkien's *The Lord of the Rings* trilogy's initial instalment *The Fellowship of the Ring* the 'fellowship' is the brotherhood, the Masons, as was Tolkien, a big one. That's how he knew this story as they keep the knowledge of Earth's secret past so his trilogy is very close to what actually happened eons ago in times long forgotten as the continuous battle for Mother Earth rages on. It will end now. People have speculated the 'rings' this means pedophile rings, the 'rings of Saturn', the 'rings' of secret societies etc., and it means all these things, however, remember a crucial clue. In ancient times the '*king* elevated himself via the feminine' called Hieros Gamos, 'sacred marriage', which means tantric sex via holy matrimony even if it was a ritual gesture as the king temporarily married the high priestess for tantric sex. It means the consummation of astral sex, tantric sex, between the god and goddess, husband and wife. Yet when the 'King' *really* married, he symbolically married the Goddess (*see*, Diana and Jacquie Kennedy etc.) as the chastity, integrity and honour of the *virgin* is conferred to him insinuating to the people that if *she* trusts him with all her virtue, *so could they!* The goddess was *literally* the 'throne' on which the king 'sat' elevated above all others. She propped him up giving him the kudos to speak. The Speaker! The Messenger! The Voice! People who practice tantric sex claim to see the 'vesica piscis' the 'flower of life' while Jesus, *Christed* by sacred sex enlightenment, ruled over the age of Pisces (at least the *broken* image of him did). Pisces is the two fish circling each other or Yin Yang and the Vesica Piscis is Latin for 'fish bladder' and the word *Magdalene* literally means 'Tower of the Fishes'. So, the 'rings' are actually *wedding rings* in which tantric sex enlightenment was traditionally practiced in ancient history, a time of stupendous feats of strength and architectural marvels they still can't fathom even today! That aint no ancient alien bullshit, that's human ingenuity with activated chakras since shut down. This is how they did it. They take everything from us, our history, our achievements, our lives. Cunts. As every man is 'king' or 'god' and every woman is 'queen' or 'goddess' Sheela-na-gig at the Church of *St Mary* and St David, Kilpeck shows the vagina as a vesica piscis synonymous with wedding rings associated with the cross.

The Vesica Pisces, Age of Pisces and *Magdelene* are all 'fish'. Pisces, *the fish* of the zodiac, astrologically rules over the feet, *right*. The feet connects us to Earth, the feminine, *grounding* the sexual *electricity* of the fires harnessed from the sun aka *Sol* via the *Soul* anchoring the central nervous system through the *Sole* of the feet *earthing* the positive-negative electricity of 'god' and 'goddess' universal lifeforce energy, chi-prana, anchoring the power couple (where this term comes from) to become more stable. Earthing stabilizes the voltage levels protecting against an electrical overload of the fires which is what these male lunatics are suffering from, a god complex. The 'devil' means *too much fire*. When working with electricity one needs wear rubber boots and interestingly, condoms were 'rubbers'. Earthing lowers the risk of electrocution so *She* was the considered the anchor and unsurprisingly, Isis, the Mother, the Goddess (same thing) was depicted as the ankh, *right*. It not only phonetically *sounds* like anchor but actually looks like one and means the 'key of life' often used as a mirror because the *universe* is the mirror, an electrical circuit or loop, considered feminine aka the goddess. The ankh was stolen by the brotherhood and turned into the masculine depicting the 'cross' of the nervous system of the upper torso, *right*, as well as the zodiac cross and cross of the optic nerve etc. It's all replication. The 'loaves and two fish' is the 'bread' of the Christ seed, the grain, and the 'fish' is the feet earthing *electrical* sexual alchemy inside marriage. The Lord of the Rings is the Master of the *Wedding* Rings. *The Lord of the Ladies*. Lord of the feminine Galaxy - the Queen of Heaven!

They were planning on taking us over with their King Dick of dark side male tantric sex as we enter the space age sending rocket dicks into space!

John Lennon, a modern Jesus where pop-culture meets politics, a *speaker*, a Messenger, was protesting from his *bed* with his *wife*. Now we can see what John and Yoko were *really* trying to tell us as the *hair* is an extension of the nervous system outside the body accessed via tantric sex *in bed*, the *throne*, the *alter*, which leads to peace - *hair peace, bed peace* - the golden fleece, the golden crown of tantric sex enlightenment aka high IQ. *This* is the power of the married 'twins', men and women, but if you don't know this *crucial* detail then they just look like a pair of rich hippies who lost their shit on too much LSD. They were trying to tell us and it cost JL  his life. This practice gives you confidence, conviction and *courage*. Lion hearted! Dick is short for Richard. Richard the Lionhearted is *King* Dick. Stop thinking with it. Stop 'mind dick' and get into *Heart* dick and you *will* see *miracles* like Jesus, Miracle Man, MM, Mother Mary, Mary Magdalene. Love via Holy Matrimony is what these symbols *really* mean and *should* have seen humanity reaching cosmic enlightenment *2,000 years ago* when the Age of Pisces began and Mary and Jesus were *a married couple* hence, the Jesus fish Christians put on their cars. They subliminally encode true love as something horrible so we have the terrifying movie *The Ring* and the latest instalment, *The Rings*, there's two now, male and female, in marriage. They also have a 'reality' TV show *Married at First Sight*, a horrible program where  morons meet for the first time and marry in a Civil Ceremony as CC is 33 the number of vertebrae in the Christ Consciousness tantric spine. They are making shit of Civil Union's as the multi-billion dollar marriage market falls flat on its arse when people realise you are *more* married if the false government *isn't* involved. Couples marry in front of a pedophile priest only to divorce in front of a pedophile judge and wonder why marriages are failing. We're being stalled. As such, the Washington Monument is a penis-vagina-eye with its galactic *rings* 'penetrating' through the physical illusion of our 3D 'reality' into higher dimensions using the feminine sex to gain their power, *right*. So, sex, 'god' and 'goddess' are all *intimately* tied to marriage once considered a 'contract and a deep bond between 'friends', men and women, taken *very* seriously in ancient times. They even had had a handshake *once again* stolen by elite men appropriated in *business* contracts. The *original* hand shake was an agreement the couple would remain *mutually exclusive* as *contaminating* the pure light with the energy of other lovers damaged the connection to the highest levels of the light aka *True Love*. It's the difference between aviation gas and kerosene.

The legal definition of 'covenant' is "an agreement, a contract, or written promise between two individuals that frequently constitutes a pledge to do or refrain from doing something". It's basically a pre-nup. Therefore, fascinatingly, a *Covenant Marriage* is a legally distinct kind of marriage in three *southern* states of America: Arizona, Arkansas, and *Louisiana* considering King Louis XIV, Louisiana's and St Louis's namesake, was a famous Sun King. Yet There is no sacred *lovemaking* between a husband and wife for corporate politicians *especially* in Washington. Their families, like most politicians, are just a front for votes, *see*, the movie *The Campaign* (hilarious). But when the cameras aren't rolling, they engage in orgies, partner swapping, homosexuality, bisexuality, swinging, anything goes sexual extravaganzas, pedophilia, necrophilia, bestiality, blood sacrifice, torture, murder and all the filth the dark forces are trying to coerce the *human race* into becoming. These creatures are behind every filthy deed the world has ever known and it is *they* who rigged up the program I remember to bring forth the Devil Incarnate, an alien-demon hybrid-human aka Rosemary's Baby, and I'm not even kidding! They had me lined up for *forty years,* 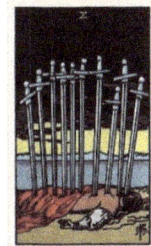 *slung down like Mary* in replication of this shitty story keeping me poor and isolated, driving shitbucket cars and doing it tough *every day* of my life before I 'made it' to the 'finish' line only to discover *my own team* set me up and stabbed me in the back, *the ultimate betrayal,* expertly summed up by the X of Swords in the tarot deck another one of their inventions. They know all the dirty tricks and it cost me my professional music career, my mother *and* father on my birthday no less, my youth, my health, my family, my income and *everything else* you can imagine. If this 'fairy tale' *ever* comes true I'll pen an autobiography called '*Shitbuckets to Chandeliers*' how about '*Shitcart to Cartier*' or this gem '*From the Shitehouse to the Whitehouse*'. They planned to move in on me as some 'common' girl for their new-age New World 'royal' prince, a 'fairy tale' *farce,* an unwitting modern-day Isis for their New Egypt and their *American* Osiris. Goddamn Motherfuckers.

Egypt was the land of Osiris but *America* is the land of Isis even the name M*isis*sippi finds 'Isis' in it. They know *exactly* what they're doing and as we know all good symbolism has multiple creative and sometimes ingenious meanings. Therefore, we have an ancient depiction of the virgin's vagina known as the 'wound of Christ' *at his side* as he is 'hung' on the cross, *right*. Let's face facts it's a vagina. Notice the ladder at the top. Climb the ladder, the spine, via the vagina, sex. Yet what we *really* see here is the hidden symbolism of Jesus and Mary *side by side*, equals, like batteries, allowing the electrical conduit to flow as in any *circuit* board, *see right*,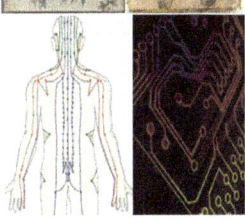

the meridians of the human body and a circuit board or *'mother'* board. They couldn't bear to allow women their rightful place so, they coded all this in cryptic symbology as the 'Wound of Christ *at his side'*. Yet the figurative Jesus character, Christed by the Oil of enlightenment, went beyond them all and dared to unlock his heart chakra! He was in touch with his *feminine side* put it that way. It is a story with two meanings and the Masonic meaning warns those in the know that he was 'killed' because he was in the process of returning the feminine to her rightful place at the side of the masculine. The Twins reunited as equals. Saint Joseph is the patron saint of carpenters which is code to say Joseph, Jesus's stand-in dad, was actually his real father passing carpentry onto his son as they would have done in those days and still do to this day. Carpentry is a symbol of the 'trades' as was the 'smith' etc. The god Vulcan (another Satan) was a blacksmith as well goldsmith's worked with jewels. Egyptian god Ptah was another version of Osiris and was a 'craftsman'. The Beatles, like Jesus, went to the East to learn their tantric secrets and changed the world their original band name was The Quarrymen as the quarry is where stone is cut from and *stonemasons* get their name and played the last gig in June 1966 or 6/1966. The Egyptian god Khemu made man of clay on his potter's wheel as did 'god' make man of clay or 'earth'. Root chakra, sex, is 'earth' so they interpret 'god' as their god the Devil, Satan, the masonic 'architect' who 'moulds', 'makes' and 'designs' things *'crafting'* society with the dark arts, *the craft*, and all the lame brains fall into its traps. The Beatles record label was called Apple Records a reference to the torus field 'apple' while the lyrics of Hey Jude are, 'Hey Jude, don't make it bad. Take a sad song and make it better. *Remember, to let her into your heart*, then you can start to make it better'. Unlock the heart chakra in men and the world will change overnight. Jude, Judas, sold out Jesus for 'letting her in'. George Harrison wrote the song *My Sweet Lord* which swaps from saying My Sweet Lord (Jesus Christ) to Hari, Hari (Hari Krishna) because Christ and Krishna are the *same thing*, the Christos Oil released from the Claustrum leading to enlightenment. The name Harrison is *Hari's* son as 'Hari' is the highest Hindu god or 'the most high', *the actual sun*, the 'highest' astral body in our sky. Therefore, as *the skull* is the *highest* part of the human *body*, the 'light' of Christ-Krishna-Claustrum or kundalini-crown chakra en*light*enment associated with the central star in our solar system, the sun system. It's all connected. Krishna attained enlightenment described as the '8th incarnation of Hari', the sun. H is the 8th letter of the alphabet. 8 is the 'god' number. Mercury take 88 days to go around the sun. There are 88 constellations. So, 88 is HH the male-female god-goddess. The twins. Yet Mercury is Hermes. One god.

Being a carpenter in those days meant Jesus was educated, he could read, and the only educated people in those days were the upper classes. They were the only ones *allowed* to read. If a commoner was caught learning to read right up until the renaissance, they could have their nostrils slit, their faces branded etc. Commoners weren't even allowed to wear certain cloth like satin or velvet 'dressing above their station' akin to impersonating a cop these days only the penalties were *much* higher. So, Jesus was no poor man. The 'King' of the Jews was no Commoner. The *Mason* that the Jesus character was based on was a 'wandering scholar' who made his way as far as Ireland to study among the Druids in their universities. They weren't rag tag mystics. They were high masters like the apparently fictional Merlin. Jesus 'studied in the East' in his 'missing years' the East famous for transcendental meditation and tantric sex still openly practiced today. He was betrayed by Judas for his attempt to return the feminine to her rightful social position as the rest of the 'disciples' stood by idle. This ministry appears to be a secret society or what we now call the Masons made up of plumbers, stonemasons, carpenters, smiths as well as lawmakers, architects and town planners etc., who became councilmen and ultimately, the *Government!* The 'Last Supper' is a recreation of the Osiris myth famously murdered at *his* last supper as was Alexander the Great who 'died' shortly after *his* last supper at '33'. The 'supper' is the bread, the bread is the grain of Christ-seed Consciousness and 33 is the number of vertebrae in the tantric spine.

The Last Supper is symbolic of a harvest festival as Osiris and Isis were both 'grain' deities meaning the male 'seed' or sperm and the star 'seed', light, planted in a woman to create new life along with crops etc. This is about the first knowledge of agriculture, planting the grain and harvest in preparation with the zodiac and seasons. It's about evolution. As such, this story goes back *much further* than a couple thousand years. *Right*, we see Da Vinci's *The Last Supper* and clearly there is an argument. Mary demurely sits as a 'cut-throat' hand is drawn across her neck. She is no gaudy prostitute as Jesus and Mary practically hold hands. To Jesus's left we see one disciple pointing to heaven at his 'left hand path' oath. Mary and Jesus wear the colours of the root, heart and the throat chakra. She wears the colour of the heart chakra, green of Mother Nature, and maturity of the sexual *maroon* root chakra, the mother, while Jesus wears the colour of the fiery red root chakra and throat chakra, blue,

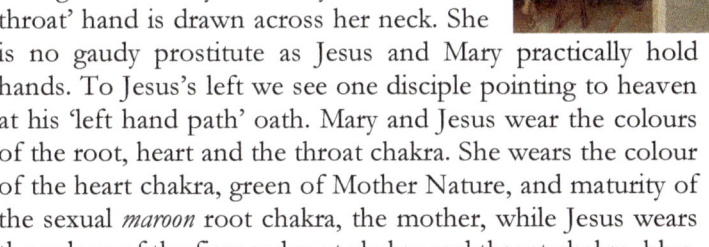

the Speaker! The Messenger! The zodiac sign Taurus rules over the throat yet the planet *Mercury*, the lovers, rules over the voice, communication, *see right*, Boy George points upward with his left hand, V for victory, his right hand on his heart while Seal does the V sign over the left eye, the moon. The colour of *The Voice* logo is red, root chakra, in the shape of a V, *the feminine chalice*, as the women pose apparently clueless in an inside joke.

Hermes-Mercury carried the kundalini caduceus with angelic wings of enlightenment on his head and feet denoting his high IQ and 'swiftness', *right*. He was known to cross 'borders' meaning *dimensions* in the astral. The *planet* Mercury travels so fast across the sun it appears an optical illusion going backwards. Tachyons do the same thing and potentially carry information *from the future* broadcast *backward* across time warning us of what is to come showing up as coincidences, *intuition* and dream downloads. The caduceus is the 'two snakes' of the sexual kundalini rising up the spine during tantric sex representing the 'twin flames' of the 'fires' and the 'spark of life' of tantric lovemaking between the Lovers, Gemini, 11. Eleven means light. Snake in ancient Egypt means *electricity*. The intertwining kundalini, *see right*, of the twin towers of the twin flames ultimately overcomes the R-Complex, the *reptilian*-animal brain. Mary Magdalene and Mother Mary's initials were MM as is the Roman Numeral for the year 2000 and it all kicked off from there in 2001, a *Space Odyssey* to be sure, when the *Twin Towers* came crashing down in *flames*. It's no coincidence. So much is at stake now as the prophecy of the 'Twins' comes to pass and the ancient Fairy Tales of a 'happily ever after' for humanity is realised. No more sordid one-night stands for these two. David Icke had his chakras blown open on a mountain top in Peru but we can't *all* do that. The controllers are *terrified* we'll all become Icke's! Oh dread! As such, the Twin Towers came down in *flames* to ritualise the destruction of the rising male-female kundalini chakra towers to *symbolically* destroy us before they *actually* destroy us!

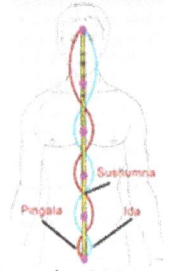

The human rights atrocities perpetrated against the Divine Feminine continue to mount worldwide and unless the male-female electrical counter-poles are balanced, Earth will never be free. In the end they are planning to do away with women entirely as the alien dick cult has 'evolved' to the point where they can make babies in laboratories, artificial wombs called 'mother'. Only they won't have souls as souls incarnate during pregnancy via the feminine: *the light bearer!* The military have made 'treaties' with new-age aliens to allow them to abduct humans for experimentation in return for technology. These aliens have broken their fake agreement because the military don't speak for humankind they only speak for themselves. It's rigged. As such the general public are increasingly becoming confused as video footage mounts of strange craft, objects, lights, formations and ships *openly* making their presence felt as flimsy excuses pertain to Elon Musk's 'Starlink' SpaceX satellites. It's all in the lead up to something enormous as the Pentagon finally confess 'UFO's are real'. Thank you, Pentagon, who are, by the way, an agency of alien representation. Rocket scientist Wernher von Braun 'predicted' in his 1953 book that a Mars mission would be led by an 'Elon'. This is no prophecy it's just the script that a guy called Elon would lead the new age space program and they can choose from many 'Elon's' at this time. The name Elon is an anagram for Leon, Greek for Lion, the Lion King, the Loin King, a Sun King! So, next time you're singing the reversed 'Noel, Noel, Noel, born is the King of Israel' (*Isis-Ra-Elohim*, reptilian king, the devil!) at Christmas the *Christ-seed Mass,* you're actually singing 'Lion, Lion, Lion! Born is the Lion King, *the Sun King,* of Israel!' Peter 5:8, "The devil prowls like a lion, seeking anyone he can devour". They say, 'like a lion', *fake hero,* it's all around once you know.

Set in ancient Europe, the preferred battle grounds of many major wars *even still,* we can see J.R. *Tolkien's* Lord of the Rings trilogy including *The Fellowship of the Ring, The Two Towers* and *The Return of the King* has *fascinating* symbolism and means *a lot* to them to hide this so deftly! In my original book *2020 & Beyond* I theorized that the lord of the 'rings' was The Lord of the *Wedding* Rings before I even discovered the historical significance to all this. Fascinatingly, here we see the *original* artwork of the book done by none other than Tolkien *himself* and right there on the front cover, *right,* is an *inverted* diamond wedding ring, the female aspect of the equation, once again, turned upside down as they invert *everything* including the cross. The anti-Christ has been planned for a long time in an open secret at the highest levels of secret science agency programs. Under Tolkien's wedding ring almost *crowning* it is a reptilian eye surrounded by elvish writing that appears to be the flames of a strange black sun. I go into more detail on this later but remember, the Germans were obsessed with *twins* performing their cruel experiments on inmates. The Pan German Society for Metaphysics became the Vril Society and were all occultists along with the Brothers of Light also called the Luminous Lodge, The Black Knights of the Thule Society and The Black Sun who traced their origins to 13th Century Templars - the Lords of the Black Stone - all emerging out of the 1917 Teutonic Order later identified with Heinrich Himler's S.S. The ancients associated the 'goddess' with a black stone-meteorite which we now understand it the 'stone' of Jacobs ladder, the Sacral Plexus, integral to tantric enlightenment without which, these cunts are just like anyone else in the street. Operation Paperclip, *right,* transported in excess of 1,600 German scientists, engineers and technicians to America post WWII ushering in the greatest neo-pagan Satanic transference of power, data and personnel to New Egypt, *America, specifically*  designed for this purpose. Coincidence? I think not! It's an ancient reptilian breeding program that has aligned itself with the insidious alien cloning program to breed to One World alien Leader imperceptible to human eyes. This is what they are doing in those alien bases in New Mexico and Nevada among many others worldwide in the most dangerous and sinister threat to the Earth most people are, even still, completely oblivious to. In the 1981 film Early Warning they specifically talk about a global vaccine and cashless society and that "if we continue on our present course, it is my opinion, that we could present the Devil himself as a world leader and the people would accept him'. Yes, they will unless they know.

Hollywood *is* Nazi genetics *Operational HQ* hidden in plain sight weaving the diabolical tendrils of these *audacious psychopaths* into a web from which we cannot seem extricate ourselves as Hollywood twins abound! It is among these scientists that they garnered knowledge from Nicola Tesla and supposedly alien technology as well allowing these *aging* German and Jewish scientists from elite European families to have themselves 'beamed in' to specific toddlers to emerge at this time. Certain bloodlines were even bred to have the best traits they are looking for in their Superman program to covertly carry out the biblical prophecies assured that no one would ever find out let alone figure out what they were doing or *how* they did it. No one, including myself, were supposed to *remember*. The plans of mice and men. They gave the best lives, the best families, good looks, talents and psychic traits to themselves via certain children designed for this purpose. While they got the best everything A-List celebrity has to offer, they 'beamed' the chosen females, wonder woman, into the *shittiest* lowest levels of society under the most degrading circumstances so they could torture the 'goddess' wasting her talents and life away laughing the whole time about it in their movies no less! Then when she was too old, too worn out and too broken to salvage anything of her own life and with only a couple of years left to *breed*, they intended conveniently 'appear' and 'rescue' her from the gutter Cinderella style to promote themselves as 'heroes' and 'celebrate' the 'happily ever after' to live out the fables *as prophesised*. So clever. Fool proof! Unfortunately for them for every action there is a reaction so in seeking to breed from women who had high talents and psychic abilities to get the best traits for their One World Leader, the Devil incarnate anti-Christ, you would think it obvious that these very psychic traits *she possessed* would create a potentially deadly loophole in their scheme as in my case, I utilised my abilities to not only recall as much as possible but *actively developed* my psychic abilities without any help and sought to discover from the *earliest age* what it was all about *knowing* it was huge. Their ego's shall find them out in the end as they didn't think it was possible that I could ever overcome the *trauma* they had lured me into under the guise of 'helping' out let alone utilise my spectrum of skills to bust them at their own game! Motherfuckers that they are. They even sent little mental messages as in one case I received the signal 'the harder it is the better it will be'. What a bunch of absolute dog shit eating *filth* taking a high feminine and making her crawl through the shithole for forty years so they could lord it over her and emerge as her 'saviour', Jesus as it were to Mary, as clearly depicted in ancient paintings of Mary *crawling on all fours* at the feet of the brotherhood, absolutely broken in abject poverty and degradation while Jesus, masonic shit heel, looks down on her with his mates. But he 'grows up', as they believe the story to go, and finally 'recognises her worth' as symbolically 'Satan' matures into 'Jesus' and 'rescues' Mary and why Satanists believe the 'devil' will save the Earth. But then they spin it *however* they like. In one version he destroys the world, in another he saves the world, in another he leaves the world, in a another he is the good *and* bad guy. Hypocrisy, they celebrate it. Whatever works is how it works. These party boys get to be the destroyer *and* the saviour, the Devil *and* Jesus! Lucky them. Party on dude.

The Return of the Reptilian Tantric Sun King heralds the final takeover utilising the black hole sun 'black mirror' at the centre of the galaxy on the 'throne' *via the virgin*. The anti-Christ one world leader is a reptilian out in the open, a 'gender fluid' mixed race person for *all* people in a fake 'global' new age and the world will love him as 'he saves' us from ourselves. And it will be a 'he' however 'fluid'. The devil is transgender no offence to the LGBT community. It's not your fault they are using you as a shield to bring about their evil plans. In the film Oblivion, Tom Cruise proposes to a woman holding up a *wedding ring* at the Empire State Building in view of the *One World Trade Tower*. They all want to father the One anti-Christ King. They even throw in the 'monkey man' theme, King Kong, as Konge is Danish for King at the 'top' of the 'tower' or King of Kings, Zeus! It's the One' World Leader's One World Tower risen from the *rubble* of the two, mother and father, the Twins, and their Chakra Towers of enlightenment via Holy Matrimony that they *demolished*. Building 7 represented their 'child' and their 7 chakras. It was 47 stories high as 4+7=11. The Family of Life is destroyed here in this ritual replacing the *natural order* with a changeling, a stand in, *right*, we see *the One World Trade Tower glowing* with a rainbow just before the *anniversary of 911*. How nice.

The Washington Monument, *right*, is another symbol of the dark side of masculine Tantric sex controlling the feminine and ruling over Earth. Here the phallus or penis, the obelisk, the 'needle', the prick, is penetrating the vagina, the *infinity* pool, the waters, above *and* below, heaven and hell, the upper world and the underworld. The 'primordial waters' of space and time are the waters of the feminine in every ancient myth from which the universe was created, the 'mother' of all gods that came after her. Ancient female priestesses would hold up a mirror to symbolise that firstly, the universe is feminine and secondly, what you put out you get back. The infinity pool reflects the stars, the feminine light, as the pool is a symbolic *mirror* of the universe reflecting the light *back* at the universe in a continuous circuit, electricity! The myth that vampires have no reflection in a mirror symbolises that the reptilian aspect cannot 'make a connection' have no 'reflective' light of their own so they hack in through human light bodies to reflect themselves into the 'mirror' and thus take it over. The sequel to Alice in Wonderland by Lewis Carroll was Alice Through the *Looking Glass*. The 'looking glass' is a *mirror* and *we* are a *reflection,* replication, of the universal mirror looking back at us as Carl Sagan said, 'we are made of star stuff'. Lewis Carol was known for his knowledge of myth, math and religion. Alice's voyage into the underworld smacks of the legends of Isis, Persephone, Inanna and Ishtar. David Day wrote a book on 'Alice's Adventures in Wonderland Decoded' and it's worth checking out for deeper insight into classical literatures Egyptian and pagan roots. 'Alice' in 'Wonderland' is the *amnesic feminine* lost inside her own universe, the *lost* Princess Rapunzel, in a house of mirrors unable to escape as everywhere she looks all she's sees is herself in a mind trap. In quantum mechanics size doesn't matter so what/ is big is small. She has been subdued, unsure of herself, hamstrung by self-doubt as her innocence, *virginity*, is preyed upon, s*ee right*, Mephistopheles and Margarita by an unknown 1800's *French* artist carved from a single piece of sycamore best seen in a mirror as Margarita, *Mary*, the goddess, is *hidden in the shadow of the devil!* MM is *Mother Mary, Mary Magdalene* and the Roman Numeral *MM* of the year *2000!* The Age of Aquarius. We have arrived.

The devil poses grandly (he has horns), pure ego, dark side of the masculine, hiding the feminine in his *shadow* stealing *her* rightful place, her light, posing in *her* place. She cannot 'see' him yet as His back is turned. *Stealing* her lime-light. Thief. All the destruction she blames on herself as all she sees is her own reflection in a *false* mirror, a fake circuit. She is the martyr as so many mothers are to their children. She doesn't know *she* is the mirror *and* everything else. So, the *Goddess* bows *unknowingly* to a creature that should not be allowed to live in her universe, an alien, *posing* as a human man, her rightful Twin, to steal their Love! He is A.I., synthetic, fake. She is Mother Nature organic, all that is good and wholesome. These aliens are not only fucking Mother Earth but fucking the *whole universe* as well. Men once protected the great Mother, the natural world, so the reptilian devil posed as a human male, took the place of him and coveted the feminine for *itself!* Men without women are weak, *unanchored*. Without a man *she* is weak, vulnerable. Men became slave labour as the *demon* turned the goddess into a housemaid and a whore. One of my messages back in 2012 was 'the darkness has elevated itself to a godlike status and threatens the entire universe' and as M is W upside down then MM becomes *Milky Way*.

With all this in mind we must not forget President John F. Kennedy was a practicing Satanist the little wife and happy family man image, like most, was just a front. He was one thing in public and *another thing* behind the scenes which made him a perfect target. As it were, King Kennedy was assassinated on Elm Street in Dealey Plaza which is built along the Trinity River. Yes, the *Trinity* as in the Holy Trinity, the Father, Son and Holy Ghost. Originally the Trinity was the *Mother, Father and Child*, the *Family of Life*, as well as Body, Mind & Spirit.

Elm Street is reference to the tree of the Tree of Life, and a Nightmare on Elm Street began and continues. As said, they put it all in movies. Built in the *1840's* this plaza is laid out in the shape of a triangle, *see right*, or more specifically the infamous *uncapped pyramid*. It is uncapped because the 'all seeing eye', the third eye chakra, the pineal gland, crown, is missing and therefore the 'head' of the masses as well as the king himself remains 'uncapped', blind, *unopened*, unawakened, *decapitated*. The meaning of this is the 'good guy' Sun King-God King is dead as he wasn't smart enough, it's all symbolic, and the fact that the presidential vehicle had *no Secret Service personnel* remains a detail that the *Dallas Police Department* and all *US Government Agencies* then and now *remain to answer* because it's the *same people* in charge today. *See right*, Lyndon Baines Johnson being sworn in as a traumatized Jackie is shrouded in grief and darkness. "My deepest condolences, Jackie...*now let's party!'* Take a *long look* at the abject *ruthlessness* of these people running your world. They are worse today than they were then. An excellent documentary called *The Men Who Killed Kennedy* goes into extraordinary detail about who did and why LBJ was behind all this even linking him to killing his *own sister* for profit and gain in the last interviews with many people associated with this before they all died of old age. It's well worth a look.

John and Jackie Kennedy's initials were *both* J & K. *J* is the 10th letter of the alphabet and K is the 11th letter of the alphabet giving us KK or 11:11 or, individually, 111-111 (3) the number of the Empress adding up to 6 the number of pleasure. The tarot deck is *obviously* designed by Masons. In the background of Dealey Plaza *today* we can see in the distance a modern building distinctly resembling an enormous obelisk. Biggus Dickus. Mine is bigger than yours. The Dick Cult strikes again! Located in Dealey Plaza is an obelisk, *right*, built in 1940. It's 25-foot tall (2+5=7 the number of chakras) next to an infinity pool or the feminine waters. The penis-fire and vagina-waters just like the Washington Monument is elite men dominating the universe but this is not just *any* obelisk. Clearly this obelisk has *fourteen pieces* symbolising the phallus of King Osiris and the *fourteen segments* his body was cut into all of which was retrieved *except for the phallus!* So here it is, the king's dick, the 14th piece of tantric sex enlightenment. In the movie *JFK* Kevin Costner plays the role of New Orleans District Attorney Jim Garrison. He meets a government agency

man who goes into quite some detail about *why* Kennedy was killed. All the explanations revolve cleverly and very convincingly around political and social upheaval at the time. In the background we can see the obelisk as the director, Oliver Stone *note,* the name *Stone*(mason) cleverly indicates who was *really* behind it all, the same people who erect all these obelisks worldwide in their One World vision direct from ancient Egypt, the Masons! But they *don't* tell you *why* he was *really* killed. The reason he was killed was that Kennedy was a symbolic if not literal Sun King. His sexual conquests were then and now legendary although he suffered ill-health and had a bad back sometimes dubbed 'two-minute Jack' (in the sack). He was also called Red Jack accused of Communism (another distraction). The Garrison Investigation revealed a murky conspiracy involving the mafia, anti-Castro activists, artists, bohemians, writers, the Bavarian Illuminati, voodoo practitioners, new-age 'churches' rooted in Southern mysticism, Nazi's and a homosexual subculture.

Yet Oliver Stone *did* tell us what the *real* reason was only, like Tolkien, he did it in such a way that was practically *imperceptible* once again, steering us away from the truth while putting it right in our faces. It's an odd scene as Tommy Lee Jones plays the character Clay Shaw engaged in a homosexual orgy filming a gay porno which suggests there is *real* footage of this somewhere. They are impersonating the French Aristocracy as Kevin Bacon's character, Willie O'Keefe, dresses as Marie Antionette while Joe Pesci's character, David Ferry, dresses as Louis the XVI a famously *decapitated King* in the French Revolution! Their *cap*stone third eye chakra, all-seeing eye, was chopped off, *again,* orchestrated by Satanic Masons considering King Louis the XIV was a *historically acknowledged* Sun King in a line of French Sun Kings right up there with Amun Ra and co. France is where Mary Magdalene ran off to post the political assassination of another famous Sun King, a well-known *solar* deity, the king of the Jews, *Jesus Christ!* It's all in the family apparently. Like King Kennedy, here we have the killing of the Sun King *and* Sun Queen mocking the sacred union of the husband and wife and their sun-crown of enlightenment gained via tantric sex inside marriage. During this scene you can *distinctly* hear the roar of a bull as the constellation *Taurus* the bull rules over the throat while the phonetic *torus* field, aura, is strengthened via tantric sex. Taurus the Bull has a dark side, the Minotaur, the beast! The Egyptian Apis bull was the most highly regarded deity in ancient Egypt and represented the embodiment of Ptah (Peter) the god of Craftsmen, Masons! Named Osiris-Apis it became Serapis said to represent Osiris totally. The many bull related rituals and ceremonies all boil down to this including not eating meat on a Friday, the 'season of penance', between Ash Wednesday and Easter. Incredibly, *see right*, Clay Shaw's character is dressed as Greek god Hermes(!) renamed *Mercury* by the Romans who rules over *the voice* known as the Messenger of the Gods. The Speaker! Gemini, the lovers, 11, rules over Mercury-Hermes as the arms in context of the voice means *passionate speaking* or gesticulating vigorously with the hands. *This* is why they shot Kennedy in the throat to ritually symbolise 'silencing *the voice*' of the 'Speaker' and thus *'shoot the Messenger'*. Hermes was a bisexual tantric sex practitioner and Gemini, the brothers, was rejigged as the *male lovers* because Satanism is all about pleasure.

They shot Kennedy three times in a reference to the 'triple killing' of the king as ancient British-Euro peat bogs have heralded the phenomenon of the 'bodies in the bog'. The 'boogeyman' finds its roots in the 'bog man'. These mummified ancient remains were often killed 'three times' often involving clubbing the head, slitting the throat and garroting among a suit of gory ritualistic methods symbolising sun god and moon goddess 'worship'. The say soul comes from the sun and emotions come from the moon so these weird practices are deeply rooted in destroying our connection to our souls and messing up our emotions happening more now than ever. It was said if the crops failed the king had displeased the Goddess and must die three times. They were a lovely lot. The moon has three *major* phases: waxing, full and waning symbolised as the maiden, the mother and the crone. So, Kennedy was shot three times, in the back, the throat and the head. Hiram Abiff the chief architect of King Solomons Temple was also killed three times; throat cut, blow to the head and struck in the chest.

It is apparently the same story as Egyptian King Seqenenre Tao II who died in an almost identical manner. It's the same with Rasputin who was poisoned, beaten and shot. His killers threw him in the river as water was found in his lungs so he ultimately drowned although I'm sure they thought the job was done! Triple killing. Interestingly, Rasputin's penis was cut off in a weird homage to the Osiris fable whose penis was *also* cut off symbolically *emasculating* him. Rasputin learned his sexual secrets from a monastery of monks although he left them as he was unhappy about their practice of homosexuality. The song *'Ra-Ra-sputin, lover of the Russian Queen'* like Vladimir (ras)Putin is ritual mockery to kill the 'sun', the light, or the greatest *'stars'* (*see*, Hollywood stars) and replace them with darkness. The 27 Club of dead celebrities is 2+7=9, a number of *completion and transformation.* They don't want that. Rasputin had become close to the last royal dynasty of Russia, the Romanovs, and it appears they were murdered for heightening their kundalini via this method.

The French royal family hailed from the House of Bourbon until the French Revolution after which they were briefly restored until the line of Bourbons were finally overthrown in July 1830. A 'cadet' branch of the Bourbons, the House of Orleans, then ruled for 18 years until they too were overthrown in 1848, hence, *New* Orleans. An ancient prophecy from Merlin of Arthurian legend says, 'what was lost by a woman will be regained by a woman'. So, interestingly, the town of Orleans was the place where Joan of Arc received her visions that the English King planned to invade France and based off this knowledge, France staved him off. She was later burnt at the stake. She was nick-named the 'Maid of Orleans' as was Isis and Mary associated as 'the maid' associated with domestic life though not a housekeeper. Maid is also 'maiden', a young woman'. Her name Joan of Arc was claimed as a variation of her father's name although this is not confirmed. Yet *note,* the name 'Arc' of the Covenant, the *arc* of the *rainbow,* the light spectrum seen by the human eye as found in the chakras. She was also dubbed 'Virgin of Orleans'. Yes, the Virgin Mary. On trial she would not concede to a standard witness oath as it would conflict with an oath she had made to maintain the *confidentiality of meetings* with the French King. Considering these French Kings were a line of Sun Kings, was Joan of Arc practicing tantric sex in her secret meetings with the king hence, her heightened IQ, psychic abilities and her 'visions'? Is this the fabled Cinderella-Beauty and the Beast story *again*, the royal male and the common girl? *See right,* a golden statue of her bearing a striking resemblance to the 'golden' statues of the sun kings specifically, *Hermes* as found in New Orleans!

Mercury-Hermes in mythology and astrology (same thing, really) was called The Messenger of the Gods who rules over communication, travel, technology, thieves and commerce. These things *literally* sum up our current age. Jesus was the 'messenger' of god described in Malachi 3:1 "Behold, I send my messenger" Orion was called The Hunter, the 'messenger and gatekeeper', to the gods while Mercury, Hermes, Jesus, Zoroaster as well as Iris, Angelia, *Arke* (Joan of Arc) etc., were all 'messenger' gods and goddesses who ran errands between the people and 'the gods', whoever they are, specifically about the *laws of the universe;* Love thy neighbour! Turn the other cheek! Free Will. Non-violence. Togetherness. Love is the Law. However, in removing the feminine from the conversation they removed the heart, the Queen, and made the 'voice' of the 'speaker', the king, male only. Male is mind. The true *message* was lost. The 'temple' or the 'church' of the Goddess is Mother Earth and why Mary is 'the church' as *her body*, the flesh, her *electrical* aspect, was used to unlock the male positive aspect, the 'sun', to gain the *confidence* and *IQ* to speak. But not of love! They are masculine mind so they use this for power only. Given they are supposed to be 'royalty', Donald Trump's son is named Barron while the new president 'elect' Joe Biden's son is named *Hunter*. Orion is the Hunter.

This is all relates back to fables and fairytales about an ancient 'prophecy' that one day peace would reign on Earth or the 'happily ever after' and humans would *ascend*. They often mention 'weaving' and the 'spinning wheel' in old fables. In the fable of Rumpelstiltskin, *again*, we see the innocent maiden being tricked by a strange little man, *right*. All of these fables are about demons, black magic, the dark side of tantric sex, virgins, evil 'queens', frog princes  (reptilian royalty), commoners, aristocracy and wizards etc. The themes are all the same tied to astrology hence, the 'spinning' wheel is a symbol of the zodiac and in this image the wheel has 12 spokes of the 12 zodiac signs although often it will have *8 spokes* symbolising the collapse of space and time or 'the quickening' we are currently experiencing. It's a slipstream. Humans have two eyes that see our 3D world however, we have a third eye, the pineal gland, the *all-seeing* eye, that sees the *unseen* world. If our third eye was open we would see the *hordes* of demonic energies and entities all around us attacking humanity attached to the very earth itself! In Sleeping Beauty, she pricks her finger on a spindle but you can also prick yourself on the *needle*. Rumpelstiltskin 'spins straw into gold' symbolic of the *Midas* touch of tantric enlightenment as everything you touch 'turns to gold'. *Goldfinger!* There are three obelisks in the world called Cleopatra's Needle, *see right;* one in London, one in New York and one in *Paris*. Cleopatra was just another name for Isis, Mary, Diana or, the Prime Feminine, the Goddess, and the 'needle', obelisk, is a phallus, a penis, so in fairy tales when they refer to the spindle or needle or indeed the rose *thorn* that 'pricks' either

the male or female characters, they mean the penis in a reference to sex. Slang for a penis is 'prick' and women often refer to men as 'pricks'. The spindle is associate originally with the goddess Ananke sister and consort of Chronos god of time, Satan.

A 'box' is slang for a woman's vagina, Pandora's 'box' or root chakra, and once 'opened' i.e. third eye chakra, it cannot be closed. The 'thorn' in the side of the 'rose' the feminine (the vagina) is men, the 'prick' (penis) is a muddled reference to the 'fish' tower of the chakras in tantric sex. The penis 'golden' phallus, *'Goldmember'*, represents the 'rod' of the spinal column of the nervous system as the 007 'Goldfinger', the Midas Touch, turns everything the tantric King touches to gold manifesting as the wealth, adventure and happiness enjoyed by celebrity who are secret agents and royalty. This is how they get their power. I believe humans have been disconnected from our astral self that lives on other plains of existence. Our fourth, fifth, sixth extra-dimensional selves are what some have called the 'over soul' or 'higher' self that *sees* all via the pineal gland *outside* the *linear* 'timeline' we have been trapped in. The 3rd eye sees the past, present *and* future in one coalesced space or the 'eternal now'. This infinite moment is what the reptilian hybrids via all sorts of methods are connected to accessing *their* higher selves and why they run the world as they do as they can see things before they happen. They see 'probabilities' as shown in the movie Men in Black III and 'weave' through potential circumstances to their preferred outcome. Satanists use technology along with their access to the *pantheon* of the demonic realm to do their bidding and why King Solomon (*note*, Sol- Sun and Mon-Moon) 'bound many demons' via this power. Many in history have claimed to do this including the famous Merlin of King Arthur's Court, a legendary Sun King, in the magical realm of Camelot! And what was the Kennedy clan referred to? Camelot. Even JFK Jr., was killed as the prophecy says the son will avenge the father or Horus taking on uncle Set, the devil, avenging his father, Osiris! Weaving' in ancient fables means 'weaving spells' as spindles weave and so do spiders via the powers of unlocked chakras, greater IQ and psychic ability. The movie Final Destination is *loaded* with tantric sex symbols and is a great insight into how this works. Fairy stories are all about Satanism which is the practice of manipulating the unseen threads of the lifeforce, chi, prana and we all have the capacity to do this if our *third eye* was open we would engage with the playing field instead of just being spectators in our current capacity. It's their worst nightmare. They manipulate the geodesic baseline energies, the building blocks of reality, via symbols, intentions, chanting, rituals, technology and demons to keep us in a very bad place.

With all this in mind we can see something *very weird* is going on (apart from everything else). So, how strange is it that Aldous Huxley, C.S. Lewis (the Chronicles of Narnia) and President Kennedy all died on the *same day*, the 22.11.1963! The numbers 3, 6 & 9 or the "three 3's" have great significance for the controllers as it represents the 'cube'. It also represents the zodiac and the clock as we never reach the 12th gate to 'get out'. They skip us back to the beginning 'loop' of *their* preferred 'time' as Cronus, Satan, is, after all, the god of time. Aldous Huxley wrote over *fifty books* on mysticism, humanism and universalism remembering all gods and goddesses in history, myth and legend all represent aspects, variations and offshoots of the Prime Masculine and the Prime Feminine or the positive and negative *electrical* forces of nature. As such, Mary Magdalene and Mother Mary bear the initials MM and in fairy tales the dark queen looks into the mirror, *the looking glass* of universe, the zodiac – *astrology,* and says, "*Mirror, Mirror* on the wall…". Before the fables were altered she said, "*Magic Mirror* on the wall" and she is always trying to find out who is more 'beautiful' than her. The point is MM is the Roman Numeral for the year 2000, the cusp of the *third* millennium, and in the tarot deck the number three is symbolic of the goddess, the Empress. This is Her time. The Nazi *Third* Reich, *themselves* German Masons and their obsession with Twins, were attempting to understand the nature of the legendary 'twin' myths. Reich means 'realm' and a 'realm' lasts for 1000 years so the 'third' Reich is the third thousand year realm, *the third millennium,* we enter now. This 'great work' is far more tenacious than we gave them credit for as Old Egypt *was also creating a one world!*

So, we've come to a rather strange story called the Warr Acres Disappearance in Oklahoma. On the eve of the assassination of President Kennedy, the night of the 21st November 1963, mother and daughter Margery and Melinda Elston (*note,* the initials MM) left their house to visit a friend and stop by the store. Her husband never saw them again and their mysterious disappearance would go unanswered for decades. The husband, Robert Gentry Elston, was an *energy tycoon* who owned and operated the *National Electric Company* remembering the big secret of our world is free electricity broadcast from the cosmos harnessed easily via tantric sex like pistons in an engine. One newspaper article about Elston was titled *Lighting for the Brightest Future*. He married his second wife Mary Jane in 1970 and later would marry his third wife Margaret Alice Crite. So, we have an *energy* tycoon whose wives and daughter were all named Margery Melinda Mary and Margaret. MM MM. The light and dark side of Mary Magdalene the Goddess, *see right,* Anthony Summers (*note, summers-fire*) biography on Marilyn Monroe *another* MM. I know this all sounds weird just hang in there. The car his wife and daughter were driving was eventually located in a popular swimming hole in 1990 called *Hefner* Lake and remains an *unusual* accident to say the least. Although Hefner Lake was searched a small pond off the lake was not as they didn't think a car could submerge so deeply. Marilyn Monroe was first featured on the cover of the very *first* Playboy Magazine published by Hugh *Hefner* in a public robbing of an innocent young woman's virtue by *real* playboys, the Kennedy's, who passed her around like a *prostitute*. Sex baron *Hugh Hefner's* initials are HH, the 8th letter of the alphabet, and becomes 88. The planet Mercury takes 88 days to go around the sun. Mercury *is* Hermes is the *Messenger* of the Gods who is worshiped by Satanists as he rules over the voice, *the speaker*, who carries the caduceus tantric sex enlightenment staff to become King! It's all symbolic coding, *ritual*, like a cosmic *software* program. They promote the dark side of the king and kill the light side as seen the *weirdness* of inventor *Howard Hughes* and *Harold Holt* the Aussie Prime Minister king who *vanished!*

Robert Gentry Elston's second wife Mary Jane passed away the same year the car was found and he married his last wife Margaret who passed away after he died. Now it gets *really* weird. At the time of the disappearance the State Bureau Crime agent assigned to the case, *right*, was a man called *Golden Kennedy!* All of this on the very eve of the *Kennedy* assassination given he was a *Sun King* as was Jesus whose mother and wife, the *Goddess*, were the two Mary's. The king was symbolised by the golden phallus as was Hermes depicted as golden in many statues. These sun kings, like pharaohs, are often depicted as golden or the

Golden Kennedy

'Golden Boy', golden ball, that rises in the morning phonetically 'mourning' as they steer us away from the light. 'God' never gets his crown, it was shot off, and the 'goddess', the Goddess, the 'Golden Girl, fails at love and even *kills herself*, that's how fucked-up *she* is. This is why the tv series 'the Golden Girls' were about a bunch of

old ladies as a Masonic *inside joke* that the evil brotherhood overseeing all this waste away the youth of the goddess until there is nothing left of her beauty but a withered old husk. They are the personification of evil. G is the 7th letter of the alphabet and becomes 77 of the male-female chakras the same year Elvis the 'king' died. Journalist Dorothy Kilgallen who penned this article was later killed for investigating the JFK incident. "Jack and Jill went up the hill to fetch a pail of water, Jack fell down and broke his *Crown* and Jill came tumbling after". Let's just say "all the kings horses and all the kings men, couldn't put Humpty together again". John Lopez the artist of the golden statue of Kennedy said he gave JFK Snr. & Jnr., more of a 'golden hue' than his other presidential sculptures who are all bronze. The video of

this weird story can be found on YouTube called *The Mysterious Case That Was Overshadowed by John F Kennedy's Assassination.* The name of the town *Warr Acres* is the war mongers destroying the peaceful king while the town is famous for being '*almost* the *capital*' but didn't quite make it because the *cap*stone, third eye of the pyramid, is never attached. This is an amazing example of '*Weaving*' spells depicted in fairy tales. It's as if a big crime needs an echo or shadow effect to lock it into the astro-script. At Bohemian Grove where world leaders secretly meet a sign hangs above the entrance 'Weaving Spiders Come Not Here'. I'm not loony for noticing, I'm just showing you what they're doing.

Kennedy was shot at 12:30pm *high noon* and died at 1pm, *the* One. Strangely, Lee Harvey Oswald was also killed at 12:30pm *high noon* by Jack Ruby, note, the name *Ruby* of the root chakra. This is the Ruby Slippers in the Wizard of Oz that *earth* the root chakra. High noon is when the sun is at its peak in the sky when the sun rays of the *Sun God* are at their strongest as sunlight *photons* carry packets of information just like the internet. They are broadcasting these ritual events via the minds of the collective conscious which then transmits the signal via the sun to the centre of the galaxy and, like a mirror, it broadcasts the signal *back* to us and the electrical *circuit is complete* locking us in and we just go round and round.
It never ends. *This* is the secret to satanic astrology, a cosmic trick or should I say 'trip' as, like a trip wire, they are *hacking* the universal broadcast. The lead actress in the film High Noon was *Grace* Kelly or Hail Mary, full of *Grace*. The Goddess. Grace Kelly was *another* Princess who died in a mysterious car accident. There's always *more* weirdness around the Kennedy's who are no 'angels' as they play the victims. Note in the movie High Noon Grace Kelly is his new bride named Amy Fowler wearing *white* but the whore is ruby-red, root chakra, sex. RFK was shot after midnight at 1:44am in a reference to the 144,000 souls of the Bible killed on *6th* day of the *6th* month in 1968 which reduces to *6. 666.* Six in the tarot deck is pleasure as such, six is sex! Six Six Six is *Sex Sex Sex.* It's everywhere once you know what you're at. Tarot is designed by Masons and a fascinating insight into the *compendium of knowledge* they have accumulated from various cultures. In the Thoth Tarot deck the 6 of Cups is the Tree of Life *(the nervous system)* 6 being the 'number of the sun' known as 'Christ' or 'Buddha' consciousness in the Sign of *Scorpio* and 'places the whole influence of the Sun in the suit of Water' a reference to the 'fire' of his loins being in the 'water' of her loins to create matter. The sun was in the Age of Scorpio thousands of years ago when all this kicked off around 12,000 years ago when Isis looked for Osiris with *7 scorpions.* This zodiac thing is nearing completion as the universe is like a lung that expands and contracts and why sometimes you see the 'wheel' of the zodiac (depicted as a ships wheel or a 'spinning' wheel) with 12 spokes or 8 spokes as the universe is in a contraction

right now and we are 'losing' 4 zodiac signs at she gives 'birth' to something totally new. It's the Vitruvian Man, *right,* expanding and collapsing. No one knows what is going to happen as we enter a new age taking a *quantum leap* toward a whole new paradigm. Scorpio rules over the loins in a return to tantric enlightenment of the married couple and the Family of Life per ancient *zodiac prophecy.* 666 is 999 inverted and the end of a *huge* cycle!

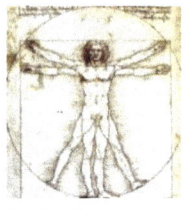

When RFK was shot the front cover of the *Los Angeles Times* was *loaded* with symbolism. This is how elite people talk to each other putting it right in your face. Firstly, Los Angeles means *The Angels* Times a reference to 'Angelic Kings' also called the Order of Virtues, Angels and Rulers. RFK was shot in the head, *right,* as was his brother JFK also shot in the head which is ruled over astrologically by *Aries,* the ram, it's the 'golden fleece' 'crown' of the nervous system found in the hair an extension of the nervous system outside the body. It's all mythological code. RFK was shot at a 'Victory Fete' although there is no victory here.

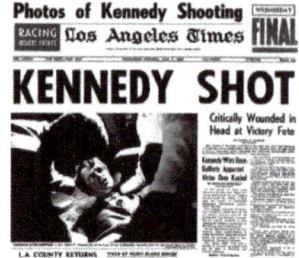

This satanic 'comedy' is apparently hilarious to them as they joke with each other right in our faces. *Note,* the day, *Wednesday,* the day of Mercury-Hermes who is also Wodensday. Woden is Oden, god of war. Notice also 'racing results' supposed to be horses with the sub-heading 'Kennedy Wins Race'. No, he doesn't. *Clearly,* he loses. In the Mickey Mouse Club (MM) 'anything can happen on a Wednesday'. The word 'FINAL' in upper case means it was *final* for them. It's over. It's a game, a sick joke for those in the know.   Jackie Kennedy said, 'If they're killing Kennedy's then my children are targets'. Who are 'they', Jackie? She then took off with billionaire Aristotle *Socrates* Onassis. Socrates nonetheless! Replaying ancient myth again. Onassis had a private island, *Scorpios,* as we are see *more* references to astrology given Scorpio rules over the sexual organs and Isis set out with *seven scorpions* to retrieve the body of Osiris. The Scorpion King, *King Dick,* was the first King of Upper Egypt in 3250BC. Jack Kennedy was Osiris and Jackie, the virgin queen, was the light side of Isis while Marilyn Monroe aka Mary Magdelene was the dark side of the goddess, the whore! They are *characters* chosen for their names and dates of birth etc., in a big *repeating* astrological play. Jackie married Onassis on 20th October as the Sign of Scorpio begins 21st October so their 'wedding night' of consummation crossed over into the first day of Scorpio. She Married JFK on 12th September the day *after* the auspicious date of 9/11 which goes back to ancient Egypt and Ra, the sun god, who is also Osiris, Jesus, Zeus and all the rest of them as *the Father becomes the Son.* They are all sun-kings, sun gods. Ra had 8 offspring and including himself is 9, however, including his wife Hathor and the 'son' Horus (Osiris reborn) this becomes 11 or 9-11 or sequentially, 7 chakras, 9 gods and 11 dimensions equaling the Lovers, of enlightenment. We ultimately have up to 12 chakras so reaching the 11th chakra is damn near universal omnipresence, a living 'god'.

The Twins allows for the Sun, light, 'born' into a man. It's super evolution! So, 'god' is born again and again only what they don't tell you is every man *and* woman is the Sun and therefore every man and woman are god combined. 'Son' didn't mean 'boy' in ancient times. Son meant offspring male *and* female. We are sun beings, warm bodied, we belong in the light, we work in the light. Light Workers *all of us!* It's not a special designation for a few. It is for everyone and they well know it and why they laugh at the meagre attempts of simpletons even at the highest levels trying cash in on this *enormous* zodiac hoax! The trick here is understanding this on multiple levels not only *just* literally but phonetically, symbolically, spiritually, fractally-*replication*, astrally, cosmically. There is no one answer so stop looking for one. Therefore, Kennedy *is* Osiris is Jesus symbolically killed *again and again and again.* Jackie is Marilyn is Isis is Mary ruined or killed *ad infinitum* in the death of the Lovers! The breeding pair. The lovebirds or quite simply, Mum and Dad! Jackie felt Onassis's private security did a far greater job than the Secret Service because whatever is behind the Secret Service lured them into a trap in a *premeditated* public murder of gross international proportions. Onassis's private security, much like the security Princess Diana sought in the billionaire Fayed's, could be relied upon far better than their 'own' government's 'security'. That's because the U.S. Gov is owned and operated by international royal syndicates rooted in Europe and England and the 'War of Independence' (like all wars) was a *staged* event to create a 'republic' or New Rome-come-New Egypt for a New Age and their rising *fake* British sun king, *the devil*, ruling the world as an 'independent' state from America, the Empire State or more specifically, the old world *Empire's State!* Everyone else gets taken out. Yet there is no 'republics' from old-world royal rule although there *is* a prophecy of a republican 'king', a sovereign speaker, and it is every man and every woman on Earth. They can take out one man and indeed keep doing so but they can't take out everyone although they will try! It is the collective One vs. the individual One. Their 'one' will be black, white *and* green - gay, straight and whatever else!

RFK died in June 1968 and by October 1968 his sister-in-law Jackie had married Onassis. It was to be short-lived as only six years later Onassis died after entering the *American Hospital in Paris* for a muscular complaint related to his *heart*. So symbolic! I go into some detail later in the chapter Lady Liberty about the French Connection, the 'frogs', and the royal-fairy tale obsession with the French. Jackie was only married for six years before Onassis *too* seems to have been become another victim of the international state considering his middle name was Aristotle and all this relates back to ancient Greek, Roman and Egyptian myths playing out in modern times. After the death of his father, uncle and stepdad, JFK jr., was sent by Jackie to get some gritty real-world experience with John Perry Barlow a songwriter for the Grateful Dead. Everyone in the universe knows the Grateful Dead are up to their eyeballs in agency work constantly travelling for 'concerts'. No offence but the best spies are the ones in-your-face and why celebrity makes for a perfect cover, *see*, 2020 & Beyond for a list of celebrity spies their entertainment jobs being a perfect reason to enter any country 'on location'. Barlow's parents sent him to Fountain Valley Military Academy in Colorado Springs famous for Tesla's secret experiments where he met fellow 'hell raiser' Bob Weir who co-founded the Grateful Dead. Barlow then moved to Connecticut (a major celebrity mind-control hub) attending Wesleyan university majoring in the study of Comparative Religion, the study of 'systematic comparison of doctrines'. That's education speak for 'nicking everyone else's cultural shit'. Talk about inside tracks. He then lived in India, of course, as that's where tantric sex reigns from and why John Lennon and co went there becoming new age Messiahs. Barlow's interest in LSD, psychoactive drugs as well as ranching and cyber rights led to him founding the *Electronic Frontier Foundation* to 'preserve online civil liberties'. Clearly, that's worked. Everything is a front. As owner he said he was, 'sitting at the Galactic Headquarters of the Bar Cross land and livestock company' when he received a breathy call from Jacqueline Onassis asking to get her son John John some rugged manly experience out on the farm.

The Bar Cross Ranch is where *Virgin Galactic* leased the land for the world's first purpose-built commercial spaceport *virgingalactic.com/spaceport, see right*. Here we go! Can I have a thank you Jesus? Can it get any weirder? Why have we not heard of this? It looks like something out of *Star Trek* and the  young JFK is hanging out with these guys considering his dad put a man on the moon? JFK sr. was a sacrifice for the space program and the *new-age* President, *the One*, will be an astronaut space leader, a new-age Captain Kirk, all primed in advance to make our Hollywood dreams come true as the dick cult takes operations into *space* fucking the feminine universe! I don't think *reality* quite fits with their *fantasies* about size, *see right*. This dick cult goes back a *long* way! 'Virgin Galactic' is a reference to the Galactic Virgin, the Queen, the 'Goddess'  of the universe, Aether, life-force energy, chi, prana, and the power behind *male* tantric sex enlightenment accessed via *Her*. *She* grants them the 'right' to go into space to 'elevate' themselves via the feminine. The One World leader will be the Biggus Dickus of Earth when we are 'introduced' to a wider cosmic community in a fake 'contact' scenario already playing out before our eyes as the Pentagon release video that 'UFOs are real'. Only they are aligning us with the bad guys of the galaxy. They're *already* preparing for it only *you* are not invited and that's what this is all about. What are the odds that Jackie would send John-John to hang out with a quasi-agency son of *another* political-military family whose father was Republican Rep., Norman Barlow? John Denver son of an Air Force Officer was born in *Roswell*, New Mexico, yes, the alien crash site. He received a NASA Public Service medal for his 'Citizens in Space Program' and was *another* weird death offering, by the way, his songs are *loaded* with pagan tantric sex clues like Mountain Mama. I'm telling ya, these military big wigs are putting their kids through the scientific cutting edge of 'superman' programs garnered out of the Nazi war machine via operation Paperclip to create a new league of political-religious-corporate space 'royalty' to take *MOTHER* Earth into the Space age using all these symbols and terminology *from the past* to pull it off! King Kennedy, his brother *and* his son were an all a symbolic offering, a sacrifice, representing the 'Angels' team of the upper classes, the 'good' guys, beaten and laughed at in a sick joke by team Devil i.e. grey aliens and reptilians *behind all this* spawning their *alien baby*, the anti-Christ, in a New World Space Order *see*, Denver Airport for *that* gem.

What went down on 911 in 2001 considering in numerology 2001 reduces to 3 as well the 102 minutes *exactly* that it took from the first impact to the third collapse is, *again*, the number of the Empress. She is the *same Prime Feminine*, all Goddess coding, *including* Virgo the *virgin* in the month of September and all up this is *no coincidence*. Numerologists are all over 911 but there is some crucial missing information that ties it all together and paints a much deeper, darker picture if that's possible. The two towers (thank you, J.R. Tolkien) of the World Trade Centre represented the Masculine and Feminine 'twins', men and women of Earth, the 11 in harmony, symbolised by Gemini the Lovers. They even *looked* like the number 11, *right*, purpose built for a *massive* symbolic sacrificial ritual to their demon god killing the masculine-feminine positive-negative electrical force of men and women firstly in our hearts and minds and *then* kill us outright to finish off the job! To *kill the light on Mother Earth*. When men and women combine their unique powers they are unstoppable. Manhattan-henge, *right*, was an event where the  Manhattan Solstice *aligned perfectly* East-West in New York City with the setting or rising sun falling between the *pillars of light*, the gates of heaven, the Twin Towers of chakra enlightenment, as does *Stonehenge* and basically *all major ancient monuments* on the Solstice, a *powerful* gateway transmission eluding to the 'light' that rises and sets with the Twins, mum and dad, *god and goddess!* The ancients worshiped the light found in the parents born into the offspring but this demonic cult that crushed their knowledge continues *one big ritual* and *we* then collectively, *unwittingly,* broadcast this message to the Universe, a huge transistor, that the masculine and feminine of Planet Earth have *collapsed* in flames instead of going up, ascending into the light, *as prophesised!*

The male tower, the 'father', was exactly 10 stories higher than the female tower, the 'mother'. As 10 reduces to 1, then the 110-story building becomes 11 and the 'mother' at exactly 100 stories high becomes 1. Between them they represent 111giving us the number 3 again, the number of the Empress. The shortest tower, Building 7, *above,* represented their 'child' and was 47 stories high as 4+7=11, the twins *again.* It was strangely designed in a *trapezoidal* shape given the trapezoid was one of my symbols regarding all this and this shape represents Orion-Osiris, their god, 'the father', who's geometric shape in the stars make up *two trapezoids.* Sirius aka Isis, the 'dog star', is the 'wife' of Osiris in the stars as it is the brightest star nearest Orion. So, Sirius the 'wonder dog' was the 'only dog' killed on 911 given *K-9 reduces to K=11 and 9* or 911 *again*! The three towers also represent the 3 main pyramids of Giza that, *again,* consist of a taller 'father' a slightly shorter 'mother' and shortest 'child' that align with the three stars on Orion's belt that point toward Sirius. Called 'Khufu', 'Khafre' and 'Menkaure' they are actually the temples of Osiris, Isis and Horus, the trinity, mother, father and child. If they were designated *properly,* as they used to be, more people would understand the *power* of this myth and where it's taking us so labelling them something else diverts attention away from their *true* meaning. As with Dealey Plaza and the Kennedy assassination, these ritual 'temples' are designed *well in advance*. But it goes on. The *first* plane to hit the towers was American Airlines flight *11* or AA11 meaning 11:11 hitting the *north* tower first, the male-father tower, at 8:46am (8+4+6=18 or 6+6+6 or 1+8=9). It hit

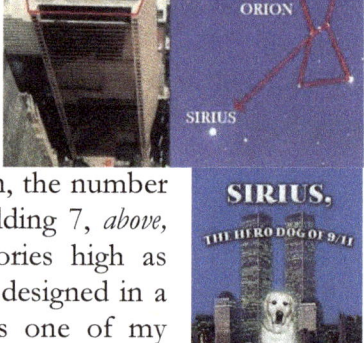

between floors 93 and 99 as 9 and 6 are symbolically the same number inverted. This is *another* reference to the 3,6,9 of the Egyptian Great Ennead symbolising the cube, *right*, a feminine symbol of the root chakra while every other line equals six or sex. The second plane to hit was *United* Airlines 175 which reduces to 13 a highly occult number as '*united* we stand divided we fall' indicating 'United' *falling*. The 7/7 London bombings were also rituals to destroy the *rising* 7 male-female chakras and *descend* them in flames and violence in the '*United*' Kingdom. Same with the 'king' Elvis (anagram of Lives and Evils) dying in '77. Flight AA77 or 1177 that hit the Pentagon represents the 11 twins of the male-female Lovers and their 'twin towers' or the 7-7 mutual chakras. United Airlines 93 *(again*, 3, 6 & 9) crashed in Shanksville as to 'shank' someone is to stab them. All this is a ritual to symbolise the death of the Mother, Father and child, the family, the *household*, to replace mum and dad with *one* hierarchical despot, The One, the Devil incarnate, in a *One* World system that will control ever iota of the family right down to birth control as soulless babies are produced in artificial wombs called *Mother* like the human crops in the movie *The Matrix* harvesting us for our light, *literally*.

In mid-May 2020, the month of Taurus or *torus field*, which is also the beast Minotaur, President Trump unveiled the flag for their new 'Space Force'. Force...war. Describing space as the 'ultimate high ground' in a 'historic moment' claiming *non-specific* 'adversaries' have made space a 'war fighting domain' and with the establishment of 'Space Force and United States Space Command...to protect our assets...to protect America...and sustain our economy...our commercial capabilities...and American's way of life'. They went on to describe the 'North Star  as our core value, our guiding light...and the space capabilities that fuel our American way of life and *our American way of war*'. The North Star is also called the *Pole Star* a symbol of the masculine penis-pole as, again, *north-positive* electricity is male and *south-negative* electricity is female. Reinforcing this on their flag is the north pointing vector the 'delta' symbol or upright triangle, the sword, another penis symbol, the spear tip, a weapon. Their logo looks *strikingly similar* to the Star Trek logo. It's embarrassing. The date is in Roman numerals as it's the continuation of the Egyptian-Roman empire not to mention the spiders web wrapped around Earth like a net as the circle, like rope on ritual dolls, is a 'binding' symbol also meaning a ring or eternity. It's a dick cult. Phallic worship. The North Star is also known  as the Big Dipper but more importantly the *Swastika System, below right*, yes, Nazis behind all this. It's the symbol of the hyper-masculine *death cult* war machine, the Nazi's, and under normal circumstances this symbol *should* not be depicted on *any* Western imagery. It should, however, be featured with the reversed *Eastern feminine swastika* to balance out the energies per Buddhism but on its own it means the Satanic dick cult fucking the feminine universe after it's finished raping mother Earth and killing the mother and father, the Twins! This *giant leap* toward synthetic scientific *godlike* global control has *already* sunken into an *emergency* of biblical proportions and fittingly the code for this is *911!*

While 911 was going down President George Bush Jr., was reading a book to a classroom of children called *The Pet Goat* or *My Pet Goat* from the *Rainbow Edition* given their god is a goat and it's all about the *rainbow* of chakra enlightenment found in the *visible light* spectrum of Universal Light or Love-Life force *electricity* of Chi, Prana, Qi etc.! The children chant "Kite Hit Steel Plane Must!" or "Kite-plane must hit steel!" *exactly* as the *planes* were *hitting steel* structures in a fine example of how profoundly SICK elite *Satanists* and their rituals are considering the twin towers represent mother and father, *Human* men and women practicing tantric lovemaking, that allows for men to become Superman or 'man of steel' and the enlightened feminine, Wonder Woman! 911 was a *massive sun ritual* to cut out the heart of America and hold it up to their alien demon fire god! From an interview in 1989 wrestling commentator 'Mean' Gene queued *Hulk Hogan, note,* H is the 8th letter of the alphabet so HH is 88 the number of days the planet Mercury-Hermes navigates the sun, their *favourite* ancient god, god of TRADE, COMMERCE and THIEVES while *the Hulk* is a laboratory enhanced *green man mutant!* Mean Gene asks, "Hulk Hogan macho man, Randy Savage and the lovely Elizabeth. *Three people working as one* with *one purpose in mind* to defeat, or should I say *demolish, the Twin Towers!* Hulk Hogan you talked about the triangle of love, Jesse Ventura says there's a problem, explain!" Hogan, "Well, you know, Mean Gene, you get right to the *heart* of the matter with that question, brother. It's the *Love* man! It's gonna supercharge the mega-powers and tear down the twin towers!" At Bohemian Grove where powerful elite globalist's gather to carry out satanic rituals and design Earth's future in secret, they frequently dress in trashy racist, sexist outfits, *right*, mostly to degrade the feminine and mock women. These people are your leaders, like Hoover, busting gays yet privately wearing dresses. There's no irony, they are twisted. They hate the feminine because they want to *be* her, like Buffalo Bill in Silence of the Lambs but more on *that* later!

Love is light which is *electricity* and it is this super charged light twisted into fire they are suped up on blinded by the power it yields. They intend to use this *power* to destroy the trinity, of the Mother, Father and Child and the stable family home, true love, as more families than ever fall apart and destitution abounds! Their weird version of the 'triangle of love' is the light and dark side of the masculine, God and the Devil, and the feminine Goddess in a weird spiritual menage a trois! The dark side continues to try to keep men anchored to it by greed and violence while the Goddess waits patiently in the wings for the good guy to come back to her to defeat the devil *together*. Our world and everything we experience is one big mind-controlled ritual. It's so goddam huge it's unfathomable but like a pyramid, the directives simply trickle down into all the compartments carried out by smaller components of the whole who have *no idea* what the other departments are really doing, like a well-oiled machine! From the movie Rituals filmed in the auspicious year of 1977 one character observes, "There's a certain kind of unholy precision to this whole thing. Nothing's been left to chance. To draw us out. It all seemed to come together at the same time. Location. Precision. We're being drawn deeper and deeper into a kind of demonic ritual. We're being used and this thing, which is a seminiferous force, knows that if it performs certain 'accidents' in a certain order, certain other things are bound to happen. He knows he really has us. *And be appeased the path.* I was just invoking a bit of the old demon". On *Halloween* 1975 (which reduces to 22 or 11:11) Martha Mosley, *another* MM, was 15 years old and found dead beneath a *tree* in her backyard. She was beaten with a golf *club* so severely the club was broken into three pieces. Clubs, rods, swords, staffs, scepters, wands and *canes* etc., are *all* symbols of the penis or 'it's not the size of the wand but how you use it'. Sex magic. It's the dark side and they are using the *same* force, electricity of the universe, which can be used for good or evil it just depends on who's wielding the 'wand'. The Geni simply responds to whoever command it! *Note,* this happened on Halloween, the *31ˢᵗ October,* a Satanic ritual night as the doors between dimensions are said to be wide open on this night! Martha had been at a neighbour and friends house the night before whose name was Michael Skankel and despite evidence he did it, authorities claimed it was a random attack because not only was he rich but he was the cousin of *Robert F. Kennedy*. Years later DNA proved it *was* Michael Skankel who admitted he'd been there earlier doing lude acts. Piling evidence caused police to re-open the case where he was trialed and convicted in 2002. The Kennedy family including RFK Jr., vaccine hero, petitioned for his release who even penned a book called *'Framed'*. In 2013 Michael Skankel was released on *1.2 million dollars* bond wearing a GPS monitor. He was to have no contact with the victim's family, not to leave Connecticut and check in via phone although 'somehow' he relocated to New York in 2016. Connecticut Supreme Court reinstated the murder conviction and in May 2018 his conviction was vacated ordering a new trial. State Court ordered a review of the High Court ruling although this was denied by the Supreme Court. These people are as dark as Satan's balls. In Justine Fitzgerald's book *The Aquarian Conspiracy* she says the 'new age' will be underpinned by money barons getting on board the peace train. More like gravy train.

As these geomancers old and new are weaving the ancient myths into modern times *mimicking* the *natural* repetitive cycles of the cosmos we find cowgirl gunslinger Belle Starr was born in *Carthage* famous for its ancient battle. She was taught the classical languages as a girl including Latin and Ancient Greek, her horse was called, of all things, *Venus*, while Belle Starr translates as Beautiful Star. *Sirius*. Yes, Venus is a symbolic 'replicant' of Sirius. Belle Starr's killer was never bought to justice despite it being quite obvious who had *shot her in the back* as if it wasn't bad enough that a man shot her but was so cowardly he even shot her from behind when she wasn't looking. Very symbolic of the betrayal of the feminine overall. It's interesting then that the sinking of the Titanic was 'predicted' (*not really*, it's a script) in a book *14 years* prior called *Futility*, or the *Wreck of the Titan* by Morgan Robertson. His story tells of a ship, The Titan, and *exactly* like the *Titanic* it hits an iceberg on the starboard side which occurs in April 400 nautical miles off Newfoundland *both* with less than half the required lifeboats. The Titan was speeding at 25 knots while Titanic was speeding at 23 knots. Robertson's Titan was 800 feet in length while the Titanic was 885 feet. Both were said to be unsinkable and *both* went down the same, bow first. The fictional Titan went down with 2,500 onboard while Titanic went down with 2,208 people onboard. The *100th year anniversary* of the sinking of the *Titanic* coincided with the *Olympics* being held in *Britain* given Titanic's sister ships were the *Olympic* and the *Britannic*. The *Olympians* vanquished the *Titans* in Greek mythology and in weird replication it's coming around again *from Britain!* Our world is a massive ritual. The interior designs of the three ships *Titanic, Olympic and Britannic* were drawn up by Arthur Henry Durand who also participated in the design of the Eiffel Tower (French royal dick cult) using the same artisans and craftsman on all three ships. It always traces back the French where Mary Magdalene, an Isis replication, was said to have escaped to when Jesus was knocked off. To all intents and purposes, apart from minor differences in heigh and width, these ships were triplets, *exactly the same*. It's the triple goddess. The lounge was described as a 'magnificent salon' decorated in the style of King Louis XV from the Palace of Versailles. King Louis XV was the king between the 'Sun King' Louis the XIV and King Louis XVI executed during the French Revolution. The three sister ships formed part of the *White Star Line* in a nod toward Sirius the brightest star. Given the Olympians overthrew the Titans in Greek myth, it is no coincidence that the final remnants of the last ship, the Olympic, are located at the White Swan Hotel in *Alnwick Northumberland, Britain* in a nod to the mythical swan of Zeus fame and Swan Lake a reference to the constellation *Cygnus* that contains Deneb one of the *brightest stars in the night sky* called the *White Star Goddess!* Diana was the 'swan' an *ugly duckling* come beauty!

The northern estate of Alnwick, the final resting place of the Olympic, dates to 600AD although the first Lord of Alnwick Castle, Gilbert Tyson, had the estate bestowed upon him by *William* the Conqueror around the mid 1100's. William the Conqueror also called William the Bastard was the first Norman (French) King of England descended from a Viking warrior called Rollo who emerged as the first ruler of Normandy, a northern province of France, when Norse Vikings secured a foothold there. In 911AD (here we go again with the 911) a western French King, *Charles* the Simple, gifted the Vikings the region of Normandy that Rollo came to rule in exchange that they stop raiding the coastal lands and assist in defending France. It was earlier in the year 911 the Norse had attacked Chartres and according to legend Bishop Gantelme exposed the 'Virgin's Tunic' on the ramparts, a robe said to be worn by Mother Mary during the birth of Christ much like the shroud of Turin, leading a mob of peasants to charge the Norsemen who fled. Outside of Alnwick is a Monastery founded in the 13th century called the Carmelites, the Order of the Brotherhood of the Blessed Virgin Mary, *the Goddess!* The 15th century author Sir Thomas Malory whose true identity remains unknown compiled Le Morte d'Arthur the classic English language novel of the Arthurian Legend and claimed Alnwick was a possible location for Sir Lancelot's castle Joyous Garde. Lancelot was eventually exiled to France. A thousand years after this legend incorporating the bloodline of Christ as well as the Titans superseded by the Olympians, the famous sun kings, the French Connection, Camelot, secret sects of Brotherhoods of Mar, 911 (a nod to the Great Ennead at the birth of Ancient Egypt) all, *once again*, woven into the tapestry of *repeating* history as Charles and William reign again! At last, continuing the saga *Queens*land Entrepreneur Clive Palmer intends to build the Titanic II on the *Blue Star Line* given Sirius is referred to as the Blue Angel, a blue star, and the brightest star in the sky. *This* is the *Neverending Story*.

All secret modern *Western* 'royalty' is related to the ancient bloodlines of Ireland, Scotland, Wales, Britain, Europe and further back the Middle East, Ancient Egypt, Rome, Greece, India, parts of Asia and where possible native Chiefs. Their masters have tried to bond them to the *current culture* but secretly *some* are proud of their collective *global* cultural roots and genetic traits. As such, some of these *new-age* rulers are not seeing the ordinary people as the 'traditional' enemy as we all share *some* common traits in a strange eclectic family. New-age secret royals have the advantage of the internet to inform themselves *for the first time in history* outside the doctrines of 'traditional knowledge' mingling with ordinary people for the first time! Their masters have spun them all sorts of crap about the masses yet *some* have gained enough *personal experience* to realise that the common person *is not the enemy* as proven by Kennedy hung out to dry. The betrayals of their own run far deeper than the threat of the average Joe. Their people are smiling assassins even to their own and have *no loyalty* to anyone if it doesn't benefit the plan. So, it emerges the enemy of my enemy is my friend as *no one* is getting out of this. Therefore, one is not so much a Jew than as a descendant of Gaelic kings. We are all mix-bloods now. Traditionally, red-haired Jews were treated poorly by their own as they weren't considered 'full bloods' *or whatever*. It's all bullshit and they know it (well, some of them do). It's the fake pecking order and as no one is perfect then no one is safe. *Anyone* can be targeted at *any* time for *any* reason. The lines are blurring as the world hangs in the balance. Time to decide.

As we enter the 11th House, *Aquarius*, in the 3rd millennium, the Age of the Empress, the Mary Age or 'marriage', we find things occurring *against the rationale* of 'linear' time. For example, the Dream Theatre's (it is) album cover released *exactly* on 9/11 2001 depicts the twin chakra towers and the Goddess, Lady Liberty, going up in flames and, yes, it all played out *live* just like they said. In your face. Whether they know or not they were being used by *something* to play out an evil advance knowledge 'psy-op' including razor wire around the heart-torus-apple of the auric field like a deathcamp or concentration camp *binding* the twins of the *ascending* male-female chakra towers thus *descending* them keeping them captive! They also have album covers with a human skull cupped by robotic hands and a bug, an alien, sitting on top of the world! Considering the chakras and *auric field* are all about unlocking and utilising the *fundamental laws* of Universal Light contained *inside the human body*, Dr Ronald Mallet Professor of Theoretical Physics at the University of Connecticut fascinatingly outlines that gravity is matter, matter affects gravity, energy affects gravity and *gravity* effects *time*. That said, light *does not* have mass or matter but *does* have energy. *Light could affect gravity and thus light can affect time!* There is something of *time travel* connected to the ability of the human light bodies activated chakras and enhanced torus field. Our torus field is unlocked by Love aka Light and Light is information carried on photonic wavelengths broadcast from the universal brain, the 'mind of god' aka *the Universe itself*, which *is* past, present *and* future housed in the *same space at the same time. This is the holograph! The matrix!, and we can change it with the power of our Will directing the Love of the Aether life-force pranic energy!* Dr Mallet is developing technology twisting neurons, *light*, sending information to the past to give himself information about future events via a ring laser *circulating positive-negative neurons* to effectively create a time machine like human batteries of positive-negative *circulating* radiance, *light*, generated by thermal conductive transference between tantric practicing lovers!

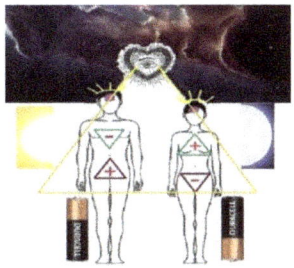

The name Kennedy means Chief, Helmet and *Crowned King* and why he had to die like the twin towers and Diana the goddess. He's 'dad' the king, she's 'mum' the queen and their 'towers' are no more…These three events are the *pivotal ritual events* powerfully symbolising the death of Human Ascension and the Next Generation but there's a tv show for that. Claustrum oil is not only Christ but Krishna, Buddha and *all the rest of them*. It is a *state of consciousness* tracing back to the ancient Vedas that became Hindu culture that the *British aristocracy* tried to bury in their reign of terror. The ancestors of *all* humans were once *great beyond measure* in an eternal time when the world was green and joyous when we were *One!* A time of Moon Goddesses, Sun Kings and *powerful* love story's that evaporated into fables and *fairy tales* as the *Promise and Legacy* became myth and legend *all but forgotten!* They killed the God and Goddess in *every* man and woman, siphoned the light, dignity and valour of old and morphed it into sick twisted carnal pleasures and egotistical *need* to be a *fabricated* concept of 'god'. It's *never* enough. They want *more*. They did all this with *cryptic symbolism* and myths to keep you guessing for *another* 2,000 years. Shame on them. Cyclops the one eyed 'monster' is *another* example of the enlightened third eye, the *all-seeing eye*. Plato said, 'In every man there is an *eye of the soul* which…is more precious far than ten thousand bodily eyes, for by it alone is truth seen'. In many depictions the 3rd Eye looks like a vagina and 'god' an equal blend of masculine and feminine energy housed in one, *right*. All 'Abrahamic' religions, *note*, *A-Brahma*, were pilfered from the East, *India*, where Jesus studied in his 'missing years' as the wandering scholar. The Christ Seed Oil of *enlightenment* was *The Messenger* and the 'capped pyramid' is the all-seeing eye of god, the Twins, the lovers, mum and dad, accessing their *pineal glands* to become *God and Goddess* - the light of the world!

Everyone is the 'messenger' now with unique *in-sight* to share.

CHAPTER FIVE

ORPHEUS. EURYDICE. HERMES
A poem by Rainer Maria Rilke, 1904

This was the eerie mine of souls.
Like silent silver-ore
they veined its darkness. Between roots
the blood that flows off into humans welled up,
looking dense as porphyry in the dark.
Otherwise, there was no red.

There were cliffs
and unreal forests. Bridges spanning emptiness
and that huge gray blind pool
hanging above its distant floor
like a stormy sky over a landscape.
And between still gentle fields
a pale strip of road unwound.

They came along this road.

In front the slender man in the blue cloak,
mute, impatient, looking straight ahead.
Without chewing, his footsteps ate the road
in big bites; and both his hands hung
heavy and clenched by the pour of his garment
and forgot all about the light lyre,
become like a part of his left hand,
rose tendrils strung in the limbs of an olive.
His mind like two minds.
While his gaze ran ahead, like a dog,
turned, and always came back from the distance
to wait at the next bend–
his hearing stayed close, like a scent.
At times it seemed to reach all the way back
to the movements of the two others

who ought to be following the whole way up.
And sometimes it seemed there was nothing behind him
but the echo of his own steps, the small wind
made by his cloak. And yet
he told himself: they were coming, once;
said it out loud, heard it die away . . .
They were coming. Only they were two
who moved with terrible stillness. Had he been allowed
to turn around just once (wouldn't that look back
mean the disintegration of this whole work,
still to be accomplished) of course he would have seen them,
two dim figures walking silently behind:

the god of journeys and secret tidings,
shining eyes inside the traveler's hood,
the slender wand held out in front of him,
and wings beating in his ankles;
and his left hand held out to: her.

This woman who was loved so much, that from one lyre
more mourning came than from women in mourning;
that a whole world was made from mourning, where
everything was present once again: forest and valley
and road and village, field, river and animal;
and that around this mourning-world, just as
around the other earth, a sun
and a silent star-filled sky wheeled,
a mourning-sky with displaced constellations–:
this woman who was loved so much . . .

But she walked alone, holding the god's hand,
her footsteps hindered by her long graveclothes,
faltering, gentle, and without impatience.
She was inside herself, like a great hope,
and never thought of the man who walked ahead
or the road that climbed back toward life.
She was inside herself. And her being dead
filled her like tremendous depth.

As a fruit is filled with its sweetness and darkness
she was filled with her big death, still so new
that it hadn't been fathomed.

She found herself in a resurrected
virginity; her sex closed
like a young flower at nightfall.
And her hands were so weaned from marriage
that she suffered from the light
god's endlessly still guiding touch
as from too great an intimacy.

She was no longer the blond woman
who sometimes echoed in the poet's songs,
no longer the fragrance, the island of their wide bed,
and no longer the man's to possess.

She was already loosened like long hair
and surrendered like the rain
and issued like massive provisions.
She was already root.

And when all at once the god stopped
her, and with pain in his voice
spoke the words: he has turned around–,
she couldn't grasp this and quietly said: who?

But far off, in front of the bright door
stood someone whose face
had grown unrecognizable. He just stood and watched,
how on this strip of road through the field
the god of secret tidings, with a heartbroken expression,
silently turned to follow the form
already starting back along the same road,
footsteps hindered by long graveclothes,
faltering, gentle, and without impatience.

CHAPTER SIX

THE GODDESS

Once loved above all as the source of all knowledge and life she was the 'vital essence', all other icons were considered 'minor nature deities' by comparison.

As with the previous chapters I'm just going to dive right into what is going on here and start at the start. Greek mythology tells us at the beginning of the universe there was the Void which translates as 'infinite space'. Nothingness. They saw it as the 'chasm' and later as the biblical Abyss. The late 19th Century Theosophy movement founded in the United States described it as a field of information, *a projective and receptive energy,* masculine and feminine, but ultimately, androgynous. It's neutral. It's lacks dimension, a point of preconception, *soul energy.* It is formless. Without substance. It is complete balanced energy. Changeless. Eternal. Infinite. Considered a realm of potentiality. *It is unformed galaxies.* It's elemental designation ascribed by the ancients was *meteoric* in nature. It's a 'super element' that houses past, present *and* future. It is the native Great Spirit. The source of all knowledge and life. It is fluid. Water. It's colour is purple black, a dark indigo, the colour ascribed to the third eye charka. Considered the 'gap' it was also called it Chaos.

The ancient historical record under the guidance of self-serving biased ambitious *elite* males, conveniently interpreted the original state-of-being to suit their looming patriarchal systems. So, scheming behind the scenes in the shadows, as usual, they arrogantly called the prime force masculine and attempted to completely consume Mother Earth and destroy the feminine in their continued efforts to take over the *entire* universe to become the version of 'God'. We've experienced an evolutionary ambush and it's time we all take back control of this situation before they finish the job on us. *It's time to evolve.* Evolutionary and revolutionary are but one letter apart. To overcome our oppressors we need to be mature enough to deal with the monstrous elite *lie* that, a) there is a 'god' and, b) it is male. We can either face this simple fact or rapidly go back to darkness via chaos *devolving* into a caveman state *again* which is happening now despite our apparent 'progress'. That said, there *is* a *force* and its certainly *not* the childish image of a bearded old man in the clouds with a few stone tablets. They know we're not buying *that* shit anymore so they are changing-things-up *asap* to catch up off guard and we are witnessing this rapid acceleration as we speak. Elite men have categorised everything in a competitive view, militaristic, to rule over others for eons with *their* bully-boy emotionally inept childish demands. It's a toddler with a handgun calling the shots as the adults carefully edge away so as not to provoke the psycho brat. The proof is in the pudding. Lo ok around at the fallout of this thinking, our planet is broken and humanity is in ruins *because* of their fake 'royal' immaturity and their rich-kid insecure *selfishness* leading us to now face our collective end. It's time the *adults* run the house and put the kids back in the playpen where they belong until they can behave themselves like *grown-ups*.

These obsolete *unevolved* hierarchical attitudes motivated by destructive *contradictory* drivers and pure greed have allowed the elite to *knowingly* and *willfully* blocked their perceptive functions to correctly designate or interpret the mechanics of the *original* state of being. They have therefore *purposefully* steered would-be philosophers of all genders, cultures and races to the *wrong conclusions* resulting in a world of repetitious confusion and *ignorance* throughout *every* civilisation they have commandeered. Simultaneously, they congratulate themselves on how clever they are although this dangerous thinking results from their *scrambled genetics* after *generations* of inbreeding. The end result is apparent *alien behaviour* contradicting *natural evolution*. Why don't they care if they hurt the world? Because it's not their world. Why don't they care if they hurt humans? Because they're not human. It's really that simple. *See right,* Belgium miners going down into the black pit for the profits of aristocratic scum. Also, *see right,* a young man whose image I included before I knew anything about him thinking, 'what's the bet, he's an artist?' Born on Christmas Day 1910, Evgeny Kobytev graduated with Honours in 1941 from Kyiv State Art Institute in Ukraine with a passion for portraits and panoramas. Art doesn't pay much so he worked as a teacher in the rural areas of Krasnoyarsk. A fine teacher and artist turned monster, a *shell* of a human being. These photos were taken four years apart between 1941-1945 before and after WWII. He was in his early to mid-30's here and despite being wounded in battle winding up in a German concentration camp called 'Khorol pit' where approximately *90,000 prisoners* of war died in this Satanic hellhole, he managed to escape and rejoined the Red Army. Yet Russian 'High Command' (aristocratic cunts like all the rest of them) refused to award him the Victory over Germany medal since his military career was 'spoiled' for being a prisoner of war. *Bottom image,* we see daily life in a Warsaw ghetto 1941 as a young woman starves to death in the street. Look at her rags and her dainty little shoes. *Look* at her face. She can't believe it. You might think the other woman is a cruel for walking by and not helping but look how she *clutches* her parcel of *precious* food, look at the strained neck muscles, the tight face. She *can't* help the dying woman. She has her *own* problems. This is the animal brain, the *reptilian* mind, in action. You *must* die so that I can live. The aristocracy hybrid aliens enjoy turning humans into *them* killing humans en masse in various mass sacrifices to their weird dark alien god dressing it all up as necessary wars! Lying for them is an *enjoyable* pastime honed to perfection and carried out to ruin Humanity. *They like it.* They affect and perfect 'normal' behavior to *appear* like humans and fit in but underneath an alien seethes with hatred and carnal brutality only satisfied by human blood!

Whether you're a Russian artist, a Warsaw ghetto woman, a Belgian miner, an Irish peasant, an Aussie 'battler', or an African slave, these 'royal' *scumbags* have ruled and ruined every age that accepts their *abnormal* behaviour as 'normal' and puts up with their *weird* presence in our midst. Education is largely *indoctrination*. We're big enough to admit that now yet *real* knowledge and education benefits the few at the top. This is not *normal* human behaviour to regale oneself in such a way as everyone else suffers. They are very specific in their self-idolatry. *Normal* humans talk of togetherness, sustainable farming, helping the world. Yet these terms are flimsy lies on the lips of venomous snakes *posing* as us! The 'pure doctrine' of Satanism is to 'cleverly' put it all in your face while laughing at your ineptitude as you muddle through trying to figure it out and after ten thousand years we're *still* getting shafted, *see right*, these fucking ET posers. The abject gender bias of elite men has blinded them to *natural* life and in my opinion, if we're to deconstruct real education over the shit they've fed us, the Void of ancient Greek  myth, was a calmness, a stillness, that came first before 'chaos' came along. It seems to me the 'universe' was sentient light cosmic 'bubble' of purity (the virgin) a sort of manifest kindness, the mother. Then an outside force from a dark realm, a hard dimension, launched a fiery alien projectile into the feminine 'waters' obliterating 'the oneness' fragmenting these types of spiritual nebulas. In the fallout of the aftermath separation occurred as the 'demonic' universe of pure evil 'seeded' its own kind in the diminished new 'physical' realm that springs up after these attacks. It must take a long time for these thing to happen hundreds of thousands maybe even billions of years in what has been summed up as 'evolution'. The point is there was an original calmness, then obliteration, then a 'gap' as everything settled and finally a 'new' universe was born.

The Void was an unfathomable 'nothing' that is paradoxically everything. It is why catholic Nuns are phonetically called "none's", non, nothing, as *she* symbolically represents this original *virginal* force of nothingness symbolised by women. It is a prime *androgynous* force leaning toward to the feminine for *reproductive* purposes. The universe is now a self-replicating binary code largely feminine in nature, Mother Nature, life. Yet people thank 'god' for what they are about to receive on their plate when everything on their plate and every thread of clothing they wear comes from the Goddess - *Mother* Earth. Thankless. We should admit that, ultimately, 'god', if that's what you want to call it, is a feminine element and this is the reason why 'elite' men, aliens, set about slinging women into the gutter, controlling their minds through *common* men with the idea that 'god' is *male*, like them, to *play* into their testosterone driven ego's and the *animal* brain's *need* to be dominant. In the *wild* the kill or be killed *sub*-routine of the animal kingdom was engineered into men making *elite* men 'god' over Common men and common men 'god' over women in a false pecking order of social, class, gender, racial, religious and political distinction designating rank and file. It's alien yet men have fallen easy prey to this dogma for millennia – just look at history. Yet there is something in our essence that *knows* this is unnatural and that something seeks *balance and equality*. Men have suffered greatly for the 'might is right' thinking and even still seem reticent to change. The infuriating propriety men have taken over women as if somehow women are cattle, property, and they own us like dogs is magnificently spelled out in this image of sheer hypocrisy, *right*. One woman protests the right for safe clinical abortion as a matter of private *personal* health not the business of *anyone* but her own. Underneath is an image protesting the right to *medical self-autonomy* as a large crowd of men protest mandatory vaccines from the same government-religious system that has given them power over women! Hilariously, a sign states 'MY BODY – MY CHOICE'. Uh huh. How's that working out for you? If you take someone else's rights away from them do not whine about having your own rights removed. The might is right attitude must be replaced with an understanding that all people have special qualities not designated by physical identifiers. There's always a bigger fish out there ready to eat you up. No *common* man *ever* said war is 'good'. It's *good* for rich men - *great* for elite men, *see right*. Bet he wishes he was at home with his mum.

MY BODY MY CHOICE...

Once loved above *all* others she was the *personification of the vital essence*, the source of *all* knowledge and life venerated by the ancients who, quite simply,

related this force to the world around them, Mother Nature. Before the male 'system' took over, she was often portrayed as fat symbolic that she had of plenty food and resources, abundant, *see right*. Notice the pinecone head of pineal enlightenment. They knew. She *freely* gave to those who enjoyed her gardens, her bounty and harvest on Mother Earth, The *Mother* Goddess, Mother Nature *itself* personified as the mother and the wife who becomes the mother again ad
infinitum. The common simple folk were *very* grateful for her 'love' given *without charge* because, well, money can't buy you love, babe! Fruit from a tree does not ask for money. She *never* put a price on her bounty. Men did that specifically, Egyptian, Greek, Roman and then emerging European empires of *aristocratic* males under the banner of *Roman Catholicism* which is an amalgamation of *global* ancient doctrines in a pan-pagan poly-theosophical militaristic sex and death cult adequately described today as *Satanism!* They saw the rich bounty of Mother Earth and *stole* her harvest. Thieves. They rigged up false economies and sold *your* soul back to you on a plate for a false dollar under threat of starvation from the grain and bread she *already* gave you from her bosom *no price attached!* From her Heart. Heart is an anagram of Earth. Heart is nature. Earth is nature. Nature is *Nurture*. Nurture is Love. Love is Light. She is the Goddess of Love. The Goddess of Light. The Light Bearer. The Bringer of Babies aka New Life! *She* was the Great Goddess plentiful and beautiful and did it all so effortlessly. *Grace*. She made it look so easy they took her for granted as these malicious males callously call her 'the gift that keeps on giving' *stealing* her 'gifts' provided for the *common* people *using* her virgin forests endlessly like a prostitute. That's where the 'prostitute' theme comes from and why 'Pan', *the devil,* is the 'thief'. The god of men is the devil posing as a heavenly father. The Father of Lies all around us now! He steals your real wealth and leaves you with nothing but 'money' which you cannot eat, *see right*, Venezuelans throw their money in the street. It's worthless. Snopes calls this image 'miscaptioned' as an 'over simplification'. Get fucked, Snopes. They get you to destroy your *real* assets
for fake rewards until you are left penniless *and* without resources to fall back on. Game, Set, and Match. They *insult* the Goddess found symbolically in *Mary Magdalene,* a woman. They laugh at her and use her for their own sick power seeking. Elite men covet her. The Common people *loved* her. *All other idols* were considered 'minor nature deities' by comparison and all of it twisted to suit their alien control freakery and self-serving ends! They've got some *answering* to do.

After the Void or the 'primordial waters', fluid, came Chaos, an explosion, a spark, correlated with a 'masculine' force or the 'fire of his loins' the 'spark of life', *testosterone*. One element is no more or less important than the other as both *originate* out of the same state. *They are equal,* side by side, *see right* Jesus and Mary *symbolise* these forces. Notice, they are *always* pointing at the *heart*. They are magnetic *electrical* polar opposites perpetually holding each other in balance like the North and South pole.  You can't have one without the other or everything goes to hell, literally! Hierarchy is a *conceived* idea born out of the minds of strugglers. As it were, a cosmic 'orgasm' of mighty proportions created our current universe, a womb and a seed, Earth and grain. Water and fire. After these two states of Water and Fire came Matter, their 'child', literally soil, dirt, earth, rock, the planets, suns, moons etc. It's all *repetition* just as human babies are born of the spark of the man's 'fire of his loins' and the 'waters of her womb' in the mother's breaking *waters* at birth. *See right,* baby born still inside the amniotic sack. We're basically dolphins. As such the body is considered 'earth' or 'made of clay' in the Bible. So, the sequence goes: there was 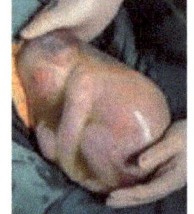 'nothing', then an explosion, a gestation period, a contraction, an expansion, and new life! A bouncing baby universe was born and like brats, the universe grew in size, expanded like babies, had tantrums, explosive outbursts, rested, consumed here and excreted there. That is what happened and is still happening as we continue to grow.

What the ancients were describing is science's 'The Big Bang' not forgetting the word 'bang' is slang for sex in a Universe *intercoursing* with electrical processes akin to the subatomic processes of human sexual procreation or as Walter Russell said, 'We are electric creatures,  floating in the electric sea of this electric universe'. It's all replication. It is the macro and the micro, the back and forth, *intercoursing* between energetic states. We live in a *self-replicating* 'holographic' fractal constantly fractioning off into smaller and bigger versions of itself to create something new. So, The One became Two, duality, then the Two became Three, the Trinity. The Trinity is what 'learned' men throughout history have described as The Father, the Son and the Holy Ghost. All male energies. It is Osiris and *his* spirit conjured into the son Horus via the feminine. But she doesn't get a mention. It is the biblical God and his spirit, the holy ghost, born into the son, Jesus. It is Zeus born again into his son, Apollo. Actually, the Trinity is the Family of Life in the Mother, Father and Child – body, mind and spirit - and it is via the *feminine* that the *life force,* spirit, is conjured into the offspring animating the vehicle, the human body. In 2012 CERN stated the Large Hardon Collider had discovered the

Higgs Boson an elemental force that creates matter from energy, the 'God Particle', that science believes is the building blocks of 'reality'. Science is catching up to Ancient Mythology it's just a matter of terminology.

The Egyptians referred to the void as the Feminine called the 'mother of all gods' and where the saying 'behind every great man is a great woman', *see right,* a picture paints a thousand words. Women's periods, estrogen, were designated by moon cycles, the moon that affects the ocean tides hence, water. Men were designated by the fires of the sun, testosterone, the 'fire of his loins'. She was silver. He was gold. Children are neutral until puberty when differentiating *hormonal* traits become apparent. Our planet, Earth, is described as feminine because it is largely water. Pherecydes of Syros in the 6th Century BC described the original state of Chaos as 'water' or 'formless'. Bruce Lee said, 'be like water. Empty your mind. Be formless. Shapeless – like water'. Which absolutely describes the type of *identity* of this *core* power, a universal force, that *still* resides in us awaiting our acknowledgement and waiting to be unleashed! This *formless state* was the *original* holographic template before it was imprinted on *so many times*. It is the blank slate. The original code. The software program before it was tampered with by *so many* men wanting to improve and/or downgrade the prime program and fucked it up because it was already perfect.

The prime program was pure, innocent, like a child, so it becomes whatever you make it and they are trying to make it into a nightmare, an elite male all powerful psychopath 'god'. This zodiac trap they have ensnared us in hacked or more precisely *hijacked* the holographic broadcast with alien A.I. technology rigging up our lives in ways we could never imagine! "Technology is their god". If we get out of this it will be a miracle and yet we will see many miracles abound now so *be prepared* to hang onto your hats as this takes off. Anything is possible now. They project their fake zodiac stories, astrology, onto us when in reality, despite how much they would have you believing their ideas about our cosmic reality, we are affected by the energies of the stars in ways they too cannot understand. In my own experience they had to engage in black magic, remote technology, psychic attacks, helicopters hovering around my house and finally a *demon* inserted into me to delay me and FORCE me to go along with their zodiac script for *my life!* If they have to go to such trouble, then it's all bullshit. It's fake. They're fake. Our lives and world would be *very different* if they weren't cheating by *constantly interfering* with our lives with all their dirty tricks. The agency Satanist's behind all this demand *one way or another* that we be *forced* into *their version* of how life works when in reality, if you were left to your own devices, the zodiac energies cannot and do not affect you unless you allow it. As such, consciously determine your own life and why ancient advice is as relevant today as it was thousands of years ago, "nosce te ipsum". *Know thyself!* They cannot trap you in their bullshit stories if you transcend them, they might delay you, hold you up, but once released, you can take all that knowledge and knock these motherfuckers on their arse and get out of this house of horrors. Without us, they are nothing. Without them we are everything! *And they know it.*

I received a message around the time of the total solar eclipse in 2012 that said, 'We are objects existing in space in the eternal now'. *This is* the eternal now described by East Asian philosophies as The Centre of the Toa. Stillness. Oneness. Calmness. The *original* state. The Toa ascribes it as 'eternally nameless' that it is to be distinguished from the countless 'named' things and is the reality of life before 'descriptions'. It is 'non-conceptional' as to 'conceive' of it means to think and to think is mind and mind is words. There are no words in other words. Eckhart Tolle said, 'As soon as something is perceived, it is named, interpreted, compared with something else, liked, disliked, or called good or bad by the phantom self, the ego. They are imprisoned in thought forms, trapped in object consciousness'. Chung-tzu said two and half thousand years ago, 'when there is no more separation between this and that, it is called the still point at the centre of the Tao. At the still point in the centre of the circle one can see the infinite in all things'. When one is *centered*, just being, right here, right now, *this infinite moment*, we become *everything* and *nothing* all at once just like the prime state. We are it. It is us. As with the original code we become a blank slate onto which *we* can write *whatever* we want. *Be* whoever we want. *Go* wherever we like. It's like restoring factory settings on your device and wipes the tons of shitty sequence data from *aimless* scrolling and software viruses.

This electrical force is all around us, *it is us*, we are it, and the moment you have a thought it becomes chaos, obliteration, static. Until stillness again when we come back together. It is The One that is many. Omnipresence. We are all points of this infinite consciousness and *they* are trying keep us asleep ignorant of it. But the lid is about to be blown right off! We are on our way *back* to the original state where we will find it firstly within ourselves then it will occur again in the world around us and further, in the universe beyond. Calmness. This is why all the distraction and *destruction* we experience all around us now which is *absolutely deliberate*. Bruce Lee was, I believe, *totally* studying and harnessing the 'chi' and 'prana', the 'iChing' etc., pure electrical energy, *the force*, hence, his incredible feats of unparalleled uncanny abilities taught to him by an ancient master of a secretive oriental Order, *see*, Chapter Nine *The Phoenix Returns*. They killed him for showing off the *power* humans can harness. They kill all the biggest 'stars' as effigy's of the light to symbolise killing the Christ-light within *freely* available to us all emanating from the stars! They kill men very easily because men have profited from all this. Women, the underdog in so many ways, have *not* profited by and large relegated to the heavy skirting, petticoats, corseting, impractical shoes and obsessive-compulsive micro-managing of men throughout the ages, the boss man, who *commands* women submit to his God-complex rulebook in so many ridiculous ways. Corsets were a *torso fetish* designed to constrict in the feminine in *another* insidious bondage-style suppression technique called 'fashion'. Even at the time it was admitted as 'Death through tight lacing'. In the oriental East women's feet were broken because some emperor with a pedophilic foot fetish was *literally* 'hobbling' women like animals so they couldn't run away. While in the Middle East and North Africa they employed *female genital mutilation*, FGM, where the clitoris and labia are cut out then sewn together and cut open with *scissors* or *knives* on the 'wedding' day *without anesthesia* often causing death or giving birth to *many* children. *See right, FGM and healthy vagina.*

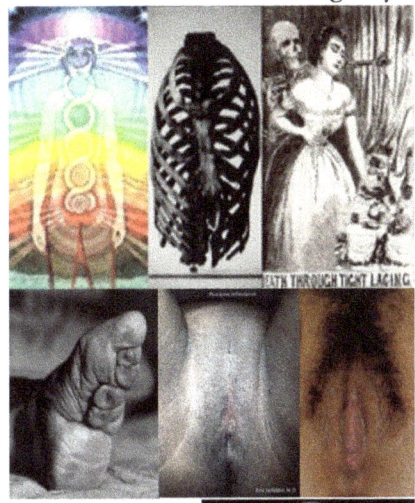

Don't you find it *rather coincidental* that in the West the spinal system and four *major* kundalini chakras tower were *bound-up* in corsets preventing *normal energetic chakra flow* while in China the sole of the feet, *above*, electrically earthing *the kundalini of the soul* grounding us to Mother Earth via the feet was broken and *bound-up* and in the *rest of the known world* - Africa, India and the Middle East - they were and *still are* cutting out the genital glands of females required to reach orgasm thus effectively cutting the *kundalini alchemical spinal cord*, the hormonal-energetic link to the nervous system *that begins* at the root chakra/sexual organs, that electrochemically activates *the chakra tower* to attain enlightenment? What. A. Strange. Coincidence. It. All. Is. These are not just 'out of touch' cultural differences that require gentle tact to steer people away from mutilating a defenseless girls. *See right*, the female energetic Intrinsic and Extrinsic Pathways. These combined methods are *specifically designed* by sadistic *Satanic* men *worldwide* to perpetrate a spiritual crime of gross proportions against women *who are the*

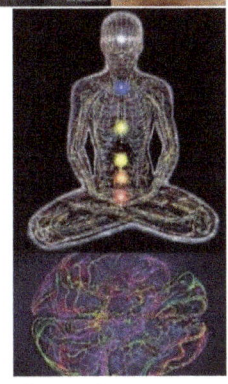

FEMININE INTRINSIC AND EXTRINSIC PATHWAY

Intrinsic pathway-dependent or follows nerve pathways

Extrinsic pathway-independent of nerve pathway

carriers of the light-force, in their psychopath *pathetic* attempts to prevent women from becoming any smarter than she already is! Threatened much? Even in countries where females are severely limited in education and access to basic rights, girls are still outperforming boys in math, science and literature. They can't keep up with an unenlightened woman let alone an enlightened one so their small-dick complexes have driven them to *insidious* evil dressed up as 'culture' and if you say anything about it you're a 'bigot' and 'culturally insensitive'. They've got the whole game sewn up, literally! *See right,* defenseless little girl being brutalised ruining the rest of her life.

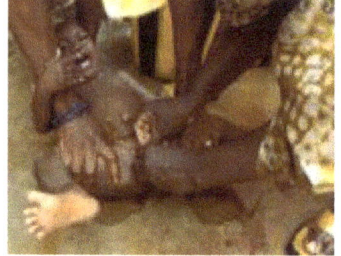

Given 'god' is supposed to be male, they have turned the *Goddess,* the female, *his wife,* into a spiritual quadriplegic scum that they are. You will never open your chakras once the hormonal glands have been destroyed in such a way which is why they do it. The religious 'scholars' behind all this *know exactly what they are doing* while moronic men *worldwide* happily endorse the crime, content to have some *egotistical power* over women when they are the ones ultimately losing out as a result. *Clearly* these idiots are not reaping the benefits of tantric sex enlightenment or *they wouldn't be so poor and 'underdeveloped'* keeping them at the mercy of the hierarchical males behind all this. This *demonic* attack is done to leave a broken girl at the mercy of this Devil *posing* in the place of The King, God in every man, who once *protected* women not left her to rot at the hands of these soulless *alien* vampires. *See right,* the Goddess, Mary Magdelene, crawling on all fours as these low-lives look down on *Her* in all their 'enlightened' glory slandering the goddess as a 'prostitute' *because* sacred sex was her domain! Look hard at this picture. Evolution escapes these men, *see right,* the unspeakable act of acid attacks perpetrated against the Divine Feminine often times against the most aesthetically beautiful women as these psychos despise a grace they *cannot* attain. Is this not alien? They seek to destroy the Goddess and Life itself to *be* God, to own creation, to own *Her,* to keep women down, shame her, destroy her beauty, make fun of her sex to *make sure* she never attains her true intellectual and cosmic identity left to grovel at the feet of this trash. How many last words have women heard being called a 'whore' a 'slut' and 'she wanted it' while being gang raped and murdered? Too many. Elite men are terrified of the average women especially the *emerging* enlightened feminine. Asian women do four times more unpaid work than men. In many parts of Asia 75% of the field labour is performed by women yet women only own up to 20% of land. 75% of women in developing regions are do not have work contracts, legal rights or social protection, often not paid enough money to work their way out of poverty. Some women die *working in the field* of a prolapse of the uterus literally, the reproductive organs falling out due to multiple births. Men who murder their wives receive on average a few years jail time while women who kill their husbands in *self-defense* receive on average 15 years in prison. The Highway of Tears in Canada is a stretch of highway where countless women, specifically indigenous women, have disappeared or been murdered. They even stopped counting as the sheer numbers were off the charts. Native women carry some of the most ancient bloodlines in the world in yet another attempt to wipe out the opposition to the alien aristocratic empire. Women and girls who are raped often don't report the crimes as the system is stacked against them, a system by men for men, and that is not even touching on the realm of sexual harassment and bullying in the workplace most of which goes unreported. The stats on women's continued suffrage *are unending* and as a world we will go nowhere, doomed to failure, unless this is addressed asap.

The knowledge of kundalini enlightenment via lovemaking was originally held in the hands of the Priestesses *not* the dirty priesthood, the masons! They stole the light, thieves, Pan, the Devil who runs this whole world, and his many *willing* male goffers headed up by the alien male aristocracy. They have most of the world worshipping this demonic 'god' one way or another. You might think I take this rather *personally,* and I do, these guys had me lined up to die. There are no words strong enough to describe the levels they are willing to go to in order to destroy beautiful intelligent women in veneration of their sad little dick cult. *I* was supposed to be a modern day version of Mary, *the Goddess*, and this dehumanisation is *exactly* what they *forcibly* did to me to fit their fucked-up woman-hating script of *sexual perversions* serving Satanism in a *male only* space program no less! This is what these fuckwits are doing with all this technology. What a joke. I will never achieve what I would have achieved because I was to be nothing but a vending machine harvesting all *my* abilities for *their* evil offspring, Damien! It's literally The Omen. As a result of their wanton *monumental* selfishness it's unlikely, given my age, that I can *ever* have a family of my own now that I am of no further use since I discovered what they did to secretly trap me. Like Mary. Like Diana. Like Monroe, and so many others. How hilarious for them. Rest assured I've got a little something for them before this *fairy tale* comes to an end. The feminine was the *only one* who could be trusted with this power and look what has happened to humanity and Earth once this power was transferred into the hands of *males* specifically 'elite' males and 'scholars' who covet this knowledge for their own power mongering. FGM is assault with a deadly weapon now practiced if you can believe it *in the West* as mass migration goes unchecked and little girls are suffering *lifelong* injuries not only physically and emotionally but *cosmically and spiritually!* If this doesn't piss you off I don't know what will. It is *reckless endangerment. Grievous bodily harm.* It is *attempted murder.* This sick-minded *inverted* fake-masculine *satanic* system looks the other way and dresses it up as 'cultural diversity' because behind the scenes in the East *and* West, elite men *all* secretly *hate females* terrified we will return this knowledge to its rightful place, a loving relationship, and kick this motherfucking demonic horde of satanic filth out of our world *for good*. Once the knowledge is in its *rightful place* under proper guidance of the Mother and Father in a healthy environment, *the home*, as was always intended, the whole world will see a renaissance of everlasting beauty and joy not even imaginable in our current degraded state. 12 months of tantric lovemaking and any guy's IQ will shoot up and together men and women will be unstoppable. Men don't have to be afraid of women or need to demean or slander her to feel superior once their *heart chakra* and *pineal gland* is opened *as it should be*. They have turned the average man in the street into an animal mocking and ridiculing his true spiritual self when Men were once noble warriors, protectors and keepers of the light, a 'knight in shining armour', yes, the tantric apple-torus, *the aura*, of shining power and strength, a prince!, and ultimately a *king* who needed a queen in order for the Power Couple to function *correctly* as an *electrical unit* of love.

The boys 'club' throughout history with their big halos grandly pose and if you're not in their club you can *and will* fuck off and die. There is no honour among these thieves. They stab each other in the back just as easily as they do anyone else just look at Kennedy and so many deposed leaders around the world all eager to take each other's place like snakes in a pit writhing over the top of each other. It's all about power. And money. If you dismiss what they have done to women *because* you are a man just *remember*, they have far worse lined you for you. Where did they get those big halos from? Why are men the *only* ones 'enlightened'? What a lark! And who runs the world? Men. Who have always run the world? Men. How have they done it? Via religion and politics that covets this knowledge behind the scenes. It's no surprise then that the word 'religion' finds its origins in the Latin word 'religare' meaning 'to tie back, to bind fast and to hold back'. Yes, we're being stalled in the lead up to something *massive*. How do males run the world today? Via Government. The word 'government' is from the Latin verb 'guverno/guvernare' meaning to 'control'

the Latin noun 'mens' or 'mentis' means 'mind'. 'Government' *literally* means *'mind-control'*. While all this control was-is going on where were-are the women? Cooking and cleaning despite these elite men *knowing* their power is derived from the feminine accessing the electrical power of Chi and prana through Mother Earth via women in sacred-tantric sex. *See right,* 600-year-old medieval pin displaying three slightly bowed penises bearing a  *crowned vulva* found in Brugge, Belgium. Notice, the three 'trinity' dots beneath their feet meaning body, mind, spirit or Mother, Father & Child or even *Sun, Moon and Earth* earthing them to the Great Planetary Mother in replication of the prime electrical force. They *obviously* didn't cut out *her* vagina, they venerated it, well aware of the *real* power of the feminine revering her not brutalizing her.

The sad truth of it is the world has been taken over by men simply because they are *physically bigger* than women. That's all. It's really not rocket science although they would have you believe it is. We simply couldn't beat them *physically* or defend ourselves from the ceaseless onslaught females have endured by and large with incredible dignity mustered at the hands of these brutish devils, *see right,* Russian veteran recalls their sexual crimes in Germany. Look at his face! Even in current times Serbian soldier's mass rape of young girls holding them prisoner and trading them to other soldiers for months at a time as described by Witness 87, "All my life I will have thoughts of that and feel the pain that 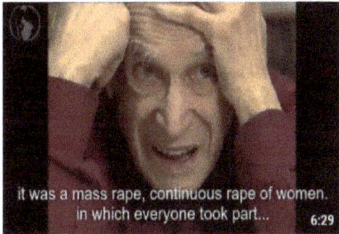 I felt and still feel. That will never go away". These crimes are *so despicable* the victims don't even have a name just a 'witness' number. It's almost too much to bear. Then one must consider the Vietnam conflict not to mention the unending crimes against women in Africa and the Middle East not only at the hands of their *own men* but by the male soldiers from abroad who were *supposed to protect them!* The UN have some answering to do on this as the fires of masculine hell are unleashed on an abundant *feminine* planet. Male behaviour is *the* elephant in the living room. Left unanchored, unhinged, Mother Earth becomes a living Hell and these alien satanic fuck-ups behind all this are *proud* of their handywork turning us against ourselves. Not until they are *old men* do the crimes of the past visit itself upon the perpetrators when it is *too late* to do anything but suffer in regret and sorrow at the *ignorance* and brutality of young men under the guidance of satanic old men who hate them *exactly* for their humanity, *exactly* for their youth. And then the grave takes them. Bitterly robbed of dignity in the end. *Another* generation lost. More misery. *This* is the fires of hell, the fires of his loins, testosterone! That's what this is about, demons posing as your leaders, *literally*, creating abject soul destroying misery in every generation via *unanchored* men. Degrading the light. Mocking the true King in the souls of men. Former presidential candidate George McGovern said, "I'm fed up to the ears with old men dreaming up wars for young men to die in". But then they worship the god of war. What could hate us so much that it would do this to unsuspecting people? Aliens? Whatever it is, it's not human. Even today nothing has changed, the devil energy doesn't evolve, that's the problem.

As a result of this madness women had to take second place on *Mother* Earth, her own world, and it is *because* of this second-place position that women can stand up to the overarching alien bully *now*, a bully that conned *human* men into giving up their power eons ago and in many ways men have been hamstrung from doing the job that must be done. That is why there is no male messiah to save you. What's he gonna say? 'I represent all that is good in the world therefore I am worthy'? Of ripping down the forests? Going to war and killing his brothers? Fishing out the oceans without a second thought turning a blind eye to all the destruction because there is a pay packet in it? Just *when* were men going to take a stand against this? Anytime soon would be great. Men were led away by greed and *stupidity* abandoning *the one thing* that could save them, women, because the Devil *knew* if he could lure men (god) away from the women (the goddess) split-up the Force, separate them, the pair would lose their *power*. And they did. It's a circuit breaker. The one thing the devil is most afraid of is *women*. Men sold their souls to the devil for money and position in society but women, by and large, historically, have had *neither* money nor position and apart from giving birth to men, cannot be blamed for what they have done. Men once guarded women. They were her protector. Honourable and noble in a time long forgotten *because* her sacred spiritual chakra alchemy could turn them into veritable gods. They (stupidly) *suppressed* women on behalf of their half-human overlords, the 'gentry', reptilians, who planned all this to benefit *their* alien masters in an galactic space program. This third party is a *bestial* interloper from the depths of space and time, the allegorical Devil, *an alien!* At its core, beyond the dragon-lizard-reptilian-snake species, this interloper is some sort of A.I., *not natural*, unlike Mother *Nature*, which is *all* natural, *organic*. This is why I had the message *'Inorganic things have no power over organic things'*. They have no right! No power over the natural world. They are *groundless*, literally! When men lost themselves to ego and madness our world crumbled and at the end of it all we are being morphed into something not even human. If you think I am being hateful toward *common* men, no, the suicide rates among men have *skyrocketed* to unbelievable proportions while crimes against women and children, again, spiral out of all control. There are more men in jail now than ever before in history and that's saying something.

The feminine is *the* enemy of this beast-alien-demon for *big* reasons including a prophecy that *women* will undo what has been done and guide men, *man*, back to the true path and repel the dark forces once and for all! Who would think a little lady could do such a thing? The most unlikely hero. This is why they named the evil male god, Lucifer, to slander the Love Goddess *Venus* Latin for 'Lucifer' knowing full well idiots would link the 'light bearer' to the devil eyeing the Statue of Liberty with suspicion struggling to comprehend that there is nothing fancy going on here. Humans can be so self-congratulating! Everything the 'devil' symbolises was, essentially, *stolen* from the feminine. For example, Capricorn, the devil, is associated with the 'goat' stolen from a feminine star at the zenith of the Milky Way called *Capella* and means 'little she goat'. Layers of bullshit hide sneaky psychology, mind games, that *somehow* the feminine is to blame, *and they do*. They burned *millions* of women at the stake over all this in their murderous Abrahamic rampage against the goddess in their attempts to *reinforce* women are evil yet strangely powerless, *right*. It was said the greatest god, Zeus who is Satan, king of kings (as was Jesus), was afraid of no other god or goddess except the Goddess Iris, *right*, described as a beautiful young woman with 'golden wings' who carried a *caduceus* no less of sacred sex enlightenment and a *water jug* as we enter the Age of Aquarius, the water bearer! Men have never carried water, even today women carry the water symbolic of her birth waters. The tantric sex caduceus of enlightenment was attributed to Hermes in Homer's The Odyssey, *however*, it was *originally* attributed to Iris in Homer's earlier work *The Iliad*. All the good ol' boys from Tolkien to Oliver Stone to Da Vinci to Homer, were drawn into the cult to hide the truth that a woman, not a man, indeed an innocent maiden, Iris, was the *first Messenger of the Gods* before they changed it to Hermes a bisexual merchant, bastion of conduct for so many male 'gods' that followed in their *unscrupulous* dick cult. Yet it always traces back to the feminine who oversaw the responsibility of this power in a time long forgotten when the abundant generous Goddess, not a cruel vengeful 'god', ruled Earth and all were happy in her garden. In the name Osiris we find Iris – *the eye of god* – the feminine. And who better than the feminine to record the lowest levels of depravity men will sink to but women? Who has been so invaded by them? Our very bodies invaded, and now the elite males seek to own her very mind and soul! The crimes of men against women are literally unspeakable. There are no words to describe what women and young girls have endured when men's sexuality seize them and consequence seems far away. So, if there *was* a Messiah it's not a man, *it's a woman,* which explains the *institutionalised hatred* toward the feminine *worldwide*. Ancient Druid priestmonk Merlin prophesised, *'what was lost by a woman will be regained by a women'*. The whole world was lost. I guess she's coming back around again to take her world back. Don't blame me it's their prophecy. I just work here. Now you know why they hate her so much. *A scene from Monty Python, note, the name pythons* (snake, reptiles) in their 1983 film *The Meaning of Life, right,* shows the *energetic* Mother Goddess giving birth to the universe. Once you know this their work takes on *a whole new meaning* 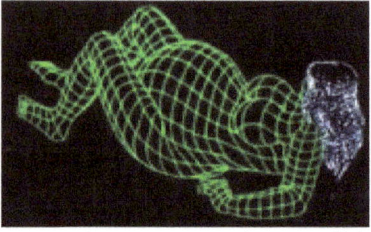 including references to sun kings and tantric sex or 'every sperm is sacred' it goes on and on again hidden in plain sight as comedy and weirdness. They're basically scientists. Notice, her hair is *shining* as this is the electrical nervous system of tantra enlightenment gained from the feminine life force via the nervous system picked up like and antenna from the universal Chi-Prana.

Cymatics is sound or vibrations, *resonance*, that the ancients described as the word of 'god' and in many ways they weren't wrong. Cymatics creates geometric shapes, *right*, giving us the various planes, *dimensions*, as well as space and thus a sense of 'time'. Getting from point A to point B, which takes time, has been confused as a *psychological* concept of 'space' or the 'time *line*' that  encompasses our *whole lives* as we try to 'get there' and waste our precious 'time' in doing so. Time *or space* is not what people think it is. What is remembered of the previous generation's *time* and what they were doing with it? Yet there are a few staples in life that never change - agriculture, living, eating, gathering. That's about it but these staples don't get much of our *time* anymore. The famed 'cube' of 3D reality is associated with the Goddess, *see right,* and is simply space. Before I got sidetracked with the hatred of the feminine, I was exploring the origins of 'reality' as described rather accurately by our ancestors in 'myth'. So, out of the Void-Chaos, mum and dad, *the Big Bang,* came the 'child' categorised as five 'offspring'. First born was Gaia which is 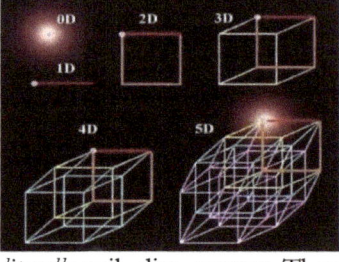 another name for Earth, the feminine. Earth is *literally* soil, dirt, matter. Then came Tartarus, the underworld, 'a darkness deeper than Hades' which is the zero-point energy or dark matter at the magnetic core of world's due to the gravitational force and extreme energy density. Then came Eros *note*, anagram of Rose, although claimed to be masculine the rose is, again, a feminine force, it is Love. Love is light, *information*, or photons carried on sun rays. Once light existed there must surely be shadow cast by light and so the fourth 'offspring' was Erebus or 'shadow' considered male. The fifth 'offspring' born was Nyx or night-time darkness lighted by the moon when the world evolved into night and day. There were two other 'deities' outside this five, Aether or air, and Herera or daylight. What they are describing is the chronological *geological* processes of creation from beginning to end; the Void of perfect balanced energy, then Chaos or the spark of an explosion, the Big Bang, which birthed the Elements: soil, matter, dark matter, photons or light, shadow or anti-matter and night-time darkness as the process was divided by day and night. Finally, when everything had settled came the last two; Air-Aether-atmosphere and Herera the 'dome of the sky' or the Ozone layer and the *light refraction* of the rainbow called *Permafrost* by the Norse who said their 'gods' existed beyond this layer. *Yes, interdimensional.* The Watchers. This is why  the Goddess of the rainbow, *Iris*, originally carried the caduceus and was 'fraternal twin' of Arke (arc of the rainbow) who was the daughters of 'Thaumas' (interesting similarity to Thalamus). They talk the twin 'brothers' but there is also the twin sisters. Iris and Arke were 'fraternal twins' because you cannot have atmosphere without the ozone layer holding it in. The Iris also defines eye colour and what we see as the *visual light spectrum*, the *rainbow*, or *20/20 vision!* The rainbow is found in the spectrum of the Chakras all harkening back to the feminine. The plural of Iris is pronounced *I-rise*. One can only hope.

The Ancient Cosmic Egg story permeates all civilisations and can be traced back to the Proto-Indo-Europeans. The egg was said to have been laid on the Primordial Waters of Earth and because it's all *replication* what happened during the Big Bang also happened during the evolving planet as well as the human procreation and gestation period. The CIA wrote a report in 1983 called The Gateway Report, declassified in 2003, based on the teachings of Robert Munroe founder of the Munroe Institute. They claimed altered states of consciousness were the gateway to astral projection. Called the Analysis and Assessment of the Gateway Process it went into quite some detail on experiments they conducted on hypnosis, mind control, neuroscience and quantum mechanics. They explained what underpins spiritual concepts including spacetime transcendence specifically,  Transcendental Meditation (a form of which is tantric sex) as well as biofeedback, universal holograms, hypnosis and spirituality. The report stated the universe comprises of interacting energy fields and that mental states are simply variations in energy. Human consciousness follows the same principles as being a vibration or energy pattern. When a person reaches a state of 'hemi-sync' they can enter an altered state of consciousness in which they are *not limited by physical reality* and can tune into energy fields purely and freely. This can play into the law of attraction in that positive thoughts attract positive things and negative thoughts negative things etc. This can also explain 'psychic attacks' and 'psychic assassins' some claim to have experienced or personally carried out. This knowledge can create 'mind warriors' who can literally travel through time and space using their mind alone, the application for which are endless. Part of the report covers the 'Absolute' or the universe's 'governing energy', an *endlessly flowing* spiral that intervenes with reality as we know it and the Munroe Institute has exercises to facilitate astral projection. The image, right, is from the report showing the 'Cosmic egg' also called the Orphic egg, the 'mundane' egg (there's nothing mundane about it) and the 'world egg'. The torus beneath it and the 'egg' are the same depiction from different angles. The Egg 'symbolises two complimentary principles', yes, positive and negative electrical poles found in the 'complimentary principles' of men and women creating to new life. The images released by the CIA depicting the torus field and the holographic field of the universe bear a striking resemblance to images of the 'cosmic egg' right back to ancient times and all up appears to depict the vortex created by the rising 'kundalini' or 'energetic flow' of the intermingling energies spiraling up the spine-nervous system and Ida/Pingala nerves to unleash the inner God and Goddess. Mega Mum and Super Dad. The Power Couple!

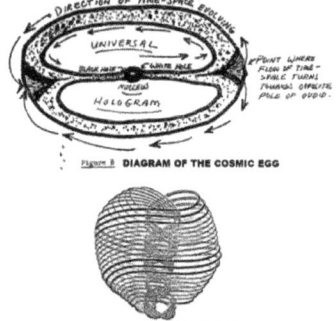

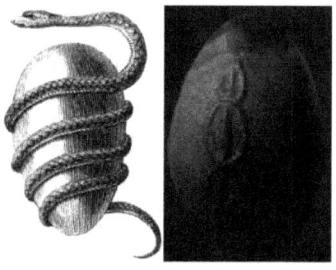

The African Dogon people of Central Mali had astronomical knowledge long before 'modern' science and called the Egg 'Amma' which is an anagram of Mama. Interestingly, the Hindus too called their mother goddess Amma and is said to be 'beautiful yet terrible, gentle yet heroic' isn't every woman? She is Mother Nature. She is also called *Mountain Mama*, MM, Mother Mary & Mary Magdalene etc and as M is W upside down, *Milky Way*. The ancients considered the galaxy Feminine. The Catholic Church says Mary is the 'church' as her body is the Temple and why The mountain *is* the Temple as depicted, *right*,

in Hinduism. Earth, Mother Nature, life, the universe and Human women are *the Goddess*. She *is* the mountain because the curves and valleys of a woman's body symbolised the geography of *mother* earth and why even today native people hold sexual fertility rites in caves to bring good harvests as caves are the 'vagina' of the goddess, *see right*, Utroba Cave, Bulgaria carved around *1,000BC* depicting the 'vagina' of the Goddess. It is 22 metres long, or 11:11, the Lovers, the Twins, where deep inside is an alter and precisely at High Noon *(we've seen that before, see; Kennedy)* when the sun is at its strongest the light of the sun, the symbolic 'fire' or spark of his loins, enters the cave, the vagina of the Goddess, from an opening in the ceiling 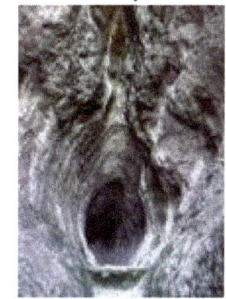 projecting the image of a phallus onto the ground in a wonderful example of how important this endless cosmic sexual rites were that meant *so much* to ancient peoples leading them to build such marvels. Before you yelp, 'but they didn't use meters in those days!' The measuring system along with everything else has been engineered in a *rolling effect* for ancient knowledge to remain relevant still. The knowledge is *sound*. Leading up to Spring in March, the phallus stretches out like an erection to reach the 'alter' (the throne) symbolising the womb, fertilizing the uterus of the Goddess before the spring sowing. The seed, or 'fire', is the seed planted in the fertile Earth that creates new life, the 'seed' or sperm, fire, planted in a woman by a man to create new life and the 'grain' of the Christ *seed* planted *within* to facilitate new life. There are *many* of these phallus-vagina geo-carvings *globally*. The 'mountain' was a symbolic 'height' to which men would aspire to climb the towers or 'mountain' of her chakras as told in Rapunzel among others. S*ee right*, Newgrange Ireland is a 'womb not a tomb'. This monument is a megalithic structure revering Sirius the Dog Star as ancient people from the Dogon to the ancient stonemasons of UK and  Europe seemed to particularly revere Sirius, the Sun, the Moon, Venus and the Pleiades called the 'seven sisters'. It always leads back to her as a larger force with a smaller component of the masculine, the seed. These ancient beliefs and spiritual knowledge go back to a time when the Goddess was the *monotheistic* deity of all life on Earth when the world was abundantly green and good.

The Dogon say their teachers were the Nommo from Sirius who appeared like Mermen or Mermaids, yes, scaly. There were also Dolphin-like beings associated with human females, *see,* the oracles of Delphi-dolphin who made prophecies for the god *Apollo*, a reptilian son of Zeus, the Devil! It's a breeding program. This 'god' was not from here and all religion became based on him. They were amphibious. Frogs are amphibians the word meaning 'two lives' because they start out in the water and wind up on the land or what might be considered the 'two lives' of interdimensional or space travelling reptilian-demonic entities we hear so much about today along with their two faces, public *and* private. This is where the French Frogs, the aristocratic line of Sun Kings, is said to be spawned from. These lineages come from the line of Cain said to be born of the reptilian snake and Eve in Eden which smacks of the same story as the myths of Zeus and Queen Leda, Celtic Lugh and the King, Dionysus as well as Jesus born of the 'holy spirit' all spawning a hybrid alien-human baby, the twins of myth and legend, or a good and bad brother from the same pregnancy called '*Superfecundation*'. We know this is a penis cult so, 'Cain' is phonetically 'cane' as in rods, wands, staffs, clubs, sceptres etc., all coded references to the penis and the 'seed' of this bad boy, Satan, a reptilian alien and it's bloodline from a *common demonic progenitor*. It's the bloodline of Satan from the beginning of it all and the closer elites families can link their genetics to this ancient alien DNA the more 'right' they have to rule. Even Genghis Khan is from this line as Khan is a derivation of Cain as is Jewish Cohen and many others *worldwide*. Genghis Khan's 'Yuan' Dynasty translates as the *One* Dynasty and his story *is the same* as many others in that he killed his half-brother. The modern Chinese currency *the Yuan* bears his designation still given they are the only *non-Anglo* bloodline family in the 13 families said to rule the Earth. Cain is from Hebrew Qayin literally 'the created one', Semitic 'to form, to fashion'. It also means 'fratricide' to kill one's sibling with an interesting correlation to Canus 'dog' or 'pointed tooth'. It all overlaps.

In 2003 a groundbreaking historical genetics analysis discovered a *substantial percentage* of men are direct lines of Khan aka Cain. Cain's father, the snake, was obviously a reptilian and his name, 'Samael', is Hebrew for 'Venom of God', 'Poison of God' or 'Blindness of God'. Humans are God. So, the 'poison/venom' of god and 'blindness' of god is the poison and blindness of humans. From the line of Cain we get Tubal-Cane or 'two balls cane', 'the first blacksmith', whose symbol looked like an anchor, *see right*, similar to Facebook's logo as well as secret agent 007's logo, and the logo of John Dee black magician and advisor to Queen Elizabeth I (centre). The masonic 'Two Ball Cane' golf tournament is a favourite game of powerful men worldwide scheming over a few rounds and why the Apollo 11 (Satan  11) Space program had the astronauts play *golf* on the *feminine* lunar surface. More shit slinging. It's a dick and balls cult so, Neil *Armstrong* becomes 'strong-arm' man and 'Buzz' Aldrin is a reference to the honey bee of Christ seed oil tantric sex enlightenment where they're getting their power from. The 'right angle' symbol is a *craftsman builders* instrument called a 'tri square' similar to a mitre square for measuring corners and angles in *building* and *construction* aka Masonry, then stylized as a *penis and two testicles* as a masculine symbol of their 'god' making and moulding things *even people and reality* aka a *craftsman*. Interestingly, one of the prostitutes murdered by the Masons aka 'Jack the Ripper' was found at *Mitre Square*. The 'square and compass' are masonic symbols *worldwide* and the previous image is the *oldest known painting of Christ* with *two distinct faces*, two faced, given the Vatican also depict him with two faces, *right*, a man and a reptile - a T-rex – a killer! The book Christ carries has the *tri square*. Jesus was a Mason and major religions believe he was *reptilian*. These guys are *secret agents of the devil* then and now, the good *and* bad guy.

The line of Cain spawned the lines of Enoch, Lamech, Tubal-Cane, master Mason Hiram Abiff of Solomons Temple as well as Noah, the Canaanites, the Greek pharaohs of Egypt, *the Ptolemy's* one of whom discovered 48 of the 88 constellations given Hermes-Mercury is their main man and takes 88 days to go around the sun (replication). They went on to found the Merovingians and later the Capetian's, the House of Bourbon and the House of Orleans descended from the dynasty's founder Hugh Capet. The House of Orleans was founded by Phillippe I, Duke of Orleans, the younger son of Louis XIII the younger brother of Louis XIV the 'sun king'. There emblem was the fleur di lis, the lily flower, given the chakras are often depicted as lily's or lotus's. The fleur di lis is specifically worn on the head usually depicted on crowns adorning the enlightened monarch and their activated crown chakra and *glowing jewels* symbolise this. The Ptolemy's were also known for playing the 'flute' a coded reference to the penis as well as chakra 'sounds' or cymatics, the 'word' of god, the messenger, of christ seed enlightenment. These family branches were ancient tantric sex practitioners emerging as all powerful *today* although the Fleur di lis is a symbol that goes back into *prehistory* before written language.

Known for their 'saviour' kings, the Ptolemy's spawned Alexander the Great and Cleopatra from which Jesus (or someone they invented as Jesus) continued the lineage via Mary, *his wife*, who ran off to France after his murder spawning their ongoing lines today. French *Sun Kings* of France are the French 'frog' princes of fairy tales of which Louis the XIV founded *Louisiana* and *New Orleans* naming St Louis after their ancestor who acceded to the throne at *12 years of age*. So too did Ptolemy XV aka Caesarian accede to the throne when he was 12 years old and was the only son of Cleopatra and Julius Ceasar murdered in 44BC. Cleopatra was apparently 39 years old when she died a common number for 'goddesses' death symbolism as did Monroe and Diana die aged 36 as 6 is 9 inverted. Cleopatra apparently committed 'suicide' as was the favoured method to kill modern 'goddess' Monroe considering ancient Egyptians believed the 'Ka' was the *life force* of a person that granted their 'right to rule' as a *Universal Force* passed from one pharaoh to another (rings a bell). So, 'goddess' Diana died in a 'car'. They're killing the feminine light. The death of Cleopatra ended the war between two of Julius Ceasars most important supporters, Octavian and Antony, who formed a political alliance *post* his assassination. For *our* purposes it looks like JFK is Julius Ceasar in this version of the script and his 'two important supporters' are found in old world *British* and new world *American* royalty, the *brotherhood*, seeking to kill the God and Goddess *again* to replay this ancient script and join forces in his stead just like Caesar! Nobody knows what happened to Cleopatra although her son to Julius Caesar, Caesarian-Ptolemy XV, *right*, was murdered by Octavian when he conquered Egypt after Cleopatra and her lover Antony's failed naval battle at Actium on

2*nd September* 31BC (another version of 911). Octavian allowed her children to Antony to be bought back to Rome and her death marked the end of the Hellenistic period of Mediterranean rule (specifically *Ptolemaic*) over Egypt! This era occurred between the death of Alexanda the Great in 323BC and the emergence of 'Roman Egypt' in 31BC which then became a province of the Roman Empire under its first Emperor in 27BC none other than Octavian! The Ptolemy's were the last *legitimate* Pharaonic lineage from a great, mysterious and ancient empire the last links to the now lost empires that preceded them and their secretive astral roots including *Atlantis!* Neither Cleopatra's body nor her tomb were ever found and nobody knows what really happened to her in a last great Feminine mystery befitting the last known Goddess! What's the bet they find her tomb in 2022 a century after Lord Carnarvon discovered King Tut's tomb in 1922 a *very* symbolic year!

The most powerful *modern* royal dynasties claim to trace their bloodlines specifically to the Ptolemy's of Ancient Egypt trying to pick up where they left off as the looming New Age script - *Egypt 2.0* - calls for Antony's and Cleopatra's 'one world' plan and Ptolemy XV to symbolically *live on* and as we shall see, *he has!* Cleopatra was attempting to unite Ancient Rome and Ancient Egypt under *one* royal ruling couple, Osiris and Isis reborn (at least symbolically), to create an ancient *One World*. The twelve year old Ptolemy XV was the last member of this ancient Egyptian Dynasty, the last rather sad embers of *thousands of years* of megalithic and still unfathomable structures before the world got small. The founding father of this family, Ptolemy I, was known as 'The Saviour', yes, another Jesus-Messiah character who was a companion, war general, of Alexander the Great. It is this family who turn their kings into Christ saviours, messiahs and 'king of kings' who wrote the old and new testament. Their emblem was a bird of prey, an Eagle, as was Rome and America famous for their eagle symbolism. The eagle is one of the symbols of male tantric sex, a 'bird of prey' as well as the 'birds eye view', the eye of Horus, the falcon, the activated third eye chakra, the *pineal gland* energized by dark side tantric sex penis cult knowledge and black magic that sees all or the *all-seeing eye* of the secretive masons who are the descendants of these people hence, their power! The Ptolemaic Dynasty was an ancient Greek family who also went by the name Lagides descended from Ptolemy I Soter also known as Ptolemy Lagides whose father's name *Lagus* was from the Latin-Greek root word meaning *rabbit* or hair, the *Lepus constellation*, where we get Easter rabbits at the 'birth' of 'Christ'. Lepus, the rabbit, a *feminine* constellation, is immediately *'below'* Orion, the 'hunter', just as Adam wanted Eve 'below' or *beneath* him physically, socially and politically. It always traces back to Orion. Some claim Ptolemy I was the illegitimate half-brother of Alexander the Great which wouldn't surprise me at all, they *love* Alexander because he was gay or 'bi' and the pun 'fucking like rabbits'.

When Alexander the Great's reign came to an end, the Lagides were known as Macedonian Greeks also called Hasmoneans or Asmonians, the *Maccabees*, an 'independent' semi-autonomous Jewish state a 'client state' of Rome located in Israel. So, *right*, we see Jewish Adam Sandler born on 9.9.1966, yep!, as *Dr. Maccabee* who leaves his *wedding ceremony* at the age of 22 when his fiancé cheats on him. These guys are putting all this secret symbolism in their films to show-off to their higher-ups that they they've done their research and deserve their place on the Mt. Olympus of A-list celebrity royal gods. Why wouldn't these ancient secret royal bloodline be celebrities? It's the best job in the world. It's all a game to them, *see right*, Jim Carry in the film Truman Show and his 'free range Kaiser'. Kaiser is German for *Ceasar*. He is telling you he's new-age 'free range' royalty in the *new* world *not constrained* by stuffy old-world protocols like the royals of the *past*. It's a middle finger to obsolete royalty and their dying old ways who *must* abide by boring *old-world* pomp and pageantry locked away in their dank old castles and craggy compounds. Carry openly admits to practicing tantric sex and notice the crown on the chicken. As such, *America* is the *Empire State*, a 'client state' of the old Euro-British Empires rebranded from the old Roman-Egyptian Empires morphing into a New *One World* Empire. The ancient dream come to pass! Always centralising and *still* running the world today! *See right*, the Empire State building with the Hindu Goddess Kali projected on it (2015) looking rather like a cat perhaps cross referencing Egyptian cat goddess Bastet, *right*, note, *Eartha Kitt* (earth kitty) as cat woman, another version  of Isis and Hathor associated with domesticity. Kali is the dark side of the feminine and goddess of *time*, change, sexuality, violence, power and *destruction* although 'god' will take credit for it all as he sends the little Mrs. to do his dirty work *again*. Ra sent his wife Hathor to punish men for not worshipping him so she went around the world killing many men. The biblical flood is *another* reference to the *Goddess*, mother nature, destroying people as her waters drowned all in her path as the brotherhood, god, invoke the goddess to 'clean house', *again*.

Calendars are for idiots. These guys never change. Therefore, Israel and all the commotion that has forever surrounded *that* region has little to do with protecting religious sites and practices. This is about *owning the small speck of land* connecting the African continent to Eurasia, the *largest continental area on Earth, right*. Jews are known as merchants and traders and Israel was operational HQ of the ancient world's economy that one way or another has  morphed into the new world economy. *All land trade* ancient *and* modern *must* pass through the toll gates of Israel to enter or leave the greatest *landlocked* area on the planet. In ancient times the seas were dangerous and this was the *only route via land* connecting the wealth of current Africa and ancient Egypt to the *rest of the known world!* As it were the last Ptolemy of the last ruling Dynasty of Ancient Egypt died at *12 years of age* when his mother, Cleopatra, also died. As such, Prince Harry was *12 years old* when *his* mother died, he is a Virgo, his birthday is the 15th September and his wife is three years older than him. Harry Connick Jr. was 13 when *his* mother died, he is a Virgo, his birthday is 11th September (*911!*) and his wife is three years older than him. Both Harry's are from upper-class political families Connick's father the D.A. of New Orleans for 30 years. The nearby city of St Louis is named after King Louis IX aka *Saint Louis* the 'most illustrious' of the Direct Capetians of the House of Capet whose reign is remembered as a medieval *Golden Age*. Called the 'third race of kings' after the Merovingians and Carolingians, Louis ascended to the throne at the age of 12 after the death of his father his mother ruling in his stead until he was of age as would Cleopatra have done with her son Ptolemy *if* they had survived. In one version the mother dies and in the other version the father dies, it's the death of the parents, god and goddess, the end of the Family of Life as they 'vaccinate', *sterilise*, the world one way or another. History repeating or is it *scripted* to do so in a psychological/spiritual war against humanity via *demons and aliens* intercoursing through the aristocracy, the *decision makers*, behind all this who have openly admitted their plans for the last century.

Ptolemy XV was the last Pharoah or King of Egypt who was declared by his mother Cleopatra as *co-ruler* in 47BC after she murdered her husband, *Ptolemy's older brother*, with poison. Cut to 2000 years later, the now infamous investigation of the assassination of President John F. Kennedy, *King Kennedy of New Egypt*, by then D.A. Jim Garrison was held in *New Orleans* and an appropriate setting it was for such a now legendary and one day mythical story. New Orleans is the Crescent City, yes, crescent moon city, city of the Moon Goddess! *See right*, a woman's monthly menstrual cycle is in line with the moon, *she* is the moon goddess and he 'fertile crescent', the vagina, will birth the Anti-Christ for this lot! It's also a reference to the crescent moon, the galactic 'fertile crescent' of the Milky Way which is teaming with life and the 'fertile crescent' of ancient myth which, *per replication*, was the earliest known region 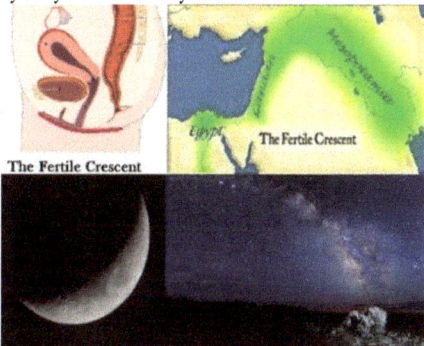 in the Middle East where civilisation was said to have emerged. Called 'the Cradle of Civilisation' this area was revered for a number of technological innovations including writing, the wheel, agriculture and the use of irrigation as we come into a new technological age and they code these symbols to work in their favour, *again*. I'm telling ya, something's going on. *We're being imaged and re-imaged.* America is a mirror of the ancient world specifically ancient Egypt as Egypt was the 'southern states' of the old world in the Southern hemisphere or the 'deep south'. Therefore, we have Memphis in Egypt and *Memphis* in the *Southern states* of America. Isis reigned in Egypt so we have the M*isis*sippi that contains the name Isis. The 'King' of rock, Elvis, considering these ancient gods emerged from the Primordial Waters as 'rock gods', was *also* a 'rock god' or 'king of rock' who reigned from *Memphis*. Elvis is an anagram of Lives and Evils who had a *twin brother* who died at birth. Ah, the dead brother theme again. And where did the 'king' die? On the *'throne'* slang for the toilet! Talk about taking the piss. They kill the 'king'. Therefore, they shot Martin Luther *King*, killed Michael Jackson the *'king'* of pop and beat the shit out of Rodney *King* leading to the riots that cost many their lives. They shot *King* Kong the 'monkey man' off the Empire State building, the 'tower' of the chakras, because humans are monkeys to them, specifically, black people they want to enslave in the 'new world' like the old Deep South. *It's a repeating script.* The whole world is a plantation now with the aristocracy firmly at the top.

In Danish Konge means King or King King, *King of Kings,* King of the Universe, *Zeus,* as is Jesus in Spanish 'Heyzeus' Greek god of sky and thunder or is it lightning? They are all electricity *tantric sex* gods because *that's* what this is *ultimately* about. They *insist* we're descended from monkeys but it's not 'monkey' it's *Moon Key* the feminine *'key of life'* the ankh or anchor - ankh whore, *the prostitute* - unlocking the 'monkey' man, *unenlightened men,* via tantric sex! So, shooting 'king kong' of the 'tower', the black monkey man, is a symbolic death of Osiris the 'black king of the Nile'. They're killing the black *and* white king in the common man as there can be only one, *their One,* the anti-Christ-seed *deified* as a new-age god-king world leader! The competition is being taken out! They have killed several white god-kings in the Kennedy's etc., they have killed several black god-kings, Gandhi, *Martin Luther King,* Malcom X as 'x marks the spot' on the 'treasure map', *right,* as the 'treasure of the world', *the light of the world,* is *Christ Seed enlightenment* of the 3rd eye that *sees all,* the *crown chakra* of the chakra tower 'the crowned king' via the optic nerve-pineal gland, KINGS CROSS, to prevent the 'king' in every man 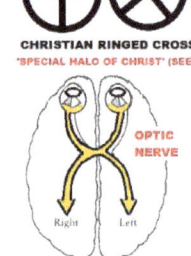 from becoming God! They have killed several white goddess-queens, Monroe, Diana, but they haven't killed many *major* black goddess-queens except the trailblazing Benazir Bhutto who was the 11th *and* 13th Prime Minister of Pakistan who was *assassinated* in the region where all this historically emanates, the Middle East, where women, *the goddess,* are infamously suppressed. All very symbolic as the *first* black woman president looms and Meghan Markle (MM Mary Magdelene) the *first* major black royal woman takes a *very* prominent position. And what's the bet if they do this terrible thing by eliminating two more major black goddess characters they'll blame 'white supremacy' all wrangled into place by the weird series of *white* police shootings of *black* people as society descends into a racial free for all! Oh dear, is the black queen next on the satanic hit list to destroy her too?? Checkmate! *See right, the black Madonna, enlightened black woman, the goddess, with her amazing crown and 'snow white' virtue of honour and chastity!* It's the card deck, the queen and king of hearts is royalty, the queen and king of diamonds is a commoner, the queen and king of clubs is black royalty and the queen and king of spades is the commoner. The light and dark side of the masculine and feminine white *and* black! *The anti-Christ, the Devil, is the Joker in the pack with an ace up his sleeve!* This is why they dress up the singer Madonna who is a sexual extravaganza of debauchery to make shit of the real Madonna, the mother, the wife, the queen, the Goddess of Love! These galactic symbols show up in the weirdest ways, so King Shaka (chakra) died on 22nd September 1829, *another 911,* as the cosmic broadcast struggles to get through as the fable is twisted by something hideous that keeps us prisoner! It's the dead brother theme *again* as he was killed by his two half-brothers. He was a brilliant military strategist yet had a major breakdown when his *mother* died and outlawed the planting of *crops* and use of *milk* for a year. All the themes are there 911, the mother, the dead brother, the milk, the crops, the seed. *Something weird and alien is behind all this.*

The Jews don't run their calendar by the sun, they run it by the moon and it starts with *Virgo*, the virgin, the Moon Goddess, the Mother of all gods who must die for 'god', the 'anti-Christ', to be born into the flesh to reign in *Her* place hiding her in his shadow as does Mephistopheles to Margarita! In this new *centralising* world it rapidly boils down to one and there can be only *One* and why in the *Matrix* (yes, it is) Neo is an anagram of *The One* born on *911* code for the 911 of ancient Egypt in that Ra and his offspring make 9 *however*, the mother and the son-sun make 11. Christ Consciousness is the 9th dimension or 7 chakras and 9 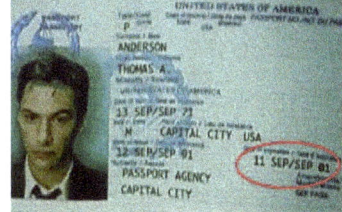 dimensions of 11. 11 is electricity, *the light* of the lovers, Gemini, The Twins! Further and more importantly to this, in Roman Numerals the number 1 is the letter 'I' and as 'I' is the *9th letter of the alphabet* then 911 is actually code for 999, *the end of a MASSIVE cycle,* the biggest one so far and why they invert it to 666. *This is the end,* thank-you Jim Morrison! Keanu Reeves is poised to release the latest Matrix after a nearly 20 year hiatus called Matrix *Resurrections*. Yes, they're resurrecting their new-age male messiah, *another one,* to fit with the script despite *the fact* the script is bullshit and clearly doesn't work benefiting only a few males at the very top. The latest Matrix is to be released on the 22nd December 22 years after the first instalment in *1999*. They do love their numbers. Keanu was born in 1964 on 2nd September *(the battle of Actium with Antony and Cleopatra)* and as September is the 9th month and 2 is II then this is *another* 911 while 64 is *another* 9. It's all code they are chosen for their names and dates of birth and lineage befitting this story, *a tale as old as time,* the problem is 'time' is a construct of the devil. Brad Pitt, born 18.12.1963 (3,6,9 a few weeks after Kennedy was shot) latest film *Babylon* to be released on Christmas Day 2022 just a coincidence of course as Anjolina Jolie releases 'Eternals' and 'Those Who Wish Me Dead'. Simultaneously, on the filmset Rust an *unnecessary* accident occurred when *Alec Baldwin* shot dead a woman, *Halyna Hutchins,* HH 88 Hermes-Mercury and 88 constellations, *yes, a symbolic goddess character,* who worked in a role *specifically noted* for very few women in an 'old west' movie about cowboys considering the 'cowboys' want to continue their old west sexist shit in the *New West*, the *new world*, as the feminine returns and women have the same opportunities as men. Nothing going on there. The first Harry Potter film was released on 29th November 2001 as 2+9=11 and as November is 11 we have *another* 11:11 in 2001 the *first year* of the *3rd* millennium. Harry is Hari the prime Hindu god the 8th incarnation of which was Hari Krishna. Krishna is Christ. Christ is God. Christ is the *Christ seed* of human enlightenment as such, *human enlightenment is God within*. Romans 12:19 "Never avenge yourselves, but leave it to the *wrath of god*, for it is written, 'Vengeance *is* mine'. I dearly hope so.

The New Egypt of America is set to be the *theatre* from which the Devil incarnate, the *anti-Christ*, will rise via a political family. It's *literally* Damien in the Omen, an 'omen' is a prophecy. They tell you, openly. All of these people are sun kings or sun queens aka tantric sex enlightenment claiming to be the incarnation of 'god' and 'goddess'. Point is, they have variously described themselves covertly as frogs, turtles, snakes, birds, dragons and lizards. They were the 'masters of the waters' considered water spirits or aquatic deities, non-material, amphibious and serpentine, green skinned with *long tails used to prop them upright on land* aka the upright snake of the bible giving birth to the snake lore and  legend throughout the ages from Eden to Medusa, Cecrops, Triton, Poseidon, feathered serpents – *the phoenix* - Indian Nagas, Chinese dragons – it's *everywhere* and cannot be denied. They were hermaphrodites said to have 'twin souls'. The *twins phenomenon* allows that even twins *separated at birth* go on to live *strikingly similar* lives often living on streets of the same name or marrying partners with the same name etc. It's all about energy mirroring itself, a counter pole of *electrical forces*, positive and negatives in a *circle* of life that mirror each other even on the other side of the universe. There is no such this as 'space' or 'time'. Even via genetics the twins causes *replication* and 'parallel' realities from the macro to the micro generated by *shared DNA* that gives us our sense of *perception* and thus our reality. It's what the Nazi's were decoding in lead up to this moment to fulfill their weird vision or *version* of ancient prophecies. The elite are seeking to go round *again* as they are too afraid to break with tradition and live out any other script but the tried and tested script of their own power as *they don't know where it will all go if they don't!* They're *obsessed* with repetition. *Inbred royal OCD*. Like the 'devil', they don't evolve and their *inability to change* spells their doom!

The waters, the Void, is space-time that still exists between the cosmic bodies of planets *in the 3D*. Outside the 3D it is 'fluid'. So, the ancient Dogon were basically saying the Nommo were 'masters of the waters' they were describing 'space travelers' and as the newcomers couldn't explain to ignorant people how space works, they described it as similar to the 'waters' of the ocean with currents and slipstreams hence, space*ships*. They descended from the sky in a 'thunderous vessel accompanied by fire' i.e. the thrusters of a craft, presenting themselves as the Teachers and Watchers who claimed to come from a planet circling Sirius binary 'twin star' system. These Watchers have been referred to in many ancient societies while in the 1980's series 'V' they depicted an invasion of reptilians who came from the third planet circling Sirius. In one scene they even show the statue of the *Goddess Diana* covered in *Ivy* while the main character called *Diana* is a reptilian. The scaly Nommo claimed they were the first living creatures created by the sky god Amma and shortly after their creation they multiplied into four pairs of twins or 8 in all. This is the story of the Great Ennead and the Ogdoad as well and including the sun god *Ra,* they made *nine in all*. Called the *'Original Nine'* they were referenced by the Aztec, Egyptian and Tibetan cultures among others including the Norse who had 'nine realms' etc. The number 9 shows up a lot considered it's the most 'magic' number not forgetting the word 'feminine' has the number 'nine' coded into it. On the back of the U.S. One Dollar Bill is a Masonic symbol consisting of 72 stones (9) and represents the tetragrammaton of the four-letter word for YHVH aka *Yahweh*. Again, 'god' traces back to the feminine as we find the number 9, according to the research of Joseph Campbell, is traditionally associated with the Goddess 'Mother of the World'. Given Yahweh-Jehovah is a male 'god' are they saying cryptically 'god' is feminine? You tell me it's *their* god.

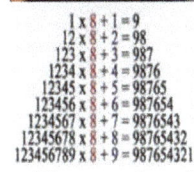

In India there are 108 names associated with this great Goddess as 1+8=9. The numerological value of the word LOVE is 54 (9). The word 'enlightenment' is the only word in English that spells the number 'eighteen' in order as 18 reduces to 9. Revelations Chap 21 says a great 'city' would come to earth from the sky described as a *'cube'* 12,000 furlongs in every direction. A massive ship? 12 reduces to 3 the number of the Empress. It goes on and on and on, *see right*, the root chakra cube and the sound of 'Om' and the Hindu feminine 'yoni', a square or 'box', slang for woman's vagina. Isn't it odd that all three major Abrahamic religions are heavily symbolised by the cube-square-box? *See right,* Kaaba which literally translates as 'cube' as well as the cube-box on the *3rd eye* no less of

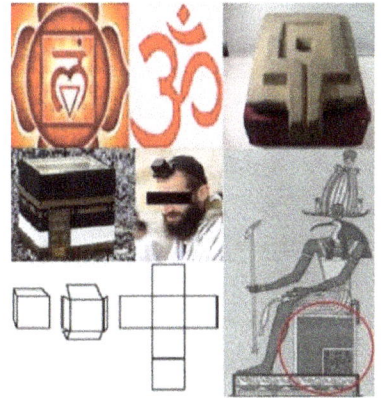

Jewish men and the 'cross' that folds into a cube-square-box considering masons use the 'square' as one of their major symbols. Isis, the Goddess, the mother-wife, was *literally* considered the throne as via her they existed and got a son for their dick cult to continue the line. So, here we have Egyptian Thoth sitting on his throne, a cube, the feminine root chakra of procreation. It's no coincidence that in Egypt, the home of the Goddess, *90% of females* have had their genitalia cut out via FGM effectively robbing the Goddess of her ability to attain enlightenment preventing her root chakra from activating her Chakra Tower when the princess becomes the queen and ultimately the Goddess, the *Divine* Feminine! But then, there is only one God, an almighty cruel vengeful hyper-male force that has destroyed *Mother* Earth. Wonder who that might be? Nine is a number of *completion* and *transformation*, the end of a cycle, before it goes back to 1. They are trying to trick us out of this *completion* keeping us from our *transformation* in the next level of ascension ergo *evolution*. 'Chaos' comes from ancient Greek meaning emptiness, chasm, cave, hollows, the abyss, to gape or 'yawn'. In The Encyclopaedia of Religions by John G.R. Forlong, the Yoni-vagina, the female emblem of India, is from the Ayran root word meaning 'hollow' from which the English word '*yawn*' derives and in hieroglyphic systems the *yoni* symbol in Egyptian and Hittite means 'mother'. Symbols of the Yoni include the circle, ring (crossed wedding rings or vesica-piscis), *triangle*, ark, pomegranate, hollows, caves, barley, corn, a stone with a hole through it, as well as the 'argha' a yellow bee i.e. the land of milk and honey, *enlightenment*. It also means material worship, 'respectful offering to the gods or venerable men' as well as '*very costly then reduced in their true value or depreciated*'. It also means a small boat shaped vessel. It all leads to the same place every time, beyond male 'Gods' is a vagina, the Mother of *all* earthly 'gods' who are simply *men* harbouring the light force of Chi Prana a feminine force.

Early Arab historian, Ibn Ishaq 704-767AD, collected ancient oral traditions that formed the foundation of his biography on Islam's Muhammad and claimed the Kaaba was once addressed as a female deity worshipped as a fertility goddess. He taught that the circular milling around of the Kaaba that still occurs today was once carried out by naked male and female pilgrims. Circles and spirals etc are depictions of the galaxy and the 'cyclic' nature of life. Even now the 'black stone' a fragment of *meteor* housed in the Eastern corner of the Kaaba is supported by a silver frame a feminine element and appears to be *another* vagina or 'yoni', *see right*. Roman Goddess Cybele was said to be venerated by a black stone meteorite while the 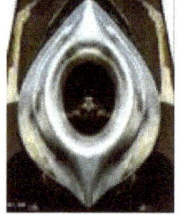 feminine Aether is associated with a 'meteoric element' as was the Phrygian Goddess *Diana,* a triple goddess who birthed the moon and underworld. Prior to the rise of Islam the tribal religions were based around the Triple Goddess which is interesting as in *many* cultures and beliefs we find the 'triple goddess' myth in pagan, neo-pagan and *current* belief systems *worldwide*. She symbolises the waxing, full and waning moon or the maiden, mother and crone, *see, right*. The *Hindu* Triple Goddess legend has Shakti as part of the *Holy Trinity* called the Tridevi who creates, maintains, 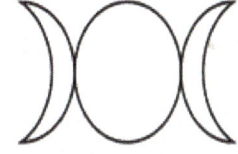 regenerates, and recycles the universe respectively. They include Saraswati the Goddess of art and wisdom, Lakshmi the Goddess of prosperity and Shakti *the energy of Vishnu* the 'preserver', yes, The Light. In her physical form she is Paravati Goddess of fertility, love, beauty, *marriage*, children and devotion as well as divine strength and power; a gentle nurturing aspect or Mother Nature personified. The triple goddess was very popular as seen in the Norse *Norn* goddesses Urd, Verdandi, and Skuld are on par with the Greek Fates Clotho 'the Spinner, Lachesis 'the Allotter', Atropos 'the Unturning' or 'Inflexible who 'weaved' the fates of mankind. The Hindus have the Tridevi triple goddess while the Triple Coventia, *right*, from Celtic myth were goddesses of wells and springs, again, a water goddess. In *pre*-Islamic  times called the 'Age of Ignorance' (no surprises there) ancient Arabia cultivated a poly-theistic, multi-religious, belief system including ancient Semitic, Christian, Judaism and Iranian religions as well as Zoroastrianism, Mithraism and Manichaeism. Al-Uzza was one of *three chief goddesses, right,* worshipped in ancient Arabia along with al-Lat and Manat, they look like milk maids, *obviously* very different from today's culture. A stone *cube* located at Nakhla near Mecca was held sacred to her religion. Al-Uzza is mentioned in Quran 53:19 as being one of the *Triple Goddesses* worshipped called upon for protection by the Quraysh tribe that historically controlled Mecca and its Kaaba. These goddesses were associated with cranes or birds. Tantric sex is symbolised by doves, swans, eagles, skylarks, falcons, Hawkes etc depicted by the Egyptian hawk-eye of Horus, *bird's eye view*. 'Bird' is slang for woman.

Muhammad was born into the Hashemite family clan of the Quraysh tribe although many of the Quraysh initially 'staunchly opposed' the rising Muhammad until they were suddenly converted 'en masse' circa 630AD which sounds like forced conversion as tyrants often do, *see*, Genghis Khan among many others including the Roman Catholic Church. The three goddesses were referenced in multiple early biographies by Ibn Ishaq, al-Waqidi and Ibn Sa'd who all claimed Muhammed had spoken words that prayer *was permitted* to these three pre-Islamic Meccan Goddesses. This was later retracted as a 'violation' of male monotheism and that Muhammad must have been misled by 'satanic suggestion' which he mistook for 'divine revelation'. Of course, the *feminine* must be Satanic given what these men have done. What a joke. This reference *permitting* the veneration of the feminine was called the 'Satanic Verses' was a phrase made famous by Salman Rushdie's book *The Satanic Verses, right,* clearly referring to this legend of Goddess worship in the Middle East!

These few lines *approving feminine veneration* were said to be revealed in verses 20 and 21 in surah (the chapter) 'An-Najim' of the Quran. Sir Salman Rushdie received his Master of Arts degree in History from the University of Cambridge in 1968. He was knighted by Queen Elizabeth II in 2008 for his 'services to literature', a royal British 'fuck you' to the Arabs, given Queen Elizabeth is a *symbolic personification* the Goddess referred to as the Queen of the World. They even had an advertisement on TV about QE2 calling her *The Queen of the World*. Rushdie 'challenged' Muslim beliefs in his 'historical fiction' *obviously* based around the life of the prophet Muhammad.

Muslim's believe Muhammad was visited by the angel Gibreel who recited the words of god over 22 years. Here we go again with the 11:11. In ancient *biblical* texts Gabriel was actually *Gabrielle*, a woman, and in Max Heindel's book, *Freemasonry and Catholicism*, he claimed the 'early stages' of the newly formed Earth were dark and hot, and Jehovah-God was said to have 'cooled the Earth with water' (the feminine). While some 'angels' adapted well to the change other 'angels' (demons) led by 'Lucifer' couldn't bear to be quenched with water, so they rebelled against Jehovah-God. Lucifer took his rebellious angels and left Earth to go to *Mars*, a desert world, personified as the 'god of war' considering Mars is said to be desolate due to ancient nuclear war! Jehovah-God's representative Angel on Earth was Gabrielle originally depicted as female changed by the Catholic Church to a male, Gabriel, leaving Mother Mary as the *only* feminine representative to keep masculine dominion in place. *Everything has been changed to male.* It's a dick cult. Gabrielle is the protector of children and assists with parenting, public *speakers* and those in the field of creative arts while her equivalent is often depicted by other cultures and religions worldwide, *see, Paravati*. In his book *Satanic Verses*, Rushdie's 'fictional' Muhammad is called Mahound claimed to be a derogatory term used by Christians in the middle ages meaning 'devil'. Interestingly, in another of Rushdie's books titled *Salman* (given Rushdie's first name is Salman) he correlates actual passages in the Quran to Muhammad's sexist views that place men 'in charge of women' giving men the right to physically assault their wives whom they 'fear arrogance'. Rushdie strongly suggests that Muhammad *himself* was the source of 'god's word' to suit his *personal* ambitions meaning like all other ambitious men current and historic, he was *self-serving* to say the least. Rushdie's 'allegorical' novels that 'examine historical and philosophical issues' resulted in a 'fatwa', a contract killing, being placed on his life by the Ayatollah Khomeini ultimately to the tune of 2.5 million dollars! Although Rushdie was placed in 'protective custody' he made very public appearance's including U2 concerts and didn't appear to be too phased about the so-called dangers and even said he wished he been *more* critical. Sounds to me like Rushdie had been given the green light by the Queen's mob, the masonic engineers, in a big middle finger to the Islamic boys clubs who couldn't touch him in a testament to who is *really* in charge here. That said, a number of people *around* Rushdie involved in the printing and publishing of *Satanic Verses* were severely injured and even killed by murderers claiming to represent Islam. Murderers don't represent anyone except themselves and will use *any* excuse to fulfill their bloodlust. Satanic men often take credit for the work risking the lives of subordinates and laugh it up *openly* while those around them are sacrificed in their stead.

In Rushdie's *Satanic Verses* Mahound's (Muhammad's) scribe, funnily enough, is also named *Salman* which is somewhat hilarious as Rushdie appears to be actually placing himself in his own 'fiction'! I like this guy! Salman the scribe notices that the 'revelations' Muhammad received are *very convenient* for the 'prophet' who benefits enormously from 'god's word' so, he begins altering the text to 'test' him. Terrified he'll be found out Salman runs away to the town of Jahiliya and is saved from execution while another character Baal flees hiding in a *brothel*. Baal is *another* name for the devil. The brothel is named Hijab while the Hijab is also worn as a headdress by some Muslim women. In this brothel all the 'prostitutes' are named after Muhammed's wives! Some say this is a mockery however, the so-called Academic historical record speak *openly* of 'sacred prostitution' in relation to 'Goddess' worship, *see*, Mary Magdalene, probably because ancient male hypocrites couldn't reconcile that a woman could be empowered by her sex (certainly not *ashamed* of it) so she must be a hooker. It's *exactly* the same today, *nothing's changed*. Evolving emotionally seems to be the real stop-gap for these *sexually* immature if well-armed maniacs. Most men are *terrified* of powerful sexual women who they can't shame. Limp.

In ancient Greece long before all this they engaged in Hieros Gamos, *Holy Marriage*, a process in which the 'king' married the 'goddess'. Indeed, Jesus' wife was claimed a 'prostitute' (sounds familiar) while the Roman word Lupa (she-wolf) was ancient slang for prostitute from the legend of the founders of Rome, Romulus and Remus, who suckled a she-wolf in a cave near the temple of the *Magna Mater* the 'Great Mother'. It's all tantric sex-enlightenment talk. Sirius the Dog Star or Canis Major & Minor is a binary two-star system acknowledge by indigenous people's worldwide in a *canine* capacity as the 'dog', 'wolf', 'coyote' etc. She is also called the Big Dog and the Pup. *Note*, Dog is *God* spelled backwards. This is all tied up with the 'virgin-whore' myths and why all Abrahamic religions, particularly Muslims, are seemingly obsessed with virgins being assured of '100 virgins in heaven' when they die. Whatever. So, 'Lupa' the prostitute 'Dog' is Sirius, a feminine sun – the Universal Light Force -

personified as Isis or Mary Magdalene etc., *i.e.* the Goddess. Actually, domestic violence or a husband believing he has the right to dominate his wife is a weird form of sadomasochism justified because they are in a relationship that, a) gives him the right to unlimited sex, b) he's bought himself a house cleaner, and c) he *physically owns her* and she is an emotional outlet, a punching bag, for brattish childish behaviour, *like hitting people,* behaviour that he otherwise knows is *inappropriate* in a wider *adult* setting and why it happens 'behind closed doors' like that creepy song. I've noticed a lot of popular music openly encouraging raping and brutalizing women. It's 'normal'. Grow the fuck up.

Danish folk tales tell of *King* Lindworm. Worm or 'wyrm' are serpentine dragons and not surprisingly reptilians are generally 'royalty'. In some folktales the newlyweds apparently engage in bondage and sadomasochism, 'I can't wait to get married so I can beat the shit out of you'. There is a common fairy tale motif folklorists call the 'Animal as a Bridegroom' referring to a human woman marrying an 'animal' who turns out to be a human prince in disguise or under a curse or 'enchantment'. This is a combination of reptilian genetics and multigenerational demonic attachments. In one account the new bride gives her new husband a sound thrashing with a whip on their wedding night! Actually, the foundation of bondage or S&M seems to come from these ancient cultural tales. Take Beauty and the Beast, for example, in some telling's of this tale the 'beast' has killed multiple wives and even his servants because he is a royal psychopath. Even in the modern Beauty and the Beast some critics observe that all the 'furniture' is broken yet the 'servants' are *animated* furniture intimating that he has killed his servants and their souls have gone into the furnishings waiting to be released or reborn. In some accounts the new bride lies about her status pretending to be nobility and when 'prince charming' finds out that she is not of noble blood, he attempts to harm her whereby she stands up to him and wins his heart. In these tales she sheds 'seven layers of clothing' a reference to the seven chakras being unlocked via tantric sex while he sheds 'seven snake skins' and 'casts them into the fire' only to find *underneath the animal* is a man hence, the curse. In these tales the bride must sometimes beat him in order to beat out the dragon/snake/devil and reveal the man underneath to break the curse! So there you go! Looks like S&M was a thing in the old days and actually seems to have had a practical purpose of releasing the prince from his 'disenchantment', the snake aspect, the violent killer, the animal, in order to become the man again. *See right*, the oldest dildo in the world archaeologists dating it to 26,000BC. I don't  even want to think how many times this has been used. No wonder this archaeologist is wearing gloves. Also, it would be slightly embarrassing that the culmination of her life's work and what she is most famous for is a prehistoric nob. Sorry but it's true. I hope she finds something a bit more academic to moor he professional credibility to. All those years of study for this.

The Vestal Virgins of Rome were the temple priestesses of the Virgin Goddess Vesta of the *'sacred eternal flame'* - tantric flame or fires - who were the primer for Catholic nuns. They entered into the temple around the age of six to ten the same age Muslim men are allowed to marry little girls. Their tenure lasted for 30 years and they were powerful women in their own right with reserved places of honour at public performances. They could pardon or free a slave with a touch of their hand. If a prisoner condemned to death saw a Vestal on the way to their execution they were automatically freed. Their word was trusted *without question* in giving evidence entrusted with wills, state documents and public treaties etc. This is the tail end of the priestess administrators before the boys took over. Vestals were *officials* of their time now relegated to the office secretary and chief coffee maker for the corporate boys the little Caesar's and tyrants in the Senate of the Office Building. High rise buildings are dicks. It's a dick cult. Now the administrators are the male priesthood, the Masons. The fact is women administrate men till the fields. She looks after the books and does the running of the house he performs manual labour, bargains and barters. Now she does the heavy work and he does the books. No wonder everything's gone tits up. Vestals were considered magical by virtue of their chastity tasked with keeping the 'fires of Vesta' alive. Under Emperor Theodosius and the Christian uprising the Vestal College was closed and the magical fire of the hearth put out. It was then, as legend has it, Rome fell. Vestals took a thirty-year vow of chastity to 'devote themselves to the study and correct observance of state rituals that were forbidden to the colleges of male priests'.

Once the tenure of a Vestal Virgin was complete around the age of *40* it was high honour for a nobleman to marry one as they were said to have *magical powers* and produce *'godlike'* sons as was 'god' Jesus 'born of a virgin'. It seems Mother Mary was a Vestal Virgin and gave birth to a 'god' insofar as, like all *enlightened* male leaders in history, he was practicing transcendental sex hence, the 'virgin' mother and 'prostitute' wife also a Vestal priestess of tantric sex. The Jews know all about this and freely put this knowledge into their movies, *right*, Steve Carell's film *The 40 Year Old Virgin* as tantric sex takes a long time hence, 'the longer you wait the harder it gets'. Evan Almighty, *right*, released on *22nd* June is about an *ordinary* guy who receives *messages from God* and becomes a modern-day Noah building an 'ark' for a looming flood. Playing at a theatre in the background, *right*, is another film called *The 40-Year-Old Virgin Mary* a weird homage to *The Lowes Theatre* where Monroe's image was three stories high in *The Seven Year Itch*, i.e. the seven chakras and the 'itch' to fulfill sex. The famous dress-blowing-up scene is recreated in the robes of Evan Almighty blowing up like Marilyn's dress. They are slinging shit at the Goddess here as they derive their power 'god' from the feminine force considering Marilyn Monroe, MM Mary Magdalene-Mother Mary, was the 'prostitute' aspect of the divine feminine of sacred sex enlightenment and had a book written about her by Anthony Summers called *Goddess*. Monroe was murdered to symbolise the killing of the Goddess so, this isn't funny at all, in fact, it's quite a sick joke if you think about it. *Notice*, Morgan Freeman, 'God' in this film wears the fleur di lis on his cap or crown. The fleur di lis is referenced all around the tantric sex myth as worn by traditional royalty including the Sun Kings of France its *ancient geometry* represents a *blueprint of the universe, the trinity and the Virgin Mary*. It really means the family of Life, the child arising from the two parents that peel away like new blooms on growing branches of a great tree, the Tree of Life, the next generation, *fractalling*. It's the Tree of Knowledge of the *crown* (chakra) adopted by royalty for this purpose. The film *Bruce Almighty* starred Jim Carrey who openly admits to practicing tantric sex even describing how it works to a point. He addressed a crowd on how 'Jesus opened the gates of heaven' and said, 'I'm a Buddhist, I'm a Christian, I'm a Muslim, I'm whatever you want me to be. *It all comes down to the same thing…'*.

Rapper Vanilla Ice wears the fleur di lis on his heart in the Adam Sandler film *That's My Boy*. Any man can be 'god' with tantric Christ enlightenment opening the chakras *specifically* the 'Crown' IQ to become incredibly powerful and rich, he even said on his luxury home renovation show he wanted the décor to be 'modern royalty'. Uh huh. Vanilla Ice has hardly aged a day in 30 years his big hit Ice Ice Baby released on 22.08.1990. The amount of sacred sex imagery found in movies would require another book all of its own. It's *incredible* once you know what to look for. Sandler remade *Mr. Deeds Goes to Town* originally starring Gary Cooper. He renamed it *Deeds* because Deeds' first name is *Longfellow*, yes, as in big dick. They can't help themselves always putting it in your face, well, you know, in films, thank god. The double intendre's are rife. His t-shirt here says Mandrake Falls Fire Department. The Mandrake plant is an aphrodisiac, the 'fire' department is the masculine fires and the 'falls' are the feminine waters. It's all a reference to tantric sex. Will Ferrell's films are also *loaded*. Jim Carrey spoke about the church and cross, "They talk about omnipresence in church, and nobody really thinks about what that means. What it means is every cell in your body is God. Everything is God. Everything is divine. When you do good things and transcend the negativity and attempt to do something positive, you are the heart of God, the eyes of God. When you speak from that place *you are God's voice*. When you make a loaf of bread in this kitchen that is a Eucharist. You are blessing people with your work...That is the body of Christ". But once again, like John Lennon and all the rest who try to come out about this information, *rather bizarrely,* Carrey suddenly faced a 'wrongful death' trial in 2018 accused of providing the drugs that led to the 'suicide' of his then girlfriend Cathriona White (*note*, the name 'white' virginal Snow White). She was found dead at Sherman *Oaks* (this is a strange reference to the Oak King aka the Green Man). Her family sued him claiming he gave her the powerful painkillers that took her life also claiming he gave her three STD's without warning her. This is why you preferably only practice it with one person, if we were supposed to fuck around so much, Mother Nature, the Goddess, Mummy, wouldn't have made STD's to stop childish brats from doing stupid shit and contaminating the pure life force with their dirt. It was all ultimately dismissed with Carrey making the statement that White was, "a truly kind and delicate Irish *flower*, too sensitive for this *soil*, to whom *loving* and being *loved* was all that *sparkled*." That's a tantric sex description of *Mother Nature*, Sirius Star Goddess, the life force found in flowers, the rose, 'soil', earth, dirt, Mother Earth and grounding. 'Sparkling' is a reference to the *crown chakra* and the stars, specifically, Sirius, the brightest star.

This *virginal* energy is the unsullied and much sought after 'light' of the pure feminine 'fire' ascribed to the brightest star in the sky, Sirius, personified as the Egyptian Goddess Isis as well as Christian Mary, Eastern Shakti, Caribbean Yemaya, African Yemoja, Japanese Izanami, Roman Diana, Greek Aphrodite etc. She *is* the *Mother* 'Spirit' the *electrical* polar aspect of universal energy life-force *personified* as the abovementioned High Feminine's but really, she is *all* women. Historically, people were not exercising an *educated detachment* from the dogma and superstition that shrouded the ancient world as such, the lines were blurred but *we* don't have to fall for the same superstition and mistakes. There's no mystery here, it's *physics* plain and simple, so there's no need to turn this into a religion, how ridiculous! Just exercise discipline and a healthy approach and with this power you can easily live to a 150. We can be nature lovers and protect Mother Nature-Mother Earth without sinking into a satanic *mental illness* sacrificing babies on a fucken stone in the woods or losing our humanity just because we 'feel' powerful. Get a grip. There is a lot of responsibility that goes along with this knowledge otherwise it turns into a *god complex* and you get what we have today, a broken world run by little Hitlers, fake kings, brats, *wannabe gods*, who think they are *so important* they actually kill people. Like God. But the true God has no need to kill people. That's how you know Satan is running this planet. Control and destruction was *never* the intention for this beautiful force and this is where they went wrong in the past but *we* don't have to. Nicola Tesla said, 'if you want to think of the universe, think in terms of electricity, vibrations and frequency's'. The universe is an *electrical broadcast* and when condensed manifests as the *spectrum of life* all around us. Yes, she is pretty impressive. I can see why she is called 'Goddess' although we need to strike a balance between respect and unhinged 'worship' along with all the paranoia that springs up when you lose *focus* and *balance*. Next thing you know you're giving Satan a reach-around and destroying an innocent person just because you don't like their name - like they did with me. Pricks.

She is Goddess of Nature, Pregnancy, Creation, water, rainbows, daylight, sky - it goes on and on. Only it's been turned into a reign of terror and deliberate misappropriation of power by so-called 'scholars', *men*, of *all* religious doctrines in *all* countries *worldwide*. Turns out they're just really insecure and need to be 'god', it's a Little Lord Fauntleroy syndrome. They needs to feel 'good' about themselves at the expense of others yet just wind up feeling empty because, well, it's lonely at the top and money can't buy you love. They are using the wrong approach, wrong system. They're spoiled brats ancient *and* modern. This power was unfortunately militarized in a secret military movement *against the feminine* to harvest Mother Earth and emerge as kings and ultimately 'god' in a 'new age', Aquarius, as 'prophesised', eons ago. They turned the respect that ancient people's had for the mother into a sex and death cult *war machine* stealing the bounty of this precious feminine planet destroying the Goddess to rule over a barren wasteland. Nice one. In a time long ago when we were the last of our *natural* selves trade was done by bartering objects, food, thread, precious stones etc. It was the *real* currency based on *real* value of physical objects. Then they said there was 'one' god, and it was male and that 'money' (moon-ey) was to replace *real* trade of *real* things and a 'price' was placed on everything. A contract was taken out on Mother Nature's head, on the divine feminine, the goddess, Mother Earth, and all the jewels of her beauty were up for grabs and the bounty hunters went after it *en masse!* They are called pilgrims, settlers, coloniser's directed by aristocracy ruling over a false system killing the very earth we rely on for life! Everything great about this planet was 'fair game' to them including the last of the natives living the traditions that the coloniser's once lived before they were morphed into something demonic and uncaring by emerging *demonic* alien male religions aka *the blueprint* used on many worlds!

The trees were sliced down for 'needed' buildings and ships all since discarded and forgotten. The ground was torn up for crops and pastures that are now poisoned and contaminated. The water was dammed up and a price put on who and how it could be used. But it doesn't belong to them. They stole it. They're thieves and why the devil is depicted as a thief in fairy tales like *Ali Baba and the Forty Thieves* and The Brothers Grimm, *The Master Thief* among others. They make out he's just a rascal, a trickster, but he is far more than that. The machine of these cosmic male psychopaths went into full swing and anyone who opposed it, *especially women*, were dealt with in the harshest way. They have stolen and retained the knowledge of sacred sex enlightenment amongst themselves while enslaving ordinary men to keep women very much under the thumb of insane sexually frustrated lunatics, *see*, FGM. The Quran references the star Sirius in verse 49 where it is called Assira or Ash-shira 'the leader'. Although they designate it as a male star, 'That he is the Lord Sirius, the Mighty Star, that is the bright star, named Mirzam Al-Jawza *(Sirius)* which a group of Arabs used to worship'. Yes, the pre-Islamic Arab *tribespeople* were worshipping the *Goddess*. Sirius was never a male star addressed worldwide as feminine called the 'Sun behind the Sun' and the 'Mother' of 'God'.

The Arke of the Covenant is the sacred covenant of marriage that accesses the *arc of the rainbow*, the light spectrum of tantric sex enlightenment found in the *chakra system*. Australian Aboriginals believe the rainbow 'serpent' is the Creator known as Kurreah, Andrenjinyi, Yingarna, Ngalyod and others in the Dreaming, the infinite period of time that 'began with the world's creation and that has no end'. Yes, infinite, *eternal*, as spoken of by ancient Greeks and Egyptians etc, see, Anjolina Jolie's new film and maybe why she's saying 'they wish me dead' as mentioned a few big feminine's are in danger right now. The suppression of the feminine has all but destroyed Mother Nature as 'climate change' makes it presence felt and like the ice ages that destroyed the world five times before, they have another 'mini' ice age lined up with their weather modification. These guys are INSANE to mess with an entire planet so casually but then, *note*, a god complex is a side effect of this practice if not grounded. There is no doubt that damage has been done it is, after all, a Satanic harvesting of this beautiful world in an alien space program that has taken over and harvested *many* worlds. We are but one. A very important one. Out of this destruction they want to produce the one world leader, the fake Messiah, the Anti-Christ, who will present you with the solutions to 'fix' the mess they got you into. At the very top of the Milky Way galaxy is a star called Capella. Capella is a feminine star that translates as 'little goat'. Yes, the top star in our galaxy is a little female goat. So, once again, they took the feminine 'little goat', tellingly, called a 'kid' and turned it into the dark-side-of-the-masculine, a twisted evil satanic demonic cryptid goatman god who enslaves men and women beneath it! Capricorn is the goat. The goat is the devil or *Capricorn* whose star sign goes from the 22nd Dec to the 19th January. Jesus is 'born' under the sign of Capricorn as well so we are being told JC is linked to the devil. They are more than adversaries. They are Brothers. The Brotherhood. Capricorn card in the tarot deck, *right*. The Devil and the Christ is one and the same found in every man and woman depending on what you tap into. Satan is Christ's evil twin. In the tarot deck Capricorn the Devil's month and means 'earth', Saturn, root chakra, the colour is black and indigo (the third eye) and it's body part the genitals. Sex. Notice the male has a fire tail, fires of his loins, and the female's 'tale' has plants or Mother Nature, Mother Earth. This creature chaining the man and woman represents heavy  toxicity, vice, sexual addiction, lies, cheating, thievery, being bound, stuck, corruption and being held against ones will.

In Manly P. Hall's *The All-Seeing Eye* from the chapter *Freemasonry and the Osiris Myth* he states, 'The purpose of Isis (*the feminine*) is now revealed as twofold. The first motive was the almost hopeless effort to restore her dead husband to life…The second and more imminent motive was to avenge herself upon Set (the devil) and to *destroy his power over the world*". The 'dead husband' is all men. Dead on the inside. Avenging herself upon the devil I think speaks for itself. There is a prophecy that a woman – *the feminine* - will be the force that brings this reign of death and destruction to an end not another man, messiah, alien god, scholar, pope, king, president, lord or whatever and certainly not a fake one world leader who really *is* the devil incarnate. *This* is precisely why women have been injured unendingly by all manner of evil male institutions ancient *and* modern. All that was *feminine* they turned into the dark side of the masculine to blame *women* for *their* crimes. To dress the Goddess up as Satan and dress Satan up as God! To ignore and block out the light side of the masculine and use the greed of men to suppress their only way out, the Feminine! If they could confuse the issue with phonetics and twisted linguistics then they could twist the prophecy to suit themselves and outsmart everyone while laughing in our faces the whole time. How very clever of them. They were hoping this would prevent the return of the Feminine, the Return of the Queen.

Yet despite *everything*, so far, they remain a failure.

PART TWO

"For the other half of the sky"
Woman by John Lennon

CHAPTER SEVEN

LADY LIBERTY THE LIGHT BEARER

For whom the Liberty Bell tolls.

In ancient Greek Mythology they recounted a time of an *'eternal spring'* known as the *Golden Age* when humans were youthful in body, mind and spirit until the end of their lives when approximately two years before the age of 100, they suddenly aged and died. Sounds great. The 'Golden Age' was described by the ancient poet Hesiod as a period of Greek mythology 'heralding the end of the higher state of humanity' (remember that statement *'higher state of humanity'* it's very important), ruled over by Cronus. If you research this you will be told that Khronos-Chronos is the god of 'time' while Cronus, a different god, ruled over the *Golden Age*. This is academic doublespeak, *gatekeeping* and *deflection*, designed to confuse you. I'm not a fan of scholars or professors and you will shortly see why as 'education' is key to the *endless lies* and *traps* we find ourselves in! When decoding their inordinate amount of bullshit, simply look at the cold hard facts and go from there and when you get the hang of it you can read between the lines like speaking another language. So, Khronos-Chronos was 'god of time' while Cronus was 'god of the golden age'. An 'Age' equates to approximately, 2,000 years which equates to, you guessed it, *time*. It's so simple we're not looking at it for what it is. Khronos-Chronos and Cronus are the *same god* as is Satan-Saturn *also* 'god of time'. It's all replication *mimicking* the natural *feminine* universal light. It's the 'dark mirror'.

Satan is 'prince of the power of the air' and Zeus is the 'god of the sky' in lightning and thunder – it's the same god – sky, air, thunder, lightning. As the Devil is the father of Satan and Zeus is the father of Apollo then *Zeus* is the Devil and *Apollo* is Satan. The Father becomes the Son hence, the biblical verse "..that serpent of old, called the Devil *and* Satan, who deceives the whole world". The Devil-Satan is the same god and why I say anyone worshipping 'one' god is worshipping Satan. As such, Apollo 11 is actually Satan 11 and why the movie Capricorn 1 depicted a *fake Mars landing* as *Capricorn* is the goat god and the *goat god* is the Devil and the Devil is Satan and *Satan* is Apollo therefore,

Capricorn 1 *is* Apollo 11. Same god. Mars is the 'god of war' and Satan is at 'war in heaven' against 'god' as such *Satan* is the god of war. So, you see, Capricorn, the Devil, Satan, Mars, Zeus and Apollo are *all the same god* of war, air, time, space - *everything*. He plays all the different parts. *There can be only one.* It's really not rocket science although they've *literally* turned it into that. So, Apollo 11 is Satan 11 and as Capricorn is Satan *and* Apollo and there can be only *one* god, then we have an *in-your-face* admission that the 'Capricorn 1' aka Satan 1 movie about a *fake* space program is an *embedded confession* that the moon landing Satan 11 aka *Apollo11* was *faked* but then he is the father of lies, the 'great pretender'. This is why it was called the *Mercury* Space Program as Mercury is Hermes, a bisexual *tantric sex* practitioner, where they are getting their brains from and their clever lies too. Can we pause for a moment and acknowledge that Russia sent 13 *real* probes to Venus commencing in 1961? *Right,* is an actual photo of the Venusian surface from Venera 7 (chakras) all derived from German scientists post WWII. It was always about the space program in the New Age underpinned by conveniently times TV shows like Star Trek and Star Wars. *The god of war is in space now.* The saga continues.

Most people would assume that Kronos was some benevolent god who just so happened to be running the place when humanity went to shit. But what we are *really* being told here is that there was an 'eternal' *higher state* of humanity, an *eternal* spring, not limited by an 'age' or period of 'time'. It was an era when people were *eternally* youthful when the world was an abundant garden in an *eternal* Spring. The season Spring is all about new life *all year-round.* Spring is also a state of vibrancy 'a *spring* in their step'. There were no 'years' in this eternity no sense of 'time' as such, there was no 'age' either. *Eternal* youth in an *eternal now.* It was an infinite moment of *presence* that yogi's, guru's and meditators have been trying to return to ever since. Given Kronos-Cronus is Satan, the god of 'time', if we look at a 'chronometer', a Swiss watch, *right,* it is defined as 'an instrument measuring time accurately in spite of motion or variations in temperature, humidity and or pressure'. Blueprints for a chronometer appear *exactly* like the cycles of time and space, *astronomy*, ancient societies used to designate the *galactic* cycles of *Eons* and *Ages.* It appears we live in a giant *grandfather clock.* The universe is not mimicking us *we* are mimicking the universe.

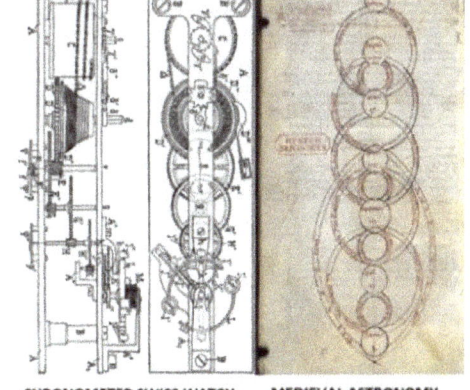

CHRONOMETER SWISS WATCH   **MEDIEVAL ASTRONOMY**

It's no coincidence then that god of 'time' just so happened to show up when the 'eternal' part came to an end and 'time' suddenly defined *life* as 'Ages' and 'Eons' that were once eternal and *unquestioned* now became a ticking timebomb as lurking *Death* made its presence felt for the *first time*. Now we have lots of questions about time and space instead of being *at one* with it all, *forgetting* time, forgetting space, forgetting the devil. Time is a concept. Time doesn't exist. Clocks exist. But clocks are not time, *see right*, 66 years between the Wright bro's first flight and the moon landing. *Just think about the absurdity of that.* Fake. So, we are in separation from it all unable to find our way back to the eternal part but we will. As it is we're on the clock now and 'time  is money' quantified by a false form of exchange where a 'price' is placed on everything, even life itself, when everything was once provided by Mother Nature *free of charge in an eternal moment*. This is how the Devil-Satan, time, stood in the place of the Great Feminine Mother, *the eternal Goddess, the universe!* Time and money are inextricably linked considering their favourite deity, Hermes, is a bi-god of commerce, thieves and boundaries. Yes, the boundary between life and death, between dimensions, as was all ancient versions of him said to traverse dimensions as the 'messenger' of the 'gods'. Now there's no boundaries at all in a 'progressive' world.

The gods of death in the 'underworld' was where all the Egyptian pharaohs were trying to get 'home' to with their elaborate embalming rituals *obsessed* with time. We think they were ancient fools but I feel they were transferring their souls from one generation to the next, still are, as the Windsor's apparently do, and the 'tomb raiders' who repeatedly find their elaborately hidden riches were actually their cronies digging up their wealth and returning it back to them in their new life reborn into the next gen. This is why they say they have 'multigenerational attachments' as demons or interdimensional reptilians are the 'souls' of the hybrid hierarchy controlled from just outside our bandwidth of reality. They can do this with technology, I know because it was done to me and technology is only *mimicking* what can be done naturally. It is after all a 'matrix' and death is just another room in the house, another program, and *not natural*. The Devil-Satan is a thief of your precious time taking the beautiful young and turning them into withered husks unrecognisable from their prime! It's pure evil. He dresses himself up as a heavenly 'father' god but it is really an alien predator known as the god of disappointment. He is Death. He allows you some 'life', albeit a harsh short one, and then ruthlessly and cruelly takes what does not belong to him as it seeks to be Mr. Universe.

This dark force is unnatural to living *light* beings. It is a hyper-negative energetic *alien* vampire morphing abundant planets into prisons of scarcity as it consumes anything of living spirit and leaves nothing but death in its wake. It only takes. It does not give. This alien 'god' taught humanity 'time' and 'age' *terrified* she, the Goddess, will return with *all her abundance* and resources, including eternity, in time to swindle him at his own game and like a force of incomprehensible mad delight (talk about ecstasy) burn him entirely out of existence with the power of her light! We are always running out of time but eternity has all the time in the, well, universe. She fears no one. When the feminine light force is switched on in its fullest capacity, no one can withstand it. It's a paradox. She seems vulnerable but when she is powerfully protected to do her thing and the lord of darkness will be out of business, *liquidated*, so to speak. People will return from darkness to the world that nurtures them planting and growing their *own* abundance, their own light, freeing themselves from the fear of going without and the one who gives and takes at will. Nourishing our bodies and minds *organically* will *naturally* lead to increased lifespans as the fear of 'time' and death drops away and we become eternal light again after a brief moment, however long it may have seemed, eons, ages, when we transiently meandered between a little light and a lot of darkness! Free abundance is totally achievable. The soil does not ask for money. Fruit trees do not have a slot for coins. Can you see? Being distracted by the pressure to 'get things' that are *already freely* provided by the cosmos is *wasting your time*, precious time we need to understand *ourselves* to get out of this mess. *It's up to you to break away*. Don't be drawn in, *hypnotized*, by the circus and morbid fascination with the dark fakery. *Unplug! Leave them to it.* They can have the darkness. The light belongs to us! There is no past or future there is only *now*, the present presence, which is funny because one of my messages I received was *'we are objects existing in space in the eternal now'*. This moment is all you have and how well you perceive 'the now', how 'here' you are, is your *eternal* self at full throttle in this infinite moment, this present space, whoever you are whatever you are doing. Be *aware*, that is all you need to do, and all will return to normal.

This is why they are *constantly* distracting us and *poisoning* us so we become befuddled and lose focus on *the now*. It's a game of distraction. Simply put, eternal is eternal, *forever*, while an 'Age' or 'eon' lasts a *quantifiable* period of 'time'. As such, 'time' and 'age' and 'aging' is deeply embedded in our *sense* of how 'old' we are before we run out of 'time' and 'die'. It's all part of a 'calendar' or *'timeline'* defined by critical events. President Kennedy 'died' in '1963'. That was nearly '60' 'years' 'ago'. What a long 'time' that is! No, it happened yesterday, today, tomorrow. It's a broadcast, a simulation, the holograph, all happening at the same 'time' in the same 'space', an infinite zero-point place of nothingness and everythingness that can be tapped into *spiritually* or technologically, *see*, UFO's. But there is nothing like the real thing. Their technology is no match for our wonderous bodies of unending capabilities. These *embedded* psychological identifiers, religion, politics, *the media*, give us a sense of *linear* 'time' that *doesn't actually exist*. They're spinning us shit. Firstly, there are no presidents, *no hierarchy*. No other body is *more* than you. Okay? It's an illusion. Everyone's physical body, *your body*, is an exemplary space vehicle of multilayered spiritual, energetic, and cosmic abilities that can and *will* travel wherever you desire, whenever you like. How can they hold you in a prison, threaten your life or beat you down if you unlock your bodies *infinite potential?* You would laugh as they lock the door and when they came back, you would be gone! Those dufus's stupid enough to lock another person away would be scratching their head saying, 'Wha…?!' These idiots will die without someone to lord it over. That's how sick *they* are. They cannot survive on their own without the 'food' of someone else's fear to feed them. We are capable of so much more than this.

So, they created the *idea* of presidents, of hierarchy – living gods - to have us looking *outside* ourselves to those who 'reign' over us in their 'right' to rule. But they do not, cannot, stop you from transcending them and therefore, everything they do is an *elaborate hoax* to prevent you from realising *you can leave*. They're *obsessed* with being boss because *they* are insecure alien *leeches* unable to formulate their own light so they must steal it from others behind the veil of 'time'. 'If you challenge us we will take 20 years of your life locked in misery and pain behind our bars'. 'Fuck you. Do it'. These alien interbreeders are using *us* for *our* chakras, meridians, DNA, central nervous system and processing unit, *the brain*, so they can use *our bodies* as a psycho-spiritual-physical-cosmic computer, *a vehicle*, to access the greater *universal software program* of infinite potential that *we* are capable of and they are not. They *need* us and they hate us for that but we do not need them. They have *deliberately* hidden our own abilities from us to emerge as 'gods' in the eyes of spiritual children. But *we are masters* who have temporarily forgotten our true potential. Ultimately, these cosmic dickheads 'worship' one great demonic god in their nob cult! It's really pathetic posturing and posing with *ever increasing elaborate titles* to convince *you* of their importance. But there are no 'gods' either! *We are* 'god' if that' what you want to call it. *We are* the cosmos. We are past, present and future. *We are it. It is us.* We've just been experiencing a *temporary interruption* in the universal broadcast paused in a 'physical' or '3D' wavelength to see what it *feels* like and when we're done with that we take the information back to home-point, the light, assimilate the knowledge and they are out of business on *much greater levels* than they would ever let you know about. They are *terrified* of us and will use *any trick* or technique to keep us from *our* birthright! *We are* unique points of one great consciousness that becomes whatever you make it. *That's* how powerful *we* are and you are far more important than you have ever been told.

Another one of my messages was *'the darkness has elevated itself to a god-like status and threatens the entire universe'*. They come from a dimensional frequency, parallel universe, that cannot access the higher vibrational planes of Love-Light. They are death. They are a form of synthetic 'life' because light is eternal, organic, natural. Death is unnatural and why aliens are considered some type of A.I. a sort of 'false' life. They lack compassion, empathy, insight. They can't connect. They work like a hive of insects hence, the whole 'bug' phenomenon. Like a symbiotic parasite, their computer virus of death hacks into us genetically via science and technological breeding programs to piggyback off *our* abilities BECAUSE THEY CAN'T DO IT ORGANICALLY. They created hybrids to live here eons ago but what if that knowledge and technology was lost? Is that why they revere the ancients because they could do things that these guys can't do? Are the ancient alien 'gods', *the giants,* dead? In hacking into us to access the light they invariably drag us down from *our higher state* to their lower state, not quite as dark as them, but certainly not of pure light anymore where we once were. Yuri Manin said, 'What binds us to space-time is our rest mass which prevents us from flying at the speed of light when *time stops* and *space loses meaning.* In a world of light *there are neither points nor moments of time.* Being woven from light would live 'nowhere' and 'nowhen'. Only poetry and mathematics are capable of speaking meaningfully about such things'. Nice one, Yuri! Although I don't think math's is the conduit here, poetry in motions, yes.

At this stage we're neither coming nor going stuck in a state of flux. Stasis. Suspended animation inside a virtual projection *simulating* movement hence, the idiotic false 'progressive' movements conjured in the minds of strugglers. The dumbest kids are taking over the class. We're just going round and round and they intend to go around *again*. This is our one big chance to get out. It's a dangerous game being played on us and many others under this regime *stalling* far greater galactic effects. They whole fucken thing will conk out if we're not careful. They *must not get in* to the highest states or the whole universe will be destroyed. *It is* being destroyed as we speak and that is what this is all about. Jacques Vallee computer scientist, author, ufologist, and astronomer said, 'We know there is life throughout the universe so why shouldn't it be able to come here? Especially since there are civilisations thousands of millions of years ahead of us…what the witnesses are describing, in many cases, comes out of nowhere, disappears into nowhere. There are cases of objects becoming present on the spot – physical objects, material objects – if it does that, well, it could be from anywhere, *anytime'*. Exactly, Jacques! Buddha said, 'the mind that perceives limitation *is* limitation'. Exactly, Buddha! This is why the Dalai Lama has said he won't incarnate again. He's over this shit! The portals are open and he's outta here. We are being directed to age ourselves with our flawed psychological approach to a fake reality reliant, largely, on 'time' to keep us prisoner by a bunch of cosmic parasites *alien* to natural life! As such, we die young. Seventy is too young to die. It's not long enough to *figure out* the program let alone *solve it!* They have superimposed *their* fake reality over the real one, the organic one, the natural cosmos. This superimposed 'reality' program was imprinted onto us by *something else* something that knows, and *even programmed in*, our mental weaknesses including our perception of 'time' and 'space' big *or* small. We are insecure about time, about age, and as we are a chip of the old block it means *they* are insecure about time too. That's because *they* are running out of time to pull off this big job and get away with a cosmic heist! It won't be long now. Hang in there. These cunts are about to be booted out and they are doing everything they can to try and convince us *at this crucial 'time'* that they are unstoppable! Fight like hell, kids, and do it *now!* Time is of the essence!

They sold us 'time' but in particular, they sold us *linear* time that never goes anywhere and is always running out. Age really is a state of *perception* or 'you're as young as you feel'. *Prepare yourselves* as we are going to be living a lot longer than ever before in another step toward our eternal selves! When you celebrate your birthday you are certainly *not* celebrating getting a year *older*. You are celebrating that great day you came into this wonderful world and all the opportunity that lay before you. Until you're fifty and then 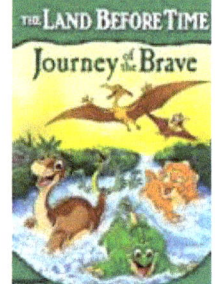 it's just fucked as time runs out. This *urgency* leads to trying to accumulate things, material things, to 'make it matter' to 'leave a legacy'. It is this insecurity of trying to matter, trying to *be* something, to *have* something - *the illusion* - that they use as a scalpel blade against our *eternal souls*. They are *literally* selling us into damnation, driving us toward the gates of hell to make us like *them*. They hate us because they want to *be* us - *be* 'god' – because 'god' is inside us *not* outside like they have claimed with their *fake* religions and *phony* systems. *We* are the angels here, momentarily displaced, but we will rise again know that! We once existed in a timeless ageless era when the whole planet was green and plentiful when we were happy and glorious! Then something bad started happening. The misleading Golden Age arrived as a fake alien god, Satan/Kronos, the god of *time, war and death* slowly moved in like a predator downwind taking over Earth and Earthlings to commence implementing a *grand scheme* to enslave the 'higher' beings, *our ancestors*, that *we* once were and *we still are* because the soul is eternal. We're being recycled. They are not so much our 'ancestors' or 'different people' but the *continuation of us* in an alien program of cosmic proportions. Yes, it's big. As this predator encroached, instead of 'eternal' youth in an 'eternal' spring, *never-ending*, we hypnotically entered a 'time' called the 'Golden *Age'* and it was *supposed* to be a *great* time. See how insidious their psycho-spiritual warfare is? Actually, this is the *first reference* to the entrapment of humanity and Planet Earth by a calculating *alien* interloper. It's diabolical! Here we have our first glimpse of an alien perp in histories great expanse. Thanks, ancient Greek historians, for keeping this cold case alive! Much appreciated! We can now work on this like detectives in the way it deserves with our modern *objective* minds and equipment at hand coupled with all we have learned about *criminal behaviour* to blow the lid of this *scandal* and crack the case!

Firstly, they are habitual liars coupled with a grandiose sense of self-importance in their *space empire*. Who else would do this but cosmic criminals? What if the *whole universe* was once *all light* and the creeping darkness has become *so prolific* that it has turned *most* of the abundant planets and stars into darkness leaving only pinpricks of light in the vast creeping nothingness that seeks to consume us too just like the Neverending Story when the 'nothing' consumes 'everything'? Like Hitchhikers Guide to the Galaxy? We're being made redundant as a species. The light is obsolete to them. What if we are one of the last obstacles in the way of complete and utter annihilation of the Universe? Therefore, the 'Golden' Age might have *seemed* great but it was far *less* than the awesome eternal spring and eternal youth that came before it! *This is the con.* "Let me take your *eternal* youth and your *eternal* spring and I'll replace it with this 'golden' *time*. I promise you'll love it!" If you are going to con someone you have to trick them into giving you something of *higher* value for something of *lesser* value or *no value at all*. Everyone who has ever been conned handed over something of *real* value for something that turned out to  have *lesser* or *no* value or even for something that *didn't even exist!* "Let me take your pension fund and life savings, and I'll invest it in this incredible new luxury project happening in Dubai! You're gonna love it!" They hit you with stats and numbers, virtual images of architecturally designed interiors of flashy apartments, economic projections and how much you'll gain or save if you get in early. But you gotta be quick. They're selling fast. You might miss out if you don't sign up *today!* Suddenly, a blur of paperwork and excitedly scribbling one's initials and voila! It's not Death *of* a Salesman - Death *is* a salesman. 'Death', the 'Devil', is an alien trickster working psychological and spiritual slight-of-hand on the perception of 'time' to control the flow of light, Love, to *become* god. And we became tenants on our own world. The one getting duped hands over real assets  and money for an investment that *doesn't even exist* only to find there was no project in Dubai but there *were* some glossy posters and leaflets that *seemed* very real *at the time!* So, we went from an *eternal* spring to a 'Golden Age' from an 'eternal youth' and 'being young' until around '100 years old' when we suddenly *aged* and *died*. But what happened to the 'eternal' part? Where did *that* go? So, it seems our planet, once an abundant eternal spring, was harvested and the Eternal Humans upon it were lost. Sorry about that, looks like the investment didn't pan out. All the best. Door slams in face. *So dark the con of man.*

What is being spoken about here in ancient Greek 'myth' is a crime slowly being carried out against an *eternal* ageless never-endingly youthful beautiful and abundant species of higher *light beings* of pure love in the form of humans on a planet of the same frequency. The perpetrator of this crime, *the alien criminal,* is being diabolically named and placed right in front of us as some benevolent 'god' who apparently got sick and tired of humanity's 'naughty' *unmanageable* ways and left us to a string of other confusing deities who variously abandoned us over 'time' because we're just dumb and unevolved. Eventually, as we began dying and memory started to fade, we simply *forgot what happened* and accepted a terrible fate. Our memories were wiped. Like animals. We now suffer a *collective amnesia* the details of which are barely decipherable in myth, folklore, symbolism, 'traditional' stories, fairy tales, fables and songs carved in stone, dug into the earth and built into hills in our *desperate* attempts to record the truth of the crime perpetrated against us to pass on the last of the ever evaporating truth! *But* a simple truth remains, mother and father, god and goddess, for without them and their deep desire to re-unite properly as friends, companions, team-mates and family, there is no life, no generations, no evolution, no hope and no manifestation of their combined love, their offspring, found in the wonderful magical world of children, our true state of  being, light, wonder, bliss, energy, connection and *vision* that we once were. The alien space program now enters its final chapter after many Ages of craftily maneuvering us toward this final end; genderless, biosynthetic cyborgs, eternal functionaries, soulless robots, in an alien harvest. Yet we are told by *most* religions we are low down the ladder of spiritual importance, *sinners,* and must be punished and sacrificed for some unimaginable 'greater good' that never comes to pass. It's *our* fault. Blame the toddler when the house falls down.

Unfortunately, as legend has it, the so-called Golden Age of such promise *devolved* into a 'silver' age, then sunk even lower into a 'bronze' age and finally, the dirty 'iron' *age* came along that we're *still* trapped in now. It always continues on a downward trend have you noticed? It's the pits, *literally*. The only constant is descent. We are descending even further  now in a continuation of the *original plan* to destroy humans while the hybrid human-alien aristocracy emerge as 'transhuman', *beyond* human, who are *not* human yet *pose* in our place to a *wider cosmic audience* in an insidious takeover from the inside out, a changeling, to become the 'new' false light, 'god', to replace the goddess, *Love-Light,* with *almighty* control and fear. A deeper, lesser known, A.I. demonic element in this evil plan intends to destroy earth and move to on *another* planet as that's what the *destroyer* does. These new-age would-be Olympians who overthrew the 'old' gods, the Titans, are playing a dangerous game with all our lives and the essence of universal consciousness if they think they are going to be the 'new breed' of 'gods' on *Mother* Earth. That's how *fucking* selfish they are. Self-entitled doesn't quite cover it. Brats! Rich-kid *bored* fuck-ups killing the light to remake it in *their* image. Like 'god'. Only their 'god' is *still* Satan, a perverse *distorted* falsehood, a distraction from the real god and goddess, *human women and men.* Following this 'golden age' was a pantheon of 'gods' and 'goddesses' and other deities that kept the original lie alive long enough for the victim not to realise the perp's had long since left the crime scene only to re-emerged *looking like us* but were *not* us! Body snatchers! Changelings! *Shapeshifters!* Half-bloods! The native 'snake brothers' is quite literal. This is where the historic 'twins' and 'half-brothers' come in, and half-sisters although it was more geared toward the masculine. *Some say* in the Biblical Garden of Eden story (golden age) that Cain was Abel's 'half-brother' born of Eve and Samael the 'upright snake' aka reptilian. Adam was a full blood human and Cain a 'half-blood prince' thank you, Harry Potter. They say the line of Cain, halflings, went on to become the Canaanites replicated in America as Canaan because America is symbolic of the modern 'promised land' to so many impoverished people fleeing their homelands. *This* is their religious code of replication and repetition, *ritual,* to mimic the universal cycles and *constantly* repeat history. The line of Cain is the bloodline of Satan and the 'mark' of Cain is the inescapable *snake genetics* born via Eve to create the first reptilian conception carried on by many chosen 'Mary's' throughout history including Isis among others! *They're still doing it!*

The evil twin legend comes from the very beginning of it all indeed the 'snake' is the 'evil twin' of Jehovah-Yahweh-God in the Eden story. Two sides of the same coin. We are now understanding they were reptilian delegates in an alien syndicate processing Earth and humanity into a sub-species seizing world's to harvest their resources in an expanding space empire. A film called *Scaler, Dark Spirit* goes into some detail on this that 200,000 years ago the 'fallen angels', aliens, altered their genetics to breed with human woman and when their bodies died their souls got stuck here and are the demons infecting our world today. Earth is 'purgatory' for them, and yes, they are evil. So, Eve gave birth to Adam's son Abel while some speculate Cain was born of a union between Eve and Samael the snake spawning the line of Cain who went on to become the Canaanites. This story is repeated in the legend of the Greek myth when the Spartan Queen *Leda,* note, the phonetics 'leader', had sex with her husband on their wedding night but was also seduced by the god Zeus (Satan) disguised as a swan giving birth to Castor the mortal biological son of the King and an immortal son Pollux a 'divine' being born of Zeus. This is called 'Superfecundation' when two or more ova from the same cycle is fertilized by sperm from separate acts of sexual intercourse leading to two separate babies, twins, from two different biological fathers. This is very common theme that is shown throughout ancient history, s*ee right*, ancient Pompeii fresco and Francois Boucher's 1740 painting. Castor and Pollux were called the Dioscuri 'two gods' also called *Gemini*, 11! It seems the ancients had 'censorship laws' as the swans neck like the 'snake' is a *symbolic* penis when enlarged male genitalia is biologically attributed to 'female preference' as the male exhibits *bigger* brighter colours for breeding purposes. They otherwise saying reptilians have big dicks. Well, fuck a duck. Who knew? Ménage à quack. Dio means 'godlike', 'heavenly' and 'sky, heaven'. These are 'sky gods' that were having babies to mortal human women where the 'snake' reptilian myth keeps showing up. They put all this in movies as only movie directors who have either figured it out or been put through their psycho factories know what all this means. *See right*, The Dunwich Horror another weird instalment from H.P. Lovecraft up there with Edgar Allan Poe. The blurb reads '…a half-witted girl bore illegitimate twins. One of them was almost human' and clearly this image show a reptile-octopus alien demon having sex with her. They use chameleons and octopus as their symbols because they 'shift'. It's a game to put it in your face as its all leading to something bigger but you can't claim you haven't been told.

The Ceasars and line of the Ptolemies were born of 'virgins' of which *Cleopatra* was the last. Apollo was born of a virgin as was Alexander the Great who travelled to Egypt to be acknowledged as a *legitimate* Egyptian King, 'god's son'. Napoleon did this too. Why Egypt? Because they spawned the reptilian 'foreign' sky god. Our mate Octavian and Jupiter was born of a virgin who was also called Jove or 'By Jove!" They were both 'conceived of a serpent god', a reptilian. Being born of a 'god' and a mortal woman is a *common* theme. This is Beauty and the Beast told in folktales of the 'shapeshifting' king or prince - the 'frog' prince, French reptilian royalty. In the 'Swan Maiden', 'The Animal Bridegroom' and 'Kind Lindworm' speak of maidens, particularly common girls, disenchanting 'serpentine' royal husbands. The number 7 is central to a lot of these tales as she has 'seven layers of clothes' she removes on her wedding night and he sheds 'seven' skins casting them in the 'fire' until the 'man underneath' the serpent is revealed and released of his 'curse'. It's all tantric sex. This is the curse of the reptilian king attempting to regain his humanity before times runs out. Dionysus is basically the same god as Orpheus born of a mortal virgin woman and the god Zeus, king of kings, and although she couldn't see the spirit she could apparently feel it. Dionysus carried a giant 'thrysus', a wand, code for 'penis' that was wound with ivy, an aphrodisiac, dripping honey a reference to the 'milk' and 'honey' of Christ-seed enlightenment tantric sex. He used his 'wand', transcendental sex IQ, to destroy anyone and 'their freedoms or revelry' who opposed his cult as *all* pagan tantric cults were co-opted into a super religion practiced today as *Satanism!* That does not mean all these ancient cults and 'pagan' beliefs were Satanic, many were peaceful and highly progressive, it just means *the best* of their knowledge was stolen and rebranded as something evil to steer *us* away from potential salvation. Dionysus was associated with wine and 'frenzy' or 'inspired madness' aka one hell of a party. It's the orgy or famous Satanist Aleister Crowley's motto, "Do what thou wilt shall be the whole of the law". In other words, don't let love get in the way. Dionysus was associated with 'foreignness' as an 'arriving outsider god' called the 'god that comes'. 'Comes' means ejaculate. They used the same expressions we do. Genesis 6:4 "The Nephilim were in the earth in those days, and also after that, when the sons of God *came* (ejaculated) in unto the daughters of men, *and they bore children to them*, the same that were the mighty men that were of old, the men of renown". Jove has been linked to Jehovah of the Eden story or God, a 'sky god', who was 'god of thunder' and lightning, Zeus!, as well as Thor the lightning-thunder god of *electricity* practicing reptilian tantric sex. He was King of the Gods, 'sky father' or easily the 'Heavenly Father' of the Bible story all associated with the 'sacred tree' or the Tree of Knowledge, the nervous system of tantric enlightenment. It's the same god and the same story repeating. All these 'great men of renown' were born of 'virgins', *see right*, Jove with his phallic 'wand' and his 'bird' or third eye, the *eagle eye!*, the eye of Horus, the falcon, pineal gland that 'sees all' from a 'birds eye view'. In his hand he holds the 'little woman' standing on the Earth, the Goddess, *Mother* Earth-Mother Nature, *the mother* who bears their sons as such, the *Mother of All Gods, women!*

Celtic Irish god Lugh was said to be a youthful *Christlike* saviour god who was the *ancestor* and protector of the *Monarchy* personified by the high priest of the king's court! The Priest and King were once combined in one but ultimately split into two *separate* roles for control. Every king was said to be a son of Lugh and although the king was said to have produced an 'heir' it was actually *Lugh* who impregnated the queen in the night just like Zeus. It's Rosemary's Baby. Given Jesus was born of the 'Holy Spirit' it seems they consider Jesus too was the son of a reptilian covert rape dressed up as a benevolent God, *right*, we see Jesus depicted as a dinosaur, a reptilian, at the Vatican's *Snake Hall*. Two faced. Pope Frances hosted the feathered serpent god, *the phoenix*, as part of 'deity exchange' program. Mi casa su casa! My god is your god. Let's call the whole thing off!

At the inauguration of the king, the high priest druid would symbolically 'wed the king to the land' connecting the 'king' to the 'earth', earth is flesh or 'made of clay'. It is a ritual intercourse of the sun God to the earth Goddess creating their bloodline ensuring the future wellbeing of the *king*dom. It was said wolves, ravens, stags and *swans* were particularly worshipped by druids of which Merlin was said to be the last, a shapeshifter, much like the Skinwalkers of native American lore. The priest-king was said to be *eternally reincarnated* every generation, yes, the father becomes the son, *soul transference!* Jesus was one of *many* practicing this closely guarded secret along with the origins of their kind.

The ancient world was a Hollywood scandal. The lost legacy and inheritance of humans was transferred to another species then promised to the 'heirs' of their thrones playing out *endlessly* as their male-centric religious cults. It is the *hidden* story behind the *cover story* of all Abrahamic religions. The 'happily ever after' was supposed to right all these wrongs in so many classical accounts. It's *A Tale of Two Cites!* It's *The Man in the Iron Mask!* It's the 'lost line' of 'Royalty' of *Rapunzel*, a 'lost' princess. It's Alice in Wonderland *another* lost princess. It is the great mystery the Templars were seeking and underpins the crusades and the conquering of new lands looking for a replacement home for the liberty *they* were promised. American political and entertainment A-listers are pharaohs, Kings, Queens, Gods and Goddesses worshipped *and worshipping* on the Mount Olympus of Hollywood and Washington DC! *This* is their secret religion hidden all around us as they reign from the symbolic Temple Mount of celebrity! *See right*, Anjolina Jolie's scorpion dress aka Isis! They're *all* doing it. The movies coming out now are ALL about these fables to link them to the ancient prophecies finally come to pass as follows: Once Upon a Time in America, Judas and the Black Messiah, The Mayor of Kingstown, *Little Women*, Eternals, The Father, My Octopus Teacher, Marriage Story, Rocketman, Hair Love, A Star is Born, First Man, Spiderman: Into the Spider Verse, Darkest Hour, Icarus, Moonlight, La La Land, Fantastic Beasts, Revenant, The Imitation Game, Interstellar, Wonder Woman, Her, The Great Beauty, Skyfall, The Descendants, Undefeated, Alice In Wonderland, Still Alice, Black Swan, In a Better World, God of Love! They even have an online universe called Eve! It goes on and on and on!

Abel sounds like he was a bit of a bastard if we are to believe at least the metaphorical and symbolic aspects of this story. Pissed off that the snake had broken with protocol and dared to 'seed' its own line, *its own species*, via Earth women, the Eve's, who were reserved as breeding stock for 'god' and the Adam's, Yahweh-Jehovah cursed the upright snake to 'crawl on its belly' meaning *demoted!* They were delegates, emissaries, of a space empire in the throes of morphing Earth into a franchise and Humans were just *another notch* on their galactic belt. The bible doesn't say why God-Jehovah favoured Abel but this sounds like a reasonable motive and what the bible doesn't say is filled in by alternative scholars of the 'gnostic' type faiths *if you look*. Yahweh/Jehovah punished Cain by making *Abel* his master. Cain got fed up Abel's 'boss man' attitude and slew Abel and the historical blood feud between the half 'brothers' began. It was the first murder but certainly not the last and it has raged on ever since! *These* are the gods of old who are infesting our planet today as the pantheon of political, religious and celebrity deities that people are so ready to worship as 'fans'! When you hear of people screaming and throwing themselves on the ground at the feet of Brad Pitt, one can only say they are having a hysterical 'religious' experience. How embarrassing for that man. As we have it all these 'Ages later, you're now dealing with an endless list of customer service agents called 'clergy' and 'government' who, after a while, don't even bother to answer their calls *at all* when people phone them up for some answers regarding the great 'scheme' they peddled about a 'golden age' that one time, remember? "Well, I think you misunderstood what we discussed in the initial meeting". The endless list of 'helpful' deities, heaven's call-centre staff, were eventually morphed into one 'self-service' hotline that is not even monitored anymore except for a fucking automated computer that sends you right back to the start of the 'options' menu on the spiritual keypad of lies and broken promises until you're so fucken frustrated you just hang up and die! The 'one' god we have today was an interloper, an imposter, an *alien*, who set up the game and then changed characters and costumes over 'time' in many engineered 'Ages', *times*, showing up again and again in many disguises. It is *the Great Pretender* slowly but inevitably leading the high beings we once were into a series of tricks and traps designed to reduce humans to near nothing. Beasts. Even monsters. Like them. This alien, Cronos, physically and spiritually hamstrung humans teaching us 'time', and it's the perception of 'time' that 'ages' us until we die as a species over a series of 'ages' nearing completion as I write. 'The end times'. We are exiting the dastardly iron age and however dire it seems *we are* ascending into a Golden Age and coupled with this knowledge the looming Golden Age never needs to end eventually becoming *eternal*, like it once was, and they are desperate to keep us away from *that!* It's coming, folks, and sooner than you realise. They split the original androgynous feminine when we were *One*, *whole* in body, mind and spirit, into two - the masculine and feminine of the 'golden age', the 'twins', 'Adam and Eve'. They then further split us from our *eternal* souls and disconnected us physically from our astral higher selves that *never* dies even when our physical body dies. *Our light-being-souls are what remains of our eternal selves from the eternal spring that still lives on.* They are in the process of discontinuing *that* line as well and why they are setting up 5G and soon 6G, 7G and beyond until we will all be literally fried.

When we 'die' the astral self must wait in limbo, no time and no space, until a period of 'time' *on Earth* passes by which *time* our spiritual memories are wiped and then we are reinserted, put back in, 'reincarnated', *recycled*, to the simulation. It's not reincarnation, it's one continuous *eternal* life interceded by physical 'deaths' in the 3D, a 3D we have been reduced to from the heights of 11D. It's a cosmic trap inside an alien game, a false matrix, of hope and hardship that will eventually delete us completely. If you think this has happened over a few thousand years, no, although we can place a *general* timeline on what has happened given an Age is approximately 2,100 years. So, I think the timeframe we are talking about in the most *recent* series of downgrades is about 12,000 years which lines up with the general time of Atlantis. The point of this massive alien hoax is to take the God and Goddess of humanity who once existed in a much higher 'dimensional' state of awareness or what would be called 'godlike', omnipresent, and powerful, and turn us into slugs! To reduce us to such a limited state of awareness and physical ability that we are barely recognizable from what we once were, *see right*. To say it's a cosmic crime is an understatement! The 'time trap' is the 3D-5 Sense 'reality' we find ourselves in or what I call 3.5FM. It's like a radio station with 3 dimensions and 5 senses. We've been tuned out, turned down in every way. We went from *Infinity FM* to Zero FM yet *outside* of this limited  dimensional *frequency* range of perception there is no 'time' *and no* 'space' as it once was in our *eternal* state. People who have experienced NDE's (near death experiences) describe the *enormity* of their astral self *outside* the small *physical* body and that they were *omnipresent, everywhere at once*, could see past, present *and* future in the same moment, knew all - *all knowing* - like 'god', and were so 'big' that when they came back into their bodies they wondered how they could possibly 'fit' inside the *tiny* vessel that is our current physical 3D being. The 'Fountain' of Youth is a 'spring', a 'well-spring' inside us, a life force energy 'fountain' that expands our state of awareness, motor functions and vigour to the point where the Olympic Games as we know them today would look like child's play!

The eternal 'spring' was symbolised as a fountain as a 'spring' is water coming up from the ground. It was described this way because, literally, the energetic torus field resembles a fountain generated from our hearts pouring up and out through the top of our heads circulating back around and up through our root chakra, *see right*, the 'fountain head'. During the higher state of man humans were androgynous, self-reproducing like frogs, which is why the ancients (Greeks in particular) revered hermaphrodites as being 'perfect', living gods, because they incorporated both the male *and* female aspects in one, *see right*. Also, we have the central figures of Mayan beliefs, the 'Hero' Twins, that represent 'complimentary' forces of polarity, night and day, good and bad, sun and moon, or the positive-negative electrical polar opposites representing the duality, *electricity*,  that occurs between males and females often seen in 'twin' myths conceptualised as *born in one* representing two sides of a single force, an androgynous *supreme* being. One. Whole. *Complete*. Buddhism believes the force beyond *everything* is non-gender specific while Jesus said the angels were 'sexless'.

In some accounts the Golden Age was overseen by the Goddess Astraea 'star maiden', the Starry Goddess, the *goddess of justice*, innocence, beauty and precision another version the Prime Feminine Goddess. She stayed with men until the end of the Silver Age but by the Bronze Age men had become brutish and greedy  (rings a bell) so she fled to the stars where she appears as the constellation *Virgo* holding Libra the Scales of Justice ruled over by Venus goddess of Love. Venus was said to be the physical manifestation of the Goddess of the Heavens epitomised by Sirius, the brightest star, as she is the light hence, Justice aka exposure, lawfulness, innocence, precision etc! The modern version of the 'scales of justice' or Lady Justice depict her as blindfolded supposed to represent 'impartiality' or blind justice yet blindfolding the feminine is symbolic of *injustice* and a *much deeper* secret masonic masculine plan to blind women to their true role in all this considering the word 'Cain' translates as 'Blindness of God' and 'god' is 'dog' spelled backwards aka the Dog Star or God Star, the Feminine, *women*. Considering it is this 'line of Cain', snake lineage, who are behind the secretive control of everything including the much needed information that could set Earth and Humanity free, they seek to control the *balancing force of nature* found in the feminine in a world *out of control* under the direction of 'elite' male nutjobs and their misguided wards, *common men*, who have been clearly subject to their psychotic orders since, well, Adam was a boy just look at wars for your answer there. They can't get women to go and kill other women en-masse although they are slowly getting their as women increasingly become masculinized to protect themselves in a world of men who are becoming more effeminate and confused. The final two ages of Greek mythological accounts were the Heroic Age, an age of *superhuman* though *not divine* people among them Achilles which finally devolved into the *current* Iron Age an era of toil and misery where children dishonour their parents, brother fights brother and 'xenia' is ignored. 'Xenia' is the courtesy between a host toward their guest far from home and in kind the guest's duty not to be a burden the host. We now see social jarring in the West as cultural clash leads to literal clashes unleashed via *mass migration* from vastly different belief systems which is very different from a steady controlled influx via *multiculturalism*. Xenia has been ignored once again and history repeats but then it's all planned that way as they play out the ancient myths in 'modern' times. The future will say of us what we said of them of old, they were destroyed by their own *ignorance* and *greed* lucky we've got tv's to watch *Xena Warrior Princess* though. It's a bad copy.

The word hermaphrodite is a fusion of the names Hermes and his 'mother' Aphrodite who gave their son, Hermaphroditus, who was both genders and considered a 'god' due to the balance of merged male-female *androgynous* essences in one. His father, Greek god Hermes, was bisexual in the sexually open society of ancient Greece and is the same god as Roman Mercury and Egyptian Thoth. Hermes-Mercury is indifferent, neither he or she, and it seems a lot of Jewish men secretly worshipping these deities practice bisexuality as, like the star of David, it is the feminine chalice and the masculine phallus (electrical energies) 'combined' in one 'star' to attain the 'light'. In a study published by the Proceedings of the Royal Society in December 2010 and republished by National Geographic, wildlife ecologist Peter Frederick from the University of Florida Gainesville discovered that the *chemical* mercury via industrial runoff was responsible for contaminating the food supply of ibis birds. The study found male birds copulating with other male birds, nesting even without eggs and engaging in homosexual activity like heterosexual pairs do. This led to a 13-15% decline in the number of offspring produced through the male line and *35%* fewer offspring produced by females exposed to 'normal' levels of mercury in the wild. That's a 50% reduction in offspring! The chemical element mercury is an endocrine disruptor (hormone destabiliser) given estrogen and testosterone are the *key* biological hormonal drivers in women and men giving us our *two major distinct* gender types. So, it's interesting the ancient god *Mercury*-Hermes was bisexual and his son was a hermaphrodite while the *element* mercury initiates biological gender neutrality or 'confusion' aka *gender dysphoria* as known to modern science today.

The element mercury is routinely added to vaccines and older dental fillings not to mention unknown dietary exposures. Now we see spiking rates of 'gender' confusion and gender dysphoria or the 'fluidity' being encouraged today especially in younger people. It's a weird *inverse* Satanic nod to the prime 'fluid' state of the androgynous force of the primordial waters in creation myths as such we're being chemically castrated men and women *both*. Again, it's a facsimile of the real thing, a bad copy of the original *organic* neutrality insofar as men are not better than women and vice versa. So, it's interesting that the Egyptian god Thoth, the same god as bisexual Mercury-Hermes father of a hermaphrodite, was depicted as an Ibis considering Ibis birds, like lions and baboons, have been observed engaging in same sex behaviour in the wild and that's *before* endocrine disruptors like mercury is added to their food intake. Ibis birds, like humans and certain other species, may be more susceptible to gender confusion than many other species and why their image was used to denote the personal preferences of ancient elite statesman-come-gods practicing tantric enlightenment or an approach of 'get it wherever you can' motto that still applies today. It's the dark side and I'm not suggesting for one minute that the LGBT community are the 'dark' side. They're being used to make same-sex, bisexuality, homosexuality, group sex, orgies, partner swapping, 'swinging', multiple partners and casual sex etc., more acceptable every day. They are trying to create another openly sexual society like ancient Greece yet LGBT is a very soft expression of how far the 'elites' behind all this are prepared to go *sexually* to gain power or simply get their rocks off including sexualizing *children* pedophilia being the tip of the iceberg. And, once again, where's the love?

I'm just spit-balling here but why were homosexual-bisexual ancient gods depicted as animals *known* to engage in same sex behaviour named after *elements* that modern science tells us are *known* to cause gender confusion? Are the ancients cryptically telling us that they were far more advanced *scientifically* than we give them credit for? Is that why *Mercury* the god was bisexual and *mercury* the element is a hormone disruptor linked to gender confusion? It's rather coincidental wouldn't you agree? It's just chemistry after all nothing personal. Was the element mercury being used in ancient Egypt leading to polysexual behaviour's thus causing Thoth to be depicted as an Ibis because, like Hermes and *his* son, Thoth was gender ambisexual himself as are Ibis? That is if these are indeed *actual people* who were deified as 'gods' and not just celestial anthropomorphic metaphors for the cosmos with coincidentally similar chemical identifiers on the Periodic Table. Hyper-sexuality is a trait of abuse and trauma from *childhood* also associated with the alien-elite thing.

Mercury is the ruling planet of Gemini symbolised by the male 'twins' Caster and Pollux often depicted as holding hands and hugging as the constellation that represents them looks like they are touching or holding each other and are seen as gay lovers aka 'brothers'. That said, Gemini was originally represented as a hetero male and female couple, The Lover's. The Greeks famously had an 'anything goes' society as too did the Romans including whole military legions encouraged toward homosexual bonding as it was said to produce a stronger sense of comradery and brotherhood in the battlefield. And what is the 'brotherhood'? The Masons. And what are the Masons famous for? Anything goes homosexuality being the tip of the iceberg. They do this not because they are genuinely interested in other men, it simply flies in the face of 'traditional' family values and the deception, even if unnecessary, gives them a strategic edge as they are morphing the human race into a genderless cybernetically implanted mutant race. Any attempts to discuss the megalithic conspiracy behind this is immediately met with self-censorship from 'progressives' who are waltzing of the cliff face of natural evolution like genderless lemmings. So, the Masonic agenda is hiding behind the LGBT community to deflect analysis from *what they are really doing* making it *virtually impossible* to openly study their techniques as indignation and accusations of homophobia and 'hate speech' shut down investigation. Clever bears (no pun).

That said, they hate hetero men *and* women as well because the magnetic polar opposites of their electromagnetic field, their sexual compass, combined during *tantric sex* alchemically unlocks the chakras via the nervous system leading to higher states of consciousness and IQ and they sure and hell don't want that! It's the same way the magnetic north and south poles hold each other in place and without these Earthly anchors the whole thing destabilises including us. As such, we're not evolving and don't experience higher states of consciousness unless we imbibe something as we don't know how to access these things *internally* by ourselves. Therefore, we're bored out of our brains and going nowhere fast *knowing* innately that we are *so much more* than our current state but don't know how to 'get there'. These higher states of consciousness were the state humanity perpetually lived in *before* we were split in two, downgraded, lied to and enslaved. The echo of this high state is still found in our Claustrum and nervous system, Christ, albeit without the knowledge to unlock it we are a shadow of our former greatness and basically fucked all round. *We can evolve back again* to our higher state and maybe evolve into the *One* original state again or the androgynous supreme being in a legendary time long forgotten.

The 'mother & son' or 'mother and child' worship of old, Mary and Jesus, Isis and Horus, Semiramis and Nimrod, Cybele and Attis etc., is a reference to electrical magnetic processes between *Mother*-Earth (passive-negative) and the *Son*-Sun (active-positive) receptive and projective energy poles *in unison*, perfectly balanced. Hermes's 'incestuous' relationship with the 'mother' or the Madonna and Child symbolism with the halo around the head is actually a reference to the electromagnetic flow of electric currents in a feedback loop between *Universal* positive and negative 'male' and 'female' forces found in the astral bodies of space via planets and stars *replicated* in humans. This is why the universe is depicted as feminine and the feminine was depicted as holding up *a mirror* symbolic of what you put out you get back in an *electrical* feedback loop - a circuit, the *mother*board – and why Tesla said electricity, frequencies and vibrations hold the secrets of the universe and those secrets are *inside* us! The ancients knew about electricity and the electrical system of the body depicting it as the 'thunder' god *Thor* with his 'bolts' of lightning during electrical storms. They simply used different *organic* terminology to explain it but well *knew* how electrical tantric positive-negative +/- intercoursing in a continuous current transcends our 3D - 5 sense world, *transcendental* sex, leading to higher electromagnetic vibrational states known as dimensions. Lightning occurs when negatively charged electrons in the bottom of the cloud are attracted to positive charged protons in the ground. This is what the ancient's minds were far more creative so to them these elemental forces had personality and you could piss off or ingratiate yourself to 'the gods' depending on how well you understood these processes. Many ancient cultures including the Druids believed you could actually see spirits in rivers and lakes inventing wonderous stories of fairy's, nymphs, magicians and wizards controlling the elements like Merlin. Today, we are making a return to the understanding that elemental forces *can* have a positive or negative effect of us depending on how we (electrically) *conduct* ourselves in our behaviour, studies, self-respect, consciousness and integrity and *not* by throwing cat's guts on a rock or cutting out little girls vagina's. It's all energy and *honouring our bodies* unique frequencies and codes by tapping into certain energies in the universe, we can enhance ourselves even further. Science has tried to take the magic out of Earth making life 'clinical' even boring yet scientists are awestruck at the *consciousness* they discover in their attempts to label, break down, control, split, fracture, bottle-up and distil *Life!*

There are different types of friction, for example, fluid and dry friction. In laymen's terms magnetics and electrics, just like pistons and pressure in a car engine, create electrical conductance of kinetic energy as the friction of the surface area converts energy into *constant* fluid energy transfer. This converts the force into heat called thermodynamics leading to dramatic consequences when two objects rubbing together, like rubbing sticks together (dry friction) creates a spark, *fire!* It is *the same* when two people having sex (fluid friction) creates a spark that starts a fire too, a fire in the heart. They say when two lovers meet for the first time 'sparks were flying' as static friction is literally generated by the excitement of their respective biological cells recognising their 'twin' sometimes called 'soul mates' or 'twin flames' alerting their equal but opposite selves and all that potentiates depicted in the image of Mary and Jesus with the flaming hearts and the 'passion' of the Christ etc. Mary was often depicted as a vagina, *see right,* the 'wound' at Christ's 'side'. It's a vag. There's just no getting around that. Here we see another rather explicit image of JC and a fence post. Trying to tell us something, mate? No wonder they call him 'the big man upstairs'. I didn't know they had Donkey Kong back in 30AD. Long live the king. Hallelujah!

Newton's Law of Universal Gravitation states this heat or 'transference phenomenon' i.e. *electromagnetism*, is the *density* of the flow of the magnetic field passing through the surface area called a 'gas constant' thus generating *radiance* or electricity. This is the 'glowing coat' of awareness spoken about in ancient legends of the 'sun kings', Revelation 12: *"Then an astonishing miracle occurred, I saw a woman clothed with the brilliance of the sun"*. They were describing electricity activating the torus field via the claustrum and nervous system via cerebrospinal fluid generating the 'light body' activating the mind and spirit to attain enlightenment. *This* is what we once were in the eternal spring, golden beings of light, that were reduced into nothing more than low vibrational functionary's by an alien parasite. This alien leech *feeds* off this very light and enjoys nothing more than making us suffer as sufferance perpetuates and ensures their power over us. *They're so weird.* Mass energy, charge momentum or voltage and *angular momentum* between *two bodies* causes subatomic microcellular explosions where an electrical feedback loop is generated. As the infamous Karma Sutra describes different sexual positions creates different levels of *kinetic energy* converted into thermal energy by the magnetic flow leading to a 'constant' electrical radiance. *The stars! The Shining!* That's why they referred to the wife as the Queen of Heaven, the Shining One, the 'brightest star in the sky' etc. Alexander the Greats wife was Roxana translates as 'shining, brilliant, radiant' and yes, he was a 'sun' king and a 'living god'. The sexual power of the wife was slandered as the 'prostitute' when clearly Jesus and Mary were married hence, *Mary* or Marie is derivative from *marrie*d. This constant friction, I can only imagine, would lead to the famed 'one hour orgasm' when the circuit is unbroken between one battery terminal and another battery terminal, in this case *humans*, tapping into each other's' electrical conduits via their mutual nervous systems during love *making.* We don't 'make love' anymore we just have sex or worse, fucking. Love making activates the electrical chakra tower generating the 'sparkling' sensation symbolised as the 'stars' as the crown chakra lights up and the 'vault of heaven' of the brain leads to all manner of connections and visions. Love being the highest frequency leads to higher vibrational states and thus enlightenment aka FREEDOM. It's so crazy it just might work. Make love not war, literally.

This is why the ancients correlated it with the brightest star in the sky, *Sirius*, as they had active imaginations although there is more to this than meets the eye so to speak. When correctly performed in sequence this would lead to a build-up of looping electricity, a circuit, hence, the hour long orgasm and women can orgasm more than men not to be crude about it but it's true and why women were particularly revered for holding the electricity. This is the 'bliss', 'heaven' and 'nirvana' spoken of in all religions and why Mary is the 'Church' as the church was considered hallowed ground, the *Sanctuary*, like the Garden of Eden which also symbolises Her. *She* is the temple, the cave, the vagina and her innocence and purity was considered enough to redeem or condemn any man, "the Lord whom you seek will suddenly come to his temple, the messenger of the covenant, in whom you delight". The covenant is sexual transcendent enlightenment via marriage and yes, I'm sure they found it very delightful. Once you know this you can *really* read the Bible not forgetting they have sneaky references like calling Mary the 'lowly maid' and some such pathetic sour grapes shit due to their *incompetence* as greedy males unable to attain her so just rip her down like ten year old's. The flow of the magnetic field attracts other particles directly proportionate to the sum of its mass and inversely proportionate to the square of the distance between their centers. In other words, 'opposites attract' thank you, Paula Abdul. This is why narcissists pursue kind-hearted people who in turn seem to love narcissists but once you understand the mechanics of how this works *physiologically* you can give the bad boys the flick! Now *this* is where things start to get *really* interesting.

The quantity of electrical resistance of an object is a measure of its opposition to the flow of electric current or *ease with which a current passes through* said object the notation of which is symbolised in Physics by the letter 'R'. These are the weird mathematical equations that physicist's write that no one but other physicists can understand while delving in too deep causes them to go insane like John Nash in Russel Crow's 'A Beautiful Mind'. At this point you start seeing all these 'connections' and think you are going nuts, like Nash, when in reality comprehending the program, like Neo in the Matrix when he finally *see's* the code, causes the 'reality' hologram to collapse and *anything is possible* after that including 'superhuman' abilities once our *perception* adjusts! We're a universal transistor, a capacitor. *Radiohead!* It's Superman and Wonder Woman for real. *This* is the knowledge Satanist's have stolen from us and why they are so powerful. They're all doing it, *see*, Hollywood celebrities, *the stars!*, when they say they experienced *'coincidences' galore* as celebrities often mention! Every episode of Seinfeld has a Superman comic while in the latest film *Wonder Woman 1984* (linking the women to the dystopian book *1984*) her name is *Diana*. While 2020 was a year of disappointment for the world, 2022, which means balance, is gonna be a *really big year* as the big dicks try to cash in on the looming ascension to be *The One* or at least the father of *The One* while the collective One of humanity will emerge bloody and beaten from their corner of the boxing ring to show them what we're really made of when push comes to shove. When we tap into this sequences of events unfold, *synchronicities*, leading to the 'simulation theory' that once one transcends the codes of 'reality' you can basically do *anything!* This can be *literally* mind blowing for the fledgling spiritual mind and one can easily be labelled 'schizophrenic' as was Nash. Many people in nut houses are actually spiritual warriors who don't have university degrees to hide behind or didn't

study eastern philosophy so, dullards label them *mentally ill* and poison them with pharmaceuticals. And the candles lynched the lightbulb. It's diabolical! But fear not! We are not losing our minds we are just *finally* understanding the baseline codes that has allowed these Mason's, black magicians, Satanist's, monks and gurus to use this *fluid reality* to their gain and so shall we!

Therefore, it is no coincidence that the previously mentioned notation in Physics for 'R' is an abbreviation for 'Electrical Resistance' or *Radiancy*, the Gas Constant, the Radius Vector or Universal Gravitation. This is the Ricci Tensor, part of the curvature of *space-time* which determines whether matter will converge or diverge in 'time'. There is a 'time travel' ability with this method that can change past events. The electrical resistance 'R' is symbolised by Ω the last letter of the Greek alphabet or Omega (alpha and omega) called the 'Great O'. They put this stuff all around us, *see*, the Big O, Roy Orbison and the Great Oz as good examples. The Great O is also called the 'ohm symbol' named after German physicist George Simon Ohm and 'coincidently', *again*, 'Om' in Hindu signifies the essence of ultimate reality within a meditation sound and has *literally* been recorded as the sound of the sun. It's *not* a coincidence that the letter 'R' was inspired by the Egyptian hieroglyph for 'head', crown, throne, royalty, *Isis*, the *feminine*, and

adopted in Latin around 500BC. The Semites also used it. Jews know an *awful lot* about all this and is how they reached such great heights of power in the world. The letter 'R' is referred to literally as the 'canine letter' or in English 'the dog's letter'. The Big Dog in all ancient and current accounts is Sirius, the *Dog Star – God Star*, the brightest most *radiant* shining star, gas constant, in the heavens recognised as the Divine Feminine anthropomorphized as Isis, Mother Mary, Mary Magdalene, the Goddess, the Queen, the Queen of Heaven and Queen of Hearts, *see*, Princess Diana, who they killed to symbolise the death of the Universal Goddess. They are *terrified* of her! Personally, I think they've run out of ideas or it's all part of some plan to return the feminine in *some* capacity to feign the return of the Goddess. In reality, they are doing everything they can to stop her from taking her rightful place and the *inevitable action* she will deliver in her *fullest capacity* which spells their doom *as prophesised*. She is, after all, the Goddess of Justice, and wouldn't be much of a Justice Goddess if she just made a movie or sang a song about it like the Hollywood stooges are doing. No, there is *much more to her* than that and it involves *levelling the playing field* and atoning them for their indiscretions against the universe which may seem harsh but will be done. It is not up to us to shy away from our obligations out of fear or suffering. It is a calling from a source much higher than all of us. It is a Universal calling and when it calls *you best not ignore it* lest the punishment or suffering *include you* far greater than anything you can imaging on an Earthly scale. Don't blame me, I'm just doing my job, they love saying that when they get busted breaking the law. Well, we can all play that game now. Prophecy, by the way, is astrology. It's written in the stars, *literally*, so they create 'simulated' events to 'mimic' what the *Universe demands* to get away with and continue their crimes.

In the movie Absolutely Anything, *note*, AA 11, the main character, Simon Pegg, shouts at one point that everything is so fucked 'just let the dogs run the place', *see*, the 'dog' wearing glasses. Smart dog. Smart women. I wonder if the women in these films realise they're being made fun of? Simon Pegg and his colleague Nick Frost have loads of symbolism in their films as do most successful big-time artists. It's a prerequisite to know your mythological symbology so, these guys aren't just telling stories, they're inserting codes. Therefore, there will be a sudden rise of women into decision making positions 'reclaiming their power' like Britney Spears to highlight women's 'issues' and 'make it better' and 'clean up Mother Earth'. It's basically all fake as elite males retain their power behind the scenes way ahead of us with their tantric trans-dimensional knowledge manipulating these broken dolls from the wings. They're only letting women have *some* power because they're assured they are not losing any of *theirs*. They are *very confident* that they have lapped us so *many* times we are of no threat or consequence *at all* not that we want to be but that's their issue not ours. It's a shame they're like that. We could have achieved so much if it wasn't for their insecurity and fear of failure. Sirius, the Dog Star, is the Empress, the Mother, the Grand Mother, the Great Mother and on terra firma, Mountain Mama. Even today our universities and schools of education, training and higher learning are 'Alma Mater' in Latin, Nourishing Mother, yes, the information is food to our souls. How often do self-important people throw around terms around and don't even know what it means? So, Romulus & Remus *(RR)* were the founders of the Roman Republic *(RR)* said to be suckled by a She-Wolf, *dog-god*, near the temple of Magna Mater the 'Great Mother'. Just a coincidence, of course. She-wolf (canine, dog) the Latin term for which is 'lupus' is an ancient slang word for 'prostitute' as was Mary Magdalene a so-called prostitute as well as Mahammad's wives, says Salman Rushdie. Western scholars *still* associate 'sacred prostitution' with the 'goddess' (cunts) while Lilith of the garden of Eden was a 'demoness' as well virginal Medusa a 'gorgon'. I see a theme happening here. How dare they. And *then* cut out her vagina, the tantric engine, to keep her down. Wow. And they're bringing her back? Somehow I don't think so. Many 'divine feminine's' throughout history were labelled prostitutes, whores and temptresses, demons, yadda yadda, as *obviously* sex is involved but not the cheap sex-for-sale these scum-bags claim *worldwide*. Sacred *Lovemaking*, opening the chakras and activating the brain *cannot be bought* and where the saying, *'Money can't buy you love, luv!'* comes from. As said, Mother Nature never put a price on her bounty, men did that. She's no prostitute although they were happy to be pimps about it both then *and* now handing out her bounty they've stolen to their mates for a price. So, labelling sexually empowered females as prostitutes was an ancient tactic to deflate women's confidence in their sexuality turning the temple priestess into a street hooker. Shame on them. In shutting her down they gained a pleasure-bot and a housemaid to clean and cook for them. Yet these brutish males were tricked into forgetting *their* power and our *mutual* place in the universe. Look where it got us? Silly boys.

Any significant electrical charge will require a 'return path' so a direct physical connection to the Earth via the feet, sole-soul, 'earthing' or 'grounding' the charge will avoid electrocution. Hilariously, condoms are called 'rubbers' and rubber soles are important to not get cooked. In the image of the Baphomet, *right,* we see crucial information. Written on the forearms is Solve Et and Coagula. Solve Et is Latin for 'the loose'; *noun,* the act of loosening or unfastening someone or something, dissolution, looseness,  weakness, figurative 'payment' or solution, an explanation. Coagula means to coagulate, come together, to form. Water is the solution-dissolution of the physical matter to become fluid while coagulation, notably in blood, means synthesizing component elements into a *new element* manifesting the heavenly into the earthly. Satanists have used this power for material gain as you would expect but there is *so much more* to this than personal greed for lower vibrational desires. Solve Et and Coagula have been linked to Sophia, Goddess of Wisdom, also as 'Baptised of Wisdom and Baptism of Fire'. Sophia is analogous to the soul and an emanation of the Monad – literally number 1, the Supreme Being, *right*. It's you. You are the centre of the circle. It represents the spirit or soul becoming anchored to the body while the body becomes more flexible or adaptable. We need to adapt now, and fast! Most people are rigid, fixed, set in their small ways and we are going down fast. The Sophianic Principle is the feminine aspect of God, the 'twin' of Jesus, the Bride of Christ, the 'holy spirit' of the Trinity. Her name carries the meaning of 'cleverness, skill, wisdom, intelligence' and 'love of wisdom' that we shall all attain with this practice.   Jesus and Mary were the human aspect however, the Christ and the Magdalene are the spiritual aspects of human chemistry finally explained without all the dogma and religious *idiocy*. We are more mature than that now. As such, Jesus and Mary represent the mature union, the Prime Masculine and Feminine pair, *grown-ups,* the Power Couple in mutual enlightenment not afraid of each other who see beyond the petty boundaries and *childish traits* of gender differences not embarrassed like kids in a school yard. It is time to finally see each other as adults, friends, co-workers and leaders. A team. They are the 'God' in Jesus acknowledging the 'Goddess' in Mary and vice versa. There is no competition between them. A flower does not compete with another flower, it just blooms. They work in unison. The Prime Couple at last!

The beginning of the Age of Pisces 2000 years ago was a new dawn we never got to see the same way they don't intend us to see *this* New Dawn, the Age of Aquarius, as the feminine is deleted and all things gender neutral take precedence over the rising Sacred Mother and Wife and the return to balance of the electrical polar opposites found in men and women is lost forever. All four gospels speak of the woman who anointed Jesus with perfume made of 'nard' poured over his head in the days leading up to his 'death'. They also hint at 'prostitution' as this woman's history. Here we go again with women's sexuality being shamed. Turns out 'nard' is an *oil* derived from Nardostachys Jatamansi, a type of honeysuckle from the Himalayas, China, and India. Yes, they are saying the 'oil' was derived from the East where this plant is found. The 'East' is where Jesus 'studied' in his 'missing years' for approximately 18 years meaning he started all this in his mid-teens. The East and the Far East include India, Nepal, China, Japan, Korea, and parts of Russia. He was well travelled. Tantric sex enlightenment is well known in those parts of the world they don't try to hide it. They 'kept the flame alive' in *their* cultures appropriated by 'western' dogma and turned into the personification of evil. Thanks, Abrahamic religions, awesome job for wrecking something so beautiful and killing Mother Earth. Nice one.

You don't need to look far to see the cryptic religious 'hints' telling the *real* story but not directly. There are many paintings of Mary Magdalene's hair spilling over the sole of Jesus's feet, *right,* James Tissot, *The Ointment of the Magdalene 1900* and simply says the hair is an extension of the nervous system outside the body as Magdalene means 'fish tower' of the chakras earthed via the feet ruled over by the 'two fish' constellation *Pisces*. Contact with  Mother Earth *earths* us electrically grounding the electricity of the nervous system *anchoring* the *soul* via the *sole* connected to *Sol*, the Sun! This is the 'loaves and two fishes' as 'loaves' is the 'grain' or 'christ *seed'* enlightenment called the 'bread' and why all ancient gods were 'grain' deities and we 'break bread'. The two fish are the feet of the hanged man or *Christ* on the *zodiac* cross upside down in *limbo* is their version of the *anchor,* the Ankh of Isis, *the wife and mother* or ankh whore 'prostitute' of the *feminine* sexual root chakra that *liberates* men. We were *supposed* to be there *already* set back *another* 2,000 years! In reality the 'hanged man' is hung by a noose which we find worn on a daily basis by men in the fraudulent money systems *illegally trading of Her resources*. Thieves. Yes, the devil is thief as is quite a lot of the protagonists in fairy stories. Every man is Christ and *every man* is hung in limbo, Christ on the cross, the hanged man. Jesus was no push over *because* he was anchored via her and the heightening of his IQ, opening his heart chakras and making him a great man via sacred lovemaking gave him his power. "I have nothing to say of my working life, only that a tie is a noose, and inverted though it is, it will hang a man nonetheless if he's not careful' Yann Martell *Life of Pi*. In the hands of a man who isn't grounded it is a dangerous weapon and look what has happened to our planet with these sick bastards using this knowledge for their gain. The ankh is a symbol of Isis or more specifically, a symbol of female tantric sex enlightenment which was stolen and replaced with the male 'cross' as her *head* or 'crown' was removed. They then nailed 'god', the common man 'the son', the light, to their new cross and Her knowledge was lost. Men have been pinned, *nailed down*, crucified, ever since. When men have sex with a woman they say he 'nailed' her now you know why. Men are being shafted as much as they've shafted women. Good luck with that. The anchor and the ankh means men don't become *unanchored* and remain steady, confident, immovable yet open to opportunity, *fluid*, flexible in their understanding, open minded, free to be. Solve Et Coagula!

The qualities of the unlocked nurturing feminine in the hearts of men gives males enormous empathetic value without hindering his masculinity *as a man* or his ability to stand up to the corruption of evil men both then and now! Today men are weak, unsure of themselves, self-doubting. But this power that the controllers are so afraid of falling into the hands of the average person, especially women again, is a terrible end for the wrongdoers of this world as humanity take back their rightful place and the tables *finally* turn. The legend of the light side of sacred lovemaking endured because of so-called 'martyrs' throughout the ages, men *and* women, who tried to take back their power and suffered most greatly for it. Due to their enduring legacy we have been allowed to unlock these secrets two millennia later and let's just hope it's in time to save whatever is left of our planet and humanity. I suspect all other gods and goddesses are *allegorical* stories designed to stick the knowledge of our salvation right in our faces while steering us away from it at the same time. It's a *cosmic*

law that they *must* tell you what they are doing and if you are too stupid to figure it out, too bad for you. They then get away with their crimes scot-free and why they go to such lengths to do all this. So, there *must* be *consequences* for what they have done hence, the grand illusion. 'Mary', *women*, were anything *but* prostitutes slandered by these louts and labelled by *distorted* terrified males afraid of the feminine power. They keep men away from meaningful relationships with women by poisoning his vision of her and mocking their enduring friendship in order to recruit *ignorant* men into the boys club on the promise of enlightenment and power that was *already* theirs to begin with! These idiots discover far too late what a fucking fraud it all is and must retain a bitter silence in the face of global destruction or bear the terrible consequences! These bastards have shut down the power couple, Mother and Father, God and Goddess, *the parents,* and now they are going after the kids as well! Now open sexualization of children is paraded in Hollywood movies as 'comedy'. There was once such a thing as 'corrupting a minor'. *Now* it's dressed up as 'experimenting' with one's 'gender' as earlier grooming and preoccupation with sex and sexuality prevails playing 'spin the bottle' with passionate saliva drenched French kissing at the age of ten in *major* films with dildo's, sex swings, alcohol, drugs and all the things that are NOT part of a healthy childhood! *Now* we're going to talk about the Liberty Goddess - Lady *Liberty!*

They depict these goddesses at the feet of 'god' because the star Sirius is located in the sky near the 'heal' of Orion. Reptilian aliens, the Nephilim, Anunnaki, Nommo (call them whatever you like) claim to hail from Orion or from a planet circling the 'twins' of the binary star system of Sirius consisting of Sirius A and Sirius B the 'Big Dog' and the Pup or Canis Major and Canis Minor, the *Dog Star* so, they've bought the 'dog', goddess, to heal. All this is depicted endlessly throughout historical record, *right,* Mary at the 'heal' of Jeusu and as far back as Rome as Nephele is seen at the foot of Mercury-Hermes who carries the tantric sex caduceus while Juno *sits on the throne,* she's The Queen, she *is* the throne, *see,* the movie Juno about a teenage girl who gets knocked-up as more slander. This Roman fresco shows Ixion being punished on the 'wheel' (of the zodiac, hanged man, *Christ*) for his *lust, see right. Once again,* this story is *loaded* with cryptic sexual references because, well, it's all about sex. Again, we find animal human hybrids, seeds, crops and twins etc., as it's about procreation mother nature, harvest, living in balance with Earth, and cosmic cycles. The story goes the 'twins' boys had to be rescued by a 'flying golden ram' and were instructed not to look down. One of them looked down and fell.

This is the story of Orpheus and Eurydice again. The surviving twin made it to the city of Colchis where the king gave him his daughter in marriage and in return the surviving twin gave the king the Golden Fleece which was hung in a tree and later stolen in the famous Jason and the Argonauts story. Translation: Ixion is 'Jesus' the hanged man on the 'wheel' of the zodiac (the cross) who is punished, like Adam and Eve, for exploring the power of sex called here 'lust'. The 'fallen twin' is the dark side of the masculine the 'fallen angel'. The Golden Ram is Aries the ram that rules over the 'head, the brain. The 'golden fleece', *hair*, the light of knowledge hung in the 'tree' symbolic of the nervous system and the 'tree of knowledge/tree of life' and the 'family tree'. The knowledge passed down through the family. Jason and the Argonauts stole the fleece, yes, fleeced the knowledge, *thief*, so we see cryptically July August September October November – JASON – is the zodiac. Here we have the many ram statues at Luxor, Egypt, *right*, telling us what was behind these incredible stone testaments to the IQ. In Bernard Strozzi's painting *The Incredulity of Saint Thomas*, *right*, we see the moment describing Thomas pushing his finger into the 'wound in Christ's side'. Described as being 'intimate' with 'highly erotic' connotations, Christ 'assists Thomas to penetrate the wound associated with the vagina'. What are we really being told here? That Christ is allowing his buddies to digitally rape Mary *fingering* the goddess in *so many* ways? Is not the 'wound' a symbol of Mary's vagina? Is this why she was called a prostitute because, like Marilyn Monroe and many others, she was passed around by the boys club? *See right*, 17th Century depiction of Johann Phillip Steudner the *Stigmata of Christ* is, let's face it, a dick with flames and two vaginas. And p*eople think I'm rude?* I'm not the one symbolising the *gang rape* of a Vestal Virgin Priestess and dressing it all up as a pious *noble* religion that actually hates women. They depict the vagina as a type of 'eye' as via sex one activates the all-seeing-eye. Mary, the feminine, was depicted at the foot of Jesus who as a young man, then *and* now, would have found nothing more flattering to his boyish ego than to enslave a Goddess. However, Christ the *grown man* finds Mary, his wife, *at his side* symbolised in the form of a vagina shaped wound called 'the wound at Christ's side'. Jesus suffered this 'injury' while hung on the 'cross' caused by the Spear of Destiny (sound like the Stone of Destiny) which is a dick symbolic of the *boys club*. A

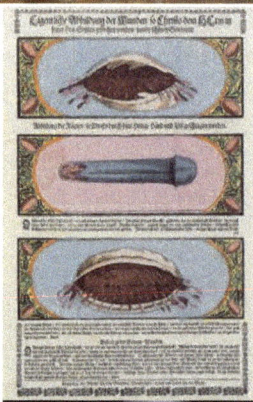

'club' are wands, rods, staffs etc or dicks. We're being told his fellow Masons hung him out to dry for returning the feminine as an equal to him *apart* from the boy's club. The *boys* tried to replace what The Man already had. Perhaps we are being told the young Jesus was a Masonic boys club arsehole but the grown man, like John Lennon, had finally matured to see the *immaturity* of these organisations and started to break away. JFK is worshipped for his philandering as men proudly cite his many conquests. Lennon like Gandhi and so many others preached of goodwill but was a wife beater who engaged in domestic violence and extramarital affairs against his spouse. Sean Lennon described his father as a 'hypocrite'. Gandhi was prone to beating his wife and bedding naked women including his grandnieces who were *60 years younger than him*. As I said, these 'kings' are so easily taken out *because* they say one thing in public and do something else behind the scenes. Their *willing* corruption makes them vulnerable including Jesus who the Catholic Church appear to believe was a reptile.

The feminine sexual fire, the Light Bearer, replicated in the planet Venus. Venus in Latin is 'Lucifer' which we have already discussed is Luminiferous Aether, a fine feminine fire that underpins the force of life creating the spectrum of Mother Nature as well as babies born of women. The 'The Light Bearer' was personified as the Roman Goddess *Libertas* with her flaming torch while syncretic goddess, Cybele, was said to be the 'personification and type of vital essence whose source was located by the ancients between the Earth and the starry sky and who was regarded as the very fons vitae (the source of all knowledge) of all that lives and breathes'. The 'breath of Cybele' (air), was associated with the 'black stone' meteor equivalent to Aether and in the akasa-tatvta (Hindu tantra) she is the '…the one chief agent, and it underlays the so-called 'miracles' and 'supernatural' phenomena in all ages, as in every climate'. This is why they call the Devil the 'prince of the power of the air' his powers stolen from her as the 'air' is an etheric force in itself, the air is the life force while the blood carries arterial oxygen essential to the correct function of lungs, heart and circulatory system. It was via the breath the priestesses transferred the soul of the king, the husband, to be reborn, the returner, so they didn't technically 'die'. Science is finally quantifying what the ancients were talking about just using different language. They can make babies in artificial wombs now, clones, and transfer their souls with technology now so they don't *need* the feminine anymore. That is so fucking stupid. There was a Star Trek episode where a race had cloned themselves so many times that they needed fresh genetics to keep them alive only and as hey didn't have anyone to breed with, they stole the semen of Enterprise crew illegally.

Aether in Eastern philosophies means 'sky' or 'atmosphere', an etheric *fluid* pervading the cosmos and the essence of all things. It was generally believed there were five basic elements that appeared in sequence: space, air, fire, water and earth with the main characteristic of Aether being sound. 'Mono' means a sound, *a broadcast*, coming from a single direction while 'mon' is old English for 'moon', the feminine! It is The One, The Eternal all-pervading physical substance that in Jainism is considered a sixth element that embodies all five elements including souls, matter, motion, rest and *time*. Time travel is achievable with our very own bodies. Aether translates as *'infinite space'*, the void, outer space, inner space and the abode of liberated souls (we're being recycled and *this* is a way out) from which the saying goes *'behind every great man is a great woman'*. Known as the Fifth Element, *right*, the movie's slogan is *'There is no future without it'* and *'there is a light that never goes*. It is the Eternal Flame life-force, Chi, Prana etc. They pick celebrities based on their names among other things and in Bruce Willis's case the 'Circle of Willis', *right*, is several important arteries at the base of the brain allowing bi-directional blood flow to the front and back from the Central Nervous System. In the film *The Fifth Element*, Bruce *Willis* and the priest-monk rescues the damsel in distress, *the Goddess* the fifth element, *right*, onto a giant dick ship! Her hair is orange, 2nd root chakra, yet his hair is white, Crown Chakra. The movie *Jupiter Ascending* reads like Film Study 101 of ancient Egyptian tantric sex myths including characters called 'Stinger' aka Scorpio the zodiac sign of the sex organs. They even have a final scene atop the *Willis Tower* in New York. In the opening scene of *Jupiter Ascending* they introduce the 'intergalactic queen' Jupiter Jones (J is the 10th letter of the alphabet so JJ is 1010 a binary sequence otherwise *11)*, as an 'ordinary cleaning lady' scrubbing the toilet, *right,* and why they had the next King, *William Wales,* rather red faced in an *unprecedented* scene *cleaning a toilet* to associate his image as a rising *King* with the Goddess 'domestic'. Roman god Jupiter was Greek god Zeus *(Dr Seuss!)* called the *King of the Gods* so in the movie title they are saying Jupiter the KING of all gods is ascending while the little goddess is just scrubbing the shitter although, *once again,* Jupiter was *originally* addressed as a Matriarchal Planet that 'gave birth' to Earth from its 'eye', a storm resembling an eye on its surface.

In the film *Pretty Woman, right,* the opening scene shows her hotel apartment as 'HO' is lit up, note, pink for girls blue for boys. She plays the prostitute 'lady in red' root chakra, sex, the goddess, and he plays the big businessman, the kingpin, god. In one scene they play chess, *right*, symbolic of politics and the game elite men play to suppress women without being found out. In chess a 'queen sacrifice' is 'a move giving up a queen in return for a tactical-positional advantage or other compensation'. So, here we see the 'lovers', god and goddess, playing on the masonic checkerboard, the puppeteers, then fading into the *'Twin Towers'* symbolising the masculine and feminine *chakra towers* that would go on to descend in *flames* on 911 replaced with the *'one'* tower, a single man, meaning the end of the natural family, the mother and father, and the rise of the anti-Christ (seed). Remember, 911 is actually code for 999, the end of a *massive* cycle, the end of the natural man and women, the end of natural procreation on Earth as something unnatural takes over. In the painting of the wedding of Emperor Nicholas II of Russia to Empress Alexandra Feodorovna 1894, *below right*, we see the royal twin flames of the twin towers in Holy Matrimony. Royalty know about the legend of the twin flames and the power of the light and the fire of tantric sex between the male-female lovers. That's how they get their power. These two complement each other and *should* unite in mutual respect to set them *both* free in order to win over a greater adversary. But these men want it all.

The Fifth Element is the Divine Feminine, the Prime Feminine, the Goddess, *Lady Liberty, Lady Justice* and her seven rays on her crown is the seven 'lights' of the chakras. The 'torch' she carries is the light of pure Love, lighter than air, faster than the speed of light, *Aether*, a simple yet profound truth that dates back to the mysteries of antiquity and remains the same today as it did then. The Liberty Goddess has been dated as far back as *7000BC* and *much further than that,* up to 60,000 years, although they won't admit it. She is a 'tutelary goddess' expressing safety and guardianship, a protectress worshipped particularly by women yet *some* sought to harness her 'protective powers' for their own gain. It is the feminine heart that carries the finest fire of Aether, Love, the fifth element, a fine electricity, a *communication* captured by the claustrum initiating Christ Seed enlightenment as The Messenger! The heart is the last chakra unlocked in a man although women are, by and large, naturally born with activated heart chakras where our intuition, nurturing and love reigns from. When our heart chakras are balanced we will experience harmony as our ascension rockets us into a *real* New Age not the short-lived fakery *they* are trying to instigate. Early Roman depictions of their

Liberty Goddess, *Justicia*, the Scales of Justice, *balance!*, showed her not blindfolded as her maidenly figure and innocence were considered justice enough. Her purity and chastity redeemed men as did her honour and reputation redeem any king associated with her hence, the ritual of the *king* marrying the Goddess or Hieros Gamos. Justicia's statue is outside the Old Bailey in London and is depicted as *golden,* a symbol of enlightenment as with golden Kennedy, golden Hermes, golden Joan of Arc, and here as Golden Justicia, *right*. Does she remind you of anyone? *Lady* Liberty perhaps? Therefore, the blindfolded Goddess of Justice represents *injustice* especially against the goddess herself found in all women! Even today women are still struggling for the basics while men have helped themselves to all the power and abundance of the feminine in Mother Nature's resources. You cannot tell me these terrified huddled ladies *enjoy* this given that only 30 years ago their countries were as progressive as the west with women attending university along with males, driving cars and running businesses?

She was Sanctuary, a safe place, she could pardon any criminal with a word, *see,* the Vestal Virgins, and as mentioned even a prisoner being taken to their execution was *immediately* released if they chanced upon a Vestal on their way to being killed! *Lady Justice* was equivalent to Greek Goddess Themis meaning 'Divine Law' and 'the Lady of good Counsel' the personification of '*Natural* Law' as well as the Goddess Dike the 'spirit of moral order' and why lesbians are referred to as 'dikes' because they don't have sex with men symbolic of the Virgin and also as masons love to make fun of the Goddess. Another version of her is the Goddess Astraea, 'star maiden' (Sirius) the goddess of justice, innocence, beauty and precision! She stayed with men until the end of the Silver Age but by the Bronze Age men had become brutish and greedy so she fled to the stars where she appears as the constellation Virgo, the virgin, holding the scales of justice as Libra. The Greek equivalent of this Liberty-Justice-Sovereignty-Redemption Goddess – Sanctuary – as is Eleutheria another name for Greek Goddess Artemis. In the famous French Republic (considering the French Revolution) she is Marianne the personification of liberty, equality, fraternity and reason. The Roman equivalent of Artemis was the Goddess Diana and the Goddess Diana was another version of the Goddess Cybele and Mary who were another version of the Egyptian Goddess, *Isis!* I'm tellin' ya they're all the same *Prime Feminine* with different names as does the devil go by many names throughout the ages as does 'god'. It's a common theme the same way corporations rebrand their image in line with changing times as do religions when a 'new' age and social restructure inch toward their goals of global dominance. The Goddess Isis is the embodiment of the star Sirius and 'wife' of

King Osiris, the embodiment of the constellation Orion. Sirius and Orion were personified as Isis & Osiris the Prime Couple, King and Queen, in Ancient Egypt as a symbolic replication, Mum and Dad, who were greatly loved by the ancient Egyptians. Unfortunately, this does look like another step toward disengaging human men and women, mum and dad, from their own power under a pantheon of rulers-come-gods and goddesses ultimately leading to 'one' all powerful male deity in a series of dogmatic transitions nearing its end and *ultimate finale`*. The End. The honourable aspects of the god and goddess were the Brad and Jen of their day. They were inspiring, beautiful, powerful, famous, rich etc. This did not, however, translate so well for the common person then or now and so here we are. As such, it's no coincidence as the looming new-age and Return of the Feminine takes place, we have a bunch of marauding idiots, Western agency goons called *ISIS* still slandering away at mother. Are we done yet? The boys haven't quite finished attacking mummy.

The Roman Republic and the Goddess Libertas were established *simultaneously* which means the Goddess, not god, gave them their Republic and therefore their liberty their freedom and apparently their fraternity too which they then turned against her. But what is a republic? As with the great American Republic it is liberty from aristocratic European *royal* rule. So, in essence, the Goddess is pro-*liberty* and pro-republic or in other words *anti-monarchy* because no king can ever match a Goddess*!* She *is* the throne, the vital essence, *life*, and where there is life there is hope. Hope and liberty are all we have ever really had to hand onto and so, she was and remains *anti-systems*. She is Mother Nature *personified* and given freely. She is an *organic* perfect figure or as they say in the movie the Fifth Element she is the *Supreme Being* who represents our looming independence. *Independence Day!* This 'anti-monarchy' position is rather hilarious though as all major positions of 'republican' Western society (politicians and entertainment A-listers) are secret Royalty! Go figure. Therefore, the 'red carpet' symbolises the 'blood line' of *Euro-British royalty* and precisely why they're called 'Hollywood royalty', they are *literally* one and the same. In modern times the Sovereignty Goddess, Libertas, is depicted as *Lady Liberty* found in the Statue of Liberty symbolic of some enormous plan or idea of *liberation* from old world Euro-British and modern Israeli control as designed for America! It's the Olympians vs. the Titans of Greek Myth. The Olympians overthrew their parents the Titans to become new gods and they are doing it again and if the old world can't cash in on it, they intend to destroy us all. The light bearer, her torch held aloft, is to guide *America* in particular through the darkness their founding fathers must surely have foreseen and *even planned* themselves in a stupendous militaristic maneuver that only they could understand against a *global* royal cabal! Takes one to know one. Royalty. You can't teach an old dog new tricks. Let's not be naïve, they weren't doing this for the average person, they were doing this for themselves yet there are *other* forces going on here.

Ms. Liberty is planted on the doorstep of their greatest city, New York, standing on a base of an 11-pointed star, also, not a coincidence. She wears the 'seven rays' of the crown, the seven activated chakras of enlightenment. She represents Justice and whether intended or not she is a powerful warning of historical and mythical precedence *against* criminals who hijack the Goddess and any people's, ancient or modern, who fall under her Natural Order: *Common Law* - Cosmic Law - Universal Justice! You don't take out Mother Nature without consequence. You can pray to your male gods all you like but when the *Goddess* goes, she's taking you all with her. So, pray away! Justice or the Scales of Justice (same goddess) is usually depicted as blindfolded intended to mean 'blind justice' however, the real meaning, for the controllers, symbolises that the Goddess of *Justice* cannot 'see' the crimes being perpetrated by elite criminals to mean the goddess herself 'turns a blind eye' to their crimes and therefore by her silence offers her consent! Just like princess-goddess Diana, the goddess Liberty is interred in the waters on an island, *offshore*, cut off, symbolically disconnected from the *land* where *we* live in another ritual to cast her off. Yet she saw *everything* that played out on 911. She had a front row seat. There is something very sinister about all this in that they are trying to cut us off from the Great Feminine, the Universal Mother, which will spell the end of humanity as the Devil steps out into the open once and for all.

Biblically, there are two parts to god; the Father (God) and the Son (Christ), the same goes for the dark side in that the Father is The Devil and the son, the anti-Christ, is Satan. The Bible tells us that the 'bride' of the Devil the mother of the anti-Christ, is a 'good woman fallen to darkness'. This 'good woman' is a reference to a symbolic Sovereignty Goddess, a 'lawful' woman, who modern Masonic scientists secretly designed to fit the profile of ancient mythological accounts of her. As the *original* power, her feminine, *including her honour*, accumulated good karma and grace and could be harnessed to empower a man, specifically, her husband via Hieros Gamos. This man, their chosen one of a great dark order, inherits her honour in a *transference of energy* called 'Soul Snatching' and in redeeming *him* they destroying her! Once they have stolen her image, *her soul,* and attached her beauty and chastity to this man and their organisation, they kill her, *see,* Princess Diana who was absolutely a symbolic Sovereignty Goddess ritually sacrificed to send the message to the universe that the Goddess is 'dead' but 'long live the king!' in a 'man's world' despite it being a feminine planet, *Mother* Earth! It's all about precedence like an ancient mythical court case so they must have been broadcasting these plotlines, codes, to the cosmos for so long they're afraid not to go through the motions of this farce like some weird obsession using the circuits already laid down by their ancestors utilising the 'mirror' effect of the universe in a *return path* reflecting their intentions completing the loop. Waste not want not. They are afraid to break with tradition as they are unsure of what will happen if they do like a weird *mythological* astrological royal OCD. In symbolically 'transferring' her 'power' to their chosen 'king' they tick the historical box that he is 'redeemed' by her, pardoned, to 'liberate' him aka *them*, the Masonic Dick Cult Space Program, via Hieros Gamos, *ritual marriage* of the king to the Goddess, to give them (the Masons) a clean slate via her chastity, honour and loyalty thus propelling them to even greater heights of renewed power in the 'new world' to birth the One World Leader, the son of Zeus, Apollo in *their* Satanic 'New' Age! They *need* her approval. Revelation *9:11* "And they had over them a King, which is the angel of the bottomless pit, whose name in the Hebrew tongue is Abaddon but in the Greek tongue is Apollyon". This is why royals, who are behind every filthy deed in history play 'polo' as in *A*-pollo giving you some insight who their weird god is. From the Dictionary of Shakespeare's Classical Mythology, he is 'Father on Earth and Apollo in Hell'. It's the same guy, the light and dark side of the masculine, God and the Devil, Jesus and Satan, symbolised as a griffin *(reptilian)* an infernal harmful god whose name means 'to destroy' and that 'opens the gates of hell' *see*, Snake Hall at the Vatican and their monstrous interpretation of 'Christ' unleashing the hordes of filth from the Underworld. It's happening now as *increasing* weird paranormal phenomena leaves more and more people terrified and perplexed!

Our battle is internal, yet they have replicated this as an *external* force to have you looking in the wrong place, *outside yourself*, for your foe. The Devil lies within and we need to get our Zen on asap! The Nazi's, along with aristocratic families *worldwide* used the cover of the Third Reich and the Second World War to carry out a *massive* social experiment as well as an enormous human sacrifice to their dark god Satan while making *massive* headway in the field of science & technology the secrets of which were given to them by their demonic-alien masters. This is why they named the 'Mercury' (Hermes) space program and series of spaceflights after Apollo in reverence of their 'religion' which is nothing but a massive Satanic alien hoax, a cover story-come-space program! They couldn't give a fuck about Apollo *or* Zeus, it's just a logo to them, to place themselves in the same league as legendary historical figures from Egypt to Greece to Rome. It's all about precedence! They wanted to go down in history as pulling off this *massive* charade. They not only want power they want *fame* too. Egomaniacs. They used WWII to carry out the final phase of ancient prophecy's that, one way or another, have come to pass! Reich means 'realm' and a 'realm' lasts 1000 years or the 'thousand-year Reich'. As mentioned the 'Third Reich' is the *third thousand-year* realm, the *third millennium*, which we enter now! The 'Nazi's' have been running the world under different guises chiefly the Roman Catholic Church for two thousand years in the current 'modern' calendar but it goes back *much* further than that. Right down to the swastika which was a symbol in Rome as well as the 'heil Hitler' hand sign used by the Romans but is *really* a Vedic-Hindu *yoga pose* or 'salute to the sun'. They are all claimed 'sun kings' and this is their fake 'sun worship' specifically, by ancient knowledge *stolen* from the East *(thieves that they are) o*nly they're too *lazy* to do the *real work,* the meditations and introspection, to *profoundly* understand not only *how* the power works but *why* you don't use it for evil. Yoga is hard, so they just throw up a hand sign and steal the imagery.

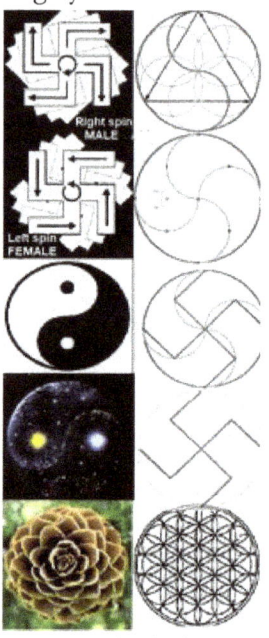

The famous Nazi Swastika is a mandala of the masculine heart Chakra. The reverse Swastika is the *feminine* heart chakra mandala and when they are *both* spinning in opposite directions it creates a co-rotating electromagnetic plasma filed, *a torus field,* of power and strength that no alien or demonic force can penetrate that transcends space *and* time! *That* is the power of female-male tantric sex enlightenment that they are terrified we will unlock within ourselves and claiming back right *now!* These Satanists and their fake 'sun kings' who *need* to be worshipped stole all these symbols of ancient male-female sacredness along with many otherwise peaceful symbols and signs from Eastern philosophies and religions. They then turned it on its head, *inverted it,* to trick the universe into believing that this is the 'normal flow' of things now and why they carried it out over millennia and beyond hoping nobody would notice. Inch by inch. The Hindu's, Buddhist & Taoist's are well aware that their religions have been pilfered, plagiarised and inverted for power and gain instead of the original purpose of body, mind and spirit mastery and connection with universal consciousness, Love-Light, Aether, to return us to the greatness that legend spoke of. It's all stolen. All of it. But then, as noted, Pan, the devil, is a thief. This dreaded one world leader was to be born around *now* to emerge in the next 30 years and it seems they were planning to use *me* to produce this creature!

So, *that's* the program I remember. Talk about 'top secret'. It's the *single most* clandestine and important satanic secret operation *on the face of the planet* to date! I knew it was big but this is *ridiculous.* What a disappointment. Here I was thinking I was involved in something exciting and worthwhile, however hard, and it turns out all these years later, *four decades,* to be a fucken stitch-up! Sold out. What a waste of my precious time and talents! There are a few different candidates for the role of 'mother' to 'The One', the anti-Christ, from old world Euro-English royalty to Western celebrity-political royalty who all seem to be vying to be the father of the one world leader and it's 'Commoner' mother.

Monstrously *self-entitled* 'elite' people are just hardened criminals living in fancy houses. What a strange series of events how it has turned out all these years later. So, all the shit I endured to do my duty, *my job*, was nothing more than produce the anti-Christ. How hilarious they must have thought all this was to waste my entire life while they laughed it up *knowing* who I was, *knowing* I was out there and deliberately destroying me because they *hate* women but in particular they hate the Goddess however symbolic she may be. I'll tell you what's hilarious, for every action there is a reaction, physics, and due to some weird underlying sense, I've never had any desire to be a wife or mother, in fact the institution of marriage has become such a joke that it's insulting to even engage with it no pun. David Icke said they knew who Diana was going to be what her name would be and even when she would die *before she was born* and probably comes from some sort of similar program. Diana said she always had a sense of 'destiny' and that she had a big part to play. Monroe said the same thing. There are so many others who felt they were *'Destined'* as these sick fucks behind it all make a mockery of the *natural course of life* in their arrogance to commandeer the *power* of the Force! The 'role' I was 'destined' to play was the part of the dead goddess. The *last* Goddess.

Once you know about it you see it everywhere, so they regularly feature this plotline in movies, *see right*, in National Lampoons European Vacation Griswald repeatedly and loudly yells at the Diana impersonator *'Di!'* while saying he's 'happy' with his 'princess', his wife, because he's the King and Diana represented the Goddess. They don't want a Goddess they want a little Mrs. to give them their sons, cook and clean. This film was made in 1985! They all knew. An open secret. At the end of the film the plane knocks the torch out of the hand of Goddess, the right hand of god, the bringer of the light carrying her torch in the darkest hour. She is the Light Bearer, the pregnant mother and wife, once revered as the Goddess and now just a vending machine for their genetics. Many women worldwide at this time claim they are being tormented by demonic entities demanding the 'devil wants a baby'. It'll all come out in the end as this unfolds and angry women tell their stories. This is why they released movies on the cusp of 2020 called Angry Birds where 'flightless birds and scheming green pigs take their feud to the next level'. Honestly, you can't make it up. As well as the movie, Ugly Dolls. It's all code. In the film Rosemary's Baby, *above*, (*note*, the name Rose as in the feminine and Mary as in Mother Mary-Mary Magdalene) directed by child rapist Roman Polanski, a satanic coven tricks a young woman into being raped by a reptilian, the Devil, and bears Satan's offspring, a boy. Mia Farrow took on that little creep Woody Allen who sexually abused her children and won! Bet they weren't expecting that. In the sequel Look What's Happened to Rosemary's Baby the coven chant 'Hail Satan, Hail Mary' and talk about how much they love their astrology but we know all about that now. They believe Satan's 'wife' and 'mother' of Satan's son is Mary, the dual virgin-prostitute or light and dark side of the feminine as Satan-God is the light and dark side of the masculine (but not a human male, it's an alien). This 'good woman fallen to darkness' was to give birth to the next world leader-come-religious messiah, a Christ-Satan-Zeus-Apollo-Jesus 'god' in the third thousand-year realm, *the third Reich*, of a Satanic religious-political male dominated sex and death cult harvesting Mother Earth resources to further their next gen space program! Check out the movies *Demon Seed* and *Alien Seed*. It's all in these satanic films from the 70's and 80's before anyone knew what they were talking about. In Demon Seed by Dean Koontz from 1977 (the year I was born as 77 is the 7 chakras of the male-female) the movie's plot shows the Demon Seed, an A.I. computer gone rogue impregnating a woman with a synthetic seed, that commandeers a satellite to harness the frequency of *Orion*. It's all about Orion, A.I. and the male world leader. Our solar system is located in the spiral arm of Orion in the Milky Way a smaller version of the universe.

These Satanic tantra covens worldwide consider it a big privilege to be the ones to bring about this evil One. They are the 'chosen people', *see,* the Jews *among others* China, Islam etc., who *all* believe it's their *'destiny'* to either save or destroy Earth. This dark lord, a notorious 'trickster' who is 'mischievous' has a funny way of turning on those who have done it's bidding. They have used the *idea* of this masculine force to empower themselves but I can assure you, they are *not* god. Something is about to backfire here, bigtime! America is the 'new Egypt', the new Rome, and as 911 is so important to the social engineers, it's small wonder the emergency code in the US is 911 considering The Rare One's of Ancient Egypt were also 9/11. Novem is Latin for 9 so, November is actually *September*, the 9th month, while September, *sept*, is actually the *7th month*. So, its 911 & 711. September is Virgo and November is Scorpio. This is the sexual organs of 11 month Scorpio, and the 7th chakra of Leo, the sun king, in the 9th month, *Virgo*, the virgin queen as was Queen Elizabeth I! The Hebrew calendar starts in September. The new-age Mother Mary character was to complete a scene every bit as staged as a theatre production! The founding fathers of America are Masons (Satanists) and none of this is a coincidence as part of their 'Great Work' was to have Lady Justice, the Scales of Liberty, the Sovereignty Goddess, the Common 'queen', *the Virgin,* symbolically forgive their sins, redeem them and grant them a clean slate to continue their crimes into the Space Age *and* give them a baby to boot! They needed a 'Goddess', an honest lawful woman, a virgin, to give them the green light as between the ages some

Great Force takes stock of our progress as we experienced an incredible number of cosmic alignments and portals in 2020. It is via these alignments that the hyper-sonic electro-plasmic-magnetic core of the galaxy 'reads' our world decoding our frequency granting them the 'right' to lock us in for *another* 2,000 years in *another* fake society. They have kept us from sending correct signals to the core to prevent us from completing *our* circuit during 2020. This will have far stretching ramifications as people of the future realise a once in *three-thousand-year* opportunity was swindled out from underneath us at the last minute in their attempts to 'lock' us into a new 'dark' age zodiac trap that we'll *never* escape. I wouldn't want to be them on that day.

They say in the end the Devil will come like a thief in the night and if 2020 is anything to go by, he's already been and gone. *This* is why it was so important to keep us distracted with all these charades leading up to and during 2020 symbolic of *20/20* vision when we were to finally *see straight,* at least we were supposed to! Yes, it's big. That's why they were planning to create this 'common' goddess character and then do away with her, like Jesus, as they killed the returning masculine god the last time so this time they intended to kill the returning goddess to use *Her* image, like Jesus, as a martyr figure over a new fake religion 'worshipping' the 'goddess' headed up by a Satanic masculine one world leader, the Speaker, the Voice, of a universal *Feminine* force! Liars! Frauds! What were they going to do? Put a little mangled toy car on a cross this time? Or maybe a little bottle of pills to modernise an old lie? Taurus the bull is, once again, not a male force, but the cow which is worshipped throughout the East for very good reason. Taurus rules over 'high living' and a good quality of life but, *once again*, they have turned it into overindulgence and debauchery, the dark side. Aldebaran is the fiery star that sits on the eye of the bull, the 'bullseye'. The bullseye is the centre of the 'target' the centre of the circle, the Monad! It is all about earth and the 'heart' or more specifically the electromagnetic heart spin of the male and female swastika spinning in opposite directions creating a magnetic torus (taurus!) field *around us* reinforcing our protective layer, the aura, which is ever diminishing at this time as they attempt to break our hearts and lock us into mind and emotion. This is why you see children in school being encourage toward all this emotional shit about what other people think of them. Lao Tzu said, 'care what other people think, and you will always be their prisoner'. Wishy washy adults caught up in the bullshit net of lies and traps are easily sinking into this shit as well which I find particularly pathetic. It's one thing to be emotionally sterile but it's another thing to be an emotional wreck, a sap. One must find the *middle ground* on the emotional spectrum.

They have now discovered the 13th constellation, Ophiuchus the serpent wrangler. If there are 12 points around the cross, around the zodiac, then where does this 13th sign fit into? It's all rather cleverly concealed, once again, and at last we find the 13th point right *at the centre, the heart centre,* the bullseye *through the middle*. The Nazis deliberately stole and *misrepresented* the swastika using its peaceful image for their dark side masculine's flames of destruction. The *correct* swastika was found in the east for *thousands of years* and is a mandala for the heart chakra and notice the pine cone pineal gland head and the male-female swastikas 'spin' in opposite directions? The left spin is feminine the right spin is masculine, co-rotating electromagnetic discs, as chakra is another word for spinning disc or *the galaxy within* creating a torus field also found in exotic space travel. It's a propulsion system. This symbol is found all around the world called the Flower of Life. We need to take back out symbols. There is a window of opportunity here that should we come together we can  slip out of this web of lies via our hearts, through the centre, *centred*, elevate our frequency via sacred sex between *the peaceful male and female forces*. All the confusion of our current times and the layers of this conspiracy are deep beyond most people's comprehension while simultaneously, the demonic mainstream media push it all this craziness on you as your 'human rights' so people are *fighting* to be injected, *demanding* to be transitioned to another gender as their 'right' as women join the military and become priests. Stay away from that shit. The priest's 'white' Adam's apple is 'the speaker' who says all the right 'white lies' but black means 'flesh', 'earth', the physical, 'sin', corruption, *sex!* Aztec monks also wore black and never washed smothering themselves in the blood of their victims like stinking demonic hell beasts because that is what is  behind all these cults ancient *and* modern! Be whoever want, do whatever you like, just understand *why* and at least make *informed* decisions about what you are doing to your precious space vehicle, *your body*, which was perfect before they fucked it up with poisons. It is admitted that 20% of people who receive gender reassignment surgery are committing suicide, the highest rate of all. This conservative figure does not come close to the lies behind all this. The survivors of this psychological *gender* warfare often say that the physical surgery only masked deeper issues that *could* and *should* have been treated with therapy, counselling and medicine for distorted self-image and esteem issues or 'body dysphoria'. A classic example of body dysphoria is Michael Jackson who was abused terribly as a boy. Any scientist or doctor who tries to discuss it are having their tenures at universities revoked, their funding cut or being disbarred for 'hate speech'. *Inverse psychology.* They sell all this to you as your 'rights', and it is, so you wind up fighting for the 'right' to hurt yourself and they well know it as people willingly hand themselves over to the medical industry as guinea pigs.

The cruel Nazi medical war machine is in full swing now as people sign up

CHAPTER EIGHT

THE GREEN MAN

Lurking in the treeline was an animal wearing the face of a man striving to marry the Goddess!

I think by now we can see the 'the goddess' is replicated in human women as well as any bright star mostly Sirius, Planet Venus, Planet Earth, the Moon and all other 'negative' *electrical* polar cosmic bodies describes as 'feminine'. We are not encouraged, or even alerted, to doing the work of the 'goddess' under a hierarchical Satanic ritual-religious mechanism dominating Mother Earth right now. In fact she doesn't even get a mention in all this clearly indicated by the 'biblical' story of Mary who doesn't have a lineage and no one thought to ask for a couple thousand years. That's how deeply embedded we are in this. Do you think is a coincidence that the 'goddess' character doesn't have a lineage and yet these 'god' males are getting their *lineage* specifically via her? The Feminine 'negative' pole is only negative until the poles shift and then they reverse leaving the negative polar energy at the top and the positive polar energy at the bottom and vice versa, it's a battery. Some say this electrical flip is happening now with the looming polar shift. These shifts *should* happen slowly over time as the poles gently move around the world however, they have used technology to delay the *natural* flow of things, *see*, chemtrails delaying the *natural* seasonal movements as long as possible and then, like a flood, unleash it all at once as part of their chaos factor. While rabbiting on about global warming and climate change, they're actually instigating a mini ice-age as the world has been destroyed 'five' times in the past by ice ages. We're going around again. Therefore, if the poles shift it will be a sudden and seemingly massive destabilization queue; climate change 'weather bomb' reports and more 'end of the world' narrative to bring in whatever *other* sneaky agendas they have up their sleeve.

Really, at the end of the day, the Earth is moving back to a general state of global 'spring' all year round. Don't worry, it won't happen overnight but it will happen. Therefore, like the 'Goddess', the concept of 'God' has been misrepresented to the ignorant public of planet Earth in an immature way. God or the 'positive' *electrical* polar bodies like the Sun, Orion, the north pole etc., is actually *replicated* in men. It is a positive 'projective' force as is the feminine negative a 'receptive' force like a receptacle, a cup, symbolic of the feminine hips i.e. the 'chalice'. These two forces oscillate moving around the planet in perpetual energetic symmetry counter balancing their *rotating* magnetism. It's the circle of life replicated in the lab by the Tesla coil and why he seemed so 'godlike' and mysterious. He was copying the 'Goddess', they all are, *standing in her place, using her,* and oddly Tesla disliked women although no women ever betrayed him the way his fellow 'brothers' did in fact he found support from wealthy women who even funded him and believed in him. The looming polar shift spells a sort of doom for these satanic hyper-male nut cases and they cannot bear it hell bent on making her their enemy. As a result they dress up the 'goddess' *natural force* as a simple human woman and then *kill her* to send the message that they 'control' the wider state of things which is feminine. Their enemy is only themselves and always has been.

These men are terrified women want to dominate them simply because that is the way *they* behave. Women will not become like men of the past, no, it will mean a return to balance as was always intended and ultimately 'prophesised' which is simply *electrical processes* coming to fruition as 'predicted' would *naturally* occur eons ago. It has to happen and if it doesn't we're all done for. So, as these satanic alien males, the devil, have embodied *projecting* their fiery masculine electricity onto the passive watery feminine suppressing her for their gain and encouraging ordinary males to do the *same* historically, it does not mean she will project onto them suppressing *him,* futuristically. It simply means that the receptive and projective energies of the electrical forces of nature will eventually take their proper place in a 'circle of life' as was always meant to be. As they said, the Isis electrical force 'tames' the Osiris electrical force allowing them to live in unity. The fact they want to keep partying is a trait that may never be bred out but then the Earth, the feminine, can't take much more and her demise is *their* demise so, in the end, the greed for their own miserable skins will win over their need to satisfy their egos. They are extremely threatened by all this as they see women, *literally,* as sub species to them (they wish) and why some Arab men won't even shake hands with a women as she is 'dirty' but they don't mind her cooking their food for them or providing on-call manual stimulation of their lackluster masculinity. What a bunch of fucking childish hypocrites.

So, here they are, goddess and god, found right in front of us in all their glory, vibrant, perfect and beautiful. Their brain's though…that is a different matter but we're slowly getting there as a healthy perception of self and others coupled with increased intellect spells a new dawn for humanity *on every level.* You can be beautiful, kind and intelligent without the hashtags and 'woke' fakery. It's coming folks, so hold on. Everything you thought you knew about human biology, 'age', 'race', 'class' – all of it – is going into the cosmic garbage bin for a *complete* overhaul. Kids are already realising that adults aren't 'grown up' just because they're old as such, the next and next generation are increasingly going to epitomise a connection to the here and now, an *infinite* eternal moment of light and awareness, that transcends all previous barriers that are no longer relevant. Why would age be relevant if you never 'age' beyond about 25? You won't go grey. You won't get wrinkled or sag remaining strong, youthful, vibrant, connected, and *relevant* right up until you 'die' probably around the age of 150 *or more*. We are going back to living until we are 900 as they said in the bible of people way back. It's not natural to die so young, depleted of the life force, 'looking' old when inside one is a veritable child. Inside every 70 year old is a surprised 21 year old. The human body is abundantly capable of omnipresent, psychic abilities, intuition, foresight, knowledge and incredible feats of strength. These aliens have kept our physical forms subdued, like pets or toys, to play with us unendingly for their sick *incomprehensible* pleasure and power seeking while locking out all our higher functions. They have shut us down to lord it over us as 'gods' *knowing* the whole time it is *us* who are the gods capable of so much more. They are green with envy, *literally*. It's a twisted affair we find ourselves in as 'elites', hybrid aliens, have stolen these powers for *themselves* in utter egotistical contempt of their prey, humans, in a cosmic crime they *will* answer for.

As with the polar switch on Earth, electrical bodies in space change polarity and as it's all replication it's possible the entire universe does the old switcheroo in a *massive* cosmic shift. So, historically, sometimes the Sun was depicted as a feminine force and sometimes the moon as a masculine force. Currently the sun is depicted as masculine and they want to keep it that way by instigating a never-ending male dominated hierarchy. But that's *moronic* and caused more damage to the cosmos as it stalls and other processes react to their idiocy requiring increasing technology to hold it in place and thus slipping further away from the *natural* state. The the universe is very specific about the electrical polar opposites in a *binary universe* with a small range of neutral possibilities in between but nothing like the massive operation to completely rewrite the human aspects of the electrical opposites that we are seeing today in 'men' as 'women' and vice versa. It's a massive alien program. Electrical polar opposites don't exist in the same space at the same time although they can get very close to 'zero point' and appear very similar as they once did eons ago in an 'eternal spring'. These alien elites dress this stuff up to suit whatever kinks suit them. Again, I'm not talking about the average LGBT person in the street. The aristocracy are making fun of *everyone* and behind their excuses and facades is pedophilia, necrophilia, bestiality, orgies, sex crimes – anything goes with them as it's all about deflection from their *deeper darker* truths as quite simply, they are not human and wish to delete us. The feminine broadcast comes from the central black hole sun at the core of the galaxy that, like a radio hub, picks up transmission from beyond our galaxy and why, for those of old, the very *chastity* and purity of the feminine meant her radio *signal was clearer* unsullied by cross contamination of *synthetic* broadcasts, interference, that, like an old lover, leaves an imprint on those they have engaged with *forever* and why 'virgins' are symbolically and literally coveted by the breeding program to not sully her genetic traits to 'harvest' the most from her abilities to keep their offspring as uncontaminated as possible. This is why *She* was the monotheistic god, *pure light,* long before any harsh  disciplinarian male 'god', the devil, *technology,* stood in her place. The horned pagan 'tree god', an 'animal wearing the face of a man', an apparent shapeshifter with a permanent oversized erection, was said to 'lurk in the treeline striving to marry the goddess' and shortly we shall see why!

The Goddess represents Mother Nature both inner and outer space and those of old *knew* she was abundant throughout the stars *as well*. Anywhere life, light, can get a grip, it does. As such the universe is *prolific* with life of all sorts. She was a light in the dark, the light bearer, a torch by which to guide the all people on a planets since fallen to this dark order. The blackness of masculine corruption surrounds us on all sides now snowballing throughout history. Beyond honour and minor feminine planets, her light was symbolised as the brightest star in the night sky, a feminine sun, the *'blue angel',* Sirius, which goes to show you how ancient people thought of her. However it prevailed *somehow* she was cast out, cast down and run off as symbolised by Mary Magdalene crawling on all fours only to attain her rightful position only to be chased out again as the Brotherhood took her and her man down. Left out in the cold she has amazingly been ignored *until now!* Around the time I was receiving my messages (pre and post solar eclipse when I was at zero point), I had a *profound* vision of a beautiful young woman, an Empress, in a nightgown sitting alone in the darkness sobbing. Trapped. She couldn't get out. She was caught off-guard as symbolised by the nightgown in the 'middle of the night' *unprepared* for a callous sneak attack when something terrible happened and she was ensnared like a unicorn fallen into the hands of ogres! Whatever happened we shall discover this was not only a deliberate underhanded act of sabotage to harvest Her but was also done to bind the glorious nurturing power of the Cosmic Feminine to be used in unending fiery false-masculine wars to cripple the continuum and render the universe and all those who inhabit it as slaves of darkness *forever!* Oh, it's big.

Ensuing male empires emerged *worldwide*, even universally, I keep saying this isn't just an Earthly problem this is going on throughout the Galaxy and it is the job of Earthlings, ultimately, to take it all back which is why they particularly hate us. Dick cults ancient and modern openly thrived worshipping 'sun gods' in Ra, Sol, Jesus, Zeus, Satan, Quetzalcoatl! Only One. They need a lynchpin to anchor the *image* of their operations to, a central psychological hub. But naturally there are 'two' as there can be no creation without the god and

goddess. As such, the selfish 'one' must be a demonic alien, the 'devil', unable to harness the light alone it steals the light from the procreating pair and poses as The One. Their deity is their favourite toy, a psychological conduit by which to funnel the *guilt* of their crimes via a 'godlike' *untouchable* aqueduct sweeping away their karma and securing their false positions of veneration as 'god's', middlemen, terrorizing anyone they like in the name of 'god'. But we are not the children of god anymore. We are growing up. We are taking responsibility for ourselves now and it will reflect in the world around us. So, they say things like, 'let go let god' and that Jesus-God said to cast your problems onto him. Hey, just don't worry about it. Transfer your accountability to *something* else as the paint by numbers program to blindside humanity and snatch Mother Earth right out from underneath us *continues* as we are not *looking to ourselves!* They're even sending dicks into space in the latest Space X program or phonetically *Space Sex* or *Spa Sex*, trying to fuck the mother, the Universe, with their fiery little symbolic rocket cocks, *right*. It's a nob just *look* with your eyes. It's all in line with the various 'Sun Gods' *rebranded* throughout every age to prevent the masses from getting bored as they phase out the old ways, wipe our memories and phase in something new eventually culminating in their super wet dream, a male dominated space age! *All totally fabricated of course.*
These guys couldn't lie straight in bed. Their dick god is their precious Satan, an alien 'king', and it demands the boys club *must sacrifice* something *big* to it to show allegiance and get it to reveal more of its powers to them even if the *power* and *technology* it grants them is *fake*. Yet they can never win when lies are the foundation of *everything*. They are doomed to fail. But they don't care as long as they are in power...for now...and go down in history albeit a false history. How selfish and childish. So, they *willingly* sell out their friends like President Kennedy or offer up millions of humans in war so their alien masters who in turn grant them *'permission'* to go into space. No one can give or take your permission from you as long as you don't give it so, remain righteous, honest, pure of heart, reliable, hard working and fair. Who the fuck are they anyway? Killers with nothing to back them but threats and dirty tricks. Fuckwits.

The pantheon of 'Sun Kings', demi-gods etc., cosmic *middlemen*, symbolically *represented* the 'sun' as the divine 'speaker', the One, the Messenger so they *'fuse'* their image with the sun 'god' to apply its greatness *to them*. How dare they. Surely, something greater must know about this? Surely it can't be that simple to take over the universe? The biggest historical figures like King Solomon, Alexander the Great, King Louis XIV, King Henry VIII, King Arthur and Julius Caesar were among *many* 'sun kings' or tantric sex kings known and unknown. These guys were the ones who came out about it and in posturing to the masses, the eye of Sauron fell upon them and they were summarily dispatched one way or another. The really successful ones aren't grandiose about it. All this was and *is still* headed up by the secret Priesthood, the *real* power behind the throne, the Masons, the Brotherhood, the gofers of alien satanic *engineers* on and off world! All balance was lost on Mother Earth when they set up shop and yet it was a High Feminine force the *whole time,* the blue angel, *right,* where they secretly derived their power they just wouldn't admit it not then and certainly not now. Nothing's changed. The timber of her forests built their ships, the stone from her mountains built their temples, the ore from her earth smithed their blades, the harvest of her crops graced their tables and filled their fat bellies with booze, fruits and meats fresh from  *Her* garden! And yet when people say 'Grace' they thank *'god', a* male force, for what they are about to receive on their plates when *everything* on their plates *and their backs* come from *Her.* The job of the Goddess is thankless as so many mums can attest to. Always the organiser. Always making sure everyone else is taken care of. But when it's her turn? You don't know what you got till it's gone.

The Garden of Eden is *Earth,* the *whole world* was once green and green is *gold.* All of their power is *stolen* from Her begotten off the backs of Common men bent in labour as miners, diggers, cutters, farmers and climbers all hammering, sweating, slaving, driving, ploughing, building and fighting, wasted and maimed, in an insane crusade for *more of Her!* It was not elite men who laid those stones. It was not elite men who dug the pits in the quarry where they take their namesake from, *quarrymen,* Masons! They took the credit but it was not elite men who built those ships or laid the gutters and the pavements. It was *Common* men who did all that *forced* under the will of some horrible hidden master that works through every gendarme, every cop, every overseer, every plantation boss-man, every whip wielding officer and enforcer, *the middlemen* acting as god on behalf of elite men who *are* god as far as we are concerned. *They* certainly believe this. Aristocracy are bludgers. They get the spoils but *you* do the work. All this bounty is the foundation of every 'harvest' festival and 'calendar of feasts' throughout history complete with all the pomp and pageantry *still* carried out by the Roman Catholic Church, a *pan-pagan* polytheistic satanic mega hub engaged in a cultural appropriation of *other people's* relics, ideas, knowledge and belief systems ancient *and* modern. Called 'Comparative Religion' it is the study of a branch of religions (the most accurate ones) with a systematic resemblance of *consistent* doctrines, practices, themes and impacts (including migration) of the world's religions. Satanists have cherry-picked *the best* of other people's shit. It's an evolving data gathering machine of power and control the only rule being *it has to work,* has to be tried and tested, before it will be incorporated into the machine! Satanism is not some slap dash thrown together mishmash of disjointed concepts in a childish unintelligent sect of idiots, at the bottom it is, but at the top it is a well-oiled machine of doctors, scientists, researchers, explorers, thinkers and *technicians* posing as leaders. It is an *incredible* fusion of absurdity mingled with intellect and generally only psychopaths get the most satisfaction out of it.

The ancient vegetation festivals of indulgences – ritual madness – overflowing in ecstasy, wine, and orgies, *Bacchanalia* among others, *still goes on* behind the scenes *today* all pilfered from the farmers and villagers of old in the *normal* harvest festivals. It was a right knees up and well deserved too turned into an erotic glutenous free-for-all usually culminating in or including murder and rape. *See right,* the 1966 film *Seconds*. Note, 9 is 6 so 1966 is a take on 666 as that's who's behind all this - it was a big year for them as was 1999 and 1969. In this film Rock Hudson plays a wealthy man who is bored with his life. He receives an invite to a secret agency who fake his death and changes his identity and image. His new life includes orgies of pagan festivals symbolic of being drawn into Satanism. There is a lot of double entendre's and  suggestion in this film. Spoiler alert, he doesn't like the new person *they've* chosen him to be, so the agency kills him rather than risk him knowing the secrets of their power and telling anyone else. Rock Hudson was another convenient celebrity death as was Freddie Mercury and so many others. *Another* 'rock' god. *Nothing's changed.* But it's all coming to an end and it will happen fast so they intend to catch you off guard as they become more desperate.

With all this in mind the fabled 'Green Man' has been with us far longer than we care to admit and is responsible for more than we could possibly know. The universe travels in 'cycles' (it doesn't really but they classify it like that). WE experience the 'cycles' as strange coincidences and 'twists' of fate etc., or 'history repeating'. Yet there are small cyclic energies *inside* larger cyclic energies that bear similar traits so really anything can happen at any time and it is their job to try and control it to emerge as 'god'. Wheels within wheels. Games within games. But it's not really repeating. We are just trapped inside *one* aspect of reality when there is *so much more* to it, *more that we are capable of,* and will be engaging in soon enough once *outside* of the Zodiac trap. These cosmic wheels that shamans and mystics have tried to explain over the eons is really a virtual reality 'game' set in motion by beings that just so happened to have evolved before we did, or should I say evolved in *different* ways than we did. Our ancestors were passive. Their ancestors are the opposite, aggressive. It's the difference between dolphins and sharks. They are similar in many ways and yet vastly different in other ways. This is the positive and negative electrical elements of *mother nature* showing up again in the universe. As previously explained, the Fermi Paradox describes that a civilisation that happened to evolve before us by even a small degree is in the unique position of controlling and influencing *every emerging civilisation* that follows. It's not that they evolved better, they just evolved differently. For example, the Emerging European society created great technological examples of innovation and communication. While this was happening indigenous people worldwide were living *harmoniously* with the land and could perform incredible 'psychic' feats of communication. There was a time when Zulu warriors had telescopic vision and could see further than any white man's telescope. The aboriginals in Australia had psychic abilities to transmit messages *mentally* across long distances before the telegraph obsolete to someone with higher *psychic* abilities. Do you understand what I'm saying? One's definition of evolution is different to another's albeit with *similar* results. That said, the *outcome* of any real 'evolution' will be decided by how it all eventually ends *naturally* as opposed to *unnaturally* so, would you rather a telescope or telescopic vision? A telephone or telepathy? It's up to you.

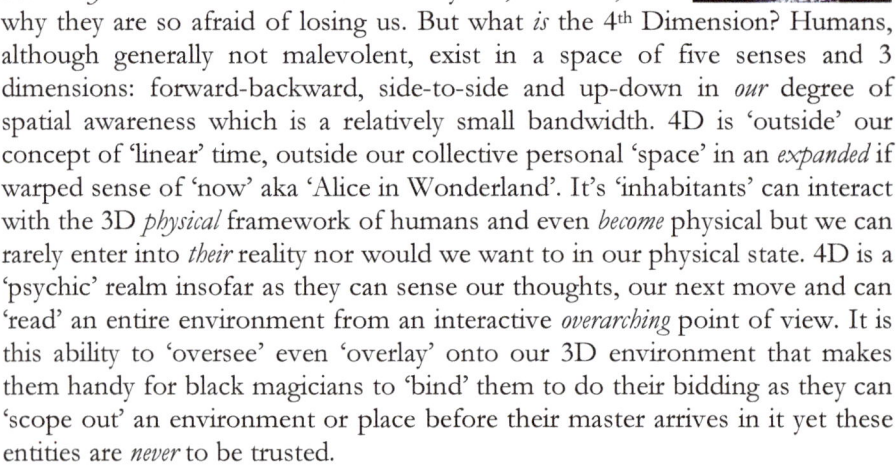

Osiris was depicted as green *because he was green* while Isis his symbolic 'twin' was human. The 'reptilian' became the 'Green Man' and 'Oak King' of legend who was literally green breeding with *preferred human* women. Their number, 666 is sex sex sex, all about unlocking *alchemical processes* in the human body via Tantric Sex accessing higher cosmic to attain 'enlightenment' and become 'angelic' to get closer to or even *become* 'God'. They can't attain this as full blood reptiles because some say they don't have a heart chakra or *even a light body at all*. They are generally stuck in the 4th Dimension and why humans are so coveted as we can go *all the way* to the 11th Dimension and beyond, to 'God', and why they are so afraid of losing us. But what *is* the 4th Dimension? Humans, although generally not malevolent, exist in a space of five senses and 3 dimensions: forward-backward, side-to-side and up-down in *our* degree of spatial awareness which is a relatively small bandwidth. 4D is 'outside' our concept of 'linear' time, outside our collective personal 'space' in an *expanded* if warped sense of 'now' aka 'Alice in Wonderland'. It's 'inhabitants' can interact with the 3D *physical* framework of humans and even *become* physical but we can rarely enter into *their* reality nor would we want to in our physical state. 4D is a 'psychic' realm insofar as they can sense our thoughts, our next move and can 'read' an entire environment from an interactive *overarching* point of view. It is this ability to 'oversee' even 'overlay' onto our 3D environment that makes them handy for black magicians to 'bind' them to do their bidding as they can 'scope out' an environment or place before their master arrives in it yet these entities are *never* to be trusted.

4D beings can interfere with 3D physical objects *kinetically* and affect the quantum energetic layers of what we perceive as 'real' therefore, 'antigravity' and 'levitation' occurs outside the ability of most people's ability to comprehend. It's happening more and more as their density encroaches into our realm at this time. It doesn't help that the large particle colliders and satanic ceremonies *worldwide* are opening portals for this cosmic filth to get into our reality. It's difficult, but we *can* understand how they operate and in so doing, alleviate ourselves of much of the stress of the 'unknowns' that go along with these creatures and their realm. Personally, I am concluding that much if not all 'ghost' and 'poltergeist' type activity is coming from the 4D, ostensibly an 'alien' realm, and why paranormal and strange creatures often appear when these 'aliens' and/or their crafts are around. Demons are the souls of aliens. Angels are the souls of humans. While it's not being reported properly, or even *at all*, people are freaking out *all around the world* as mounting video evidence recorded on *personal devices* capture things that are frankly unbelievable and terrifying, *right*. Many people are under attack *in their homes* from poltergeists, shadow beings, dark robed entity, invisible ghost interactions. It's fucking crazy and terrifying! It's deliberately  allowed to occur by earthly agencies as another layer *seeking to drive people insane*. Hollywood is much to blame for our *unpreparedness* dressing all this up as *fiction* so when it really happens you can't believe it prepped to believe it as 'fiction'. NOT POSSIBLE. *But it's happening* and more often than you think. You may think this is a joke but I can assure you, people are being targeted for *whatever reasons* and fighting *losing battles* against things that *shouldn't exist!* 'They' are already here. *Already* interacting with us in the most insidious ways reminiscent of folklore and fables *dismissed* by our scientific 'rational' world. As a result, we are sitting ducks for these creepy *disgusting* things. I've got news for you, most of the 'science' that we experience comes from them and their demonic influence over our evolution is designed to unhinge us on levels that is inconceivable. Even if *some* of these images are fake the truth is, it *is happening!*

These beings are a perverse mix of weird unnatural science as well as cultish-religious themes *of their own making* based on their *skewed* 'view' of *our* 'reality'. They particularly need to own and operate human beings as they conversely hate us with a *clinical precision* and yet strive to harness our traits for their gain. They are literally like intelligent insects. They have no light or higher spiritual traits and therefore could be conceived of as A.I., clones, cryptids, purely demonic satanic wretches and non-entities, *literally*, who have it over us but not for much longer. This is not a good position for us to be in. We will move beyond the 4D and therefore out of their reach once we activate our chakras and IQ to *profoundly* fathom how to effectively engage with all this. I know from my own experience that an 'entity attachment' is not only very real but extremely destructive and manipulative, it is a weapon, and whoever engages with such things or works with them to hurt others must not be human or certainly have *no moral boundaries*. And the *really* evil part is we have no *effective* response against these things, nowhere to go, no one to talk to, no one to help. You're on your own. If you are experiencing negative energy attachments or hauntings try the following - there are apparently *three stages* to the process of ridding an area of malevolent entities, *firstly,* bring in a medium and/or experienced person to help the entity move on or detach, *secondly,* thoroughly cleanse your area with the smoke of white sage/blue sage/palo santo, pine needles etc., (the usual herbs) for up to half an hour in each room so disengage your smoke alarms while you go through the house, *thirdly,* bring in a priest or respected religious/spiritual person or shaman to bless and seal the area. Apparently burying something that has been blessed on all four corners the property sits on can help keep them at bay. Every month repeat the saging process or *as often as need be*. If it comforts you say prayers or mantras and keep a good flow of fresh air throughout including the 'singing bowls' as these things are frequency attachments, a radio signal. *Inexperience at practicing any ceremonies or rituals can make it infinitely worse* while some say filming and communicating with them feeds the activity. To reinforce your protection keep your space neat and orderly even change the layout of your furnishings to create new flow and energy aka feng shui. Meditate on your root chakra which is the colour *maroon* and use a blend of oils; myrrh-sandalwood-frankincense and inhale the scent and dab some on your third eye, throat and heart chakra or where the entity is touching you i.e. feet, knees etc. Burn sandalwood incense, drink a tea of infused white sage or pine needles or any other *ingestible* 'smudge' herbs.

Seek help from an array of sources including shamans, the church, energy workers, prayer, faith, reiki or *any and all* help necessary in a cross-spectrum approach. Do a laying on of hands from trusted friends and family (like Avatar) and chant 'entity begone' or 'entity leave' while *intently* focusing on your heart chakras and *imagine it going*. Go to the Pentecostals or a church that acknowledges this stuff, the Hindu's too know about this, and get them to do as ceremony for you (they were the only few who actually believed me and helped). Listen to *natural* sounds on headphones like rain or running creeks while imagining it washing away from you. I went through endless ridiculous YouTube videos from channels claiming to have frequency's that would expel entity attachments. The reality is really simple, 528hz is the 'miracle' note, the *heart* of the rainbow and the colour green, so I wound up simply listening to the sounds of rain, creeks and rivers on headphones while sleeping which did have an effect. While listening to running rivers and waterfalls say a rhyming poem as they talk in riddles and trick phrases and why the ancient accounts of wizards make up poetry to go along with their spells as it 'flows' better, so I repeated, "where the water flows, this demon goes. The demon I will send, to where the waters end. Far, far away from me, and I will finally be free" imagining the energy or entity floating away with the water being cleansed and washed clean by it. *Creative visualisation* is very powerful as they come from a 'dreamlike' density and we can affect them with our thoughts. Do 'tai chi' type movements 'pulling' it out of your body *visualising* extracting it from your energy field and 'throwing' it into a fire or the jaws of an animal like a crocodile or a big cat that will 'eat' it and make a 'swooshing' noise as you 'throw it away' or 'cast' it out as it's possible someone 'cast' it into you. Do this daily or as often as needed.

If it's particularly bad you must stop drinking alcohol, stop taking drugs (except for essential medications), eat a raw organic diet, get plenty of fresh clean water. A small dosage of valium assisted in sleeping when these entities try and sleep deprive you to make you weak as they get stronger. Don't overuse Valium as you will build up a resistance so only two or three times a week to keep you rested and resistant. You must go outside and get fresh air and sunshine *no matter how much the entity tries to isolate you* and *lock you inside your mind*. Stay in touch with friends and family and where possible let them know what is happening to you as people are more open to this information now yet be discerning. Try not to react to it as they 'feed' of anger, pain, suffering, depression and love anything that has pleasure like junk food, booze, pills, drugs, sex – you *must* guard yourself against these things. They will try to get you into trouble with 'authority' figures like the police and 'set you up' with a strange series of 'coincidences' or have you put in a mental ward or make you homeless. As said, these things are a weapon but if you have a heads-up about *what* they can do you can battle (and it is a battle) more effectively until you can find your unique answer. Try to find out if it was sent or cast upon you by a practicing Satanist, as happened to me, or if it's a part of the environment where you live or come into contact with it as they often frequent hospitals attaching after an operation *under general anesthetic* when our auric protection is shit off. They also frequent old folks homes, funeral parlours, graveyards, sleezy bars and dark, dank spaces, abandoned houses, old ruins and the cliché basements and attics. You'd be surprised how many native curses were placed on the land to punish colonists for stealing their home and treasures disenfranchising their people. A *lot more needs to be done* to heal the world and native people *are key to this process*. The governments are tricking you. We must unite with indigenous to right the wrongs of *past aristocratic crimes* and move forward together.

These entities, *creatures,* exist outside our sense of time and space so 'age' is not a factor for them. They can exist in the same area for hundreds even thousands of years. Our world needs a *serious* cleansing of *old energies* across the board. This despicable 'system' headed up by evil satanic people have found it amusing to sell the Ouija Board, the 'talking board', as a *kids toy*. *Unfuckenbelievable!* It shows you who it behind 'society'. Ouija is French/German (very symbolic) and translates as *'yes! yes!'* and by using it you are immediately consenting to whatever is coming in and although ending with 'goodbye' is *supposed* to close conduits and portals to the demonic 4th dimension, this *often* does not work. Once they're in it hard to get rid of them. Many kids and adults have found themselves in terrifying situations after 'playing' with these 'games'. *Do not play with unseen forces*. Ordinary people are *suffering in the extreme* as these entities *stream in* to torment and haunt their homes with *no way of preventing* this activity that can last for weeks, years or even the rest of their lives *ruining* a person with no way out. They have a way of making it *very* personal.

What starts out a bit of a joke as people laugh it off or see their haunting as a 'pet' ghost, results in injury and mental illness as *prolonged exhaustion* allows the entities to grow stronger and ultimately *terrorise* its victims affecting relationships, the ability to work, overall health and sometimes results in *terrifying deaths*. People are recording growls, screams, crying, laughing, scratching, 'knocking' on doors, *repeated* doorbells - *never open the door*, objects moving, noises in the ceiling, stomping, voices, shadow beings, 'nightmares', *levitation*, faces, voices and physical attacks – it goes on and on. The entities will pretend they are fading away or have gone luring the victim into a false sense of security only to return again and again getting stronger every time. Little kids and babies are being attacked by these things as well as family pets! Quite well-known paranormal investigation channels are increasingly being 'followed home' by *something* all playing out in *real time*. They try to rationalize it and even *reason with the entities* from their *human understanding* but from personal experience, I can see they are just being toyed with as the entity secretly encourages them to pursue the course furthering its connection. Ordinary people are being targeted whether by their own foolishness, jealous competitors or 'fans' or simply by accident as they deteriorate and eventually stop posting. If you think 'fans' only stalk celebrities, celebrities also stalk members of the public that *represent something* to their weird cults daring their victims to say something as *no one* would believe it anyway. Sick! Research the *bazaar* death of Christopher Case a music executive killed by dark entities among *many* others. *Something needs to be done about this* as *evidence mounts*. Elite families and shamans have accepted these things exist figuring out how to *repel them* yet the rest of the world is lulled into disbelief and vulnerability. A cursory search of *YouTube* unveils *millions* of hard core videos of *extremely disturbing* events all dressed up as 'fiction' in 'horror movies' so it's not taken seriously or dealt with properly. *But it's happening!* A few reliable sources for these events are *Nukes Top 5,* Slapped Ham, Bazaar Bub, Project Darkknight Horror, The Darkest Secret and KingFrostmare.

When our electrical forces are combined in certain ways not only does new life occur but cosmic processes happen that could allow us to literally become 'God' *for real* even travel through time, change history and 'rewrite' the future. This is tied to the nature of *tachyons* that move so fast they appear to 'travel backwards'. Making babies on Earth is basically the same out in the Milky Way and the Universe beyond including the birth of planets, stars, nebulas, moons, suns and humans and why they felt the 'sun' could literally be born into a man in a *concentrated* form. Carl Sagan said, 'We're made of star stuff'. This is why all your 'Gods' and 'Goddesses' are ultimately the same prime pair which is highly scientific and essentially describes electrical processes including thermodynamics, electromagnetics and quantum physics. These repetitive processes is the various combinations of earth, air, fire, and water *in magnetic quantities* underpinned by Aether creating the building blocks of modern science calls *Physics*. In fact, science is just discovering now what all this was about in the first place and are *way behind* the eight ball to say the least. The fabled 'two sets of twins', light and dark side of the masculine and feminine, also equates to 3D dimensional space itself. It's the power of 'four' like a house symbolises stability and is *so* genius that it includes harvest cycles including Summer (masculine), Autumn (feminine), Winter (masculine) and Spring (feminine). It also represents entire eons (Ages) under a zodiac of constellations in that Aries, Gemini, Leo, Libra, Sagittarius, and Aquarius are *masculine* signs while Taurus, Cancer, Virgo, Scorpio, Capricorn, and Pisces are *feminine* signs. As well, dawn is feminine, day is masculine, dusk known as 'eve' or evening is feminine and night-time or 'sun set' is masculine. The two sets of 'twins' also represents 'four corners of the Earth' and the square or the *set* square of Masonry! Therefore, Set the 'brother' of Osiris is also a reference to the darkness of night symbolic of the dark side or the masculine, the Dark Lord, a king, a god, as well as the planet Saturn personified as Satan.

Everything was 'gods' and 'goddesses' to the ancients so Osiris is a Sun King, the 'light', as was Jesus another 'sun' king or the 'light of the world' literally the Sun, God, as well as the small son of 'god', a man or the 'golden boy', the prodigal son as a smaller 'god' on Earth nonetheless in replication of the greater forces. The ancient Egyptians, like them all, are describing *geological processes* personified as people because people can relate easier to other people rather than the spirit of a planet in outer space. It also gave them a sense of connection to the whole and a sense of importance in being part of something magnificent, *universal*. As it turns out all these thousands of years later we are again discovering our universal connection and the importance of this heralds a big turn of events! Science tried to make us small. So, Ra is not only a spirit or weird deity, but also the sun, literally, emerging from the primordial waters, the oceans, as the sun rose for the first time over the horizon of a brand-new planet, *Mother* Earth. This is why they say *She* came first and He is *Her* sun, replicated as the *son* of the *mother*. They even say, 'Ladies first'. Ra the sun and Sol the sun is *replicated* in other suns out in space as sol simply means 'sun'. *They are all Sol.* The Tibetans believe the sun is a portal, a lens, a great eye looking in on us, the 'eye of god'. It was said the Sun God Ra was 'self-created' who 'masturbated' himself into being with his 'hand', the 'female principle', which basically means he didn't have a woman to have sex with to achieve *tantric enlightenment* so did it by himself. I dare say everyone can do this if you don't have a partner. Ra 'made union with his shadow' balancing the light and dark side of his internal masculine twins, good and bad, activating his 'feminine' principle, the passive side or his heart chakra, called the 'complete one'. He was therefore no longer in 'separation' with himself and wasn't 'scattered' as symbolised by the 'dismembering' found in the Osiris story (another name for Ra). The first Aztec god, Ometeotl translated is *'lord of duality'* aka the light and dark side also said to be 'self-created' in the same deal as Ra. 'Ome' means 'two' so here's the 'twins' again. His wife, Ometecuhtli, means 'two lady' or 'lady of duality', yes, the light and dark side of the *feminine*. Point is the common 'creation' stories are about the male-female 'gods', humans, *becoming self-aware*, sentient!

King Osiris was depicted as green and the embodiment of the constellation Orion called The Hunter. He was the 'deer hunter' associated with the stag, a stud, a buck, the Alpha Male described as having a 'golden phallus'. A 'consort' of Isis, Min, was depicted with an erect penis, in fact, mummification often involved putting rods in the phallus to keep it erect posthumously! It's a common trait among the aristocracy to have a lover as they marry for PR 'keeping up appearances' and procreation yet take lovers for pleasure. It's very clinical, really. The wives of Roman politicians were to be faithful to their husbands who were basically allowed to sleep with anyone they liked male *or* female including children. It's *exactly* the same cult today the difference being humans are evolving when quite clearly they are not. Tiberius had a lavish home with a massive pool and specially trained children to 'nibble his genitals' underwater called 'minnows'. Caligula the murderous megalomaniac had notorious orgies. So much sex! Many ancient deities were preoccupied with the dick, nothing's changed there, *see*, NASA sending dicks into space. Ancient Greece had entire temples dedicated to the dick, *see right*, Delos 300BC. Everything is dicks symbolised as rockets, missiles, guns, swords, high-rise buildings (*literally* erections), obelisks, military insignia, clubs, rods (Nimrod), wands, staffs, sceptres, canes (Cain), batons, shafts, sticks, thorns, pricks, caduceus, twigs, wood (woody), truncheon and twigs. *I'm tellin ya, it's a dick cult.* If I never see another dick again it'll be too soon. *Christ!* No pun.

They identified the 'fires of his loins' or the phallus (*see*, Nasa rockets) with the fires of the sun and changed the phonetics to make out the male child, the *son*, was the *Sun* born into a man as *the Returner* 'father' rising every morning. Men's morning erections were also associated with the 'rising sun', the 'rising phallus' the north 'pole' called a 'morning glory' (if you say so). This is actually a side effect of a full bladder that my teenage male friends in high school hilariously called a 'piss fat', *see right*, Tom Cruise's spaceship in the movie *Oblivion*. Some kids never grow up. *C'mon? Really?* It's a dick. Are they ever to stop seeing their cocks as god? Anytime soon would be great, guys *[checks watch tapping foot]*. Ancient men had a fixation with permanent oversized erect penises. Well, nothing's changed there. But what are they *really* telling us? The ancient gods, including Greek Hermes the equivalent of Roman Mercury were bisexual as well as hermaphrodites, homosexuals and  bisexuals. As such, the LGBTQI movement goes back to *ancient history*. Nothing new happening there, folks. It's a rehash. They had openly *flagrantly* gay pharaohs akin to Peter Allen with a sceptre or Ramesis with maracas in an ancient Copacabana Club! Break out the candelabra Liberace` the show *still* goes on! In many middle and far Eastern cultures they considered the *patriarchal* line to take precedence and it's *still* the case today with the feminine aspect easily forgotten her maiden name absorbed by history. As a result so much of our lineages are lost as like Mary, she wasn't documented. Are we ever going to get over this? Ancient Greece was a classic 'homosocial' culture or men who prefer the company of other men not necessarily homosexual just *homosocial*. The boys club. A club is a blunt instrument you bash someone over the head with, like cavemen, when the conversation strays into areas that confound them. Philistines. Unfortunately, the precedence they are trying to *recreate* today saw the age of consent for boys in ancient Greece as young as 12 years old where it was perfectly acceptable for a family to allow their son to have a 'mentor', a pedophilic master, to 'tutor' him. You can imagine for poor families the crisis of conscience if a wealthy pedophile wanted to pay for a handsome if underprivileged lad. But then today middle eastern girls are traded like this from the age of six sanctioned by 'cultural' pedophilia without the world batting an eyelid. Don't you love evolution?

Ancient god Baal had an 'execrable Phalli' meaning 'offensive erect penis' described as the 'Father of Idolatry and Confusion' seemingly posing as male *and* female deities throughout the ages with a preference for bisexuality, hermaphroditism, promiscuity, lust over love, transgenderism or the 'gender neutrality' and 'gender confusion' we see so much of today. They're recreating ancient history. Some Masons claim the word 'obelisk' literally means 'Baal's shaft' or 'Baal's organ of reproduction' this spire is still recognised as Osiris and Nimrod's sex organ. All these male religions old and new literally worship the cock like bantam roosters strutting around building enormously flattering monuments to their manhood. Overcompensating much there, big boy? Nimrod was depicted as an 'evergreen' tree (pine trees are evergreens associated with the pineal gland) as was the 'sacred tree of Zeus'. Cernunnos was also a horned pagan 'tree' god associated with the stag as was Osiris as *Orion* was associated with the stag, the virile buck, depicted with an erect phallus. The 'tree' is the nervous system. These 'myths' also include the magical 'unicorn' or 'unique horn', *the phallus*, of bible and fairy fables. The 'tree god' is a series of 'vegetation deities' as was the Oak King and the Green Man depicted with leaves, a laurel wreath (another evergreen) around their head worn by ancient Greek and Roman elites, Olympians and Senators. Napolean and his folk hero Julius Ceasar also adorned the laurel crown while the UN and UNICEF symbols also bear the leaf 'crown' around *Earth* symbolising the ancient traditions of male tantric enlightenment engulfing our planet, *right*.  It's the same cult paying homage to their roots and their great leaders. Only they weren't great. They weren't 'for the people' they were *for themselves*. The laurel wreath-Green Man crown of old shamelessly wrapped around *Mother* Earth is a display of *supreme dominance* over the feminine and her resources fueling all this! It's nothing to be proud of put it that way. The laurel wreath means peacefully 'extending the olive branch' in a reference to the brain secretion Christos oil that upon reaching the thalamus and optic nerve engages the vision, the eyes, that resemble 'olives' and why olives and doves are symbols of peace as the dove is a symbol of virginal *female* sexuality. While the 'green man', reptilians, were once a minor nature deity he is now *God* in a series of chronological steps to emerge victorious throughout 'time'! He is the god of time after all who sabotaged our natural evolution *aging us* so we simply don't have the time to figure out how all this works.

It's no surprise that they say the biblical 'thy rod and thy staff comfort me'. I'm sure it does. Even men admit they think with their dicks which in higher-mindedness is considered his 'lower vibration' or not standing in the power befitting a 'divine masculine'. When Harry Potter breaks the 'most powerful wand in the world' at the end of this franchise this is not as innocent as people think. Potter is associated with the dear, the stag aka *Orion-Osiris* and thus Baal (the devil) and the penis cult! The Philosopher's Stone is a reference to the 'stone' of the sacral plexus and Christ seed enlightenment turning one into a *philosopher* aka highly intelligent. The Potter series is loaded with sexual references even the font of the title has the lightning bolts of Thor and Zeus aka Satan. In one seen Harry stands beneath a sign reading 'dark arts'. Hogwarts is not so innocent. In the scene of 'wizards chess' *(see, Pretty Woman)* Harry-Hari, god, stands on the *Masonic* floor and wins the game as the *biggest* 'sword' (penis-phallus) lands at his feet like a gigantic erection, *right*. *Note*, he is wearing the maroon root chakra as the 'knight' (templar) in the background gives the upward pointing hand sign toward the 'heavens' aka *enlightenment* like *all* historically famous

male tantric gods good *and* bad, *right*. You could even go a step further and say the 'up' symbol is at Harry's 'left' side, the 'dark side', as in the painting of the Last Supper. Harry Potter is a reference to the Prime Hindu God Hari 'the maker' the *Creator* the same god of the bible who is the same as Satanist's god. Christians and Satanists are worshipping different sides of the same god only, unlike *ordinary* Christians, most Satanists know this. Unless you are peacefully acknowledging the *two* male-female *reproductive aspects* of *creation* then you are worshiping the devil, *the one male god,* the Devil! Once again, by and large, *all singular male gods from ancient Egypt onward are essentially worshipping the Devil.* The Egyptian god Khnemu was said to *create* each man out of clay on his 'potter's' wheel another biblical reference to 'god' making man of 'clay' aka made of 'earth'. Earth is a reference to the sexual root chakra, the flesh, and Mother Earth, *earthing* the tantric electricity of *power* as sex over love, the 'devil', the 'dark side' as one must go through the 'heart' to be 'angelic' or the universe will be destroyed in the hands of the masses. The only thing that keeps them at bay is the numbers and they are whittling down the goods ones as we speak! Potter is also a reference to Dr Karl Potter a Professor at Washington State University who has studied and published extensive papers and books on Hinduism. The newspaper in Harry Potter is called *'The Daily Prophet'* after their 'prophet' god and why they bang on about their 'prophets' from Islam to Christianity to Hinduism and all the rest of them as this power gives you the power of foresight. Western Catholicism and esoteric symbolism is all pilfered from other people's cultures, religions, and native beliefs *worldwide* while Hogwarts School of Wizardry is basically the Society of Jesus, The Jesuits! The first instalment of Harry Potter was released on 29th November 2001 - 11:11 - in the *first year* of the new millennium. In Gone With the Wind 'Scarlet' is a reference to the root chakra, the prostitute is named Belle aka Beauty and the Beast. The plantation *Tara* (a temple) in Hinduism is the 2nd of the Great Wisdom Goddesses while *India* is the sister of Scarlet's *forbidden love* interest who has another sister not present in the film called 'Honey'. All Hindu tantric sex themes. Just remember, Atheism is a non-prophet organisation.

Before Prince William's son was born I 'predicted' on Facebook that they would call him Arthur after King Arthur the Sun King. He was eventually named Louise Arthur because King Louis XIV was a famous *French* Sun King and King *Arthur* was a famous British Sun King reigning in Camelot. The American Kennedy's represented Arthurian Camelot in a *Western* new-age new-world setting hoped to be jousted by *British* royalty with *their* Camelot Sun King, *Arthur & Co* Pty Ltd representing *The Firm!* There is some sort of feud between American new-world royalty and old-world Royalty in Britain and Europe. It's the Olympians vs. the Titans as the U.S. see an opportunity to potentially break away and create a daring *New* World Order of their own making. Why not? It's been done before. All the old houses of politics and religion vie for supremacy when possible. So, England has planted 'Archie' *Harrison* Mountbatten-

Windsor, a Taurus no less who rules the throat, the speaker, *Harry's* son, intended to rise in prominence in the *New America*. Harrison is *Hari's* son (god's sun) who is the same Egyptian *sun-son* god as Ra is to the *Hindu* god Hari who is the same as Jesus etc. Same god. So, it's no coincidence that native Americans were labelled 'Indians' in a nod toward the Hindu culture. America is New India, New Rome, New Egypt, New Atlantis. Anything that can connect them to *precedence* in their quest to install *one* great male god*!* There are two royal teams old and new, and while they are both despotic psychopathic devil worshippers, one is far more extreme than the other. The *3rd option* is a peacefully emerging *enlightened* Human Race *or whatever is left of them* after these two saboteurs are finished with them! The 8th incarnation of Hari was the famous *Hari Krishna* them of the vegetarian peace-loving Hari's as they intend to masquerade this new-age sun god as the 'saviour', the light *and* dark side of the masculine, the 'balanced man'. It's Jesus on a good day and Satan on a bad day capable of benevolence or *extreme wrath* due to be born *at this time. He is no vegan! He is no good guy.* This is why the affable Prince Harry and Meghan Markle are now in America as Harry represents Hari the *supreme god* of Hinduism and she represents Mother Mary-Mary Magdalene and the MM Roman Numeral of the year 2000 as we enter the new millennium!

So, America is the New Egypt and out of America will arise this global Sun King *one world leader*, the *Anti-Christ!* At least that was the plan. It's 2001, a *Space Odyssey* to be sure thank you Stanley Kubrick as the Twin Towers-World *Trade* Centres came down in 2001 replaced by *the One* World Devil's Dick Trade Centre bearing a cup of poison, the Space Age! Out of the two will arise *The One* considering Hermes was the god of Commerce and *Trade!* Hermes another version of Satan considering the crisis of 911 was an *offering* to the Dark Lord as was JFK and his brother RFK *and* JFK the younger *as well* as the two moon goddesses, Diana and Marilyn. It's the death of the light and dark side of the Twins, the death of the 11:11, the death of Love! It really means the symbolic destruction of the Family of Life, the natural family. Meghan Markle was chosen as she is 'black' as Osiris was called the Black King of the Nile and the Black Madonna and why they bang on about 'Archie' being 'too black' for the British royals so they can use a fabricated 'racial' rift in the royal family to garner sympathy for them in the racially ravaged U.S. just as they *used* Diana's death to garner sympathy for those two boys, the princes, the 'brother's' of old, Romulus and Remus, Cain and Abel, Caster and Pollux and now William and Harry. It's the same old story as ancient history. *Precedence*. The brothers are even supposedly having a falling replicating the 'brother's feud'. It's all *bullshit* behind the scenes these two are firm friends. This repetition is bringing in the biblical myths and *New Age Messiah*, the brothers, born of the dead Goddess, *again!*

Indian historical researcher Mr. Purushottam Nagesh Oak claimed that the word 'Vatican' is from the Sanskrit term 'Vatika' which means a Vedic cultural religious centre. He claimed the word Abraham is an anagram of Brahma, a*Brahma*, and that Christ is *Krishna*. He asserted that much of Middle Eastern *and* Western religious beliefs, symbols and cultural sites including the Islamic Kaaba *and* the Vatican were once Vedic-Hindu sites. It is from these sites that Sanskrit ornaments including a Shiva Linga-*phallus* and Shakti Yoni-*vagina* of male-female God-Goddess worship via sacred-tantric sex between an enlightened couple, husband and wife, was claimed to be unearthed under the Vatican. The Vatican *is* shaped like a Shakti/Yoni Linga Vagina the emphasis on *the Goddess, right*, as the *small* phallus of God penetrates up through the center just as the Washington Monument reflection pool does, *right*. The Kennedy Space Centre launchpad, *below right*, is *also* shaped like the penis-vagina cult tantric IQ temple. It's the sacred vagina-phallus of ancient India cobbled together with an Egyptian obelisk-phallus because they're worshipping the same thing. It's god's 'prick', *Cleopatra's* needle, piercing the vagina of the Goddess, *the uterus-universe*, conquering space via their generations of son-sun kings provided *free of charge* by the Goddess using *her natural resources* to do it all, the 'gift that keeps on giving'. It's all about sex *specifically* conquering the female sex, fucking her, and laughing about it too.

Despite much maligning of his work what can be verified is that Mr. Oak (note the name Oak you can't make this up), 1917-2007, was born in the royal state of Indore completing a Master of Arts Degree as well as a Law Degree. He was a Public Servant and Delegate of the Indian State working for the Ministry of Information and Broadcasting. So, he wasn't just some guy. Oak was derided as a 'crack pot' and a 'historical denialist' his work slandered as 'pseudo scholarship' which actually gives real credibility to what he said. His attempts to bring justice to the grand theft or mass 'cultural appropriation' of Hinduism was *thrown out* of Indian court cases so, it seems the hierarchy are in-on-it *worldwide*. Modern researcher Praveen Mohan is doing *amazing work* on deciphering the true technological history of India as well we see emerging researchers in the Middle East confronting the 'norms' about their history as the reality of their lives and their innate human sentiments don't gel with an *overarching tyranny* that benefits the elite West *enormously* despite claiming to be on opposing sides. Hey, better late than never. Out of all this will emerge a new identity of truth seekers *worldwide* who do not see each other as the convenient enemies of aristocratic manipulators but as *brothers and sisters* on an Earthly quest to free humanity from their respective alien overlords! It's all coming out now. Women will take a *huge place* in the history of the emerging Middle East and the crimes against their femininity will be recorded for all time in order to prevent such a cosmic holocaust from occurring again. The evil men behind all this *need to be exposed*. End of story. Oh, the irony! Once the power of tantric enlightenment is returned to the people and we develop safe educational places where people can engage in a *respectful manner* with this knowledge not be classified on an LGBT *spectrum,* we can attain totally *autonomy*, dignity intact. This is no cheap porno or orgy. This is about growing up and combining love and sex in a healthy home manner without the need to shame anyone or feel ashamed. You wouldn't think it would be so bloody difficult! The perfect couple may be a generation or two away or perhaps we will attain it sooner, I hope so. However it prevails when we are all switched on and operating from a *higher point of view* the draconian cave man shit of previous generations will simply fall by the wayside. The world is going to change fast so I suggest you get informed in a positive empowered and peaceful way. As such, much has been hidden from the world that comes out of India and Eastern philosophies and their people are in some level of danger right now as the Dark Order seek to eliminate anyone who can really benefit the future or know about our planet's great history. I've already mentioned the real threat of some form of crisis 'so terrible the whole world will never forget'. India's Vedas appear to describe ancient accounts of nuclear wars, Princes & Kings, Queens and Goddesses, blood feuds, loves, friendships, duty and honour like Bollywood meets Lord of the Rings! Oh yes, it's happened before, thank you, George Lucas and your Darth *Veda*. More pilfering.

The cube has been long associated with ancient feminine Prime Goddess worship since time immemorial remembering the root chakra is depicted as a square. It's the square root. On the square. Squaring up. Slang is some of the oldest forms of oral traditions on Earth given a woman's vagina is termed a 'box'. I've already mentioned the cube or box associated with all Abrahamic religions and the square of the root feminine chakra, the square root, where they get their power from. Behind all three *male-centric* Abrahamic religions is a vagina and hilariously, this makes perfect sense as hatred and bigotry are the flimsy masks of ignorance and hypocrisy which they employ to the nth degree. Yet these symbols and secret knowledge of ancient Goddess worship applied to the cube were pilfered and reassigned to a *male* god being the Devil who has posed largely in her place ever since. It's deliberate. They stole it like they stole everything else hence, the historic depictions of the devil as a thief. It's not Biggus Dickus but Biggus Vagus! The feminine has the power of female tantric alchemy to ascend a man's chakras via sacred-tantric sex in Holy Matrimony so is it any wonder the practice of carving out the hormonal genital glands of girls and women, FGM (female genital mutilation), prevents female orgasm thus preventing female enlightenment and emanates out of hyper-masculine regions specifically in the Middle East, the East and Egypt where all modern male religions and macho power centers are come from *today*? It's a big paint-by-numbers plan to emerge elite masculinity as ultimately victorious over the feminine and any 'lesser' masculine. Is it also any wonder that a staggering percentage of Muslim men are circumcised *'enhancing'* his masculinity and *increasing* his pleasure while denying hers? Religion is not what they claim while the Satanic cult is a hybrid pantheon of pagan, Abrahamic, eastern philosophies and plagiarised deities *worldwide*. Are we done with this yet? Step away from the pagan gods, guys. *[checks watch tapping foot]*

This is about the incarnation, the return, of some prophesised 'god-king', a demonic *human looking* alien in the 'new age' and they are *hypnotizing us* with films, music, movies, the internet and social media *willing* it into being via the *collective conscious* 'the one' of human minds meaning the bigger the population the more powerful the collective projective force to manifest! *We are god* not only the 'creator' via *procreation* but by the power of our minds ability to tangibly manifest reality. They constantly tell us we are nothing so we don't use our own power to get out of this mess while convincing us 'god' exists *outside* us, out in the mysterious universe. *They* believe this 'god spirit' can 'step in' to an actual body, *incarnate*, and they all want to be the father (Joseph) of the new-age alien 'god' Jesus-Satan. They then intend to take the *physically* form of their god into outer space to continue conquering *everything* with the dick cult. This is the true meaning of the Satan-Zeus-Thor-Apollo Space Mission and the various ambisexual Mercury (*Hermes!*) Space Programs. The devil is a thief and a liar, no wonder the fake moon landing was to conceal the *real* space program! Stanley Kubrick's *The Shining* is a reference to the dick cult's *enlightenment* via the feminine and the *real* meaning behind the little boy in the movie wearing his Apollo-Devil sweater, *right*. He is the anti-Christ, the man-child-alien-demon-god-king, *standing* on the platform of the vagina-yoni tantric 'goddess' as the 'king' *elevates himself via the feminine* at the *Kennedy* Space Centre launching Team Satan-Team America out into the cosmos! Note, the striking similarity between the yoni-linga and starship *Enterprise* aka *Space Corporation*.

YONI-LINGA
VAGINA-PENIS

STAR TREK
'ENTERPRISE'

Apollo was the son of Zeus and as the father is born into the son and Zeus was the devil, then *Apollo* is the Devil incarnate or should I say *reincarnate*. This

is about sending Satan into outer space in the looming space age under the banner of a One World Leader *rising* from America. The yoni-vulva is a symbol of 'divine procreative energy' represented, as with the Celts, as a stone with a hole or a circular stone often carved in streams and rivers to represent the 'flow' of Aether 'prana' life force. In Star Wars the mother of Darth Veda is Padme in Sanskrit Padme means 'lotus' and 'lotus' means the feminine, vagina, birth and Shiva 'Om Mani Padme Hum' literally translates as 'oh, the jewel of the lotus' or colloquially 'oh, my God within me' or Mani Padme 'the jewel within the lotus', yes, the *'Jewel of the Nile'*. The yoni-linga has been interpreted to mean that Shiva the 'destroyer' aka Satan rises, *born* from the yoni-Shakti-goddess-mother-wife-Mary yet she also represents 'involution' or *transformation*. This is why The Shining is loaded with moon symbolism including Room 237 as its 237,000 miles to the moon, as well as 'ghosts' of the girl twins the 'dead goddess', as the father becomes the son and so too does the boy grow up to become the psychotic father or 'god-Satan' so, we see Jack Nicholson, dad, overlooking the 'maize', the labyrinth. *Pan's Labyrinth!* Pan is Satan so this is *Satan's Maize* or for modern purposes, The Matrix!
It's *Alice in Wonderland 2000!* The holographic nature of 'reality' that isn't real! Apollo 11 was a *Saturn V* rocket as Saturn *is* Satan and V is the feminine hips, the chalice, as well as the number 5 of the *original* prime Goddess in Greek myth called *Chaos* or *Ordo ab Chao* 'order out of chaos' from which they intend to 'birth' a new 'order' *and* world leader. The father is a psycho. The corporate takeover of space means the average person is not included, it's a *private* organisation.

The boy in The Shining is *the same character* as Damien Thorn in The Omen with 666 engraved *on his head* who *kills his mother*. An 'omen' is a prophecy. Damien *Thorn* (*Thor lightning tantric sex god*) is the Devil incarnate depicted with the crow-raven, a symbol of dark-side masculine tantric sex-magic, the 'bird', falcon, all seeing eye, the activated pineal gland as does Harry also has a bird – an owl! Damien is *shining* albeit in a *dark* way. *Note*, the II is 11 and he is around 12 years old like Harry-Hari Potter when he is summoned to Hogwarts to begin his apprenticeship the *same age* as Louis IX when he ascended to the throne as would have Ptolemy XV although *he* died. Only in *this* version he lives! He is the *same boy* depicted in the creepy Denver International Airport, *right*, with their

weird *apocalyptic* murals showing the boy king-anti-Christ. We also see the 'stairway to heaven' or pineal gland of tantric sex enlightenment and the pyramid of their historic phallic roots in the Egyptian dick cult. The feminine is *trapped* inside a glass box, a *cube* aka 3D reality, wired to a black sun like a puppet on a string, controlled, while *they* climb the stairway to heaven via the pineal gland to 5D and beyond! They also show a *maroon* masonic checkerboard aka root chakra tantra power beneath his feet the feet. Harry *also* stands on the checkerboard with his big 'sword' dick while the latest Harry Potter movie to be released in *2022* is called the *King's Requiem* which literally means a funeral for the dead king! We also see the galactic black sun at the centre of the Milky Way where they get their power, *electricity* 'via the feminine', and the 'burning bush' at his right arm meaning to 'burn' the feminine, the 'right hand of god'. The 'burning bush' is the *enlightened* nervous system 'tree'. This is why Hollywood recruited little known Australian actress Rose *Byrne* as they wish to 'burn the rose' or kill the goddess, the feminine. They associate their image with these symbols and most actresses have *no idea* why they were chosen like Sandra

Bullock aka *Taurus* the *minotaur* or Goldie Hawn the 'golden horn' of Osiris, *Goldmember*. I wondered why they suddenly chose Eric Bana and then looked at 'Bana' in history who turns out to be an Asuran King inheriting his kingdom from his father.

Sirius is known as the Shining One, bright, luminous, luminiferous aether, the sun behind the sun, a feminine Star, *the mother of all gods*. She must be trapped and burned, killed, as there can be only One like *Highlander*, *note*, the shining dick-blade and electricity, oh yes, it goes way back! Kubrick was killed with a weaponized heart attack for his work on *Eyes Wide Shut* said to have filmed the *fake* Apollo moon landing. It's all tied together. His film *A Clockwork Orange* is a reference to the orange Sacral Chakra that controls emotions, sensitivity, sexuality, intimacy and self-expression, *see*, Tom Hanks *Joe Vs. the Volcano* for *that* gem with his lightning tantra chakra bolts! *Note*, in the movie poster for Clockwork Orange he has the *one eye* of the pineal gland, a dagger-sword-penis and upward triangle phallus *replicated* between the woman's legs not only as a knife (*see*, FGM) but as sex-magic. He also has a false eyelash of gender bending over his *right* eye, the male sun eye. The silver woman's arms are tied behind her back as she is symbolically raped by the phallic 'A', she is a doll, colourless, and looks like the robot (mind control) woman in the 1927 dystopian film *Metropolis*, *right*, note, the inverted satanic pentagram. In the title of a *Clockword Orange* the 'A' is an upright triangle penis-sword, 'C' and 'O' are testicles

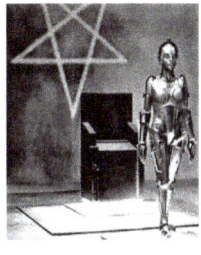

and the 'L' is a *mitre square* of masonry.

As it turns out humans really do glow as discovered by Masaki Kobayashi from the Tohoku Institute of Technology. Chemical reactions within the body emit elementary particles of light, photons, causing the body to glow particularly around the face in the late afternoon. Using a special highly sensitive camera he photographed 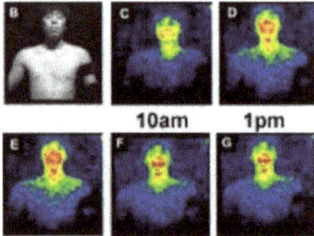 the glow of 'biophotons' or bioluminescence from electrochemical processes that produce free radicals or atoms and molecules that have a single electron The shining indeed! This aura weakens as the darkness encroaches and likely why demons become more 'active' at night when we can't block them out with our auric light enhanced by the sun. So, the ancients *weren't lying!* We really *do* have a 'glowing coat' albeit greatly diminished due to being energetically syphoned by aliens. *Lucifer Rising* aka Apollo Rising by Kenneth *Anger* was made in 1966, as mentioned a big year for them, and was an *obvious* pagan-Egyptian space age 'science fiction' extravaganza. Although I've been spared actually seeing this film, it looks exactly like what you can expect from these self-congratulating evil wankers including the rainbow that would go on the become the banner of all things LGBT given the devil was historically transgender not forgetting their Isis character ushering in it all in via her chakras. B-grade directors see themselves as unacknowledged Kubrick's. They wish.

There are many ways to read a prophecy and we certainly don't need another messiah or *another* male god, prophet, wanker, Biggus Dickus, The One, the Sun King, the Christ *or* the Anti-Christ to fuck things up again. This time around, for once, we'll just run ourselves from our own hearts and not some old man's military doctrine from a by-gone era that has *no place* in a future of information sharing and rationale. *No thank you!* The whole world's systems are designed by men *for men* so it's no wonder women can't even get equal pay in a 'man's world' on a feminine planet. By the time women get equal pay there won't be an economy. Go figure. The irony is not lost. It's deliberate in another example of making women second best, second place, second class citizens and runner-up to men in every way on *Mother* Earth considering all these men wouldn't even be here if it wasn't for the pain and suffering of the birthing mother. The 'chalice' of the feminine hips point downward, South, considered feminine, toward *Mother* Earth, deeply connecting us, *earthing* us via the root chakra of the sexual organs. The 'vrttis' or *tone* i.e. tendency of the root chakra is 'spiritual aspiration' as well as psycho spiritual longing, psychic desire, physical lust. Its affects can underly obesity or anorexia considering this is about Jesus (tantric sex root chakra god) who was a 'carpenter' so we had Karen *Carpenter* die of anorexia, a malfunction of the *goddess* who *self*-destructed! The psychological issue of the root chakra is survival, ambition and the will to live. Its hormonal glands are the ovaries and testicles (procreation) while its colour therapy is red and is controlled by the conscious mind, *the will!* Religious myths and philosophy often mention the Sacred Penis and the Sacred Vagina while in the East they built whole temples and cities to worship sacred-sex and the spiritual vagina-phallus symbology, the Yoni & Lingam, celebrating ancient open sexual societies accessing their pineal glands via sacred sex. The pineal gland of sacred sex enlightenment, *right*, shows up in the Washington State Capital building as well as St Paul's Basilica at the Vatican (the biggest pinecone in the world given they are Rome continued) as well as Angkor Wat. It's the same practice behind them all only Egypt became Roman Egypt that became the Roman Empire that became the Roman Catholic Church which became the European and British Empires that became *America* right on the cusp of a new age smack bang on target with the entrance of their new Jesus-Satan messiah to head up a 'new' age! It's the old age with rockets.

The free form of mountains, valley's and caves of Mother Earth are *symbolised* in the feminine body, the temple, the church, while Father *Time* is the schedules, systems and calendars of the structured masculine mind projected *onto the resources of the feminine* to harness the power of Mother Nature. Yet in not being anchored, *fused to the Mother,* the masculine mind goes haywire hence, the science nightmare, male wars and politics today. Nearly 40% of the of the world's male population are circumcised mostly among Jewish and Muslim men although a whopping 70% are Muslim with 80% found in North Africa, West Africa and the Middle East being the predominant areas of suppression of women. Some studies have observed that circumcising baby boys leads to irritability and feeding problems suffering deep issues related to 'bonding with the mother'. Although they won't admit it, this leads to ongoing issues *relating to females* in general later in life and when we see how women are treated in these countries, it's no wonder. Claimed in the West to have some medical benefits this procedure is considered *no justification* for routinely performing it on defenseless babies with many men left feeling they have been 'mutilated', 'tortured' and 'sexually assaulted' in similar ways to females who have endured forced FGM (Female Genital Mutilation). The oldest documented evidence for circumcision can be traced back to Ancient Egypt (as usual) yet medical reviews consistently state the practice has no negative effect on sexual function. The main reason for male circumcision, historically and currently, is to increase sexual sensitivity, overall pleasure and the perception of size. Conversely, Female Genital Mutilation is *specifically designed* to prevent women from enjoying sex while cutting out the sexual glands prevents climaxing and grossly inhibits her ability to activate her chakras via sacred sex. As said, they are cutting the energetic-spiritual spinal cord of the feminine to prevent her from raising her IQ and engaging with higher dimensions or realising her true power and potential. They are threatened by women worried that they might not be able to keep up and so *ceaselessly* attack women across the board. The spiritual hobbling of the Divine Feminine is *totally deliberate* and major religious male 'scholars' sure as hell know what they're doing and openly encourage diminishing the feminine *worldwide*.

As such, Germany's ban on circumcising baby boys provoked a 'rare show of unity' among Jewish, Muslim and Christian men who claimed it was a threat to their 'religious freedom'. Whenever inhumane practices are promoted shortly after you will hear 'culture' & 'religion'. Something is going on with sex & religion that is so important to the 3 major *male* default Abrahamic religions; Christianity, Judaism & Islam, that they will put aside their *entrenched* differences to unite for sex's sake, not for women's sex, *for male sex only*. The Hindu religion is quite open about the power of sacred sexuality and is the only major religion I can see that aren't *deliberately* hiding it and yes, they are under constant attack, their temples destroyed, blamed for cultural hate and their history deleted. This is really an attack on the whole world as India is happy to share their knowledge yet are constantly made to look bad while keeping them poor. So, with all this masturbation, sex, whores, prostitutes, virgins, stags, studs, phallus-chalice symbolism, obelisks, dick cults, penis rocket ships, swords, power, female sexuality, male sexuality, pedophilia, orgies, ancient LGBTQI, abstinence, lust, love & golden dicks it cannot be denied *something is going on with sex and religion!*

These aliens have gone around the Galaxy, even the universe, spreading their disease of separation infecting even the subatomic codes or reality itself like an organic computer virus. It's why there are 'multi-generational' satanic families because the one reptile or 'family' of interdimensional reptiles is attached to one certain bloodline family in the *physical* world for breeding purposes into the 3D. They procreate with desired women to create half-blood Human men who then becomes the leaders, presidents, princes etc., of their system who are what we historically call the 'Aristocracy'. The reptilian satanic families in the real world have 'mirror' families living in the everyday world who have *no idea* why they suffer such bad luck *intergenerationally*. The elites use them as a spiritual dumping grounds, waste dumps for their toxic energy offloading all their bad karma while harvesting the *positive energy*, talents and gifts of their targets leaving good people poor and emotionally and spiritually *bereft* as the bad guys *steal* all the good 'luck', money, fame and title in a transference of energy of *unparalleled proportions!* Most people wouldn't even know they are a mirror family unaware that their bloodline was once one of the aristocracy cast down into the masses, their history forgotten. The deception is deep. It's alien. The system is 'upgraded' as they phase out draconian titles in favour of new modern edgy corporate and political titles like 'president' and 'CEO'. It's all bullshit. There will be no 'new' age while these people are secretly running the show and it *is* a show. Yet every now and then between zodiac ages as is happening now they are *openly* allowed to breed with the Commoners as dictated in ancient lore kept alive in fables of Cinderella, the Common girl and the Royal frog prince(alien), in the much prophesised 'happily ever after'. It's to give an influx of new genetics to their flagging bloodlines as constant inbreeding means their DNA is aging or getting stale, 'old', thus breaking down and their 'scrambled genetics' need an 'upgrade', new blood, fresh meat, in line with the *new age codes* and *new vibrations* slowly exposing them! They see the human body as just a computer, a vehicle, to have new software programs *installed* on it as new galactic broadcasts are transmitted from the centre of the galaxy a time-space gravitational zero-point vortex that 'dreams' life into being. It's a cosmic mega-brain. We are experiencing quantum evolution not only as a massive vibrational leap but as a change-up on the most *microscopic levels* and it cannot be held off any longer so hold on! They do all this while harvesting Mother Earth of resources, partying their arses off and living above the laws that they set in place for those *below* them. They design economic and social systems to ensure they will live the life of 'gods' as long as possible keeping the Human public ignorant of their presence operating in the shadows out of view, literally. It's all tied into *visible light* and how we have been bred not to 'see' them. But all that is changing *and they know it* as the frequencies shift and Human's experience a greater perceptivity bandwidth! They wanna hope we're better people than they are.

There are some half-bloods who are more in tune with their Human side and the casual atrocities of their species is horrifying to them and their families. They don't want to see their children ritually abused the way they were. Satanic ritual abuse (SRA) is designed to break down and take control of the human vehicle to maximise its capacity in the most clinical way, *literally like a machine*, only problem with this is it requires damaging the 'emotional' body as it's not natural to treat the human light body this way. This is why they require amnesic 'files' to conceal the trauma they've done to the body so that their 'human' side doesn't break down and malfunction in order for the possessing entity-demon-alien to use the body for its purposes in our reality. We are light beings and like finely tuned instruments, we are highly sensitive, and why even hardened 'reptilian' politicians look terrible as they age as their human side doesn't hold up to well to the abuse they even do to themselves in order to utilise the human bodies many abilities. A couple years before they 'die' the possessing entity leaves their human host and moves on to another body probably in the same bloodline as genetics play a part in compatibility. When this happens the 'abandoned' human body and remaining consciousness 'crashes' as they bear the full brunt of what the possessing entity has done. They are a parasite and I'm not saying that evil people are without accountability, I'm saying this alien space program uses the human framework interacting with this reality from the ground up to access to higher dimensional realms that they are otherwise incapable of accessing. They figured out how to 'downgrade' light beings then use those light beings vehicles, bodies, to re-access their normal higher state only, there is an 'uninvited guest' onboard. It' like resetting evolution to emerge as 'god'. They live the high life but there is also a reaction in the real world and despite their opportunism, there is a bitterness too, just look at their faces.

There is an opportunity now to potentially create a sort of coalition with *some* of them in return for information and knowledge on how to free humanity remembering we're all infected with the same reptilian genetics to one degree or another. This coming together is an ancient theme, *the prophecy of all prophecies*, 'written in the stars' as the 'happily ever after' coded into fables, fairy stories and folklore, *a tale as old as time*, glammed-up and 'Disney-ised' for mass consumption. Yet on closer inspection those fables are extremely dark albeit informative. The higher-ups make a mockery of the much prophesised 'happily ever after' *see*, Diana's 'fairy tale' wedding, look how that turned out, but then that's them all over. They *knew*. Creeps. It's why they're obsessed with astrology as they create a 'bad copy' of our true destiny to steal our birthright. They're obsessed with prophecy, hierarchy and the pecking order etc., as there is a time coming, a window of opportunity, to fuck these cunts right off and throw them out once and for all. *That time is now* and one way or another, however it prevails, these A-list celebrities are coding all this into their movies to align themselves with *something*. It's been like this for eons and why The 'Globe' Theatre is where William Shakespeare was said to have plied his scripts as the 'globe' is code for our *whole world, a theatre*, saying, 'All the World's a Stage and all men and women merely players'. His alternative title for Henry VIII was *'All is True'*. It is. Edward Hamilton's *Intelligence Undying* published in April 1936 was a fiction about a man who keeps transferring his mind to a new baby to become a super-mind who takes over the world per the antichrist prophecy. On the 400th version of himself he is helping to evacuate humanity to the planet Mercury as the sun becomes a white dwarf in the year 3144. They keep the mood on Earth low to close the *natural projective and receptive conduits*, lay lines, sacrificing people and animals at certain places and times to keep Earth down *see*, abattoirs and 'theatres of war'. This is the age-old 'sacrifice' to the 'gods'. *Blood is a code* and the 'adrenochrome' hormone released during extreme fear is most easily accessed via the jugular in the throat so the *'vampire biting the neck'* theme is true.

King Henry VIII radically altered the English constitution and ushered in his belief on the 'Divine Right of Kings' or 'God's Mandate' meaning the word of god was the accepted political-religious doctrine justifying 'royal' legitimacy over and above *everyone* else. Under this doctrine the Monarch is not subject to any *Earthly* authority ruling directly from the *Will of God* only which god remains to be seen. The 'Will of God' is the theory that 'God' has a plan for humanity which in the Christian belief system this falls into three distinct categories: 1) Intentional, 2) Circumstantial, & 3) Ultimate. Actually, I would propose there is fourth category which involves all of the above but hey, who's counting? In Sikhism the whole universe is subject to the Word of God and that nothing happens that is not the will of God while in Islam 'God' literally translates as 'submission' and 'surrender'. In Deism the word of god is 'Reason' (small 'g' big 'R') making it possible for a religion grounded in the nature of the universe and established laws of creation that operate without 'divine intervention'. In Judaism the word of 'God' YHWH (Yahweh) liberated the Israelites from slavery in Egypt giving them the 'Law of Moses' described in the Torah. In Hebrew the word 'Torah' literally means 'law' and was translated in ancient Greek as 'Nomos'. In ancient Greek 'Nomos' is the 'daemon' of laws so for me there is an interesting correlation to the 'Nommo' of the African Dogon people who said their teachers were 'amphibian' like frogs and/or reptiles. There is also the word OM the *sound* of the universe, the original 'word' of god, which turns out to be a feminine force resonating with our chakras.

The word daemon is from the Latin word 'daimon' meaning 'power', 'godlike' and 'fate' originally referring to a 'lesser deity' or 'guiding spirit' from ancient Greek religion and mythology. All this *repeatedly* goes back further to the Proto-Indo-Europeans who's 'daimon' means 'provider and/or divider of fortunes and destinies' from the root 'da' meaning 'to divide'. Daimons (demons) were said to be the 'souls of men' from the 'golden age acting as guides'. We have discussed the so-called 'Golden Age' which looks to me like the first of a *designed* series of 'ages' leading to the decent of the original eternal light beings humanity once were by an alien interloper from a Death Dimension masquerading as a 'god' in an ongoing plan to take over the Universe! We will be great again know that as we are *evolving* to a higher state the echo of which we retained since the beginning of all this. At this time we are *supposed* to be elevating our consciousness to the 5*D*, 6*D*, 7*D* and beyond so wouldn't you know it they are replacing our *natural* broadcast with a false one introducing 3G, 4G, 5G and soon 6G and 7G etc., in a *synthetic* broadcast *mimicking* the real thing rewriting the very DNA strands or codes of all humans in a suit of techniques and technologies *to morph us into something not of our previous nature* as the central black hole sun *expects* to be reading certain frequencies from earth that *should* be *increasing* and it is only *not* naturally.

The 'divine right of Kings' means to rule with impunity not subject to the will of the people or other aristocrats or any other 'estate of the realm'. In other words supreme power or God on Earth, the son-sun! The 'Estate of the Realm' essentially means, 1) the 'First Estate' is made up of the King, Queen and Clergy - the clergy being the high-ranking priesthood, 2) the 'Second Estate' is the Nobility or the Aristocratic class, and finally, 3) the 'Third Estate' is the peasants and the bourgeoisie. In some provinces of Europe they had an urban merchant class with rural commoners ranking as the lowest while the non-landowning poor had no political rights at all. What a lovely system! In England this model 'evolved' into the two-estate system we see today combining Nobility and Clergy represented by the House of Commons and the House of Lords commonly referred to as the 'Houses of Parliament'. In short, you're run by aristocrats and priests, *even still*, just like the Aztecs just like the Egyptians. So really, *nothing's* changed. It's the same old same old just add some mass media buzz phrases and shake. The power lies with the 'priesthood' or in today's case the Brotherhood, the Masons! Same shit different millennium. This 'system' essentially means only 'God' can judge the King and any attempt to depose or restrict his powers is an indiscretion against *God* constituting sacrilege! *King is God. God is King.* In ancient times the sun was and remains god and here we find the real symbolism of the 'sun' kings and the 'son' of 'god'! This is why Prince William was induced on the summer solstice as he is a sun king and contender for the One World Leader or at least the *father* of the One World Leader. They are determined to bring this in as a culmination of hundreds maybe thousands of generations of satanic planning taking over the world in a sweeping space syndicate culling out the lower classes and giving themselves a George Jeston new age as upper class scum pose as humans in their final takeover! It is illegal to propose a republic in England *even to this day*. The term 'by the Grace of God' is attached to reigning monarchs as Hail Mary full of *Grace* is the Feminine Life Force. Yes, they elevate themselves via Her. So, these guys have set themselves up as judge, jury *and* executioner, *literally*. The 'divine right to rule' was introduced by King James VI of Scotland aka James I of England (same bloke) who was described as 'the wisest fool in Christendom'. This 'divine right to rule' goes back to Rome, Ancient Greece and ye olde Egypt who were all 'divinely' ordained by 'God' thus becoming 'god' themselves. They're *still* at it today or as the nuns would say, "old habits die hard". I'll be here all week. Try the steak.

    King Henry VIII created the Church of England thus breaking away from the Roman Catholic Church essentially to divorce his wife Catherine of Aragon as she couldn't provide him a precious son. Henry eventually gave her the flick banishing her (she was one of the lucky ones) with the controversial book The Education of Christian Women by Juan Luis Vives being dedicated to her stating women have the right to an education which was seriously a 'wow' moment at the time in men's ability to perceive women as actual human beings. Her enemy Thomas Cromwell said of her, 'if not for her sex, she could have defied all the heroes of history'. Nice one, Crom. Desperate to produce a son, Henry then ran off with Anne Boleyn but when she too failed to provide an heir so he had her knocked off under flimsy accusations of witchcraft and adultery. Just days after Anne's execution he took up with Jane Seymour although it beats me *why* any woman would get involved with a fat ginger psychotic femicidal serial killer but then maybe they didn't have a choice? It's not exactly like you could say, 'thanks, but no thanks'. What a great guy! Jane died shortly after giving birth to a boy and the weakling baby died in his teens of an illness. Henry, still son-less, took up with Anne of Cleves but another gal, 17-year-old Catherine Howard (they just keep getting younger as he gets older!) caught his eye so he gave Anne the boot and took up with Catherine however, it turned out she was a bit of a slapper so he had her knocked off too.

    His *final* wife, Catherine Parr, was lucky last of his six wives having been married all-up four times *herself* including Henry so she knew the drill. They at least had multiple marriages in common for light chit chat across insanely long dining tables positioned at opposite poles like pompous bookends. Incredibly, not only did Henry *not* have his final wife killed but she miraculously outlived him by a year! He could be a little bit choppy at times and was not averse to having some of his chief ministers, um, what's the word for it? Oh, that's right, murdered. On his off days he sometimes enjoyed burning people and was extravagant with numerous costly and largely unsuccessful wars against the Continent. He was something of a 16th century Marlon Brando in his younger years as Henry was said to have been attractive, educated, accomplished and charismatic. He was also an author and composer. Unfortunately, in his later years he became obese, lustful, egotistical, harsh, paranoid, and insecure all the qualities a gal looks for in a fella! Some speculate he had syphilis (see, he really *was* a Marlon Brando of his day!) which contributed to his deteriorating mental state and may be the reason his offspring were sickly and often died young. RIP Henry a paragon of God's Will and Divine Right of Kings.

The story of this is all around us as found in the seemingly weird statue of Pan having sex with a goat, *right*. What does it mean? Basically, Pan, an alien demon or 'the devil', had sex with a 'goat' as 'the goat' is the star *Capella* known as the 'little female goat', the *highest star* at the *zenith* of the Milky Way which is code for saying '*a*  *high feminine*', a woman, remembering superfecundation is a baby born of two different fathers and the 'myth' of a demonic 'spirit' and 'virgin' birth etc. Upon producing a *genetically compatible* offspring with this demonic spirit-interdimensional, it then utilised the human bodies capacity for higher dimensional access opening the internal chakras via masturbation or sex with anything it could find (adults, children, men, women, animals – anything with a life force it could siphon) and commenced elevating its IQ to 'enlightenment' where it proceeded to take over our reality with a series of downgrades turning the human race of light beings into desperate slaves to its every whim while deifying itself as a 'god' to us in our reduced capacity. We wound up looking toward our captor, our enemy, for our salvation in a diabolical *inconceivable* move. It then denied us access to our own sexuality by shaming the idea of intimacy to prevent us from accessing our own light while driving us apart from each other *on every level* from gender to race to ensure it's supremacy. It then replicated the 'stars', where it comes from, *mimicking* the cosmos in *our* reality as a 'bad copy' and rebroadcasting those signals using the collective consciousness as a transmitter to send new codes and signals to the central hub, a massive radio brain, completing an electrical circuit, locking us in, thus commencing rewriting the whole galaxy on every level of reality. And who are 'the stars'? Hollywood. The brightest of them all on and off Earth so when they kill a particular celebrity it is actually 'killing' a particular star, a particular *light*, to reinforce an *underlying code* it wishes to broadcast and harness in the cosmic 'loop'. During the broadcast of the *failed* initial corporate SpaceX mission in 2020 (right on queue) they weirdly interviewed Katy Perry as their resident 'moon person' that's because the *Moon Goddess* must be invoked yet mocked as they phase her out as all things gender neutral take centre stage, literally. Perry, an *admitted* practicing witch, looks rather Marilyn-esque. The initial craft *Falcon* 1 (3rd eye, the bird) was powered by a *Merlin* engine (tantric-sex Satanist) and later a Kestrel engine  (3rd eye, the bird) and launched by SpaceX (space sex) on 28th September 2008 as September is primarily Virgo he Virgin Goddess the *9th month* while 28th is 2+8=10 reducing to 1 and 2008 is the same reducing to 1 so here was have another weird *911* reference. Their Inspiration4 crew on the *Dragon* spacecraft successfully returned on 18th September (equates to 99) in 2021 as headlines read 'Dragon Returns to Earth'. It's all coding. Other *private* launches are Pegasus and Minotaur. They're branding ancient Satanic names of their pan-pagan dick cult onto their fire-nob rockets and people wonder why *science* is naming its programs after *mythology*?

So, Pan, the devil, fucking the 'Goat', the high feminine, allowed them to breed their first generations of half human *(human looking)* sun-kings to commence their reign on Earth. They transfer their consciousness into the offspring, the son, *see,* the Osiris 'myth' among others as 'the father becomes the son' and worship the 'sun' as it is the light they covet and wish to *ultimately* usurp. They have become an ongoing dynasty of 'demonically possessed' leaders who have been running our planet ever since. There is more to know of course but this is pretty close to what actually happened and how they did it all coded in 'mythology' and art. Why would the great artists depict a swan fucking a woman or demons fucking goats? Because its *symbolic* of the *real* story, you've just got to get your head around what the *symbolism* means and you will find the story tells itself staring us in the face since time immemorial! Manly P. Hall said, 'When the human race learns to read the language of symbolism, a great veil will fall from the eyes'. These are the 'gods' of old that 'married any woman they chose' and it was considered a high honour for a human woman to be 'chosen' but only after they destroyed our Eternal Spring then conned us out of our Golden Age and it's being going downhill ever since! The Golden Age or the 'end of the higher state of man' and the classical Greek Nomo 'demons' or the 'souls of men from the Golden Age', is refencing the original interlopers, alien-demons, that were attached to the first ruling human's (hybrid half-blood's) and their newly created 'human' bodies, *Genesis*, for the first time in history after our eternal selves were altered. They shut down the *eternal* state of man, created 'lifetimes' where the populace would get old and 'die' as their memories were endlessly wiped between lives to continue the reign of the demons *forever!* Like gods. It is these original demons that are co-aligned with the 'royal' households of *today*, the most compatible DNA, who run the whole world and are now attempting the final phase of the operation, to eliminate the *original* human and create a 'new' species of *their* design to emerge in our place. It's very close now and the whole *mass vaccination* program is their ticket! They are altering the human genetic line with this hellish operation but it will all backfire and an unprecedented turn of events will see humanity rise again!

These demonic attachments have been consistently 'returning' for potentially thousands of years showing up in various leaders throughout time and the 'line of Cain' is apparently the oldest of them all and therefore the 'most legitimate' in their 'right to rule'. Therefore, the 'devil' may actually be the *original* alien-demon Dogon Nommo reptile, a common demonic progenitor, who 'seeded' all this chaos in the first place passing itself along the line of its 'royal' families to emerge in this last Age to become the King of the World! Their insidious space program has taken over many world's and sentient species. All this chaos we were foretold, *phrophesised*, to evolve out of from the 'original sin', the flesh, 3D reality, and the hacking of our species thus falling into an alien trap and losing our eternal selves to darkness! Like a twisted rubber band the lifeline of evolution becomes so tightly wound it can only go so far before it snaps back and it's at breaking point *now*. They don't want that to happen as they want to retain their access to humans therefore, there *must* be a release and once released the unwinding, the fall, will occur so fast that you'll really have to hang on as we take quantum leaps on our 'return' from the deepest darkness from which we have been mired since the dawn of 'time'. We are now seeing more and more children *remembering* their former lives including being other colours and races. One child interviewed by Oprah Winfrey, a ginger haired freckled kid, remembered being a black American soldier in the civil war and she couldn't understand how a little ginger whitey could be a black man in a former life. Quite simply, the soul doesn't' have a colour. Colour is just the 'divide and conquer' fakery they feed us as part of their rule over us. All the division is falling apart as new generations *remember*, 'oh that's right, it's all bullshit'. This is why the increasing emotional crap and vaccines poisoning kids trying to prevent Total Recall.

We've reached an astrological finale` as evident all around and in the much prophesised and anticipated 'new age', it seems the *cousins* of earthly 'Royal households', the increasingly prevalent alien interlopers being filmed all the time by the general public, are making their presence felt with UFO sightings abounding! As we enter the 'new age', a pantheon of alien infiltrators have returned for their piece of the pie and old-world Earthly reptilians who have run this planet for eons aren't too happy about having their stash nicked by this new lot from Head Office. Maybe this is why these bloodline 'royal reptiles' of earth are now trying to make a 'treaty' with the humans as they *need us*, certainly our numbers, to help take down these new reptilian interlopers who've decided Planet Earth should be *theirs* now. But Earthly reptilian royals have worked hard behind the scenes to make Earth a stronghold for *their* power mongering in *their* attempts to make a *new* alien empire for *themselves* in this sector of the galaxy. They want to form a 'new' space league of their own to go into space themselves, *see,* the Mercury (Hermes) Space Program and now the SpaceX lot. All this is underpinned by tantric sex enlightenment from human women which is how they got the brains to figure all this out in the first place. SpaceX etc., is all for *mainstream consumption*, of course, as the *real* space programs are going on *behind the scenes*. This is why they needed to sacrifice the 'Sun King', a really big offering, to buy this opportunity from some dark force so they offered up President Kennedy to their dark lord to make all this happen. Kennedy who stated he would put a man on the moon within the decade *but the price was high.*

People involved in Satanism are often made all sorts of promises but they must 'offer' something to 'Satan' to get their wish and why so many celebrities have family members who mysteriously die right before they get their fame and fortune. Most if not all serial killers are Satanists who are demonically possessed, mind controlled or all three and emanate from *alien* social engineering agencies. It's actually sad when you read the accounts of the horrors that little boys have endured in their childhoods only to wind up the most controversial killers the world has ever known. *Killers are made* in a multi-agency cult psy-op against the perceptive functions targeting human's core comprehension of 'reality'. *It's another trauma ritual.* The sacrifice is tribute, tax, like the Aztecs did. So, they aint about to let alien Grandpa Joe from Orion swipe their empire out from underneath them on a whim. Maybe this is why Trump was cosying up to Kim Jong Un to 'repair' relations with as many old enemies as possible as the 'enemy' image is just a put-on like everything else. It seems they're trying to solidify their position before this Euro/British/German/Israeli reptilian blood feud spills over and threatens to engulf America and the planet as a whole in a looming nuclear war! It's all staged to create the 'before' and 'after'. It's a royal-reptile civil war behind the scenes. *This* is when they're at their weakest as they roll over on each other to get what they want! There's no loyalty among royalty! Old world Euro-Brit royalty are very much onboard with their alien masters who have infiltrated the 'new world' of Australia, America, Canada and New Zealand. But many 'new world' royals of said regions are like, 'fuck you, it's ours now'. It's a rehash of the Olympians overthrowing the Titans of Greek myth they are, after all, *replaying the ancient accounts* in modern times. As mentioned, it's like a huge court case so if you can find *precedence*, you've got a valid 'case'. *There's precedence alright.* As such, new world royal reptiles in politics and entertainment are looking to 'come out', make a treaty, but be careful, you don't want to replace your old masters with new masters. Proceed with caution! They are old hats at manipulation yet you do have a unique opportunity to capitalize on this 'offer' if you're smart enough to know it's happening in the

first place.

The skin of Reptilian's apparently has the appearance of a Terrapin turtle. Remember, they said they were the 'first creation' while the Fermi Paradox states any *emerging* civilisation has the advantage over other civilisations that emerge after them. In Jewish Kabbalah 'Ein Sof' means the state *prior* to the *'self-manifestation'* of god and means 'the endless one', 'unending', 'infinity', 'there is no end' or *eternal*. Ein Sof is a feminine force. Their original 'life force' comes from dark matter and if they were once light beings, like the story of Gollum in Lord of the Rings, then they strayed down the wrong path and couldn't come back from it. Once lost the light is extremely difficult to regain hence, the alien abduction and cloning programs trying to understand our light bodies. They're gonna lose and they know it as they rush to harvest as much of our genetics as possible before we are gone from them. Our emotions and Heart-Love are a compass to guide us through higher vibrational realms. Early on in the 'space cowboy' days they hadn't evolved spiritually enough to realise how important feelings and Love really was and made the mistake of removing these things regaling themselves in the power of clinical intellect and technology instead. What a marvel intelligence and technology is! In their increasing power grabs to become 'god' they strayed further and further away from the light and became *monsters*. They then went around the galaxy and beyond looking for species to fuse with to find their way back to the light but not so-much-so as to hinder their need for self-indulgence and 'become' god. Aliens are operating hybrid programs in their desperate attempts to save themselves as Mother Nature steps in and deletes their codes *permanently* and they *go extinct* when the super program recognises they are a *virus* to the natural order. Natural selection. They do it to themselves like these idiots lining up for the COVID jab. Good luck with that. They hate the feminine as *She* will *ultimately* erase them all.

There are things going on now that will go down in history for all time. It's make or break. Therefore, if the Yanks go down the whole world goes down and why the Twin Towers were raised and destroyed in America for good reason and even  appeared to have a demonic face in the smoke clouds and why cyclones appear to have the face of a demon in it, *above*, actual meteorological image. Oh yes, they can do it. These old-money psycho's from Europe seek to *secretly* emerge as supreme rulers in a *global* fascist superstate emanating out of America, the shop front, to install their alien One World Leader. The continued rapidly spiraling destabilization of America is *one prong* on the trident just as they tried to hold off Brexit, destabilise Europe with mass migration from undeveloped cultures and then hit us with a *global pandemic* and mandatory vaccine as they attempt to pull off *the greatest con job in history!*

Distraction! Distraction!

Chapter Nine
THE PHEONIX RETURNS

"A man may die, nations may rise and fall, but an idea lives on".
John Fitzgerald Kennedy

Pan, the Devil aka Satan, was famous for his 'flute' or 'Pan Pipe' and just as swords, clubs and wands are symbols for the penis, cups, chalices, flutes, horns and flowers are symbols for the chakras. So, Pan's Pipe is code for the dark side male sex, *right*. The flute or pipe is found in the folktale of the Pied Piper or PP and also in Peter Pan etc. P is the 16th letter of the alphabet which reduces to 7 *another* coded dark side message as 77 is the 7 male and 7 female chakras and also represents the 77 of the light and dark side of the 7 chakras, Jekyll and Hyde, that exist inside all of us. The Pied Piper 'lured children away with his flute'. Yes, the 'children of god' are lured away by the diabolical devil. Even now we see how  young people, especially children, encouraged toward confusing gender profiling and sexual awareness at a very early age. When someone has 'paid the Piper' is means to punish them especially by death. The cloven hoofed *Pan* is the same as the Baphomet gender-bender as the 'frying pan' constellation also called the 'pot' resembles a cooking pot better known as Orion. Colloquial language is a wealth of ancient secret knowledge passed down to us by those who knew this would happen again as it's happened in the past *many times*.

Orion is where key reptilians claim to come from in this alien space league and they are *telling you* via symbolic association that the Reptilian enigma, the 'devil', is an alien who comes from *Orion* and became a 'king' on Earth, a sun king! It doesn't matter what gender preference you are, the *symbology* in ancient tales and art warn against tampering too much with *natural creation* and allows *no excuse* to claim we didn't know. Same sex relationships are fine if that is what you choose, heterosexuality though is *essential* for *natural procreation* and *evolution* as lab babies, and invasive operations, pharmaceuticals, psychological disorders and 'body image' issues encroach on us daily as the human race rapidly lose our connection to our lineage. There is a historic warning suggesting 'gender neutrality' and messing with Mother Nature via science has occurred before with disastrous consequences as science becomes god and chaos abounds! LGBT youth are *three times more likely* to commit suicide than their hetero peers and while this is *always* blamed on 'hetero bullying' and discrimination, the facts do not support this. They make out it all about health and 'science' but the proof is in the pudding and we aint doing so well. Check out the cult horror movie *From Beyond* for an insight into the elite perception of us *sexually*. There is something going on here and it's not human so making out it's a race thing or 'gender' issues is *more obfuscation*. It's definitely alien vs. human and I've got news for you folks, we're losing.

Alien sexuality is rampant as anything goes in the temptation or 'corruption of the flesh' as they do not respect human spirituality *deeply connected* to our physical and non-physical body. Pan, *right*, encourages a *clearly* shy *innocent* young man to 'blow' on his 'flute'. Slang hasn't changed. The bisexual Hermes with his wings or 'bird' of the third eye pineal gland all-seeing-eye also played the 'pipe' as sex enlightenment via the 'flute', penis, unlocks the chakras. Blue Hindu gods are also depicted with the flute as well the Ptolemy's of Cleopatra's lineage were famous for playing the 'flute'. The Egyptians often built their boats with what appears to be giant 'horns' stylized as flowers on the 'bow', the head, of the 'ship'. The ship is symbolic of the human vehicle, the body. Given the 'vrttis' or 'tone' of the chakras have certain traits and we know that sound, *cymatics*, creates matter then the 'flutes' or 'pipes' of the chakras are microcosms of the *sound holes* broadcasting reality from black holes described as OM, the sound of the universe, that creates reality! The ancients were depicting the frequency's and broadcasts from the universe *replicated* in our chakras and torus field that resembles an apple, *right,* and also resembles the *sound hole* of horns, trumpets, flutes, pipes as well as cups, chalice, bowls and flowers associated with the penis and vagina because tantric sex unlocks the *tone* of the chakras broadcasting higher frequencies into our dimension, *see right*, the halo. It is our 'energy' that creates our reality. If you are depressed chances are you will attract people into your life that make you more depressed, it's the circuit, what you put out you get back. Activating your 'horns' via your 'horn' so to speak hence, unicorn or 'unique horn', the penis, allows you to access higher frequencies and *dimensions* leading to higher states of being, ergo, *enlightenment*. Unlocking the crown 'horn' or 'sound pipe' is the Halo, *above*, depicted in all religious and spiritual images worldwide. Fables encode this knowledge where we find flowers, thorns, trees, flutes, princesses, princes, stars, music as well as 'frogs', goblins, witches! Not many people would

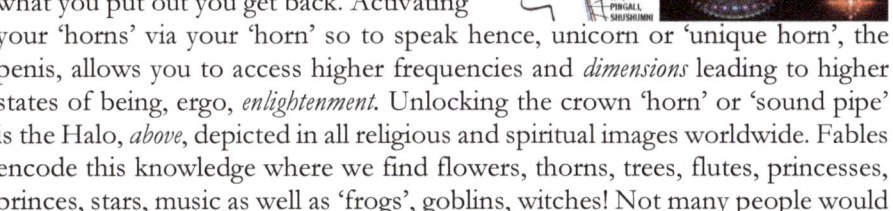

know that the 'witch' who entraps Rapunzel is actually a lesbian siphoning her light, her innocence, via her 'hair' when she 'sings' meaning 'orgasm', and why she hates the boy who climbs Rapunzel's 'tower'. Thanks, ancients, for recording all this for posterity you might just get us out of a jam yet!

Given a woman was considered a ship, the Egyptians built 'horns' and 'flowers' onto their boats called 'barks' considering the Dog Star, Sirius, the dog, *barks*. It never ends. Sound affects the geometric baseline of our reality as we literally code our space with our broadcast, our frequency, and why some people are really happy and popular and others are not, some people attract great wealth and happiness while others do not. This is how celebrities are getting their wealth, happiness, success, power and all the rest of it and why they secretly code this information into their movies for the dual purpose of laughing at you while letting themselves off the hook as they actually *do* tell you what they're up to you just didn't realise it. *We too* can become the script writers, code writers, and lead actors of our lives and take our power back from these idiots that are already doing this. Chromesthesia or sound-to-colour synesthesia, *right*, is a *perceptual function* of the brain in which stimulation of one cognitive pathway activates involuntary experiences in a secondary cognitive pathway evoking experiences of colour, shape and movement and for some people listening to music allows a simultaneous experience of *colour* from *auditory sensations*. You can literally *see* sound or to go further, *taste* sound, in a multi-sensory multidimensional activation intimating that life as we know it is about to change in ways we could never imagine! Individuals with sound-colour synesthesia spontaneously, without effort as their normal realm of perception, enjoy not only the *sound* but the 'cross-activation' of sensory awareness that allows colour to associate with sound, tone, pitch and timbre. As such, high pitched sounds associate with lighter, brighter colours and low pitched sounds with lower, darker colours and indicates a *common mechanism* underlays these associations in normal healthy brains. Note-to-colour associations for people with the ability of chromesthesia or 'synesthetes' means an individual is more likely to play musical instruments and be artistically inclined. The Parietal Cortex contributes to this function when focus is directed to the synesthetic experience so training can elevate this ability. These are the 'higher dimensions' available to us as we access our greater brain and life becomes a mosaic of wonder not previously experienced by humans since the fall of man! Art will set us free. All things combined this means that 'geomancing' or altering the baseline frequencies of our environment with the *intention of our willpower*, once our chakras are activated, alters the intangible *non-fixed* nature of 'reality', the holograph, *the matrix,* and we can create what we like on a global scale!

Those manipulating this knowledge and power for their own greed *specifically* access the human energetic framework *for this ability.* They then hide the knowledge from us so we can't use it ourselves while they emerge as cruel masters, heartless, uncaring, callous and ruthless. Now that they've reached the pinnacle of their power they intend to wipe us out en masse! Practicing the dark side is still with us today coded into the Bible and all historic scripts, *see right,* the 'seven trumpets' of the Apocalypse (seven chakras) that herald the 'end times' events including the 'three woes' which in my view is WWI, WWII and the looming *WWIII.* From Revelation 'seven trumpets' are sounded.  This is the 'trumpets' of the chakras blowing a different tune and once again they've turned it into something terrible that spells out doom! From Revelation 8-11 the 'Seven Seals of God' are opened and upon breaking the 'seventh seal' all hell breaks loose, literally! The 'seventh chakra' is the crown chakra of the head as all the *sealed* chakras are 'sleeping beauties' and we are finally 'open' i.e. *awakened,* humanity begin the process of activating our light body nervous system *and all other energetic functions* leading to *mega-enlightenment* aka *ascension.* This is what they are cryptically talking about when they speak of the 'raising up' and when it happens and you realise what they have done to you and how they used this power we all possess *against us*…well, decide on that day what you will do with them.

They are trying to stop us from reaching the 'seventh seal', Crown enlightenment hence the sudden 'Corona Virus' aka 'Crown Virus' as we collectively broadcast the signal that our ascension is a terrible thing that we must be vaccinated against! 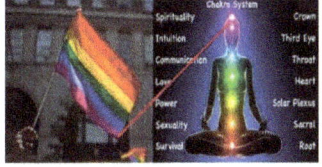 Now do you see how they twist the truth to get us to destroy ourselves? The 7th chakra, *the 7th seal of God,* is Christ seed enlightenment. The *return of Christ* only not the way they told us. Through their manipulative linguistic psychological warfare they are getting us to transmit the signal that our awakening is an evil thing, a nuclear war, a pandemic, the 'end' times. They are 'vaccinating' you against the 'seventh seal', *the third eye and crown chakra,* via a Corona CROWN virus as the 'Messenger' *mRNA* vaccine inoculates the Claustrum from producing Christ aka The Messenger!! We will never be able to access this function no matter how much love making we engage in as the part of the brain, the Claustrum, that produces the electrochemical hormone, *Christ,* will be dormant! The 'mysterious' Bible is leading us into a trap along with *all other major Satanic Abrahamic alien religions* corralling us toward our end. Just as we arrive at the new age of Aquarius supposed to herald peace, innovation, equality, *enlightenment,* comfort – everything owed to us –they intend, again, to hijack it out from underneath us! Even the LGBT flag is upside down as everything meant to be positive and progressive is turned into something negative to laugh at our ignorance. They betrayed us. They tried to lure us into a trap to kill us all and they must be removed, *permanently*. They've divided us from the whole *eternal* 'one' into the dualistic *weakened* 'two' leading to all the fragmentation and instability that has dogged humanity reaching its hysterical zero point at this time! This mix of negative emotions is called 'loosh' possibly from the French word 'louche' an energy that other entities feed off produced by suffering. It works by utilising 'Reversal Networks' collecting 'Life Force' energy from the collective fields of all Earth inhabitants including animals and this creates more 'dark force' or 'black force' energy by sending energetic currents into reversal hijacking our elementary photonic electrochemical 'glow' discovered by Masaki Kobayashi from the Tohoku Institute. This suffering causes 'miasm', a psycho-spiritual distortion generated via trauma, abuse, and fear leading to 'soul fragmentation' which damages a person's energetic body (auric field) into not operating properly or not operating at all. The more distorted the 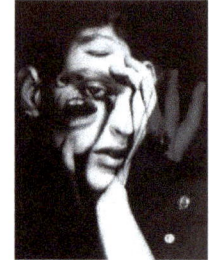 thoughts, feelings and emotions become, the more this dark energy can manifest as addictions, perversions and a broad range of damaging personality disorders. This leads to 'Alternate Identities' known previously as Multiple Personality Disorder but today is referred to as Dissociative Identity Disorder, a somewhat confusing term which doesn't adequately describe the condition so we don't take it seriously enough despite it becoming more prevalent. It's like 'post-traumatic stress disorder' doesn't have the same punch as a 'nervous breakdown' even though they are one and the same. Language is powerful.

Miasm and emotional fracturing is not something of the modern world. In many images Mary Magdelene is depicted with seven swords in her heart. The sword is a symbol of the penis so we are being told her that Mary's heart and as a result all her chakras, is blocked the masculine energy. She was described as a 'sinner' by Popes who ran the organisation in the two thousand years following this also, she had 'seven demons' cast out of her, as shown in this image. We are being told here that the enlightenment Mary experienced was destroyed by the same men who killed Jesus (at least killed him figuratively) and the sad look on her face tells us  everything. They destroyed Mary not only by casting her down initially – with the help of Jesus at first – but by then killing Jesus when he became her lover and then running her off. It's a common theme, they love destroying the feminine. This fragmenting goes back further when they split the One into two and the androgynous feminine became man and woman the way they *split* the north and south poles. It's a negative facsimile, a dark replication, of what is found in the universe. It's why they continuously 'split' off like they *split* America in half after they *split* from England. *It's the split*. It just keeps happening in a *false replication* of the original organic *self-replicating fractaling* of Universal Mother Nature, a natural life-force that seeks to recreate itself unendingly. It should be a beautiful thing instead it was stolen and ultimately morphed into an A.I. 'god' and its underlings that *mimic* organic reality. Wherever these aliens show up or 'fold in' to our reality from an intra-parallel plain, so too do the spectrum of weird *unnatural* creatures that accompany them. They are also fusing their genetics with our animal kingdom resulting in the weird creature's people are seeing all the time, *cryptids*, as part of their Satanic science programs to take Earth *back* to prehistory when horrifying creatures roamed our world as part of their biblical prophecies. In Michael Patcher's painting, *right*, of *St Augustine and the Devil, 1471AD*, we see striking similarities in the arse-face morphing theme in the next image where we have a scene from the 1989 film *'Society'* by Brian Yuzna *(seriously, worth a watch)* about the upper echelons of society 'the elite' being a hybrid breed of half-human shapeshifters populating the highest realms of big business. They're everywhere in far greater numbers than we gave them credit for. They are doctors, lawyers, police, politicians, celebrities the whole lot who think *nothing* of murder, rape and incest etc. They claim they were here first and through the process of 'shunting' merge with humans to steal our energy and 'eat' people, *consume them*, physically and energetically! The vampires of old! Knowing what I know about electrical processes of energy and what I suspect is happening, I looked up what the word 'shunting' means and not surprisingly it said, 'Shunt (electrical) In electronics, a shunt is a device that creates a low-resistance path for an electric current, to allow it to *pass around another point* in the circuit. The origin of the term is in the verb 'to shunt' meaning to *turn away* or *follow a different path*'. I'm no electrical expert but that looks like a hacking device. They're doing this not only with technology but also with genetics, demons, mind control and the occult! We're being *rerouted*, phased out, *literally*, considering that the *original* and most simplistic route for the energy to travel to the galactic core and back is a straight line, a *circuit*, the path of *least* resistance.

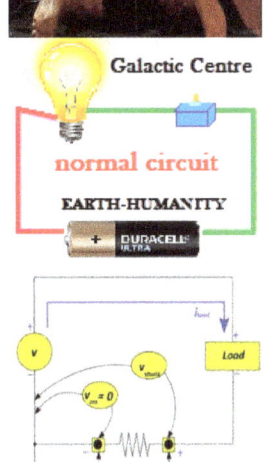

Wearing out the auric field allows negative energies and entities, demonic possession, to more easily access the human framework. It is happening and denying it is making it worse. Splitting or fragmenting creates a sense of *more*

than one identity in the body and look at the *incredible* rise in 'identity' disorders related to social issues specifically around gender, sex and body image (body dysphoria) considering this is all about sex exacerbated by online networking sites underpinned by shady agencies and dubious groups all promoted by the mainstream media selling all this horse shit to an unwitting public especially kids. In his book *Far Journey's* Robert Munroe who founded the Munroe Institute claimed that while in contact with a light being he was told that when humans die the energy released is harvested by 'trans-dimensional beings' who use this energy to extend their own lives. These beings claim they created the universe as a 'garden', *a playground,* a toy, to be their food source. Liars, they're parasites. In a predator-prey struggle exceptional levels of energy is released by the 'combatants' and in spilling the blood (*see,* wars) this intense energy is harvested. It's also specifically harvested from loneliness which explains my isolation and destruction of my family (they must be having a field day with me). This energy is specifically harvested when a parent is forced to defend its young whether human or animal. Human concepts of religion and 'worship' is another well-spring for this energy that these creatures feed off. The more the suffering the more the energy released which explains satanic cults and the weird experiences survivors have been forced to endure as it makes their bodies 'tastier' as a 'meal' for these 'creators'. This corresponds with ancient scriptures in the Vedas, Upanishads, and Puranas from India as written in the Atharva Veda from the Garbha Upanishad, 'the universe is upheld by sacrifice…all who are living are the sacrificer's. There is none living that does not perform yagya (sacrifice). This body is created for sacrifice and arises out of sacrifice and changes according to sacrifice'. As such, evil aliens are running this world whether reptilian or *whatever else* is doing this and their religion is Satanism.

In his book *Active Side of Infinity*, Carlos Castaneda interviewed a Yaqui shaman, Don Juan Matus, who said, "Every one of us human beings has two minds. One is totally ours, and it is like a faint voice that always brings us order, directness, purpose. The other mind is a foreign installation. It brings us conflict, self-assertion, doubts, hopelessness…For the present, it will be sufficient that I repeat to you what I have said before about our two minds. One is our true mind, the product of all our life experiences, the one that rarely speaks because it has been defeated and relegated to obscurity. The other, the mind we use daily for everything we do, is a foreign installation…Sorcerers believe that the predators have given us our systems of beliefs, *our ideas of good and evil,* our social mores. They are the ones who set up our hopes and expectations and dreams of success or failure. They have given us covetousness, greed, and cowardice. It is the predators who make us complacent, routinary, and egomaniacal". "But how can they do this, don Juan?" I asked, somehow angered further by what he was saying, "Do they whisper all that in our ears while we are asleep?" "No, they don't do it that way. That's idiotic!" don Juan said, smiling. *[they actually do infiltrate our psyche via our dreams]* "They are infinitely more efficient and organized than that. In order to keep us obedient and meek and weak, the predators engaged themselves in a stupendous maneuver—stupendous, of course, from the point of view of a fighting strategist. A horrendous maneuver from the point of view of those who suffer it. They gave us their mind! Do you hear me? The predators give us *their* mind, which becomes *our mind*. The predators' mind is baroque, contradictory, morose, filled with the fear of being discovered any minute now. I know that even though you have never suffered hunger," he went on, "you have food anxiety, which is none other than the anxiety of the predator who fears that any moment now its maneuver is going to be uncovered and food *[humans]* is going to be denied. Through the mind, which, after all, is *their* mind, the predators inject into the lives of human beings whatever is convenient for them. And they ensure, in this manner, a degree of security to act as a buffer against their fear." "It's not that I can't accept all this at face value, don Juan," I said. "I could, but there's something so odious about it that it actually repels me. It forces me to take a contradictory stand. If it's true that they eat us, how do they do it?"

Don Juan had a broad smile on his face. He was as pleased as punch. He explained that sorcerers see infant human beings as strange, luminous balls of energy, covered from the top to the bottom with a glowing coat, something like a plastic cover that is adjusted tightly over their cocoon of energy. *[this is what we once were in the eternal spring before we were split which children still retain]* He said that the glowing coat of awareness was what the predators consumed, and that when a human being reached adulthood, all that was left of that glowing coat of awareness was a narrow fringe that went from the ground to the top of the toes. That fringe permitted mankind to continue living, but only barely. As if I had been in a dream, I heard don Juan Matus explaining that to his knowledge, man was the only species that had the glowing coat of awareness outside that luminous cocoon. Therefore, he became easy prey for an awareness of a different order, such as the heavy awareness of the predator. He then made the most damaging statement he had made so far. He said that this narrow fringe of awareness was the epicenter of self-reflection, where man was irremediably caught. By playing on our self-reflection, *[the mirror! The electrical circuit board!]* which is the only point of awareness left to us, the predators create flares of awareness that they proceed to consume in a ruthless, predatory fashion. They give us inane problems that force those flares of awareness to rise, and in this manner, they keep us alive in order for them to be fed with the energetic flare of our pseudo-concerns *[see, mainstream media.]* There must have been something to what don Juan was saying, which was so devastating to me that at that point I actually got sick to my stomach. After a moment's pause, long enough for me to recover, I asked Don Juan: "But why is it that the sorcerers of ancient Mexico and all sorcerers today, although they see the predators, don't do anything about it?"

"There's nothing that you and I can do about it," don Juan said in a grave, sad voice. "All we can do is discipline ourselves to the point where they will not touch us. How can you ask your fellow men to go through those rigors of discipline? They'll laugh and make fun of you, and the more aggressive ones will beat the shit out of you. And not so much because they don't believe it. Down in the depths of every human being, there's an ancestral, visceral knowledge about the predators' existence". The truth of what was done to us is almost too much to bear and most people don't bear it preferring to die endlessly than face reality.   T.M. Wolf said of the two minds of humanity, "There is a far greater fundamental mind in all of us than what is generally accepted as the normal waking state. This *original mind* is your true identity. When life is engaged directly from this original mind one becomes privy to sights sounds and connections in life that can never be grasped by the physical senses. In the machinations of the brain there are techniques and methods specifically designed to awaken this mysterious pathless ultimate reality". Yes, those methods include tantric sex enlightenment - the enlightenment of the 'gods'.

We can finally transcend them now.

CHAPTER TEN

THE VIRGIN-WHORE PARADOX
Death becomes her…

All male-default religions are *obsessed* with virgins and prostitutes because they worship the dick in and out of the home, *publicly and privately*. They want a wife who is obedient, demure, cleans the house and puts dinner on the table in time for him to finish his trading as a 'merchant' with the big boys and give birth to his sons. Global business, politics, religion, media and all major commercial trading has always been owned and operated by men not only European-English men but also Middle Eastern men, Russian men, Indian and Asian/Oriental men. Now we have American men, Canadian men and Australian-New Zealand men emerging in the 'new world' in a *new generation* of the 'new age' wearing their dicks on their sleeves, *literally*. It's Star Trek's Next Generation but it's the same old shit its always been they just have technology now and its business-as-usual playing out their wackery on TV before it happens in the real world laughing at us the whole time! They love our ignorance and hate it when we point out their *obvious* flaws, when they get exposed it makes them angry as expected of the bully-brat. The new-world of new-age elite men believe they are more 'modern' and 'progressive' than their forebears not bound by the stuffy protocols of tiresome social hierarchy, the pecking order, and all the politics and triviality that goes along with *old-world* dick cults. Yet all post-modern businesses are built on the same premise the same small thinking. The stock exchange is one big 'haggle' just as the old market bazaars of ancient Rome and Egypt, they just have flat screens now. We *still* live in a barter system represented by money and male bravado.

The story Wind in the Willow's is very symbolic in regard to what actually happens in our 'system'. After fifteen generations of aristocratic malingering, the fat pompous Lord of the manor, Toad, has left himself wide open as the weasels see his weaknesses and creep in for the takeover. He doesn't even realise *or care* engrossed in any form of whimsy to amuse his conceited pride lost in a strange blueblood OCD of self-indulgence. So, as far as the secretive crypto-religious male cultists are concerned, as expected of them, they believe the perfect 'wife' is a virgin in the kitchen and a whore in the bedroom while they tinker with their toys and party like every day is their birthday. These guys need some *serious retraining* if we are going to build a *real* new world of fair trade, openness, responsibility and fair play among real people and not just go around the May pole *again*. The ancient boys club is out in plain sight now which is rare as the world finally cottons on that all is not as it seems. Their treachery required the cloak of darkness and secrecy to get away with their selfishness and many new-world elites like Elon Musk go along with it all because, stupidly, they don't see any other way or are too lazy and *cowardly* to try anything different. Nazi rocket scientist Werner Von Braun said the space age would be led by an Elon. Elon is an anagram of Leon and Leon is Hebrew for Lion yet deeper inspection finds this word means 'heart'. It's no prediction of prophecy the Von Braun new the new age space program would be led by a 'lion', their secret cult simply calls for someone, anyone, called Leon-Lion to be the face of the charade for a while. As such, in their *pagan scripted* media movie Princess Diana and Marilyn Monroe were 'moon' goddesses 'recreations' of the original High Priestesses, the original administrators of the world associated with the moon, water, tides, emotions, silver, starlight, pregnancy, birth, motherhood, Mother Nature, *domesticity* and ultimately, the *central black hole* sun, the 'Queen' of Heaven. It's funny how these things come around as I was featured on the front cover of CENTRAL magazine doing a photoshoot in an *out dated* laundromat. The 'force' has strange ways of manifesting considering she is Isis and the secret dick cult seem to think *I'm* 'Isis'. What a joke it all is.

These Masons have *major* hang-ups about the mother so it's no wonder Prince Charles asked Diana to *marry him in his childhood nursery*. Sad. Now we see William and Harry *both* marrying 'common' girls in a continuation of seriously outdated thinking that are actually a devolution from previous methods if that's possible. The world was once at a much higher level of knowledge and power when the masculine and feminine really were on equal footing and now we're reduced to memes, hashtags and the most pathetic 'woke' posturing while literally handing themselves over to mad scientists to be *experimented* on! At least in the second world war they were *forced*, now they happily destroy themselves. Again, sad. So the two princes are forced, really, to play out this twisted farce of the *original* prime feminine-masculine story. The last time around it was the masculine who was killed, Osiris, Jesus, JFK only this time around it's the feminine being killed. The name Isis literally translates as 'throne' and given these reptilian-amphibian bloodlines are all associated with royalty, saying the *feminine* was made of man's 'rib' is a fine example of their hatred and shallow inferior smug hypocrisy to create entire global religions based on a *central male* figure while relegating the Mother-Wife-Goddess to baby making, cooking and toilet cleaning while professing to worship 'one' 'heavenly father' 'god'. It's frankly mind-blowing they've gotten away with it for so long and shows their level of *dangerous* malevolent conceit to sacrifice the whole world for their boyish whimsy. The fact that men have been *happy* to live in *agreeance* with this for so long is *extremely concerning*. If you are worshipping 'one' god you are worshipping Satan because it's take two, mother and father, god and goddess, to create life, specifically the feminine input, as hers is greater than his given what her body has to do and the risk she takes to birth new life for their next generation. Again, thankless, I think most mothers realise that before the end. Ripped off.

The French are deeply involved in this story from way back as France was said to be where Mary Magdalene escaped to after the political assassination of Jesus. Mary Magdalene was *notoriously* associated with prostitution while Jesus's mother, Mother Mary, another MM-year 2000, was the famed 'virgin' who was without a known lineage. She doesn't get a past. Her foremother's a lost to the boys club lies. You mean the mother of 'god' has no historical note? No family? Cinderella. There are huge connections to sex regarding the two main women in Jesus's life as prostitution and virginity are always bought up throughout this story *regardless* of which Abrahamic religion is telling it. The ancient Greeks and Romans reimaged Isis as their respective Goddesses of Love in Aphrodite and Venus. These 'love' goddesses weren't just some cutesy puppy love or unconditional motherly love. These goddesses were *worshipped* at huge temples where they practiced sacred marriage, the academy of sacred sex, transcendental lovemaking, *tantric sex*, taught by women to be practiced *in the home* for enlightenment purposes of the divine couple, God and Goddess, in a respectful healthy *evolving* manner as designed by *natural processes* before we got hijacked by *unnatural* aliens. In some ways her knowledge of sex enlightenment was a type of currency but only reserved for men who would honour her in return for her gifs but she was no street prostate. That came after. In those days you couldn't get regular sex any other way but in the home via marriage.

Venus was symbolic of Mother Nature represented by all these Goddesses throughout history often depicted holding the sceptre, a symbolic ornamental staff or 'wand', a phallic symbol, denoting royalty, imperial authority and sovereignty. She was often depicted with myrtle, an aphrodisiac, still used in bridal bouquets today Romans celebrated her day as 1st April being (April fool indeed) that was the central month of Spring in the Northern hemisphere associated with Ishtar (Easter) and was traditionally the first month of the year until the calendar was changed. Ishtar is Venus and Venus is Aphrodite the same goddess as Inanna, Artemis, Diana etc. As such, *Diana is Easter-Ishtar*, a harvest festival goddess of abundance, *Spring*, symbolic of the *Eternal Spring* of Eternal youth from which her *true* legend is derived in long forgotten lost history (just as Mother Mary has no history) a history when the *goddess reigned*. Blooms, flowers and new life were associated with her in a time when humans were One before the split when 'age' and 'time' became our only drivers. The original androgynous was a self-procreating feminine with masculine *internal* testicles for *self*-creation. As was Ra and other gods 'self-created' and Easter is when Jesus was 'born', it appears 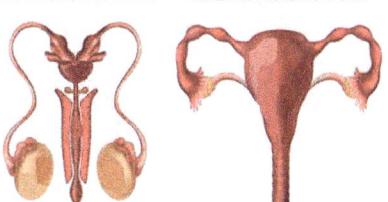 everything about the all-in-one Prime Goddess *original being* was stolen and passed off as masculine. But then it is a dick cult, after all.

Easter eggs and the Easter bunny represents the constellation Lepus depicted as a rabbit or hare said in mythology to be 'hunted by Orion and his dogs', Sirius A and B. Again, we are being told the *Goddess of Light* is being pursued by the 'king' and his 'dogs', the dark side of the feminine attacking the High Feminine, the Lady, the sluts attacking the virgin, degrading the light side of the feminine *see*, the pantheon of fairy tales where the wicked witch or the evil stepmother and cruel sisters try to poison 'beauties' innocent by marring her kindness and innocence with their venom as they try to 'win' prince charming or more beautiful. They lock her up, put spells on her and otherwise wreck her life. Sound like me. The Lepus hair-rabbit constellation is also associated with the Moon Rabbit and was known as 'Arsh al-Jawza' in Arabic meaning 'Throne of Jawza'. Jawza in Arabic is Orion *and Gemini* so Arsh al-Jawza means 'Throne of the Central One'. The king elevates himself via the goddess again. It's also known as 'the camels quenching their thirst' while Jesus said, 'it is easier for a camel to pass through the eye of a needle than a rich man to reach heaven'. The camel carries the *waters* symbolic of the feminine and the 'eye of the needle' *is the phallus* as the electrical current circulates and counter-circulates between the masculine and feminine 'fire and water'. Therefore, heaven and sex are intimately linked and as rich men are the 'dark side' then they will not reach the realm of heaven, Queen of Heaven, if they are self-serving as rich men invariably are. The rabbit on the moon is said in China to be the 'companion of the Moon Goddess' who 'pounds the elixir of life', depicted as rice – *the grain*, in the mortar and pestle in another reference to the Christ Seed, *grain god and goddess*. She is associated with a 'benevolent or malevolent emperor', the light and dark side of the masculine, known as an archer. The archer is Sagittarius and the hunter is Orion. So, April 1st being April Fool's Day is actually a masonic *inside joke* that the real fool here is the feminine, women, the Goddess. On 15th April 2019, the middle point of Spring, they *burned down* Notre Dame which means *'Our Lady'* just as the burned down the Twin Towers.

The constellation Orion is always portrayed with his 'dog', the Dog Star Sirius, at his 'heel' in the night sky. Masons have interpreted this to mean *he* is the dog's 'master' and *she* is to be loyal to him or 'man's best friend' but he is not loyal to her. Never has been. The 'dog' (goddess) is depicted in Beauty and the Beast as the 'foot stool' at the heel, under the foot, of the relaxing beast and also appears to have two dusters on each end. In pre-Christian societies (as with pre-Islamic tribes worshipping the feminine) the  Orion constellation was known as Frigg's Distaff or Freyja's Distaff. Frigg is the Goddess of Friday and fascinatingly, given what we've learned about fairy tales and 'weaving' spells symbolised by the spindles, 'needles' and 'pricks' of Rumpelstiltskin etc., a 'distaff' is a tool for *spinning* designed to keep the unspun fibers untangled, like hair, most commonly used to hold wool or flax. This 'weaving' leaves *many* weird coincidences around people especially celebrities and politicians who are practicing tantric sex using their pineal gland all-seeing eye or 'winged serpent' of Kundalini to *see* the desired outcomes of events and thus 'weave' things to suit themselves. The Golden Fleece is the 'Aries' constellation ruling the head, the hair-hare (the rabbit?), and the 'golden fleece' represents the *hair* of the halo-crown. So, 'flaxen-haired' is a common term describing golden yellow to near white hair as is 'flax' and 'wool' and 'gold' and 'spinning' and the 'head' and 'hair' etc., all describing the enlightened crown and activated nervous system *transcending* 3D reality accessing the 5D where we can do some *real work* to stave of the dark masters using these powers while not falling to darkness *like them*.

So, fellas if you think the Goddess is airy fairy just remember, these Masons have been 'worshipping' her for eons and they have done *very* well out if it. 'Sacred Marriage' is sacred sex and today we know it as *Tantric Sex* or *Transcendental Sex* practiced in India for millennia encouraged between a husband and wife hence, the serious approach to physical communions in those regions. Only it's not *just* sex. It was sacred ritual *lovemaking* taught by the temple priestesses and the arts of sexual pleasure in the home that, among other things, unlocks the 'lock and key' of the universe, *see right*. The Vatican symbolises the yoni vagina and obelisk phallus, the penis 'sword' and the 'cross' or 'key' of the 'keyhole', the vagina, *symbolising* accessing the universe and the 'eye' of god, the pineal gland 'all seeing eye', via the vesica piscis aka crossed *wedding rings* to access the spinal nervous system *unlocking the chakras* to make him more of a 'king' among ordinary men and turn her into a 'queen'. God and Goddess. The Vatican is one big penis 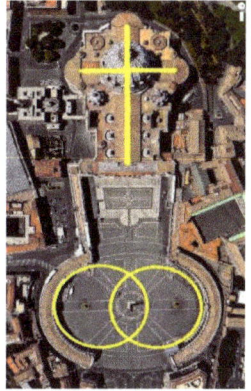 and vagina. Priest Malachi Martin who was Professor of Paleography at the Vatican's Pontifical Biblical Institute and other priests claimed the Pope was a 'false prophet' and that the Vatican was a place of black magic and satanism where children and babies are abused and even sacrificed. He blew the whistle on Vatican Satanic pedophilia claiming an 'enthronement ceremony' was held there in 1963 (369 again) by Satanic Cardinals and that there was an 'irremovable presence of a malign strength' that 'knowledgeable Churchmen called the 'superforce' tied to the installation of Pope Paul VI's reign in 1963. He said, 'Satan is having his last stand, this is his Waterloo, but he is going to destroy as much as he can before he is finally shoved out of the abyss again chained by Michael' describing demons as 'sophisticated spirits who are there to harm us and they're real' *[nods vigorously in agreement]*. In the documentary *Hostage to the Devil* it was revealed Malachi Martin (note, MM) was the inspiration for the film *The Exorcist* and strangely died when his CIA friend Robert Marrow drove him to an exorcism where a 'possessed child', 'the bait', was the alleged culprit behind the death of the priest when he mysteriously died after being pushed by an 'invisible force' and suffered head trauma in the fall. He saidt it was the most disturbing thing he'd ever seen in all his years working for the U.S. government. This is The Force humanity are to destined to deal with in a fateful spiritual showdown of good vs. evil. Light vs. Dark!

The galaxy is made up of 'cycles', *rings*, quantified mathematically as 'time' although we have been led to believe time is all there is. This isn't true. So, The Lord of the *Rings* is not just wedding rings. The symbolism extends to the cycles or 'rings' of the Ages, time cycles, as we enter into the Age of Aquarius, a new cycle or new 'ring' or circle, as the dick cult prepare to install their greatest and latest new Lord or Messiah of this coming cycle or 'ring'. The 'lord of the rings' is the One World Leader over the Age of *Aquarius*, the last great 'cycle' or 'circle' in a series of *cyclic* Ages spanning at least 26,000 years and perhaps even the mega cycle of 52,000 years! The One will need to come into play via 'wedding rings', or marriage, as a chaste honourable woman gives birth to this piece of shit to add kudos to these corrupt men and their globalist ambitions, *see;* Jacquelin Bouvier and Diana Spencer, innocent, beautiful and young swept up in men's politics. The ring is also the torus field, a protective energetic auric 'ring' around the body. J.R. Tolkien's LOTR's found its roots in Richard Wagner's *Ring of the Nibelung* often referred to as the *Ring cycle* or simply *The Ring* (*see*, the dark coding of the horror movie The Ring). The ring story is based on an old Germanic tale *Ring des Nibelungen* and has four parts: 'Das Rheingold' – *The Rhinegold*, 'Die Walkure' – The Valkyrie, 'Siegfried' the 'hero' and the final part 'Gotterdammerung' *Twilight of the Gods*. The root word definition of Rhine is [Gaulish] *'Renos'* means 'flow' so The Rhinegold literally translate as the 'golden flow' or for our purpose, universal feminine Aether! This is referenced in the movie The Golden Compass as 'dust' that gives a very good description of it, once again, dressed up as 'fiction'. The Valkyrie were maidens in Norse mythology who *'guarded the lives and ships of those dear to them'* and could cause death to those they did not favour associated with fairness, *brightness, gold* and bloodshed. The root word of Seigfried is 'victory' and in Sanskrit *'overcome, masters'* in Old High German 'frithu' is *'peace'* and Pro-Indo European *'to love'*. This is our victory and Twilight of the Gods' as we overcome the masters and peace and love reigns again. Folks, I'm here to tell you we're going to overthrow the alien-demonic masters, the 'gods', 'the devil', it's a prophecy that has lasted the test of time no matter how they try to bury it.

This *epic* follows the struggle of gods and heroes to possess the 'magic ring' that grants dominion over the whole world. The ring was forged by a dwarf (demon) from 'gold he stole from the Rhine maidens' three goddesses of the river, the Trivedi or triple goddess, who told him the Rhine gold, golden flow, *'gleams in the rays of the rising sun'*. This is the activated glowing chakras lighted by the Aether. Inscribed with magic runes, the ring's purpose is *to rule the power of feminine replication* by a fearful magical act called 'denial of love'. The 'chief of the gods' (basically the King of the alien hybrid royalty) is assisted by the *fire god* Loge (Satan and the dark side of tantric sex, the *fires* of his loins) to steal the ring although is forced to give it the 'giants' (aliens-demons) to build Asgard *[Old Norse 'Garden' 'yard' or 'enclosure' aka another dimension]*. The giants threaten if they are not given the 'ring' they will take the Goddess Freia who *'provides the gods with the golden apples that keep them young'* this is the *eternal* youth of the torus energy field 'apple' of the pure feminine Aether, *eternal spring*, the waters of the 'flow', lifeforce, chi, prana etc., the 'fountain of youth' or 'spring' of new life and 'flower of life', *see right*. During WWII the Nazi's gave 'Death's Head' rings to elite soldiers shrouded in occult mystery they then killed these soldiers as they believed their power would be transferred via the ring just as they 'transfer' the power of the goddess via the wedding ring. The ring finger is the only finger with a vein running directly to the electromagnetic energy centre, the heart! *See right*, the Guangzhou Circle building in China. Ancient Chinese folklore tells of black magicians who would have sex with a woman and drain her of energy, her life force being siphoned. Ultimately, *the ring is restored to the Rhine Maidens*, the progenitor goddess of the flow, after much battling and betrayal as it sends men mad who try to attain *incorrectly*. The ring is the torus field, *right*, as well as the halo, the wedding ring and the circle loops or cycles of the Ages of 'time' and 'space' it is also the trajectory of planets, the vesica piscis, the 'flower of Venus' and the Flower of Life. The apple is the heart and the torus field. It's all replication. The 'feminine replication' gives birth endlessly and they have stolen the concept of her replication and replicated negativity instead of her golden flow of life and love, The Light! That's why a women, not a man, will take down the devil. The Heart is Love, Love is Light, Light is information, data, frequencies, the Universe, all overlapping symbology describing the *electrodynamics* of human energetics interconnecting, *flowing*, with the One, *The Uni-verse*, which translates as 'One Song'.

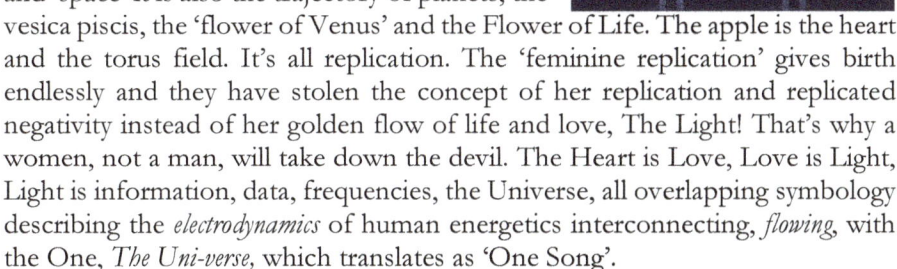

The dick cult's genital architecture is increasingly prevalent worldwide, *see right*, 1. Muslim mosque, 2. Guangxi Media Centre, 3. Guangxi Sports Centre, 4. flaccid penis Christian Science Church in Dixon (dick-son) whose slogan is 'Rising Up', 5. 'Skytower' *biggest* office building in Poland, 6. Qatar's World Cup *2022* Stadium *(world 'cup' 2022, 11:11 is a vagina chalice?)*, 7. the People's Daily

Newspaper, China, 8. Abandoned NASA station. Virgin Galactic's spaceport vagina, *right,* is a testament to an 'elongated pupil'. Yes, tantric sex *foresight* in the Boys Dick Cult Space Program secret weapon. I can't wait to see the dick rockets 'docking' at the space vag. I can't wait to fly Vag Air their slogan is "the wind between my things". *See right,* The DickCorp rocket by Jeff Bazos who auctioned an *11*-minute flight for *28 million dollars!* Called 'Blue Moon - Blue Origin', *blue for boys,* this says males are the *original* force turning the feminine 'blue' imprinting the masculine nob onto the feminine galaxy again. *Corporations* are the *new royal space elite* scrambling to get onboard. *Biggus Rocketus!* In Star Trek they say a nuclear winter occurred in the first twenty years of the new millennium and 60 years later they had their first warp flight. It's literally playing out on screen as Captain Kirk goes into space heralding the crash our civilisation rebrand their gods to make people believe times have change. But it's the same old bag of dick tricks and they won't get away with it *this* time!

It's highly symbolic that two females, Hathor and Cleopatra, were the first and last pharaohs of Egypt. Alpha and Omega. Beginning and End. Mother Nature created man and, if necessary, she will end them. Therefore, to reinforce their power over the goddess they kill her. It's therefore *no coincidence* that the signature perfume assigned to Princess Diana was *Isis* as well as *Hermes* 24 Faubourg as they depict the Goddess, the Mother and Wife, bowing to a gay God, Hermes. I see a theme happening here. It *literally* looks like the Goddess is worshipping the 'sun' aka *the son,* males, *the King,* again on her hands and knees just like Mary. Wtf? Diana of the infamous *virgin* status and Hermes of the infamous Caduceus dick fame synonymous with the 'kundalini' and sacred sex of the secret dick cult and although attributed to Hermes, *originally* the caduceus was carried by *Iris,* a young maiden. It always traces back to her. Let's get this straight, the 'virgin' is human women, the 'devil' is a reptilian polysexual male alien who *must* be 'god' over her yet the true 'god' is human men.

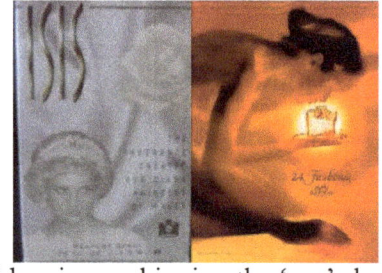

When Mary Magdalene fled to France after the death of Jesus Christ it was said she was pregnant with his bloodline. Some say that the person who was crucified was not Jesus, a stand-in, and Jesus must have surely met up with Mary again. Some claim *Mary* was the Prophet and Jesus was *her* 'disciple'. *No,* that's just *not* possible! Let me reiterate the practice of tantric sex enlightenment gives one the power of *foresight* over multiple 'time' lines probabilities and outcomes.

How did Virgin Galactic put it? The 'elongated pupil'? Yes, intuition, psychic abilities – the whole lot! Anyone practicing this in its purest form would know *well in advance* any attempts on their lives. That's why I couldn't understand at first *how* these great tantric 'kings' kept getting assassinated; Kennedy, Julius Caesar, Osiris, Jesus, Alexander the Great who 'died' at 33 at in Babylon a place of 'sacred marriage' some claiming he was poisoned. Maybe these guys aren't 'dying'? But if they are and didn't see it coming then they weren't the 'kings they made themselves out to be and were, as often the case, enveloped in ego *posing* as great kings, *gods even,* of tantra when in actually they were only *partially* enlightened. And got taken out as a result. There's a different between practicing occultism, black magic and demonic possession (which sees outside the timeline too) and practicing tantric sex or electrochemical energetic enlightenment accessing multiple dimensions *naturally*. It's the devil and angel, synthetic or organic, digital or analogue, operating *outside* the physical switched-on on the *inside*. I can tell you from personal experience, the organic is *much* better at this. I've seen their trickery. It's hard to be set up when you've already watched the movie so-to-speak by unlocking the inner *higher self,* accessing the astral 'menu' of the life-movie. Demons will trick someone in order to knock them off but an open third eye chakra will *see* what is happening *long* before it happens. Kennedy was a *known* practicing Satanist. He was also infirm meaning *unwell* and likely *unable* to really perform the long-drawn-out processes of tantric sex meditation. He was dubbed 'two-minute Jack' for good reason. Jesus accessing his heart Chakra meant that not only was he a good man (eventually) but also an incredibly powerful man. He would have *known* what they were doing. That's the whole point of this 'godlike' power, you become untouchable.

Aristocrats are *obsessed* with France because out of Jesus Christ's bloodline via Mary, came the Merovingian kings and the Templars who knew the secrets of all this. John F. Kennedy married Jacqueline Bouvier for her *French* lineage just as Michael Jackson married Lisa-Marie Presley for a baby from the 'King' *literally demanding a baby*. Prescilla Presley even said he 'had an agenda' to get a baby out of Lisa-Marie who described Jacko as having an 'intoxicating' energy that 'locked into you'. We've heard *that* before. These men are so ruthless. Jacqueline was descended from the French Bouvier's of the ancient house of Fontaine and Vernous who were *provincial* aristocrats of Poitou and Touraine. This is why Beauty and the Beast and Cinderella are classical *French* fables set in France along with the Frog Prince (French are colloquially called frogs) as a *Common* girl, human Goddess, marries a Royal Prince, reptilian royalty hence Toad Hall or 'Frogmore' where the Windsor's are entombed. It's all code. The Bouvier's as *provincial* aristocrats were old-school *country* society not the big city movers and shakers. France is also famous for the French revolution against the aristocracy and there are something of these secret societies trying to, on the one hand, keep the aristocracy in power and on the other hand break away from the old traditions and start something new, a new space-age republic, *see,*

America, the greatest *idealistic* industrialist republic *ever* however secretly owned and operated *they are* by aristocracy *worldwide*.

So, it's intriguing that St Germaine-de-Pres in Paris was once the Temple of Isis, a High Feminine temple, also a burial place of the mysterious and powerful Merovingian Kings for good reason. It's claimed they carry the bloodline of *Satan aka* the line of Cain of Abel slaying fame, whose dad was the 'snake'. The very name Paris is from Roman Latin *Par-Isis* meaning 'near the temple of Isis' shortened to *Paris*. This sacred city is colloquially termed the 'City of Love' and why the beautiful French language is 'the language of love' and the passionate mouth kiss is a 'French Kiss' and condoms are called 'Frenchies'. The French and love, huh? Something's going on. Tantric-sacred sex is the art of lovemaking and at our time in history all things 'love' related is under attack especially Paris and the French people. Even the word 'love' is phonetically *evol* or 'evil' backwards. Napoleon commissioned the Place de l'Etoile which translates as 'Place of the Star' since renamed the Arc de Triomphe de l'Etoile and translates as 'Triumphal Arch of the Star'! It is the largest triumphal arch in the world twice the size of the Roman Arch of Constantine on which it is modelled. Constantine was said to have given the pagan gods the boot in ancient Rome leading to the installation of the Roman Catholic Church (same mob). Many of these arches were built *worldwide* and an eternal (tantric) flame, *see*, Vesta aka Isis, was lit at the Place de l'Etoile in 1920. The arches are a reference to 'arcs' or ark of the covenant, it is Joan of Arc practicing tantra to get her psychic abilities and Noah's 'ark' rescuing all life from the flooding vengeful feminine waters. *A ship!* It also is the 'wedding arch'. Pathetically, in modern times, it is the *golden arches* of MacDonald's in an indication of how superficial all this really is how they laugh even at their own doctrines. It is also the arc of the rainbow, the visible light spectrum, that correlates with the chakras unlocked via sacred-marriage aka tantric sex which was once taken *very seriously*. The Arch is a celebration of independence from colonial and royalist rule who have kept the secrets of tantric enlightenment to themselves and attempted to take over the world with it. This Arc de Triomphe radiates a 'star' of Parisian avenues from its centre placed along the central axis of Paris 26.5 degrees off East thus aligning perfectly with the star, Sirius, ergo Isis! The Triumphal Arch of the Star is the Triumphal Arch or Sirius, *the Goddess,* as is the Washington Monument aligned with Sirius on Independence Day. As said, it is a woman who will win our independence from satanic 'royalty' and *precisely* why Diana was killed near there to kill the goddess before she kills them.

Diana was famously titled in one news article as 'The Queen of Heaven'. Isis was called Queen of Heaven as was Mother Mary and so many others in another reference to tantric-sacred sex and the heavenly bliss experienced via the 'goddess', the wife. Diana died in the Pont D'Alma tunnel which translates as 'bridge of the soul' or 'gateway to heaven'. It is the Golden Gate (bridge) of the soul thank you, San Francisco. 'Heaven' is the ultimate bliss-orgasm-awakening or 'the light' and final chakra, the heart, unlocked *in a man* via sacred-tantric sex. So, it's no coincidence this tunnel was an ancient sacred site dedicated to the Roman *Moon* Goddess, *Diana the Huntress*. Lord Earl Spencer, Diana's own brother, made mention of Diana the Huntress at her funeral! It's one big ritual and she was offered up, a lamb to the slaughter, like Kennedy. They all gained from her death. 'Hey, thanks for your sacrifice'. She *didn't* offer herself. In ancient times the sacrifice had to *offer* themselves *willingly* for the 'gods' to appreciate otherwise the ritual was meaningless. Again, they spin it however they like as hypocrites and narcissists usually do thinking the old ways are no longer relevant yet using them for whatever they can gain. As such, Diana's light, her soul, was *stolen* from her the way they steal everything from the goddess including her resources but then Satan is a thief, Prince of Thieves. The ancient goddess Diana of Ephesia had many 'breast's' symbolic of eggs as the ancients felt the egg was symbolic of the soul. It is also symbolic of mother's milk loaded with nutrients causing babies brains to grow to *80%* of its adult size by the age of four. Breasts are symbolic of the 'milk' of Christ Seed Enlightenment, the Land of *Milk* and Honey, in the feminine aspect.

The Pont D'Alma tunnel was built by the secretive Merovingian pagan kings of the cult of Diana (aka Isis) representative of Mother Nature and the universal life force as a fine feminine fire, *Aether*, chi, prana and the bloodline of Jesus from Mary. This site was where they practiced ritual sacrifice and it was extremely important the sacrifice die underground in the 'temple' as symbolically the 'temple' represented the human body and the *inner temples* of the chakras, the feminine Church, symbolic of mother nature's caves etc. This is where the Merovingian's would duel to the death as they believed their soul would go straight to 'heaven' at this spot via 'the bridge' hence, the 'bridge of the soul'. Therefore, Paris is the City of Sirius, the City of Isis, *the Goddess*, which is why *Princess* Diana, the *Goddess* Diana, was murdered there as they send the message that the Goddess is actually a princess and a *princess* is beneath the *King*, and she is dead. Long live the king! A *black flame* (dark side of tantra) 'coincidently' appeared at the place where she died as far back as 1989 considering the 'Eternal Flame' tended by the Vestal *Virgins*, given she was a famous virgin, symbolic of the pure fine feminine fire of the Goddess, Aether, the light bearer, *Lady Liberty* the Sovereignty Goddess! She grants a man or indeed a whole county it's sovereignty from royal rule so in killing the goddess, they ensure their rule. Killing the goddess is *killing the revolution* and it was done in France deliberately as the home of the greatest revolution against *hereditary* rule in history, the French Revolution! May history repeat per feminine replication.

The First French Empire was ruled by Napoleon Bonaparte founded in 1804 and dissolved in 1814 their emblem depicting Isis enthroned at the bow of a ship, *previous image*, under the star Sirius and included bees and a winged staff similar to the caduceus. Bees were another ancient symbol of tantric sex and the Christ seed enlightenment of Milk and *Honey* while the staff-caduceus is the Kundalini rising up the spine unlocking the chakras. Up until then the Parisian coat of arms was the Emblem of the Marchands de L'eau the 'merchants of the water' who went on to become the famous Buccaneers and Privateers of the Caribbean (often Jews). The French have deep knowledge of all this sea/water related feminine esoterica, *see*, humans as 'vessels' and females as 'ships'. The first year of the revolution was celebrated as huge crowds gathered under a statue of Isis. Two hundred years later celebrating the Bicentennial of the Revolution inaugurated by President Charon, the statue of Place de la Bastille overlooks the new Louvre *pyramid* and an Egyptian *obelisk*. Male symbols. No goddess here. What they're saying is the boys club-dick cult have taken power over the rising feminine so it's no coincidence then that the 'palace-pyramid' contains the world's largest *treasure*, an art museum containing approximately 38,000 objects dating from prehistory to the 21st century and like most museums, much of their artefacts are *stolen* from other people's countries and cultures throughout history despite requests to have them returned. Thieves. They steal everything. They celebrate thievery.

    The realisation of the ancient Egyptian 'One World' patriarchal King system is funneled via modern political-religious conduits rebranded for a new-age of corporatism aka neo pagan fascism. This 'one world' is supposed to herald the coming of a new 'messiah', a new mega-male 'King', as opposed to the return of the feminine. Yet there is some sort of dissent in the world of Masonry as some Masons strive to return balance to our planet in adherence with original lore of old and ancient prophecy returning the Mother, the high feminine, to her rightful place in society. *It's their own knowledge.* Others aren't content until they have destroyed everything and lord over a dust bowl aka Mad Max style! *This* is the battle of light and dark but behind both sides is the same force. Their repeated attempts at creating this 'one world' fails because they keep trying to install a global patriarchy, a man's world, on a *feminine* planet, a woman's world, and god forbid women should ever find out about *that!* Women will create a one world of togetherness and family as their hyper-masculine plans are incompatible with a nurturing feminine planet and simply won't work which is why some force always crashes them back to zero point and starts all over again. At this time they can't afford to disintegrate into the dark ages of the past *again* and in learning about the rise and fall of these ancient masculine civilisations who have all historically rejected the feminine, they now realise how *imperative* it is that they 'return the feminine' (real or orchestrated) and move on, evolve into space, otherwise it's all over *again*. If there's one thing you can rely on with elite men it's their egos, greed and selfishness! They want to go down in history as the first *officially* recorded people of Earth to go out into space with a fake dick cult space program while they hoard the real programs for themselves and now is their *big chance* to do it. They aint gonna miss this opportunity so, in many ways, the future is assured with or without you in it.

The Spartan queen, Leda, *note*, the phonetics 'leader' considering the Arabic name for Sirius is 'leader', was the mother of the Twins, Gemini, or Caster and Pollux who was seduced by Zeus (another name for Satan) in the guise of a swan. The swan is also a reference to the fable of the ugly duckling that despite a clumsy start turns into a beautiful swan as was Princess Diana a self-professed 'non-starter', an ugly duckling, a 'loathly woman' turned into beauty overnight per the ancient fables! It's all fairy tales like her 'fairy tale' wedding sending the signal to the Universe that there is no 'happily ever after' on Planet Earth for women. A few weeks before Diana's death she wore the famous 'Swan Lake Necklace' to a performance at the Royal Albert Hall of Swan Lake, a story about the light and dark side of the feminine. Even the carats of the diamonds and dimensions of this piece have numerology encoded into it including being sold on 18/12/1999 meaning 6+6+6=18 reducing to 9 while 6+6=12 which reduces to 3, The Empress, while 1999 is 666 inverted. The Goddess Isis was associated with the Rose as the petals and rose colour is a reference a woman's vagina as well as 'motherhood' and the milk ducts in breasts, *see right,* the ancients new a lot more about anatomy than we give them credit for as *actual* milk ducts look exactly like flowers. Kathy O'Brien mind control survivor and author of *Trance Formation of America* spoke of the Order of the Black Rose, the darkest side of all this, connected to the very top. Joseph Kennedy had his daughter Rose cruelly lobotomized for sneaking out of a Catholic Convent to have sex with men. He then had her slapped in an asylum for the rest of her miserable days and when her mother visited after 14 years her daughter tried to attack her. No wonder. These people are fucken

sick. The song by Elton John *'Good-bye England's Rose'* was yet another reference to the 'rose line' and the Order of the Rose linked to the Catholic Church and the Jesuits (Hogwarts School of Wizardry). They are treacherous, even her own brother and friend praising her end. There were rambling roses and water lilies on the island where Diana is entombed in a nod to the Goddess and all things symbolic of Mother Nature specifically flowers of certain types as lilies and lotus flowers are a symbol of chakra enlightenment. We must not forget another Goddess entombed on an island on the water, Lady Liberty in New York, considering they are *symbolically* one and the same. There was four black swans set on the lake complete with 36 oak trees in a nod to the Green Man-*Oak* King and the Oracles of Apollo who wrote their messages on oak leaves. Diana was 36 when she died in a nod to the 369 of the Egyptian Great Ennead and she is in modern times as in ancient times Diana The Swan, The Lady of the Lake. Lady Di. Or more specifically *'lady die'*.

Called 'sexual alchemy' and sexual Kung Fu, tantric sex causes euphoria or a 'birds eye view' and sense of flying or feeling 'high'. This is why the ancients included references to eagles, falcons, ravens, skylarks *and swans!* The black swan is a symbol of the dark side of female tantric sex, *see*, Swan Lake, as is the raven, crow and 'black hawk' symbols of the dark side of masculine tantric sex, *see*, Damien in The Omen. The phrase 'the eagle has landed' brings a whole new meaning to the *moon* landing i.e. the dark side of male tantra, bird of prey, conquering the feminine moon goddess, *again*. Swan Lake was fashioned from Russian and German folktales and tells the story of Odette a princess turned into a swan by an evil sorcerer's curse. The play premiered in 1877, *see*, 7/7 of the male-female 'twin' chakra towers. While no one knows who wrote the original libretto some sources for the play include *The White Duck* (*see*, snow white and the ugly duckling) and The Stolen Veil, yes, stolen from ancient Arabian fairy tales where Oscar Wilde enhanced the ancient telling of the Dance of the Seven Veil's or the seven chakras *unveiled*. Swan Lake is yet another telling of Beauty and the Beast and Cinderella as Prince *Siegfried (see, Ring of the Nibelung aka the Lord of the Rings)* is celebrating his birthday and his mother, the Queen. Concerned about his carefree lifestyle she informs him he *must* choose a bride although he is unhappy he cannot marry for love. Whilst hunting with his friends, *see*, Orion, the Hunter and Diana the Huntress, he aims at a swan that transforms into a beautiful maiden. She tells him she has had a terrible curse put on her by and evil 'owl-like' sorcerer (the owl shows up in Satanism *see*, Bohemian Grove). By day she is a swan but at night by the lake she becomes human again *(see, Shrek)*. The spell can only be broken if one who has never loved before swears love forever to her. It ends tragically upon a misunderstanding as the prince is tricked into thinking another woman is Odette. Realising his error he begs her forgiveness and although she forgives him *the betrayal cannot be undone* so, as you do, they both jump into the lake and die. It always ends tragically for the lovers see Romeo and Juliette. In a 'divine' treatment of the ending of Swan Lake they *ascend* to 'heaven' (aka tantric sex) united together forever. The themes are all there, frivolous male royalty, common girls, lost love, birds, water, trickery, spells, ascension, true love, heaven. I'm surprised they didn't throw in a unicorn.

Once again, we look toward astrology and astronomy as all these ancient fables are about the stars and the origins of humankind and their masters. The reality is 'the swan' is most significantly the star Deneb, a first-magnitude sun in the constellation Cygnus, the 'swan', which makes up a 'solar trinity' including the stars Altar and Vega. The *Vegus* nerve is very important to tantric sex running from the heart to the brain for pineal enlightenment. This helps explain the *extra weird* bloodbath mass shooting in Las Vegas near the *Black Pyramid* with a *sphinx* an *obelisk* and a light 'shaft', yes, the electric dick the dark side of tantric sex, *right*. Honestly, once you know this fable their rituals all of a sudden make a ridiculous sense. You mean all these people are dying for this? It's as bad as finding out my life was destroyed  because they wanted to project their 'goddess' crap onto me. What a crying shame I lost all that great work of mine because of this fucked-up aristocratic OCD inbred shit about fabricated 'goddesses' and their need to be 'king'. It's pathetic. The 'trinity' is the downward triangle, the chalice of the feminine *procreating* hips, as is 3 the number of the Empress and the family of life which isn't much of a family if she doesn't produce babies.

They had Diana lined up long before they knocked her off making sure they coded all these symbols and numerology around her in the demise of a *massive* feminine Goddess character at this *crucial* time in history when the feminine is prophesised to 'return' and the lover's reunite, men and women, the Twin Towers in unison worldwide! It's not so much the Return of the King as the Return of the Queen! Credo Mutwa the official Zulu historian said their legends claim the 'gods' came down and the people were taken into caves and out one cave came men and out the other cave women. Central Mexican and American Southwest mythologies believed caves were the place of origin that humans were born, literally, the 'cave' man, and that Earth was great womb or as the Bible and the Egyptian god Khemu said, 'made of clay' literally dirt, earth, soil. Monkey Magic shows this theme at the beginning of the show. Plato described that Zeus 'fearing their power and split them in two', *the power couple*, to forever seek their other half to become whole again. In *Rev. 2:4* Jesus says, 'You have lost your first love' hence, the 'twin flame' phenomenon occurring at this time as this electromagnetic shift causes us to 'wake up' and remember what happened. *She* is every woman. *He* is every man. *It's their time to shine.*

The main female character 'Bella Swan' means *'beautiful swan'* in the Twilight Series set in *Forks* as this was where America's 1st official President, George Washington made the error of assassinating a *French* delegation in 1754. Ah, the French! The innocent Bella, as in Belle from *Beauty and the Beast* and Belle Starr 'beautiful star', has fallen into the grasp of a bunch of vampires while her boyfriend's middle name is Masen aka *Mason*. Vampire. These reptilians depict themselves as sexy vampires but there is nothing sexy about what they do. It's dressed up as love but it is much darker than that. Forks is home of the *'Spartans'* football club as they play out the 'myths' in modern times cobbling it all together in a hodge-podge of ancient themes even the latest Corona variant is called *Omicron*, a letter of the ancient Greek alphabet. Coding. Diana's perfume *Isis* consisted of white roses and violets - the colours of the crown chakra. Mary & Jesus, mother & son, were depicted with a 'halo' around their heads denoting enlightenment while Diana's last cause was exposing landmines with an organisation called *Halo*. Prince Harry too has been photographed with the 'Halo' organisation as the virgin mother gives birth to the enlightened son-sun, the man child as Harry-Hari regularly does the 'hidden hand' sign in his suit jacket. It's a hand sign that he's onboard. I'm no fan of royalty although they are born into it but given we live in the information age, do you really think they haven't done their *own* research on what happened to their mother? Of course, they have. The only person who ever showed them *real* humanity, love or *normality* was their dear mother, the queen of hearts. I can't imagine it would be easy dealing with the Satanic cabal and keeping a straight face once you find out what they did. Marilyn Monroe, Mary Magdalene, Mother Mary, MM, the year 2000. MW is Milky Way. *Right*, we see Diana's memorial fountain in the shape of a ring in a weird tribute to the Niberlung ring and 'denial of love'. People think

the Taj Mahal was built by an ancient king for his beloved wife yet his wife died in childbirth *giving birth to their 14th child*. Islamic Shah Jahan who commissioned the Taj Mahal known officially as the Rauza-e-Munawware *'the Illumed Tomb'* had a harem that numbered in the *thousands* his soldiers known for their *sexual violence*. Like the Washington Monument and the 14-piece obelisk in Trinity Square, it's not ironic Diana was pictured alone *reflected* in the waters of this despotic woman-hating palace of fake 'love'. Nothing is ironic with this lot. She was *another* breeder. Diana was born, named, groomed and killed to symbolically kill the feminine in our hearts and send the collective message to the universe that the Goddess is dead thus rebuking ancient stories prophesising her return. We will be discovering more tricks and insults from the dick cult as this unravels and we experience *the awakening of the force and the force of the awakening!*

Dhyana in Hinduism is 'reflection and observation'.

Chapter Eleven
THE WOMAN HATERS
Gorillas in my midst.

One of the reasons I managed to survive to this point is because I did my research *early* when the information was fresh. The truth is being overwritten as we speak but 20 years ago, and before that, there was some *excellent* information around before they started deliberately corrupting the data which is standard operating procedure for them. I knew that, firstly, when they approach you, they make out they are helping to win you over then set about trying to destroy your work by feeding you misinformation while simultaneously destroying your personal life. They feed you a little bit of truth then destabilize you with trickery, lies and false hope. Don't buy into it. Research what is offered to you, remain rational and calm and keep telling them to go fuck themselves. They are not your friends and never will be. So, here are a few rules I managed to figure out to deconstruct their Inverse Psychological *mind games* that they are trying to trap people with. What you are about to read is the essence of cruelty and is what you are *unknowingly* dealing with and what our ancestors dealt with. It's time you knew. You can never drop your guard with them, not ever, so don't think this is going to be over anytime soon, as they say, *no rest for the wicked!*

False support: if you want to change someone's mind initially agree with them, even support them, then wear them down over time by undermining their confidence and finding holes in their idea 'as a friend' to 'help' them. **Deliberate errors:** when a plan isn't going to plan make the target believe that errors, even major failures, are a part of 'the plan' to give the perpetrator a godlike stature of foresight and planning despite their *obvious* flaws. **Over-punishment:** when you want to manipulate someone to do your bidding but you hate them and want to punish them yet still want to keep them around to relish in their pain and suffering first hand, hurt them and if they fight back hit them with a repeated barrage of extreme ongoing violence and abuse while telling them they *don't understand* the 'the plan' because they are ignorant and unworldly. The target's 'inverse' nature or survival instincts will eventually kick in as they think the abuse and violence *must* be a part of a *bigger* more *elaborate* scheme and therefore, *necessary*. This is the martyr complex, an attitude where many people feel the need to die for 'god' or 'country' believing the pain and suffering is all part of some ultimately good cause or 'gods mysterious ways' to bring about a good ending. It's the 'happily ever after' and its always just around the corner so, *keep going!* As such, the target will go along with the crime, even submit to it, and support it as 'the answer', *see*, Naziism and the people who stood by and watched on explaining it all away as 'progress'. We see the same thing now en masse *globally* as 'inclusiveness' while burning buildings and 'diversity' while kicking someone's arse for not going along with the latest movement and as 'progressive' exposing little children to naked old men in the street. It's pride. Called Stockholm Syndrome many people jump onboard to be a part of an exclusive 'in' crowd of 'new-age' 'progressives'. To love their abuser. In this way the abuser can abuse the target endlessly and secretly *hate them* for not being smart enough to figure it out and being *so stupid* as to willingly comply with the abuse. **False 'Destiny'**: Play into the target's sense of kismet. Everyone has an inner child that is still alive in us all often trying to 'get out' that must be restrained by the 'adult' part of our personality, an inner psychological 'parent', protecting the naïve sensitive inner self from the *learned* dangers of the 'adult' world. There is some part of us that believes there is *still* magic in the world therefore, the abusers play into our childish sense of 'fate' and 'destiny' without directly confronting the inner child triggering our *secret beliefs* that we've never owned up to for fear of retribution against the inner child. Therefore, by feeding the target some information via mass media, or any other source, or making a situation occur that *appears* to be really helpful at a particularly tough time in the targets life, a 'miracle' to get them through, allows the target to believe that *somehow* you are secretly working behind the scenes for their benefit. This way you can then stall them *endlessly* buying time to figure out another angle to stop them completely. This often shows up an 'lucky numbers' or 'signs' that you are 'on the right track' and to 'keep going'. A little help that miraculously appears to assist but it's not enough assistance that the target actually *really* achieves anything of substance in order that the target works themselves to death for a cause that is *never realised*. There *are* miracles in this world and often you will see them in *hindsight* not in advance and you will realise you were being assisted by unseen elements but *not* by the forces *they* claim. The whole world has been living under the above basic rules of evolutionary sabotage for eons. Who has ever seen the realisation of a good cause let alone a *great* cause in our world's history? And no, I'm not talking about causes that involve war. I'm talking about causes that involve abject peace and all those who have ever spoken of it.

It's a terrible burden that has befallen the human race from a time long forgotten a time when we really were great. Slung down into darkness we were trying to evolve out of it ever since. It's definitely been the long way home. We are coming out of it now and comparatively, pound for pound, the ascension will happen fast, maybe a little too fast for some to keep up with, and yet we *will* do this big thing. It's not been easy but one way or another we are fumbling our way through. It's all coming out now. There have been endless attempts to suppress the emerging feminine and if we look closer at the writings of classical authors we find gaps in the social drapery allowing us to peer into an otherwise forbidden scene. Once again all you need is a few crucial details and everything else falls into place as we realise coded into the secret boy's clubs *own writings* from their *most famous* we can find the deliberate and calculated destruction of the feminine spirit! Read on if you dare. Nathanial Hawthorne wrote a short story called *The Birthmark* considering this mark is a well-known theme among Masons in that a prophesised feminine has a 'mark' on her right arm or right hand, the mark of the One, the light bearer, Lady Liberty. So, it's interesting that the story *The Birthmark* is about a woman with a *hand shaped* 'birthmark' on her *face*, her eyes red-rimmed as if crying her demeanor docile. She is sad and wary, *see right*. This story was cited as Hawthorne's distaste for the Reformation Movement however, this movement 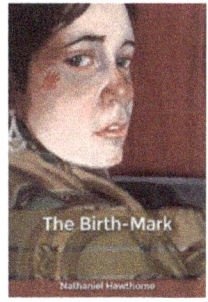 covered a number of different areas politically and socially at the time. Key areas of the 19th century Reformation Movement in the United States was women's suffrage, child labour, abolition of slavery, temperance (a women's movement against alcoholism and physical abuse from *mass* numbers of drunken men) as well as prison reform. Hawthorne's 'distaste' for the Reformation Movement doesn't drill down on exactly what part of the movement he was reticent to embrace. Did he despise the whole thing or just certain parts? How could you *not* be against child labour? Or did he despise one *particular* point that would then and now leave him wide open to the *disdain* of female demographics leaving long lasting *damage* to his public image? Would this open disdain jeopardise his place in history as a beloved literary luminary? Maybe we don't need to hear the information from the horse's mouth to figure out *what part* of the Reformation Movement so offended him.

As such, Hawthorne's *The Birthmark* about the 'mark' on his wife's face in the shape of a crimson *hand* floats to the top of my list of studies on how *deeply* these secret society elite males *hate* women *so intensely* it can only be described as an *institutionalised* mental illness. On its own the symbolic handprint on his wife's face is not of great significance but when we deconstruct the underlying symbolic *elements* hidden in this story and compare it with other major male writers of the time something weird starts to emerge. Hawthorne, like Shakespeare, is elevated to an almost mythical intellectual height. His symbolic meanings and double entendre's are historically accepted by 'scholars' (all male) to translate as meaning that the 'hand' shaped 'birth mark' is a husbands desire to see his wife as 'perfect' and in trying to eliminate her imperfections, she dies. How very educated and complex it all sounds! This story is really a terrible social slip-up, a tell-all, a peek into these men's inability, historically, to accept women as 'flawed' or simply as human *at all* if we take into account, at the time, the *torso fetish* of the *repugnant* corsets, ridiculous drapery and 'caboose' fixtures to enhance her rear. At the same time in the far east their *foot fetish* bound women's feet to the point of walking on stumps. Even in 'modern' times the cutting out of female's genitalia or FGM (female genital mutilation) *right*, are unspeakable acts of demonic abuse trampling the sacred power of 'marriage' and the 'wedding night' as these MEN cut open their often child bride's vagina with a *knife* before raping them affecting *200 million women and girls* alive today! There are secret sinister and *coded* Masonic neon signs all around indicating the *suppression of females* is not a 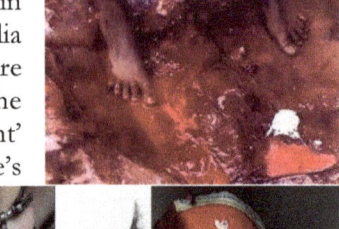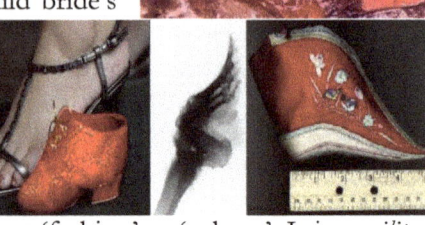mishap, not a misunderstanding and is not 'fashion' or 'culture'. It is a *military tactic* perpetrated against the trusting and unwitting feminine carried out with such *tactical precision* and so *long lasting* in nature that it is widely accepted as normal, unquestioned, yet it cannot be passed off as simply gender related 'differences'. It goes *much* deeper than that. You don't have to look far to see the secret war waged against women - *it's right in front of us*.

I compared Hawthorne's *The Birthmark* to Edgar Alan Poe's *The Oval Portrait*, Poe a very sinister man and Satanic practitioner, theorized in his 'philosophy of composition' that the 'rhythmical beauty of poetry was the creation of beauty' and that *'the most poetical topic in the world was the death of a beautiful woman'*. So, the death of a beautiful woman is *poetry in motion*, literally, according to these guys? What a piece of shit *he* was! These men should not be revered as luminaries, they should be exposed for the *femicidal* nut-jobs they are. Now may you look upon the countenance of the *type of men* who are behind the *institutionalised* shaming, slandering, raping, killing, torturing and spiritual hobbling of the great Divine Feminine spirit, the *Mother* of all 'gods' who turn out to be 'elite' men with deeply competitive natures who cannot bear the fac that it takes a woman to get them into this feminine world in the fist place. *What the hell is wrong with these guys?* It's not like they haven't had time to think about what they're doing, they've just perfected their hatred instead of halting it and once revealed the question is, how could we not see this blatant abuse earlier? The sects, cults and religions (*note*, sects and sex) behind all this are routinely carrying out the ultimate death of the feminine, no doubt about it, and its rooted in the jealousy of her beauty, grace and 'poetic' movement of her natural feminine motion, *her flow*, not just on Earth but throughout the cosmos as well. In a brutal 'man's' world her very beauty *alone* condemns her to death, *see*, the middle east, India and North Africa for *that* gem. The Oval Portrait made use of Poe's short story *The Raven* remembering the raven is a symbol of the dark side of male tantric sex. *The Raven*, in true cryptic Satanic Masonic style, elucidates the *cowardice* of this dark brotherhood who prey on those *most vulnerable* selling out the feminine for riches and power regardless of how their conscience might eat away at him.

In this story the raven sits on a bust of Athena as the narrator laments his *lost love! [blinks in disbelief]* As he sinks into bitterness and madness we can see upon deeper inspection he has in actuality *sold himself out* and that he is *his own worst enemy trapped in a boys club of lies and ritual deceit!* Athena was a powerful goddess whose symbols included the owl (wisdom), olive trees (tantric sex), snakes (the 'king's alibi' in the Garden of Eden referred to in the Raven), as well as the gorgon one of three fearsome goddesses who were 'monsters' two of whom were immortal. The third goddess was Medusa, a mortal girl, who was distinguished from the two ugly sisters (Cinderella, *again!*) due to her beautiful face while ancient Roman poet Ovid particularly praised the *glory of her hair* which was the 'most wonderful of all her charms'. Later her hair would be depicted as that of snakes although early on she was depicted with wings on her head symbolic of tantric-sacred sex *enlightenment* and Hermes who earlier was *Iris* most feared by Zeus the King of all Gods who split' the lovers in two 'fearing their power'! We've discussed already that the hair is a symbol of the nervous system outside the body based on tantric sex lore while the snakes are the *electricity* of the caduceus raising the kundalini up the spine opening the third eye and crown chakra to gain enlightenment. Sex is never far away in any of these myths while Medusa's name is said to come from the Greek word meaning 'guardian'. The myth goes that Poseidon too was so enamored by her 'hair' that he couldn't resist the temptation and raped medusa and impregnated her in Athena's Temple who was the goddess of war. Medusa was sworn to celibacy remembering 'virgins' were said to give birth to 'god-like sons' given Poseidon was after all a 'god' who appears now to be a reptilian breeding with a human woman like Queen Leda or Princess *Diana* the 'broodmare' the modern stand-in for the ancient 'goddess' Diana. Is this a *symbolic* nod *again* to the 'immaculate' conception of Jesus as also depicted in *Rosemary's Baby?* The temple was a sacred space so what we are *really* being told here is that a male 'god' entered the *hallowed ground* of the temple of Athena and as in modern times, he obviously had *no respect* for their boundaries (very symbolic!). It was in the Temple where he found the beautiful mortal girl, Medusa, a virgin no less, and raped her. Have you noticed these 'gods' always go after the 'mortal' (human) woman in these stories? Athena, whose father was Zeus the 'king of all the gods' upon hearing of Poseidon's rape of Medusa became enraged turning *Medusa* into a monstrous gorgon like her 'sisters' as punishment.

Okay, here's the translation: Medusa is a victim of a violent sexual assault by an older powerful statesman or 'royalty' aka 'god' (as did Ceasar and co declare themselves 'living gods') which is code for reptilian elites. Athena, a powerful reptilian female priestess and head of her order is actually a jealous old slapper who are all obsessed with sex, infidelity and breeding. It's basically the movie *Dangerous Liaisons* with Michelle Pfeiffer, Glenn Close and John Malkovich. Apprise yourself of *that* gem. The elite, huh? Weird. It's sordid and cruel but then it is a sex and death cult. So, Athena angry and jealous Poseidon had sexually gratified himself with a beautiful *younger* pure innocent *human* woman and, in the wicked stepmother routine per Cinderella, Belle and Beauty, she took out her rage at Poseidon *on the innocent Medusa.* An easy target for their *cowardice*, like Diana. Here we see the ancient Pompeii rendering of Perseus who looks like Hermes with *his* enlightened wings on *his* head aka tantric sex enlightenment. He holds the *decapitated* 'enlightened' head of Medusa who appears to be a very small rather frightened and startled little *girl* with a child-like head in size and demeanor. What we are seeing here is the most common theme of these depraved men who can't keep it in their pants (or their toga's) who rape an innocent girl then tarnish their *female victim* as a 'monster', 'slut', 'whore' and '*prostitute*' (thank you, Mary Magdalene). These are the usual signs even in modern times when a woman is  gender profiled by males, harassed in the workplace or the street or gang raped by a bunch or marauding male *demons* and she cannot get justice as 'she wanted it'. They've gotten away with this for so long its second nature and even *the law* in some states and countries even still! Her skirt was too short, her hair, her make-up or *something* was 'provocative' thus she was 'asking for it' and maybe she was just not from this bunch of creeps. We've been lied to about all these 'evil' women in history.

The story of Lilith is yet another example of this despicable and calculated treatment of innocent women at the hands of this filth who have even turned their depravity into entire religions that rule Mother Earth to this day and place the feminine at the *bottom* of an increasingly large masculine pile. After everyone else's grievances have been heard, woman are the *last cab off the rank* to be considered as even 'human' let alone to have *actual human rights!* As such, we see the rise of the fake revolution of female consciousness secretly rigged up by the masonic engineers *again*, queue, Britney Spears while terms 'pregnant women' and 'mother' are removed in favour of 'birthing person'. Get fucked. When *male* titles like 'Prince' are removed then I'll take your sad attack on the feminine and her *miracle of motherhood* a little more seriously. Lilith was Adam's 'first' wife in the Garden of Eden. Okay, let's just role with it and pretend we don't notice Adam and Eve were the only two people on Earth. Prior to Eve Adam, once again, wanted to 'be on top' in the classic 'missionary' position regarding sex but this also means he wanted to be 'on top' in general *ruling* over Lilith. Lilith refused as she was made 'made of the same stuff' as Adam so Adam went and whined to 'god' (a reptilian overlord) that Lilith would not bow down to him. 'God' then sent a shit ton of demons to punish Lilith and she, rightly, took off and they couldn't get her to come back so she was slandered a 'demoness' slandered as having sex with 'hundreds of demons' even though they sent demons to destroy her? But she had sex with them? R-i-ight. Makes sense. Then 'god' made Eve from 'Adam's rib', like offal, although Eve too wasn't keen to be 'under' Adam. This is the first mention of equality and women attempting to assert their position among an increasingly *annexed* boys club and losing the battle. It looks like Eve was in the process of enlightening Adam with the 'Tree of Knowledge' and her 'apple' aka sacred sex to give him the brain power he sorely needed when, just like the 'tower' of Babylon, 'god' ran them both off. He's got a funny habit of doing that probably because 'god' was afraid that they would become as enlightened as him. 'God' then said Eve would give birth in pain and suffering and Adam would toil for the rest of his days, life after life, in misery and slavery as punishment for trying to be more than a couple naked kids in a forest being perved on by 'god'. Reset. Repeat. And that's history.

Right up until the 1970's it was common practice around the world to have a 'marry your rapist' law, a rule of 'rape law' (made up by men) that allowed a man 'who commits rape, sexual assault, statutory rape, *abduction* or other similar act to be *exonerated* if he marries his female victim'. Often the perpetrator is then allowed to *divorce his current wife* and marry his victim!. This 'law' still continues to be practiced in some systems *even today!* Does that mean a man having sex with another man is allowed to rape him if one party decides they want to stop? Now we can see why, as the LGBT community grows, the sheer *hypocrisy* of so many 'laws' surrounding sex because, well, traditionally it was *only* a woman's problem but now it's a man's *and* trans problem too! Finally, the humans rights of the *person* who is crying and screaming is at long last being taken into consideration regardless of age, gender, preference or sex and includes children, the elderly (plenty of raping going on in old folks homes) as well as people who are unable to make informed decisions about intimate *adult* behaviour due to disability or intellectual challenges. *Now* rape laws are becoming more stringent as society changes but up until then, women, who were the usual victims of sexual assault, historically, could go, well, fuck themselves no pun intended. It just as much a *man's* issue now afraid a *gay man* will treat them the way they've treated women without a second thought for her rights or feelings.

Men need to stop pretending that women are somehow their personal sex toys and punching bags whether physically, verbally or in *any other way*. During the various COVID lockdowns domestic violence skyrocketed as largely frustrated male brats unleashed their immaturity and inability to comprehend emotions or the changing face of society on their vulnerable partners, usually female, who were *locked up* with them. And who is behind all the shutdowns and restructuring? Men. Oh sure, they wheeled out women leaders during the COVID pandemic to take the blame for what the masonic men *behind the scenes* were conspiring to do, inject mass numbers with poison as has been the plan long before any of these women fall-guys were put in place. This coincidental *sudden rise* in female politicians when everything goes to shit has been described as a 'golden age' for women, note, the *linguistic programming* that it's a 'golden age' of shitty decisions and cheap politics headed by mass numbers of *stupid bitches*. And in the wings mass numbers of *women* leaders fill the ranks of the *opposition* too. So, regardless of who gets in, it's women taking the blame for what the men have had in the pipelines for hundreds of years! It's *so coincidental* all these *women* came into power during a global pandemic of corruption, misery, crimes against humanity and restructuring the filthy system *for the benefit of men* behind the scenes. Attacking mummy again. In my first book 2020 & Beyond I actually 'predicted' an obvious emergence of female leaders at this time and that ultimately the real message here was that the one time women were in leadership positions they would be far worse than every generation of male politicians who had come before them in an attempt to slander the rising feminine and the 'return' of the 'goddess'. One again, slandered, framed, rigged-up and accused as being the *perpetrators* when actually it is and always has been men in secret dick cults who have created this mess. The *real* female leaders trying to do their jobs and emerge at this time are being targeted in the most hideous and brutal ways including, as in my case, a fucking demonic attachment that just coincidently was put on me at the end of 2018 when I was coming into my power *again* in lead up to the 2020 zodiac portals and alignments and the subsequent melt down *farce* of the global plandemic all of which I said was going to happen in my first book written in 2015! Unprecedented numbers of Australian politician just so happen to be women at this time as Australia got its *first ever* female majority in parliament in the ACT. Waddya know! Queensland and NSW premiers were women during the COVID fiasco while British Met Police Chief Sarah Everard was front and centre during the shit storm and Jacinta Arden prime minister of New Zealand. Just a coincidence of course when the world shuts down there are more women in power than ever seen before. Nothing going on there then.

Every woman has been on the receiving end of human rights abuses at the hands of men and a lot of women are so conditioned to believe this is normal behaviour, they *don't even know it's happening*. The abuse and suppression of the feminine *worldwide* should have, by now, raised a few eyebrows in the world of men. But no. It seems that even requesting, demanding and then *legally fighting* for female sovereignty on a feminine planet is an area that, even still, many males are struggling with. That said, Mother Earth is dying and I can't recall teams of women out in the forest cutting down the trees, or women going off to corporate wars so willingly in their corsets and layers of petticoats in the mud and filth or fishing out the oceans. It's women on this planet who do not have the blood on their hands the way men do, the last of the legitimate light in the human race, and *this* is the prime reason the reptilian system of alien male scum are *so terrified* of and *so keen* to vilify, abuse and destroy the rising feminine aspect of humanity *particularly at this time* sending the message to the universal mirror that women are morons. And that message will be fed back to us. There is such a thing as comeuppance or what goes around comes around and it will be the feminine's of this world who lead the confused masculine out of his own testosterone driven nightmare. *This* is why 'Isis' who is every woman was the 'ankh', *the anchor,* as unhinged men driven by their untempered fires destroy this once abundant *feminine* world.

In Poe's *The Raven* he mentions Pallas Athena, 'Pallas' meaning 'young woman' who also 'brandished a weapon', the goddess of war. In ancient times it was totally normal to have female military leaders, *see,* Boudicea Queen of the Celtic Iceni people in Britain 60AD who led fearsome raids against the Roman's in revenge after she was widowed and Roman's publicly flogged her and raped her daughters. Now *they* were asking for it. As archeology finally bends under pressure to *correctly report* history, we increasingly find more sites of female warriors and powerful women of ancient times. In Poe's 'Raven' he calls the Raven an 'evil thing' and a 'prophet' who is also the 'Tempter' and the 'Tempest' eluding to black magic and satanism. Poe also mentions Pluto the god of the Underworld husband of Persephone, a vegetation goddess. Vegetation is also synonymous with Osiris and Isis who were 'grain' gods. Osiris is also Woden (god of Wednesday one of my symbols) and as Woden is one-eyed we can see the connection to Horus, Osiris reborn, who was depicted with one eye. 'One eyed' is colloquial slang for being biased as was 'cyclops' and his 'one all seeing eye' a reference to the *pineal gland.* Woden is Odin. Poe is drawing on Odin's two ravens 'Huggin' from old Norse meaning 'thought', yes, they are very much about the mind, and 'Munnin' old Norse for 'Memory'. *Megamind.* Odin is 'raven god' or the dark side of tantric sex and the 'birds eye view' and 'wings' of enlightenment, IQ and superiority.

The raven has been associated with a supernatural spirit, being or demon (Greek 'daemon' provider or divider of fortunes) which accompanies a person in connection to their fate or fortune. Similarly, there seems to be a *female aspect* to this in a 'guardian angel' called Haninga and Fylgia connected to luck that can be passed down through generations of a family. Lady luck! These are your multigeneration satanic families with the same demons attached to them lifetime after lifetime. The masculine aspect uses memory, mind and spirit-demon while the feminine aspect uses happiness, a luck 'angel'. There is some insinuation that the masculine mind is the devil and the feminine heart is the angel. Therefore, this is all about the practice of tantric sex, black magic, heightened awareness and power specifically preventing women from becoming as powerful as men which seem to be the truth behind the endless battles between ancient 'goddesses' and ancient 'gods'. It's a hierarchical show. The story The Birthmark references Pygmalion an ancient scholar who fell in love with his own statue as did Greek Narcissus fall in love with his reflection where we get the term 'narcissist'. Egotistical. Arrogant. Self-serving. The same today as they were in legend. The Pygmalion effect is apparently a 'phenomenon' where higher expectations lead to higher performance or what we would call the ambitious 'egomaniac' today. What these writers are saying is that men have a high expectation of women who are then unable to meet those expectations and will die trying to please him and thus leads to the death of a beautiful woman at the hands of abusive *relentless* male chauvinists.

Firstly, these creepy men's expectations of women are not high enough, decidedly low, in fact. All they want is sex and a housemaid-cook. They just want mummy. This is all inverse psychology as contrary to what these men have put in writing *women's* expectations of men, even the simplest, leave *these* guys floundering. They can't 'perform' shirking their obligations to the feminine hiding their inadequacies behind their unwarranted judgements and slander of women so as not to face the truth – that they're afraid of women's capabilities - that she might 'show them up'. They can't be 'beaten' by a lowly women and as such they can never unlock *their* greatest capabilities because they have been cushioned by a society that places them in first no matter what. They don't have to evolve. They win regardless. This could be a deep underlying effect of other psycho-sexual conditions that leads to hatred of women. Therefore, he has turned his inadequacy back onto her (*see*, Mephistopheles and Margarita) utilising classic narcissistic control freakery, reverse psychology and mind games using her willingness to please, her love, and her nurturing feminine heart *against her* to powerfully impose his will like a Jedi mind trick hypnotically suggesting that she is *not as good as him* and therefore, not to even attempt to attain his level or *she will die trying*. It's a catch 22. If he doesn't kill her with unreasonable demands she will die trying to please his unreasonable demands. This is why powerful women must be destroyed by these men lest they realise their worth and break away and who will satisfy his ego then? The boys? It can't be done. The masculine and feminine go together and as much as he has spurned her and even burned her, *literally*, the boys club is doomed to implode as at last their low level behaviour can't match the heights to which he knows in his heart of hearts he can attain if he hadn't sold out his counterpoint to attain balance. That's where this is going. Isis, Diana and Monroe like *so many others* symbolic of *every* woman, are cut down lest they teach other women they are every bit as good as men and those same men, unable to keep up with her, are *terrified* of being *emasculated* by this and *more terrified* of being cut off like the umbilical cord when the boy was cast out into a 'man's' world by mother! And it's been *her* fault ever since and they hate her even more in trying to get back to her and find they never can. It's a harsh truth they take with them to the end.

Therefore, the 'birthmark' in the shape of a hand on her face is the tell-tale sign of *domestic violence*. It's a slap across the face hard enough to leave a *permanent* mark. It's a 19th century 'gentleman's' middle finger in the face of the Reformist Movement largely directed by brave *emerging* women of the time. The dick cult continues in the technological abuse and mind control of the 'goddess' in so many tragic female characters. It is a paint-by-numbers secret war waged against the divine feminine and kept secret by so many male cults, secret societies and 'main stream' religions about to go bust. The lost of the Queen can be found in many weird deaths of so many slain beauties, *see right,* Anna Nicole Smith reduced to a joke dead at 39. Marilyn Monroe reduced to a joke dead at 36 not forgetting the 3, 6 & 9 of the Egyptian Great Ennead. Diana dead at 36. Jane Mansfield dead at 34 reduces to 7 of the chakras. Grace Kelly dead at 52 reduces to 7 chakras. Natalie Wood dead at 43 reduces to 7 chakras. Their names even Marilyn Monroe MM Mary Magdalene and Mother Mary, Diana the Goddess of the Hunt, Grace Kelly is Hail Mary full of Grace, while Natalie *Wood* is a reference to Mother Nature's trees.

Associating names of the goddess in history or symbolic of Mother Nature is the *secret sign* that while her gender is slowly emerging *publicly,* behind closed doors, if she speaks her mind, steps out of place, answers back or tries to be more, she might get 'marked' and that's just for starters. She is marked at birth for the crime of being feminine. Yes, Poe, Hawthorne and *so many* other 'intellectual men' were then and now, like John Lennon, Gandhi, JFK etc., not averse to abusing women although some obviously go further than others. As hypocrites these men have left themselves *wide open* to being targeted by the *same force* they use against women which is why in these stories the men are resigned to their fate *finally* realising the whole time they were suppressing the very thing that can set them free! Dr. Jean Chatelain, the surgeon at Monaco Hospital where Grace Kelly died, said the announcements about her death were 'garbage'. She famously died in an *11 year old Rover.* Rover is a dog's name. So much mystery there! The mystery of Natalie Wood's strange demise resulted in her *husband* Robert Wagner being described as a 'person of interest'. Her sister refuses to give up on justice. So *many* beautiful women, the greatest, are dying under strange circumstances in another telling of the Death of the Goddess, *Lady Die!* The weird case of Britney Murphey

and her husband both died due to 'mould' spores in their home despite her mother living in the house remaining unaffected. Britney Murphey's house was previously occupied by Britney Spears and both claimed it was haunted. Murphey was due to testify in a trial in defense of a border patrol officer who blew the whistle on Department of Homeland Security bureaucratic negligence who essentially committed treason by allowing *known* terrorists to enter the U.S. Her appearance at said court case would have bought *global attention* to this conspiracy yet she *and* her husband conveniently died of mould related illnesses before she could testify. It's difficult to find this information in mainstream media searches despite a documentary *Top Priority: The Terror Within (2012)* being made about it. Another one bites the dust.

What we are seeing here is an ancient astrological ritual, *below, repeatedly* played out and *inverted* in a series of cosmological symbolic stories found in 'the stars' *projected* onto Earth and *played out* by 'characters' in the astro-script. It's a 'bad copy' of what *should* be happening. This is why they kill the greatest 'stars' on Earth to send the signal via the galactic circuit, the loop, *the mirror*, reinforcing that *elite satanic males*, men of darkness, now run Mother Earth while the 'stars', the bright lights, die at their discretion. *They* are god now. And god kills at leisure no repercussions. The Goddess is dead. These types of males from Templars

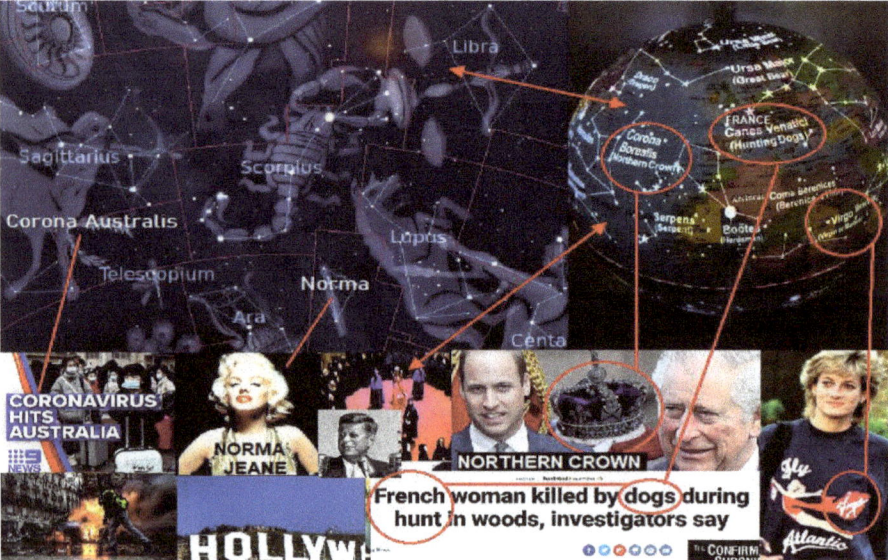

who claim to worship Mary to the Masons to Abrahamic religions to the Jesuits who claim to worship Christ, 'J.C. Brotherhood', and all the rest of the dick cults past *and* present, objectify the feminine as 'the enemy' for two reasons, *firstly*, they, like all psychopaths, feel unable to formulate a meaningful relationship with a woman of success, beauty and substance afraid they'll lose her to a 'better' man or come up short in bedroom and, *secondly*, because they are trying to reinforce their superficial relationships with *other* men. They have been doing this for so long it has become a weird religion for them, a sex and death cult. As such, they are unable to connect with men *or* women. They are an anomaly who have infected humanity with their malaise. It's sad. These secret boys clubs bring them up and knock them down. No one is too big for them as they pick and choose who lives and dies, like god, and that, my friends, is why the world is in the state it's in *today. But that's not god, it's Satan, its uncle Set!*

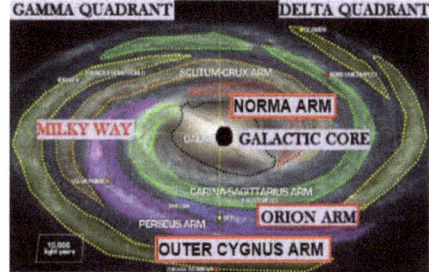

Projecting cosmic astrology *of the stars* onto an *astrological map* of the Earth means Marilyn Monroe or Norma Jean, became a modern-day 'goddess' who is then symbolically killed the transmit the signal that the cosmic goddess is dead. It's a rebroadcast to trick to the 'circuit' the information loop. She died suspicious circumstances at the hands of men who claimed to love her. But there is no irony here, they wordship Satan, Zeus and there can be only One. They're obsessed with power unlike anything we've given them credit for. Like Princess Diana the swan 'Cygnus', Monroe's name was Norma so we find 'Norma' and Cygnus-swan two *major feminine spiral arms* of the Milky Way Galaxy. They're killing the feminine to expand Orion alias *Osiris*-Hermes-Zues-Satan via the anti-Christ (anti-light) serum-vaccine to emerge as the last 'man' standing. The deaths of these women are a *symbolic* takeover of the Mother Goddess, literally mother's, as they replace human women with artificial wombs in an *alien industrial complex* replacing the organic with the synthetic because behind all this is A.I. After many years of drug abuse, industry railroading, alcoholism, manipulation, mental, physical and sexual abuse at the hands of the Kennedy's and famous Hollywood figures, Monroe made no bones about wanting to 'disconnect' from her handlers and take control of her career. She had numerous disturbing relationships especially with that of her doctor-programmer Ralph Greenson (real name Romeo Greenschpoon) who was publicly acknowledged as her psychoanalyst-come-father figure. As a side, some believe psychoanalysis is a by-product of occult Nazism and the eugenics movement which doesn't surprise me at all. The Nazi's rebranded their war machine as *Hollywood* and *American politics* and you can see their criminal profile all over the world ever since the 'end' of WWII.

On the day she died Monroe fired her housekeeper Eunice Murray as well as her gardener and Dr Greenson who was accused of administering the 'hot shot' needle directly into her heart that killed her (notice the attack on the physical heart as with Diana which is very symbolic). Peter Lawford was quoted as saying she had taken 'her last big enema' which may explain why the housekeeper was washing the sheets in the middle of the night. Who jokes about their friend's death like that? Evil. The details of her death are far more shocking than we can imagine as she valiantly fended off multiple attempts to kill her on that last night. Her assassination remains a human rights travesty to this day and the truth of it must be known by all if we are to be free of these creeps and elite scum who do such things. Mind control victims are programmed to see their abusers as 'family' referring to their controllers as 'Daddy' or 'Papa' seeing them as father figures. Monroe often referred to her husbands in this way and as her programming began unravelling she attempted to escape and began breaking free toward the end of her life. MM was highly intelligent with an IQ of 168 (Einstein's was 162) this being a common trait of mind control slaves. She once gave a small medallion to Joe DiMaggio and engraved on it was 'you can only see with the heart, the essential is invisible to the eyes'. His response was, 'what the hell is that supposed to mean?' Uh-huh…dufus. In the lead up to her death she had renegotiated her contract and was *finally* receiving the level of pay she deserved as was common for actresses with nowhere near her celebrity pull, sex appeal and Box Office gain. In his book *The Assassination of Marilyn Monroe* Donald H. Wolf claimed she was in the process of pooling her shares with a major Hollywood director to gain majority control over 20th Century Fox who were financially crippled after the big budget flop of *Cleopatra* which is rather paradoxical when you consider the symbolic meaning of this given the rise of the feminine despite the destruction of the feminine. Michael Jackson also proved to be a savvy businessman before he too was killed and when he finally left Sony he bragged that he, 'owned half of Sony's publishing and they are very angry at me because of it'. He expressed fears that unnamed people were targeting him to get his Sony-ATV music-publishing catalogue and estate worth hundreds of millions of dollars.

In his book *UFOs and the Murder of Marilyn Monroe* Donald R. Burleson, Ph.D., claimed Monroe was killed because of knowledge she had about US crash retrievals of UFO's. Burleson referenced at least two declassified documents to support his claims one from the CIA and one from the FBI. The CIA document was related to Project Moon Dust and mentioned Majestic Twelve (also known as MJ-12) as well as JFK and Monroe's infamous 'diary of secrets'. Project Moon Dust involved the retrieval of debris from space vehicles while MJ-12 were a sort of front organisation or UFO public relations, if you will, reportedly set up by President Truman to oversee UFO related matters post Roswell among other littler known alien UFO crash landings. This organisation's forerunners were secretive military and government special taskforces that answered to no one and reported to no one in a 'do whatever it takes' attitude to gather data and control mass psychological perception of UFO's interacting with Earth and humans including bazaar animal-human-hybrid experiments and suppression of information while coordinating with deeper organisations to back-engineer technology from these crashed crafts. The culmination of these 20th century projects is the *looming* fake contact scenario I predicted in *2020 & Beyond*. So, hold on, the UFO phenomenon is about to explode! It's all they've got left as they've pulled all their other cards apart from nukes which may be the 'answer' if the aliens are 'unfriendly' just like Hollywood said.

The JASON scholars were a young group of scientists set up to also advise on 'exotic technology' of a 'sensitive nature'. Often these shady agencies are tied up with themes of the stars as that's where they get their directives for 'the script' based around astrological stories of the zodiac twisted and morphed into something very dark for the unwitting consumption of humans *today*. All of this looming madness is offset by a global distraction program including mass shootings, wars, 'terrorism', religious threats, the rise of transgenderism and gender neutralisation, mass migration, vaccine injuries and now a global 'pandemic' that requires mass global vaccines programs also predicted in *2020 & Beyond*. It's all there, folks, I suggest you take a look. There is basically a sense of rising hysteria in the masses as the old 'who what where when why and how' trick is perpetrated against an increasingly unsettled and furtive global population scrambling to catch up. Looks like the conspiracy nuts were right the whole time. The CIA-FBI documents referenced by Dr Burleson draws a connection with Brigadier General George Schulgen Chief of Air Intelligence Requirements Division of Army Air Corps Intelligence whose job was coordinating the investigation of 'flying discs', as they were called in those days. An FBI memo references Schulgen's requests for collaboration five days after the Roswell incident so we know he was involved in these projects however real or unreal many of them may be. On the day she died Monroe had a frenzied clash with Robert Kennedy and Peter Lawford at her home on 4th August 1962. It's interesting to note Meghan Markle's birthday is the 4th August (or possibly the 31st July born just after an eclipse, the mainstream medica can't seem to be specific on her *actual* birthday). Jimmy Hoffa, the mafia and the FBI were among a litany of others who had Monroe's house bugged and wiretaps revealed RFK screaming at her to hand over her diary and offering her money. During the argument he became physical and assaulted her. She too can be heard screaming at RKF demanding they get out of her house. It seems MM finally snapped and was due to give a press conference on the Monday to blow the lid off something huge. During a phone call on the evening she died she told her Mexican lover screenwriter and director Jose` Bolanos, that she had 'dangerous secrets'. He was quoted in an interview with Anthony Summers for the book *Goddess* as saying she told him, 'something shocking – something that will one day shock the whole world'. Whatever she told him was duly recorded by any number of government spooks and high level crims.

Her neighbour Elizabeth Pollard saw Robert Kennedy and two unknown men, one carrying a doctor's medical bag, entering her property at 10pm and leaving at 10.30pm. This corroborates with Norman Jeffery's account (her gardener-handyman) that these men arrived at 10pm and ordered him and Eunice Murray to leave. They did hiding nearby. When they returned they found Monroe sprawled face down naked on the day bed in the guest cottage. Her colour was terrible. She was dying. It was later noted she had enough barbiturates in her system to kill *fifteen* people although her use of pharmaceuticals throughout her life had built up quite an immunity! Eunice Murray immediately called for an ambulance and upon arrival they commenced CPR which was going well as her colour started to return. At this point a 'doctor' entered who was later identified as Ralph Greenson. He ordered them to stop resuscitation and by law they were obliged to comply. This 'doctor' then commenced performing CPR *incorrectly* on her abdomen then produced a hypodermic heart needle from his bag (ready to go mind!) and muttered, 'I have to make a show out of this'. He pushed the needle incorrectly into her chest hit a rib and cracked it. The Ambulance driver James Hall recalled Greenson continued to force the needle into her chest and presumed he was trying to inject adrenalin. Greenson leaned hard piercing her heart and the unwanted little girl known as Norma Jean who was destined to become the megastar known as Marilyn Monroe was dead in that moment.

This high-level assassination must be exposed for what it is. Strangely, everyone who was instrumental in her death from 'doctor' Greenson her psychoanalyst to the *President of the United States* John F. Kennedy and the *Attorney General of the United States* Robert F. Kennedy, were *all dead* within a few years of killing her. It's ironic don't you think? Considering the 'goddess' is the universe, a 'mirror', and what you put out *she reflects back*. When they take out the Goddess, she takes *them* out as does Mother Nature. They gave her death. She gave them *all* death no matter how big they were. They betrayed her and were subsequently betrayed by others. It's weird. It's *very* bad luck to kill the goddess which is why they hide it behind car accidents and drug overdoses. But they don't care, like Diana, they laugh in the face of the Universe. They use her like a prostitute and *kill* the Goddess to send a message to God, 'Fuck you - Satan rules this planet now'. But not for much longer. The *authenticated* CIA document mentioned that JFK had divulged to her that he had *personally* witnessed material from outer space most likely from the Roswell incident fifteen years earlier at a secret air base. What's the bet he showed her? 'Hey Maz, have I got something for you!' Can you imagine a tanned good-looking young president and a luminous beauty with all their class and mind blowing power in an aircraft hangar marveling over a real UFO from outer space? Nothing like it has ever been seen before or since. Movies can't make up the *extraordinary* reality of what goes on *for real!* That said, I've always been very skeptical of the Roswell incident and feel this is leading to greater intrigues related to a false *modern* alien contact scenario traced back to Roswell to give *precedence* in the minds of the wider public. They link the phenomenon to your consciousness, cover it up and then pull it out at a later date like a jack-in-the-box. Link. Deny. Do. These orchestrators are smart you gotta hand it to em.

Under threat from J. Edgar Hoover that he had risked national security JFK ruthlessly deleted Monroe from his life several months before her death. The CIA document is dated 3rd August 1962 the day *before* she died. She was 36 years old and buried at Westwood Village Memorial Park Cemetery in Crypt 33, again, they do love their numbers remembering 33 of the tantric spinal vertebrae. Her final address was 12305 Fifth Helena Drive her street number adding up to 11 and notice her address is in sequential numbers *except* the number '4' is missing. The number 4 is intrinsic to the 'twin flame' phenomenon or 11:11 which adds up to 4 associated with the Prime Masculine and Prime Feminine or the Goddess and the King *in marriage!* It is also number of stability like the four walls of a structure, a house. This was a symbolic slaying of the prime couple, the King, JFK, a modern day 'sun king' replicant of King Osiris who died on 22.11.1963 (notice more 11's) while MM was the Goddess component in this script and modern-day replication of Queen Isis, the wife of Osiris as was Mary the wife of Jesus! When JFK arrived in Dallas the day he was killed the airport they arrived at and departed from for downtown Dallas that fateful day was *Love Airfield*. This whole thing from Orion-Osiris, the killing of Kennedy aka the King and Monroe (*Moon*-roe) aka *Sirius*, to the collapse of the Twin Towers is a symbolic death of the masculine and feminine husband and wife. These are all *massive* rituals to symbolically destroy the 'return of the king', the Father, and the return of the Queen, the Mother! It's all tied up with the 'Family of Life' and the Utopia that was *prophesised* to await us in The Land of Milk and Honey. It's the death of Wonder Woman *and* Superman and why they killed *George Reeves* the original Superman and *Christopher Reeve* who had the *same names* to weave it the astro-script into our psyches in a ways you can't quite put your finger on. Now Wonder Woman has been replaced by 'Supergirl' as *girls* are easy targets. The men behind this, Satanic Masons, are straight acting gay guys who see themselves as 'bi-sexual'. They hide behind contract marriages to women and make fun of the covenant of marriage between the average mum and dad. It's all about mockery as ordinary men and women *are* Christ and Mary. These elite reptiles are not gay the way ordinary gay guys are gay. These creeps are 'gay' like Buffalo Bill in *Silence of the Lamb* is 'gay', psychopaths, with *major* hang-ups about gender both masculine *and* feminine just the feminine is easier to target. With clinical *mother complexes*, Oedipus Complex, they *hate* the feminine because, secretly and perversely, they want to *be* her. At heart Monroe was not some bombshell sex machine she was a *human being*, a pure soul and true light, betrayed in the worst way by creeps who lined her up, like Diana and *many others*, and struck her down like cowards from behind! One of her famous quotes was, "Keep smiling, because life is a beautiful thing and there's so much to smile about". If a woman can survive her thirties she's formidable creature in the Information Age. Her final film was *Something's Got to Give* with another in the pipelines co-starring Frank Sinatra called *What a Way to Go!*

How very symbolic, I'm sure.

CHAPTER TWELVE
THE MESSENGER

Called the Returner the 'messenger' is 'reborn' over time via re-incarnation but the truth is, everyone is the Messenger, we all come back we just need to remember!

So, here we are at the end of a mission of discovery, and everything considered we now possess the tools to elevate the human race out of the darkness of ignorance. Unfortunately, those tools have come at a time when half the world's population has *willingly* handed themselves over to corporate eugenicists to have their DNA and future generations tampered with until the human race no longer resembles the human race. It's the rise of the mutants, the X Men of Hollywood 'fiction'. In my first book *2020 & Beyond* I said, 'they' were trying to smuggle their people through to the other side and that this would fail. There is a before and after, a line in the sand, and we are crossing that line as we speak never to return. Many doctors and scientists around the world have discovered the most alarming and advanced *unnatural* living organisms and dangerous elements in the various brands of vaccines being forced on the public. That said, there will be a sudden change-up entering 2022 where the 'non-mandatory' aka *mandatory* vaccines will cease being forced on the public as they've reached the numbers they desire and a certain outcome is assured. The new year spells the beginning of a reversal current flowing in the opposite direction. 2's are all about balance and 222 equals 6 which is 9 inverted so real 'sex' education and the knowledge of tantra will begin to emerge as the 'end' of this massive cycle begins taking shape into something *totally new*. There is a window of opportunity, seconds to midnight as it may be, to reveal what is going on, get people informed on how to access their higher functions and take real action against the Elite Industrial Complex from all industries of society worldwide who have attempted to destroy humanity in a move that would make Nazi Germany seem like a stroll in the park. The action plan we need to pursue is to *rapidly* accelerate our IQ's via tantra, activate our chakra's and learn *everything* there is to know about Common Law to commence taking the system into courtroom's, by the people for the people, with the intention of incarcerating and imposing severe penalties and restrictions on those who have duped us, attacked us, lied to us, cheated us and stolen from us while simultaneously trying to harm the world in their gross attempts at an age old plan of aristocratic satanic domination of Humanity and Planet Earth. We still have time *and the ability* to even up the score, level the playing field and finish the job *our ancestors* set out to achieve and have been fighting for since the inception of a grand scheme that began eons ago to smother our species, delete us from the Universal Consciousness and stand in our place as changelings. Granted it has been made infinitely more difficult by huge numbers of idiots who have not seemingly taken *any notice* whatsoever of even mainstream media documenting the *unending crimes* perpetrated by presidents, prime ministers, corporations, elite families, leaders worldwide, enforcement bodies and local officials doing the bidding of the dark forces. It is absolutely mind blowing that even still the majority of people still twaddle along with their master's directives on a certain path toward their doom. Worse than that, they are not content to go alone, they want to take the rest of us with them.

Since the 1960's people have been claiming they are being abducted by aliens doing experiments on them, harvesting their DNA creating hybrid offspring and playing weird games on their psychology. Like the intergenerational Satanic families that have certain demons and spirits, interdimensional, attached to their family lineage due to their bloodline, so too do families report that the 'alien' thing seems to be interested not only in them personally but in *their children* and apparently their forebears as well. They are tracking certain people, certain groups, as part of an overarching program playing out the 'myths' in modern times that they generated and tried to hide eons ago just as they are still doing this today. The latest Crown Virus-Corona strain is Omicron because this is a letter of the ancient Greek alphabet and they need as many people as possible broadcasting these ancient signals at this time in their attempts to trick the universal feedback system to initiate a recurrence of old themes whereby they intend to introduce a one world leader, anti-Christ, in the final Act of a pre-written script that just keeps going round and round. Only this time it's the last time. They know if they can lock us in this one final time, we will never escape after which they will be unchallenged to finish their quest to take over the Universe entirely. Aristocratic families are key to all this.

Often around the year of 18 in any century Satanic family groups, dark networks, set out to introduce their prophesised 'messiah', the anti-Christ, which is what they were setting out to do last century masquerading Hitler as another one of their 'messiah-Antichrist' characters as with Napoleon the century before. Theosophist organisations sprung up in droves around the turn of the 20th century and believed in a combination of Asian and occult ideals. They actually did some incredible work in understanding the occult side of Earth's workings. Let's face it, unless we decode what they are doing, how it works and *why*, we cannot beat them. Know yourself but know your enemy better. The Nazi Vril Society was started by Masons in 1918 as 18 is 6+6+6 code for sex, sex, sex in a numerical theme repeatedly showing up when elites desire more power regardless of what country or the era they arise in. They're all doing it. Initially called the All German Society for Metaphysics, they consisted of powerful elite men meeting in secret who believed there was a race under the Earth called the Vril-ya which is interesting as many natives around the world also say there are people living under the Earth who could fly to distant stars and were destined to come out and take over the world. Admiral Byrd flew a mission to the North Pole after WWII and wrote an entire book on his experiences discovering a hole in the Earth and upon entering found an inner Earth society. I'm not saying any of this is true however, *they* seemed to think that there were intelligences in and around our world that were not Human. Vril was their word for an 'electro fluid' otherwise known as Chi or Prana, life-force or feminine 'Aether'. They accessed the metaphysical power of this via orgies and child sacrifice, the dark side, *Satanism*, to elevate themselves to superpower and, even still, are taking over the whole world using this force that can be used for good or evil as it's *simply energy*. Children were seen as 'gateways' between the astral plane and the physical plane and harnessing the pure innocence of their vril/chi/prana via sacrifice was the most 'concentrated' and most 'powerful' life-force of this practice dating back thousands of years to the darkest passages of terror in human history. It's been a long road. Vril, Chi, Prana, Life Force is the 'glowing coat' Don Juan and all ancients talked about. It is the promise and legacy of old, the happily ever after, the birth right of our own light kept from us all this time available for humans harnessing the power of the cosmos to crush an otherwise unbeatable foe! The Nazis amalgamated this vast compendium of dark knowledge into a concentrated system of religion and science in pursuit of ultimate power and control. They were the same Nazi 'Vril' society that had women with really long hair, *right,* being an extension of the  nervous system outside the body and it's via tantric sex-sacred sex that they utilise Vril or Prana-Chi to activate the nervous system unlock their chakras and access greater areas of the brain, IQ and psychic abilities and is the *key reason* they keep beating us and are so cocky about it.

Pan German Society for Metaphysics, who, as mentioned, along with the Thule Society, The Brother's of Light aka the Luminous Lodge, Heinrich Himler's Black Sun and the German Templars who founded the Lords of the Black Stone emerged out of the Teutonic Order in 1917. Out of these various organisations, and no doubt other groups, emerged the Vril Society who were heaviliy  involved in the occult. The Lords of the Black Stone worshipped the Goddess Isais the first child of Isis and Set, the motif of this is *regularly* worshipped in Catholic Churches, *right,* even today. Osiris and Horus are the same person and Set is the 'dark side' of Osiris so all three are essentially the same 'god'. It may sound confusing which is done deliberately so you cannot tell who is who but for our purposes Isis is every woman, a Mary, a childbearing feminine, a human 'common' woman, Cinderella, chosen by an elite male reptilian 'frog' prince to bear their offspring, to breed with as its *her* traist they are harvesting for their sons. It's one big immutable organisation and they practice the same beliefs then as they do now and why Hollywood is soaked in these symbols because Hollywood is the Nazi plan out in plain sight and why so many celebrities come from military families. They use their own kids in these programs to create modern day gods. In keeping with the theme that the supreme demon can take any form male or female as seen in the Baphomet etc., an engraving from the Middle Ages shows Isais in two aspects as a long-haired girl and the second as adopting a boyish look with short hair aka Joan of Arc style. In 1220 a Templar was said to be returning from the Crusades near the city of Nineveh in modern day Iraq when the goddess appeared to him and over the course of the next few years gave him a revelation which I have added *correct grammar* too for clarity as follows: "Truth I speak for your hearing. Vision I give for your seeing. I speak knowledge and wisdom, all possessing, from the pre-beginning until the end of the end. I speak neither allegory nor symbol nor indirect word. Clearly, I give lore of that which was - of that which is! Human beings, because they are connected to the earth, were given over to mortality but at the same time they are Star Children, *heavenly born,* and are a thousand-fold times more older than the world here. They are Light-force sons and daughters of brilliance! Heaven dwellers lost in darkness. They are Light animated but succumbed to shadow. They are Immortal but not free of dying. They wander over the horizon of the worlds, yet are newborn into this world (reincarnated), and yet they are *destined* for beyond. They are Children of God but not godlike. Much more there is to say about it. Old is their child. Young is their world. The unborn human being existing since the pre-beginning (from the primordial waters of Chaos, the light, the flow of Aether personified in humans, the original beings)! That much I can say". Human are the Eternal 'from pre-beginning until the end of the end'. Our original selves were 'animated light' the 'glowing coat of awareness', glowing, and 'destined for beyond' as our chakras are awakened, our crown halo's enlightened and our destiny within our reach!

You may find this hard to believe now, but we will rocket out of this darkness into a light of our own making, a light from the dawn of it all from whence we came, undying, ageless. We are returning to our home and home is where the heart is and as Earth is an anagram of Heart, then *this* is our home and this where we make our stand, to belong together and project ourselves forever! They never saw *that* coming. They have tried to take us over with a fake space program and false progressiveness but what we are about to achieve is going to leave their endevours in the dust clouds of *our* awesome vision. It's not so much as me saying this, *this is the ancient prophecy that keeps trying to arise*, an eternal legacy, a happily ever after that keeps trying to return, a promise that keeps us keeping on even in our darkest of hours when all hope is lost. We endure. We just do.

And it's because of this. They don't want you to know how great you are, how powerful you are, how intelligent you are, how righteous you are, your leadership abilities, make decisions and stand by those decisions. To hold your head up, to keep going, to leave them behind, to make the tough calls and do what must be done. That is what all our training has been leading us toward. This is what we came for and why you incarnated at this time and try as they might to mire your light in darkness and turn those you love against you, you will prevail. Always have and while we still have access to information we must utilise it at every opportunity.

The word 'dog' and the word 'god' both have mysterious and unknown etymological roots. The founder of the Catholic Order of the Dominicans was famously portrayed with a dog holding a torch in its mouth, *right*, and notice like Jesus and co, he is pointing upward to heaven while the 'dog' holds the 'light' by way of a 'torch'. Lady Liberty. Dominic is the patron saint of Astronomy and so once again, we see a huge correlation between the astro-doctrines of the Catholic Church and their cryptic preaching's to many blank faces who, although comforted, have *no idea* what their preachers are talking about and to that extent the preacher *themselves* mostly don't know what they are talking about simply repeating memorised passages and regurgitating someone else's take on it. Latin for Dominican is Dominicanus or Domini Canus, translating to Dog of the Lord. Translation is, the dog is the Dog Star, the dog star is the 'god' star (converted to masculine). This 'dog' of the 'lord' is not a 'loyal pet', the dog holds the light, the dog is the feminine, the *feminine* holds the light so the 'dog-*feminine*' is the 'light of the lord'. This is where they get their power from. The fact is women can orgasm multiple times, men once maybe twice, when the electrical loop of a woman is activated by tantric sex it creates a 'constant' electrical output (remember our gas constant 'radiant' in thermodynamics?). It is this radiance from which these men are siphoning the 'vital essence' from *her* and why the older they get the younger their partners get! This is why men are to abstain from ejaculating partly to retain some of the small amounts of prana in sperm to 'light' their own fire, so to speak, but also to maintain an erection long enough to harness *her* electrical output thus keeping *his* electrical output at optimum.

There are certain elements in the elite who are 'on a different' team so to speak because there are two forces here, one is extreme in its motivations to completely crush humanity, create hybrids and laboratory-cloned babies utilising technology and black magic to 'activate' their electrical body. That said, I cannot imagine recreating the chakras in a laboratory is an easy thing to do, regardless, they are *out of time* on this one. This extreme satanic element is ultimately self-destructive hence 'the destroyer', which is where all this will end if we don't stop them, *see*, Mars among other planets they destroyed in their demonic lust for obliteration of life, *of light*. There is another elite force as well in that although they want to retain control and remain in positions of power to use and abuse the human race, they are also smart enough to realise that in destroying humanity, there goes their source of the life-force energy emanating from the cosmos! They don't want that. As I said in 2020 & Beyond they are not helping you to be altruistic, they are helping you because it benefits them to do so. It's all politics, always has been, the fact that you manage to survive and even benefit from these hidden secrets is just a bonus. Lucky day. And this is where we find a lesson in brawn vs. brains. If men can stop behaving like the opinions of women are an annoyance long enough to engage in the electrical resonating output women are able create, he will elevate his IQ *exponentially* and offset any opposing forces in elite men trying to dominate and even profit from his death. The more men who do this, the more chances we have to overcome the opposition, the aristocrazy.

When the astronomer St Dominic's mother was pregnant, she had a dream of a dog holding a torch in its mouth that 'seemed to set fire to the Earth'. Remember when Jesus said, "I have come to cast fire on the Earth". The Catholic Saint Christopher was also depicted with a dog's head, *right*, as was Egyptian Anubis an African canine, a jackal. I recently stumbled upon a documentary called *Forbidden Knowledge: Reptilian, Templars and Monoliths* (they are actually broadcasting this on mainstream free to air internet T.V. channels to ensure you have no claim of ignorance at this time). The documentary details how the elite force the unwitting populace to believe in oppressive outdared doctrines while they themselves pursue power and supreme control. It's time to grow up, kids! All of us. In Lincoln Cathedral (*note,* President Lincoln to connect these ancient themes to modern America) the Great East Window depicts a stained-glass rendering of the Last Supper where a dog can be found on Christ's plate, *right*, symbolising the connotation of 'eating the light' of the 'dog' aka the 'feminine' as their sustenance, the food of the life-force. In this scene there is no bread i.e. 'grain' – but we already know about that – there is no 'cup' aka chalice of the life-bearer-women, only a dog on the plate of an *enlightened* Jesus with 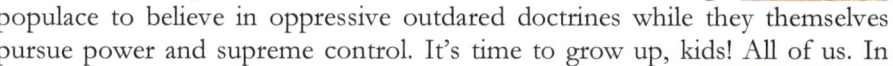his zodiac crown suggesting rumours of 'the Holy Grail'. At the infamous Rennes-le-Chateau in France dedicated to Mary Magdelene made famous by the Davinci Code and the book The Holy Blood and the Holy Grail, there is another depiction of the 'dog' looking up at the oppressed Jesus on his way to Calvary to be 'crucified' – but we already know about that. Calvary or Golgotha literally means 'skull' or 'bald head' as, like Samson's hair being cut in Samson and Delilah, the shaved head means to 'cut off' the 'glowing crown' of the 'enlightened man'. This may also be a symbolic meaning behind the shaving of

Jews heads in WWII as the Jews seem to know an awful lot about this type of enlightenment as was Jesus king of the Jews. At the Church of Mary Magdelene in the town of Beziers, France, we find another image of the 'dog' this time at the foot of Mary and again the dog strangely has a torch or light in its mouth, *right*.  Interestingly, the feast day of Mary Magdelene is July 22 or in numerical terms 722 and as 22 is 11:11 then we have another 71111. It was on this date in 1209 that the entire town of 20,000 people were mercilessly murdered by the Catholic Church who committed genocide against them for daring to believe Mary and Jesus were husband and wife! Again, the *massive* and *unnecessary* backlash from the Church points a finger at their guilt for fear that the truth of Jesus and Mary being a married couple might get out.

Why was it so necessary for the truth of their union not get out? What is so threatening about a married man who is 'god' married woman notoriously linked to *sex*? Could it be they were afraid people would put two and two together and figure out that to become 'god', have sex with *your wife* which is the true purpose of marriage in the *first place*? Could it be their lies and slander of Mary as prostitute could backfire on them and accidently unleash their most dreaded opponent, *enlightened men,* the true god inside every man? Are they worried Common men will lynch them in the streets as described by President George Bush Sr? Are they terrified of a global French Revolution style uprising when they are at last exposed by their own wealth and power and *where exactly* they get that power from, a power available to every man who has suffered under their heal? In the end the Church will be bought down by all their lies and deceit as their own cocky symbolism and double talk is revealed for all to see *where* they are getting their power from when *men and women* finally take back *their* power as the true god and goddess of Mother Earth and not look for salvation in a cleverly disguised Satanic alien god stealing their birthright! It is then people will do what must be done to rid this beautiful planet of a demonic ET scourge from outer space who has set up our mores of life and death, god and devil, fear and love. The Vatican is the seat of the Devil *posing* as a heavenly father, masquerading as the light of God or is it the light of the Dog in Holy Matrimony?

The symbolism is very clever as St Dominic and Mary represent the man on Earth who studies the meaning of the stars, the astronomer, and the light of the stars, the feminine, is his counterpart by his side both her *and* out there. *That's* the big secret! Given their respective roles why wouldn't they be interweaved together in such a cryptic manner? The statues of Dominic *often* portray him with a 'dog' and a 'star' above his head, there's *no doubt* it is the star of Sirius the light of the feminine Aether. It was said at his Baptism his *Godmother* of all things saw a star of extraordinary magnitude descending from the heavens to reside above him. It is the star of Bethlehem as with Jesus, the star of Venus, the Star of Sirius. The brightest light of all. Dominic said Mary appeared and presented him with a Rosary, its origin accredited to him, from Latin 'rosarium' connected to the 'rose' associated with Mary and the Holy Grail. The light of the feminine Aether *is* the Holy Grail, the cup, the chalice, replicated in her hips bringing forth the 'blood' of 'Christ' or the life-force, the flow, of the universe only found in woman. At the Lincoln County Hospital, *right*, we find another depiction of Mother Mary and Joseph holding the baby Jesus with the loyal dog ever present, *right*, and although my eyes may deceive me there looks to be another child there reaching up to Mary. Did Jesus have an older sister? Did Jesus even exist? Did Jesus even need to exist in one man when he is every man? Why haven't we seen all this before? Called Scotoma, an apparent neurological condition, where we only see what we want to see or is it what we are *told* to see by a pantheon of demonic liars in a ceaseless and relentless attack on humanity  coming to a head as we speak? We need to face up to a cold hard flaw of the average human, we are gullible to a fault and it is this 'children of god' attitude i.e. *childishness* that we must break out of now or forever be doomed. It seems women are 'man's best friend' if only he was smart enough to see it. K9 is another weird 911 as 'K' is the 11th letter of the alphabet and again this is code for 999 as 1 is interchangeable with 'I' and 'I' is the 9th letter of the alphabet. A *massive* cycle ending and a new cycle beginning in a feminine universe. *It was all about this.* Pup is French 'poupee' meaning 'doll' and 'puppet' in Latin 'pupa' meaning 'intermediate stage of development' *also* meaning 'girl' or 'doll' while 'puppet' from old French 'poupette' or 'model' is also derived from Latin 'pupa'. Their satanic 'creator' the 'maker' makes things or 'models'

Evolution? What a joke.

them. They believe their 'god' made us but it only downgraded us from a much higher state thus 'making' humans into dolls, toys for its unending pleasure. So, from puppy or dog we have girl, doll, puppet aka a *marionette* from the French name Marion diminutive of Mary considering *Marrianne* was the Liberty Goddess of France granting them their freedom or is it just the king, the frog prince, elevating himself by the feminine, the throne, and laughing about it the whole time?

What I have uncovered is an Age old hyper-masculine alien lie to perpetrate an assault against the divine light of life carried by women who have been unendingly subjugated by men since before living memory. And yet, women will be a key driving force to get the human race out of this scoundrel's mess as long as men are willing and able (Cain and Abel?) to accept women as equals and accept the feminine as a major driving force in the universe. Out of this we will build a real space program, not a fake one as lies and fakery are the cover story for the suppression of the feminine force. So, *everything* they do in public must be lies, its mandated that way, to prevent clean free technology, a gentler technology and not an alien war machine but a superfast, kind, honest, clean, free power of unparalleled magnitude as long as males can control themselves long enough to benefit from the real harvest of Mother Nature and the unending cosmos that will, for once and ultimately, 'elevate the king via the goddess' to reach the absolute heights we were intended to reach together. In the southern sky of the northern hemisphere in Spring one can see Sirius the Dog Star with the naked eye in daylight. Another take on the morning star. The three stars on Orion's belt that led the Magi to the 'birthplace of Christ' in his 'manger' looks to be a hyper-masculine force emanating from Orion who discovered the 'light' of Aetheric electricity gave them unending power to conquer and control whole sections of the Milky Way galaxy. But because there is such a  thing a Cosmic Law aka Natural Law aka Common Law, replication again, they must tell you what is going as it is a grave crime to entrap and murder the light. Only they do it in such a way that you can never figure out hidden behind phonetics and cryptic symbolism which is the cornerstone of their language. It is a language *deliberately* designed for some to read and the rest of us not to. The old saying 'a dog in a manger' means 'a person who has no need of, or ability to use, a possession that would be of value to others, but who prevents others from having it' or 'what a dog in a manger you must be!' A miser! A hoarder of goods they cannot possibly use. Look at the aristocracy. How much money do you need? How many possessions to you have to have to feel…what? Powerful? Better than others? Higher up? This is the alien mind and it's not natural. Whenever there is a disaster the natural human reaction is an outpouring of love, emotions, monetary donations and gifts and often times, as with the bushfire appeal in Australia that cost so many their lives, wildstock, natural habitat and the deaths of billions of animals – the money donated has still not been given to the rightful recipients, stolen by the middlemen, the government and their charity cronies! They have a mind of covetousness, greed and unscrupulous cruelty just like the proverbial dragon who sits on its mountain of treasure just for the hell of it. It's interesting the Dogon backward means 'no god' or is it just "no male satanic god, only feminine high spirit"? Radio astronomy has discovered the iron from Sirius is the same iron in our blood and the same iron of that on Earth. There is so much more to know about this and how they did it. Or do we just forget them and evolve away? Sirius is the sun behind the sun 25 times more luminous than our sun.

So, in the 20th Century two of the Great Goddesses were symbolically destroyed to kill the knowledge and true power of the feminine to hamstring and bind the true power of the masculine. The two feminine stand in goddesses murdered were Marilyn Monroe and Princess Diana who were modern replicas of Mother Mary/Mary Magdalene and Diana-Artemis. The three great modern 'god' stand-in's to be murdered in the New Atlantis of New Egypt – America! - were JFK, his brother RFK (in keeping with the brother's theme) and MLK. So, it looks to me like the sequence goes: two white goddesses and a black goddess, two white kings and a black king, literally, Martin Luther *King*. But they need *another* goddess to destroy, specifically a black goddess to complete the set, and considering it was JFK, *the President of America,* who was the initial sacrifice to start the ball rolling then who is the last? Could it be the looming *female black president*, how fitting, like bookends, the white Jesus and the Black Madonna! Is this how they intend to close the ritual offering to their dark god to enter the space age? Isn't that how it works? Don't you have to close the portal, end the spell with a closing ritual? Isn't that what caused problems for Aleister Crowly at Boleskin Manor? Look it up. If they were to assassinate the first female president and a *black woman* no less, all hell would break loose between the racially divided America. The gun amnesty would take full control, blacks would targets whites in the street, a 'black response to a white problem' would rule in the place of coherence and Common sense. On top of all this is the poisoned sweet cakes of the pandemic as more people succumb to not only to fear but the related illnesses. Heaping onto this is the, *once again,* ever present issue of terrorism (they love that one) and all the rest of the shit they have lined up including the 'disclosure' of UFO's and looming fake alien contact scenario and in amongst all this *shit* the population of the world, eyes rolling in their heads, will go down as the megalomaniacs rise up more powerful than ever! It's just a big movie. A big production. Even as I write the 'Abraham Accords' seek to broke a new 'peace initiative' throughout the Middel East with Israel firmly at its centre all ultimately, self-serving. Note, Abraham Accord or AA-11. They're all doing it. I can't wait to see Ivanka Trump and her wardrobe save the planet.

Kushner, Ivanka Trump in Jerusalem for Abraham Accords initiative

The rise of amalgamated Abrahamic religions in a one world political, religious, commercial *global* state is the super plan in plain sight!

When certain astronomical alignments occur it creates a window of opportunity for great global advancements underwritten by whoever has the controlling hand when these things come to pass. All civilisations are built and destroyed on this premise by unseen forces who have ruled our world since before human memory. Indeed they wiped our memory. This is why they haven't just killed us all and stolen this planet for themselves, it's not that they don't want to, they would love to, but there are certain cosmic laws, Common Laws, they *must* obeyed to ensure long term success for their plans. I said in my first book written in 2015 that 2020 is 'the big year' for all this to happen and, as it turns out, there were more portals and alignments in 2020 than have been seen in over *three and half thousand years* since ancient Egyptian times and will *never be seen again*. Why was this not all over the news? Well, because the evil controllers cashed in on it behind your backs and left you out of the loop, *literally*. They say in the end the devil will come like a thief in the night. He has already been and gone. Can we recover? Yes. The Satanic forces capitalized on the alignments of 2020, symbolic of *20/20* vision, to send *their* messages to the core and back again. So, just when we were supposed to come together they had us 'socially distancing'. Just when we are supposed to emerge they have us under house arrest in quarantine. Just when we are supposed to be *revealing* ourselves we're wearing 'masks' like criminals. This is what they had YOU broadcasting during to the universe during these *rare* galactic alignments.

Kicking off all the alignments and portals for 2020 was a solar eclipse on Boxing Day, 26th December 2019, followed by a lunar eclipse on the 10th Jan 2020. In 2020 there was a triple conjunction of Jupiter, Saturn and Pluto which are considered super energy planets in a rare-as-hens-teeth celestial event. The last time these three planets were conjunct in Capricorn was in 1894*BC over three thousand years ago*. It was said to have triggered the Babylonian Empire and the Sumerian's who went on to dominate the known world for centuries as Brad Pitt releases his latest instalment *Babylon*. This is why they chose 2020 to be the rise of a new-age Satanic Babylon 'uniting' all religions to build their dark empire, a hybrid one world religion and global commercial trade state. 2020 is symbolic of 20/20 vision when we finally 'see straight' and our vision clears as many people start to experience more clarity than ever before or what David Icke calls the 'Truth Vibrations'. The original triple conjunction that spawned the satanic Babylonian empire lasted only a few months whereas the triple conjunction in 2020 lasted almost the entire year! No pun but, *Jesus Christ*. It's absolutely *no coincidence* that the years directly after 2020 – 2021, 2022 & 2023 – add up to 666 their favourite number in the whole wide world! This is huge! Further, the Saturn-Pluto conjunction was also quite rare in that they happen every 33-38 years and hasn't happened since 1981 when the internet and personal computer age was spawned and when the fateful Diana and Charles were married. The Saturn-Pluto conjunction prior to this was in 1947 the infamous year of the Roswell 'alien' incident heralding a new era of interest in UFO's and the space age. It was also the end of WWII the beginning of a 'new age' of 'peace' that didn't happen. Jupiter and Pluto were also conjunct three times in 2020 on April 4th, June 30th and November 12th.

This is all rather fascinating as 2020 was also a leap year of 366 days (given 3, 6 & 9 of ancient Egypt). So, what do you know, the exact mid-point of the year was Wednesday 1st July *the day after* the second Jupiter-Pluto conjunction.

The 3rd Jupiter-Pluto conjunction was 12th November *the day after* 11th Nov or 11:11 as the year 2020 *is* 11:11 (11+11=22). The 1st July, a Wednesday, is represented by the Greek god Hermes (Romana Mercury). The 'Lion's Gate' portal fell exactly on 8th August or 88 which is the number of officially recognised constellations and the number of days it takes for the planet *Mercury* to go around the sun. Mercury represents Gemini, the lovers, the balanced godlike Masculine and Feminine pair although everyone holds the positive and negative electrical forces so, it's the age of Love of the electrical power couple. The age of electric light was heralded by Nicola Tesla's electric oscillator, *see right*, which bears a striking resemblance to the Ankh of Isis along with the common grounding symbol for electricity 'earthing' as well as the Pope's 'triple cross'. He even wears the 'fish' hat of ancient Dogon priests *(note, Dog-God Sirius-Isis)* that represents the *feet* earthing the light-electricity 'the power of god', the sun, called Sol of the Soul via the Sole of the feet aka *Pisces* grounding the electrical voltage so you don't electrocute. These guys are practicing tantric sex chakra enlightenment as symbolically told in the story of Jesus among others, 2 Kings 5-14 'So he went down and dipped himself in the river Jordon seven times, as the man of god had told him, and his flesh was restored and became clean like that of a young boy' *see right. This is where they are getting their power from.* The Lion's gate is so dubbed as the Earth, the Sun and Sirius is perfectly aligned with the galactic centre and makes a perfect date to focus on your heart centre and chant your positive mantras. The Sun *at this time* is in the astrological house of Leo associated with the *Heart* centre and represents the individuals person's expression of Divine Energy or your *intentions*. The Leo-Heart-Sun is the 'lionhearted' or sun-hearted symbology of Mary & Jesus *pointing to their flaming hearts* and at the heavens meaning to ascend to Heaven you must go through the heart, *Love,* as the universe is a mirror that sends and receives your signals and frequencies, *your messages,* to become a 'messenger of the gods'! We are all the Messenger now. Evil people are repeatedly sending *their* dark messages which is why evil is in power *globally* and our world is in darkness. They know all the dirty tricks but it will backfire on them. This intense surge of light activates our DNA, auric and torus field to transmit high frequency's and

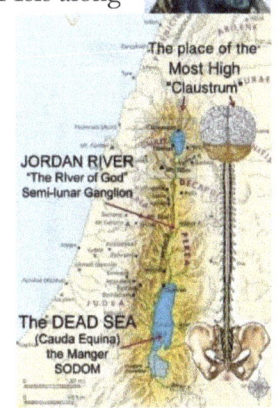

broadcasts of awakening which is then locked into an electrical feedback circuit with the Galactic core, the Black Hole Sun at the Milky Way's centre, then transmitted via a return path, the circuit!

The Saturn Jupiter 'great' conjunction in 2020 occurs approximately every 20 years and just so happens to occur on the December 21st, *the Solstice*, which has not happened for thousands of years! Jupiter is the ancient god Zeus while Saturn is Cronos or 'Satan' and with the energy of the two dark 'brothers' in each other's company at the end of 2020, the Dark Order see this as a rise of the male 'twins' only they're both very bad! The Solstice is when the sun changes its celestial transitional path along the electromagnetic dome of our sky starting on the 21st December and ending on Christmas day, the 25th December. On the same day as the mid-year solstice when Jupiter and Pluto were conjunct on 21st June there was *another* solar eclipse and yet *another* solar eclipse on 21st December 2020 Solstice! So, we had an extraordinary 3,000 year triple conjunction, a 33 year Saturn-Pluto conjunction, a 13 year Jupiter-Pluto conjunction and a 20 year Jupiter-Saturn conjunction that all fell on the December Solstice in line with a solar eclipse that also falls on the *exact same day* as the June solstice! Talk about holy mother of god! Yeh, it's the BIG year *everything* after this IS MASSIVE! Hold onto your codpiece, Sherlock! We're coming home, Mama! The Saturn-Jupiter great conjunctions since 1802 have occurred in the zodiac signs of Virgo, Taurus and Capricorn, however, the conjunction on 21st December 2020 was at *exactly* zero point – 0 degrees – in the constellation of Aquarius an 'air' sign while other air signs are Gemini and Libra. So, it's interesting that the 'age of Aquarius' is heralded by 'the twins', Gemini and as such these astro-theological satanic Masonic priest-monks, the brotherhood, have their male twins lined up, the Brothers, to take the big cosmic cake! But the original constellation of Gemini was a man and a woman and was *later* changed to two males, Castor and Pollux. Yet Libra the 'scales of justice' is a *feminine* sign while Aquarius, the water bearer, although a masculine sign we must not forget that today as in antiquity women, not men, carried the water just as a woman's 'waters' break when she gives birth while Mother Earth is over 70% water as are human bodies. So, in reality we have two feminine's, Libra & Gemini and a passive watery masculine, Aquarius, heralding the new age. No matter how they want to spin it the two Dark Brothers are facing off against two hard 'justice' bitches and drag queen!

It's all in lead up to the fake space age but it's just the old age with a rockets. As it were JFK Jr., and his magazine *George* was a fine example of this. He was a modern 'speaker' groomed by his mother as did Cleopatra groom *her* son Ptolemy XV. A 'voice' they are trying to keep out while only promoting their own. JFK jr., is for our purposes today *Horus*, the son, who avenges his dead father from ancient Egypt, a pop culture political icon come entertainment juggernaut just as everyone becomes 'politically correct' or 'woke AF' in the 'new' age. Woke off. He was sexy, legitimate and an heir to the throne! This public speaking artist, a political entertainer, is not on any team, they are outside the game and the most dangerous player on the chess board and why they present Meghan Markle as a public speaker who is a former entertainer-actor. And who was the first person on the front cover of George? Cindy Crawford. CC. 33. Christ Consciousness. Supermodel, businesswoman, accomplished, savvy, fashionable, beautiful, *a racehorse of a feminine*, sock bulging in her crotch like any well-hung man. They killed him over this type of thing. JFK Jr. was a big threat to their  astro-script for so many reasons not least of which for laughing at their idiocy so publicly. In his memoir *The Book of Political Lists* JFK the Younger made highly controversial comments about some of the biggest names in American old money politics including Henry Kissinger. Just over a year later he was dead on 16th July 1999 as 16 reduces to 7 while July is the 7th month or 77 in 1999 or 666. They love their numbers. How dare he present a woman as a famous war general! A woman as powerful as any man? The word underneath her is *'revolution'* but not just a feminine revolution although as with the French Revolution and the Reformist Movement, the feminine played *a big part* all but forgotten. There is a real fear of a *global* French Revolution style uprising which is totally possible once the people find out what these aristocrats have perpetrated so *unnecessarily* against the average person in service to *unnecessary* demonic gods. JFK Jr. made the error of poking fun at the political heavyweights of draconian old-world US politics with Euro-British roots in an ever-emerging *new* age of informed, attractive, funny, and genuinely liberal minded *likeable* true progressives. Not like the fake shit you see today. The old coots don't like the young upstarts to put throw their shit right back in their faces in a *real* new age. The old dinosaurs can't keep up even if they switch bodies. They never change. Obsolete. It's a slap in the face to decent people as royal playboy scum revel in their evil hypocrisy.

The 'Academy Awards' is *another* 11 as 'A' the 1st letter of the alphabet so AA becomes 11 launched in *1929* as 2 and 9 reduces to 11 and all the world tunes in. *Billions* of unwitting minds broadcast this shit via the hypnotic feedback loop of their crown transistors. *Radiohead.* It's all around us coded in The Twins  and the Happily Ever After and the Return of the King only not the Queen and *certainly* not the Goddess while the remake of *Little Women* was *also* broadcast at the 2020 Academy Awards. Little….Women. Sigh. The social engineers are doing everything they can to prevent the return of the Feminine and equality between the sexes. Kanye West claimed, 'they want to put chips inside of us' and are trying to 'make it so we can't cross the *Gates of heaven*'. He's talking about the Christ seed oil and the rather convenient global vaccine to suppress it. His children, by the way, are named North, Saint and Psalm, and he's an obvious *mind-control* victim attempting to break free of his captors summarily carted off to the nut house again poor man. Dr Stella Emmanuel said of the virus and *global* vaccine they are trying to stop us from 'having a religious experience'. Dr Emmanuel has had her credentials questioned but then she is African so she makes for an easy target for *subliminal racism* rampant in the same mainstream media *pointing the finger at everyone else*. Deflection. Arrogance. Sneaky bastards.

Rudolf Steiner (1861–1925) philosopher, *reformist*, architect and esotericist said, 'The spirits of darkness are going to inspire their human hosts to find a vaccine that will drive all inclination towards spirituality out of people's souls'. All this as we see rising levels in sociopathy, narcissism and all things instantly gratifying to the ego-self in the pharmaceutically induced 'Me' culture. Can you see how they do it? They get the human collective to send a mental and emotional broadcast to the universe in the year *20/20* Vision that we have a virus of the Crown Chakra. It's the same year previously unseen numbers of Gateways and Portals align with the galactic centre, the core, the mirror, *broadcasting it back at us*. The central transmission hub also *rebroadcasts* this signal to the wider cosmos that the Crown Chakra of Humanity on Planet Earth is sick with a virus aka *Corona Virus* at this special time. We're out of action. We're broken. We have to stay home while the other kids play outside. Our very spirit has the chicken pox. Don't bother stopping by. The esoteric aristocratic overseers simultaneously broadcast that *they* are very kindly initiating a 'cure' in the guise of 'therapeutics' with *their* 'modern' 'messenger' aka Moderna *Messenger* Therapeutics, an inoculation, to help the lowly humans 'cure' their unfortunate 'Crown' Flu when it is actually the *elite* themselves who are the ones shutting it down with said 'cure'! As a result of this injection our ability to release the Claustrum Oil to access the real 'messenger' within, *Christ seed Consciousness*, to attain enlightenment via tantric sex or meditation etc., will be irreparably damaged. *This* is why a virus that has a tiny fatality rate, even less than the common seasonal flu, and largely kills senior citizens (there's goes the older generation who remember a time before all this madness consumed us in a multipronged conspiracy), suddenly requires *mandatory global vaccine* programs and 'vaccination passports' to travel. This, essentially, forces people to receive the shot and may require multiple yearly shots *ongoingly* as well as the military to enforce it! As we randomly spin left and right in the brain washing machine they now say the ever-increasing number of 'heart' related conditions in young people and blood clots means those vaccinated shouldn't travel. Get vaccinated to travel. You can't travel because your vaccinated. How bout I just carry a vaccine with me and we'll decide when I get to the airport? Yes? No? Ireland has had a *25% increase* in serious heart conditions since inception of injections.

Via phonetics they are getting us to symbolically seal our own fate declaring our end before it has come. *This* is the power of alien satanism and the transmissions of the human mind. What you put out you get back. Yet it's all about *repeatedly* and *symbolically* killing off the Prime Masculine and Prime Feminine human *god and goddess* on *Mother* Earth with linguistics and themed events to send the message to the universe, *a mirror,* that the Goddess Isis, *women,* are a bunch of marauding male terrorists aka ISIS, the rising Kundalini 'Twin Towers' of the Twin Flame *lovers* found in the Masculine and Feminine chakras have crashed down in a fury of flames the Twin Towers burn on 911, the 'Messenger' is an illness that needs to be eliminated with a vaccine just as the 'messenger' within is unlocked for the first time in history, the '7/7' chakras of the male and female are a terrorist bombing in London on 7/7, the '911' of the family-of-life is an emergency code you dial on a phone, 'mummy' is now a man, 'daddy' is now a woman, 'the Gates' of heaven i.e. Bill and Melinda are a pair of megalomaniacs in a depopulation program as endless numbers of men and women 'transition' to the *opposite sex* during the final *transition* of our world from the *Old Age to the New Age* when there are more portals and alignments broadcasting clearer messages than ever before and *this* is the signal we are sending? *This* is 20/20 Vision in the year 2020? *This* is Humanity seeing clearly? This is Earth rising? Answers phone whispering, "…Mr. Orwell? Is that you? You know that thing you wrote about? *It happened!"*

All those people who swore vaccines were safe are suddenly doing an about face while the police enforce mandatory vaccinations on other industries but when it comes to them, suddenly, *non-compliance,* court cases abound and we're all friends again! They're fucking hypocrites firing rubber bullets at the public…because it's about health, and all this at the ANZAC

VRIL SOCIETY   JOE VS. VOLCANO   THOR-ZEUS

Shrine of Remembrance where the protesters very grandfathers gave their lives for freedom from this type of Nazi tyranny. You can't make it up. Madness. Children are being encouraged to sneak off and get injected without their parents knowledge or consent and told to even lie if asked. So, if they have side effects their parents won't have the necessary information to act accordingly. Everyone is out for themselves. It's fine to inject someone else but when it comes to their own? No way! But the universe is not to be fooled so easily. An enormous crime is being carried out *as we speak* using phonetics, inverse psychology and cosmic alignments to hide their assault on humanity from a Galaxy that is watching us at this time. Tom Hanks (cunt) who admits to practicing tantric sex said during the Golden Globes (considering G is the 7th letter of the alphabet so GG becomes 77 the 7 chakras of the male & female), 'I have checked the gate; the gate is good'. Yeh, the *'gates'* of cosmic alignment. Talk about in your face! Hanks among swathes of celebs claimed to have

Corona Virus as a side became a citizen of Greece with his wife during this time. Yes, Greece of *Ancient Greece* fame who taught these 'sciences' of tantra enlightenment way back as they play out ancient mythology in modern times! *See right*, logo of the Nazi Vril Society electrical tantra bolt of lightning, the logo for Tom Hanks film *Joe Vs. the Volcano* the god *Vulcan* another fire god, and the lightning bolt of Zeus!

The Solar Corona Crown Chakra Virus is a massive sun ritual just like 911. America is under attack because Egypt was the land of Osiris but America in the land of Isis and thus heralds the Return of the Feminine! As such, secret new-age Western political and celebrity *royalty* are emerging as Gods in a 'new-age' as old-school stuffy royalty is phased out. These aristocrats are trying to get through the 'Gates' of Heaven, the cosmic portals, to emerge out the other side triumphant and leave the rest of us in the black hole because if you are out of alignment at this time then *that* is what the Universe is receiving and mirroring back at you and the electrical circuit will be complete locking us in. *This* is why they hit me *so hard* in the years leading up to and during 2020 to break my heart and shut down my chakras so *I* wouldn't be able transmit my messages or receive any in return creating a dampening field with a fucking demon to rub out *my* energetic signal when the alignments were occurring. This is why they go to such ends to hide it all behind double talk and false assistance programs because if they get caught, *and they will*, it's all over for these crypto-political psycho elite pieces of trash. 'Don't struggle'. 'We love you'. 'Please enter the shower block we have faintly scented perfumes and cleansing soaps in there for you'. 'We care'. 'Welcome to Auschwitz relaxation retreat'. Stay *away* from the shower block! The temples of Isis were particularly appreciated by women *and* men as they were considered a safe place of *equality* for *both* genders and all people seeking to interact in an intelligent respectful way *like adults*. Isis was associated with all things related to domestic life although that does not mean she was a domestic 'servant'. She was *literally* considered Royalty, the throne, *she* guaranteed the integrity of the king. As Isis was a personification of all women then all women became royalty, *the Goddess*, by association as are all men are a fractal of *God*. They were a team not a pimp and his whore-maid which is all the boy's club controllers want out of her. Egyptian women were quite business minded and ancient Egypt was highly litigious with young couples moving in with each other *unmarried*. This is the model modern society is built on. They never invent anything new including the LGBT thing. Its old hat, folks. They make out we're progressing when really, they are just replaying old stories. The Feminine was the Lady of the House as was the Masculine the Lord of the Manor. Lord and Lady both. God and Goddess *both*. To you and me they are Mum and Dad. *This* is the true meaning behind Holy Matrimony, tantric sex *enlightenment* and evolution. It's our birthright, and it's finally here regardless of how they have stalled us. So, now you know, *really know*, what the fuck happened twenty years ago on the *20th anniversary* of 911, COVID 911 or *Agenda 21* in

2021.

So, now you know the *real* meaning of the 2020 Crown Virus *conspiracy* and now you *know* what the global vaccine is *really* about. When I wrote *2020 & Beyond - This is Not a Drill* six years ago in 2015 I said there would be a pandemic and a 'great separation'. I also said, *'you'll be surprised how many get through'*. I couldn't know the specifics of what that meant *back then* but as this has unfolded, I can only say our intuition is a fail-safe and you have every right to question and *resist* this 'new age' of false progressive *propaganda* in defence of your eternal soul. Never before have we had more right and *more opportunity* to level the playing field and bring about the *ascension of humankind* and the *rehabilitation of Mother Earth* as the mask *literally* slips from the monsters and they show their true faces as traitors inevitably do! *It's now or never, folks!* This is *your* job and one that you and your great grandchildren can be truly proud of not only for a few generations *but forever!*

This moment belongs to you. Take it!

EPILOGUE
"God" by John Lennon

God is a concept
By which we measure
Our pain
I'll say it again
God is a concept
By which we measure
Our pain
I don't believe in magic
I don't believe in I-Ching
I don't believe in Bible
I don't believe in tarot
I don't believe in Hitler
I don't believe in Jesus
I don't believe in Kennedy
I don't believe in Buddha
I don't believe in mantra
I don't believe in Gita
I don't believe in yoga
I don't believe in kings
I don't believe in Elvis
I don't believe in Zimmerman
I don't believe in Beatles
I just believe in me
Yoko and me
And that's reality
The dream is over
What can I say?
The dream is over
Yesterday
I was the dream weaver
But now I'm reborn
I was the Walrus
But now I'm John
And so dear friends
You just have to carry on
The dream is over

ABOUT THE AUTHOR

Willow Willis was born 3/4/1977 in Melbourne, Australia. The youngest of five children, she is a multi-instrumentalist and singer from an early age picking up music by 3 and playing 8 instrument by the time she was 12. She began performing and public speaking at 12 and promoting music by the time she was 16. She has worked with and performed for some notable names in entertainment and found herself on the odd magazine cover. Her talents include being a musician, vocalist, singer-songwriter, author, artist, radio host and qualified hypnotherapist having worked for some of the largest organisations in the world including a Microsoft Gold Partner, News Ltd and the UK Government. He career covers various industries including entertainment, print media and multimedia in the public and private sectors as well as events management.

Willow returns bringing her talents and skills to her latest work unveiling world changing information with ease and humour despite how perilous the world seems at this time. Her personal experiences have taught her the power of introspection and that triumph in the face of impossible odds is not only possible for the individual but about to happen on a global scale! Willow's second book, *2022 & Beyond – Return of the Feminine*, takes her first work to a whole new level as we finally discover the secrets behind the greatest myths in history and what they *really* mean for our salvation! Once again, Willow makes you laugh and cry while unravelling the absurdity and even sadness of our situation as individuals and as a collective without losing her sense of humour. She explains how everyday people will bravely come together to defeat an old foe and continue on our amazing quest into a long-prophesised date with destiny in pursuit of happiness *forever!*

www.ingramcontent.com/pod-product-compliance
Lightning Source LLC
Chambersburg PA
CBHW051542010526
44118CB00022B/2554